Total Cost Management Framework
An Integrated Approach to Portfolio, Program, and Project Management

First Edition

Edited by John K. Hollmann, PE CCE

2006

Total Cost Management Framework
First Edition
Copyright © 2006
By AACE International
209 Prairie Avenue, Suite 100, Morgantown, WV 26501 USA
Phone: +1.304.2968444 Fax: +1.304.2915728 E-mail: info@aacei.org Web: www.aacei.org

Printed in the United States of America

ISBN: 1-885517-55-6

A Special Publication
of
AACE International – The Association for the Advancement of Cost Engineering

Total Cost Management Framework
An Integrated Approach to Portfolio, Program, and Project Management

First Edition

Edited by John K. Hollmann, PE CCE

A continuing project of the AACE International Technical Board

2005/2006 Technical Board Members:
Larry R. Dysert CCC (Chair)
Peter R. Bredehoeft, Jr.
H. Ernest Hani, PSP
John K. Hollmann, PE CCE
Stephen M. Jacobson, CCC
Todd Pickett, CCC
Kul B. Uppal, PE
Associate Members:
Valerie Behrendt
Steven G.J. Boeschoten
Wesley R. Querns, CCE
Richard A. Selg, CCE
Joseph W. Wallwork, PE CCE PSP

AACE Technical and Production Staff:
Christian Heller, Staff Director Technical Operations
Marvin Gelhausen, Managing Editor
Noah Kinderknecht, Graphic Artist/Designer

Copy Editor: Cheryl Burgess

The AACE International Technical Board and Committees

The Technical Board is responsible for planning, facilitating the development and maintenance of, promoting, and monitoring Association technical products and activities. Technical products include those needed to establish the technical basis of education and certification programs of the Association and to advance the science and art of Cost Engineering. Technical activities encompass documenting and maintaining recommended practices, standard approaches and methodologies, common terminology, and references, as well as facilitating and promoting technical research, development, and publication. Technical committees and teams are appointed by the Technical Board to perform those activities. AACE members interested in working on the Technical Board or a committee should contact the Chair of the Technical Board at techchair@aacei.org, or Christian Heller, Staff Director Technical Operations at cheller@aacei.org.

The following organization chart shows the current Technical Board and committee structure:

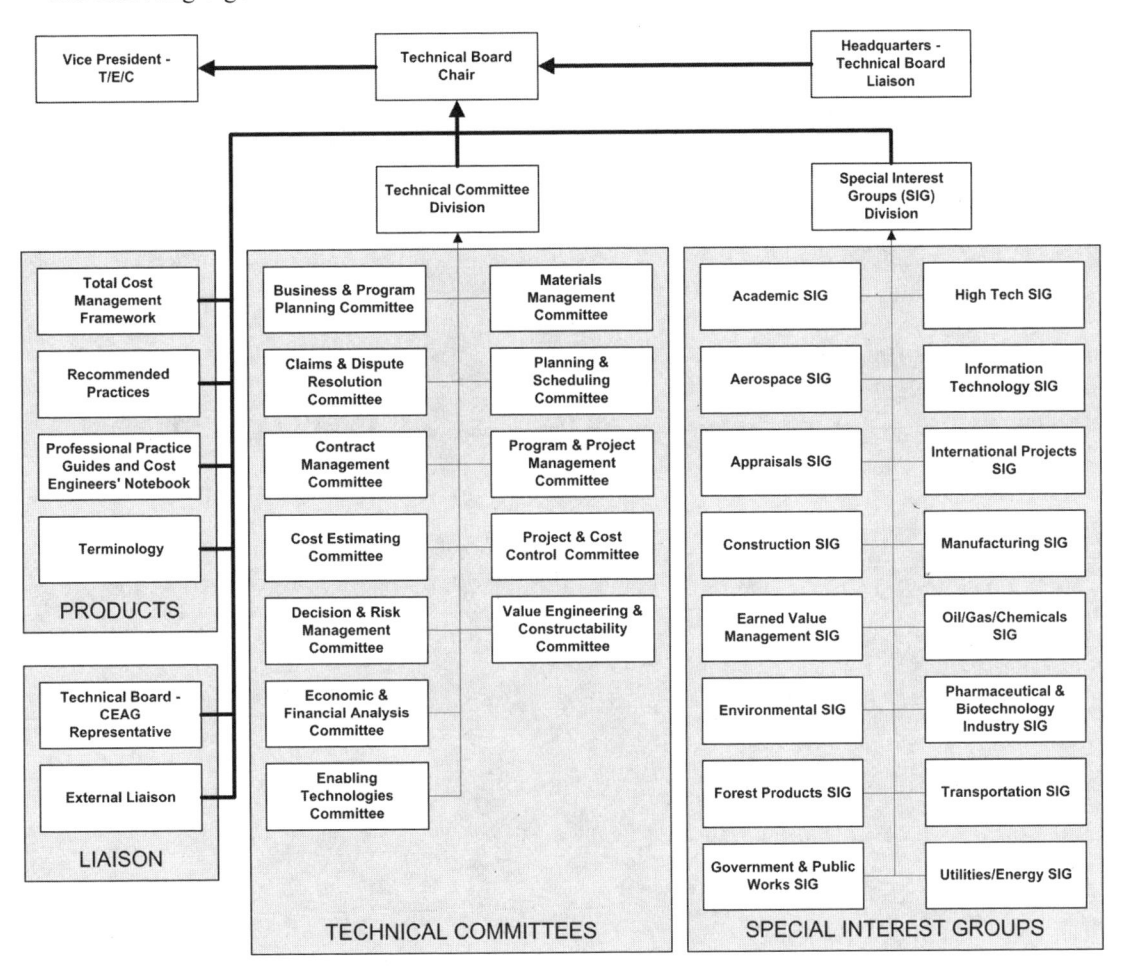

Technical Board Structure:

- Vice President - T/E/C ← Technical Board Chair ← Headquarters - Technical Board Liaison
- Technical Board Chair oversees:
  - Technical Committee Division
  - Special Interest Groups (SIG) Division

PRODUCTS:
- Total Cost Management Framework
- Recommended Practices
- Professional Practice Guides and Cost Engineers' Notebook
- Terminology

LIAISON:
- Technical Board - CEAG Representative
- External Liaison

TECHNICAL COMMITTEES:
- Business & Program Planning Committee
- Claims & Dispute Resolution Committee
- Contract Management Committee
- Cost Estimating Committee
- Decision & Risk Management Committee
- Economic & Financial Analysis Committee
- Enabling Technologies Committee
- Materials Management Committee
- Planning & Scheduling Committee
- Program & Project Management Committee
- Project & Cost Control Committee
- Value Engineering & Constructability Committee

SPECIAL INTEREST GROUPS:
- Academic SIG
- Aerospace SIG
- Appraisals SIG
- Construction SIG
- Earned Value Management SIG
- Environmental SIG
- Forest Products SIG
- Government & Public Works SIG
- High Tech SIG
- Information Technology SIG
- International Projects SIG
- Manufacturing SIG
- Oil/Gas/Chemicals SIG
- Pharmaceutical & Biotechnology Industry SIG
- Transportation SIG
- Utilities/Energy SIG

PREFACE

What Is the Total Cost Management (TCM) Framework?

Total Cost Management (TCM) is the effective application of professional and technical expertise to plan and control resources, costs, profitability and risk. Simply stated, TCM is a systematic approach to managing cost throughout the life cycle of any enterprise, program, facility, project, product or service. The *TCM Framework* is a representation of that 'systematic approach".

The *TCM Framework* is a structured, annotated process map that for the first time explains each practice area of the cost engineering field in the context of its relationship to the other practice areas including allied professions. As the book subtitle says, it is a process for applying the skills and knowledge of cost engineering. A key feature of the *TCM Framework* is that it highlights and differentiates the main cost management application areas: *project control* and *strategic asset management*.

The *TCM Framework* is a significant, original contribution to the cost management profession applicable to all industries. It is an AACE cornerstone technical document that joins the current body of knowledge literature for related fields such as project management, operations management, and management accounting. It is also consistent with the latest organizational and portfolio thinking which ties all practices and processes back to overall business strategies and objectives.

As a "framework", this document is not a "how-to" instructional guide, but a conceptual representation that provides a structured, integrated overview of cost engineering. As such, it will guide AACE International's development of more detailed technical products including the following:

- *Recommended Practices (RPs)*: original, peer-reviewed documents that define the specifics of particular methods or procedures outlined in the *TCM Framework*,
- *Professional Practice Guides (PPGs):* a set of structured, edited compilations of selected AACE publications on specific areas of cost engineering,
- *Cost Engineer's Notebook (CEN)*: a single structured, edited compilation of selected AACE publications that provides an overview of all the key fundamental areas of cost engineering.

The *TCM Framework's* structure will provide consistency and support development of AACE Education Board (e.g., *Skills and Knowledge of Cost Engineering* and *Certification Study Guide*) and Certification Board (e.g., certification examinations) products.

Those working in the project management field will find similarities with the Project Management Institute's (PMI) *A Guide to the Project Management Body of Knowledge (PMBOK Guide)* as project control is a subset of the field of project management. With a greater focus on project control, the *TCM Framework* adds richness in many of the processes. More importantly, the *TCM Framework* addresses *strategic asset cost management* practices in business and capital planning, operations and maintenance, and product cost management, both upstream and downstream of the project processes. Asset owner companies will particularly appreciate the enhanced coverage of areas such as historical data management, cost modeling, economic and decision analysis, and value analysis.

The intent is that the *TCM Framework* will be studied, applied, and continuously improved by a worldwide audience from all industries, thereby advancing the profession of cost engineering and cost management.

The Value of the TCM Framework for AACE International

In 1994, AACE added total cost management to its constitution. The AACE Technical Board was charged with defining TCM as a *systematic approach*. Without such an approach, it has been difficult to effectively describe the scope and purpose of the cost engineering profession. One study described the challenges this way: "...for the advancement of the field, more emphasis should be put on the creation of novel mental images and the development of a generalized syntactical and conceptual structure." It added that we must have a "clear methodology of what it does and how its data are collected and interpreted," and "a full, structured set of ideas that is dynamic, developmental, yet consistent."[1] These are the challenges addressed by the TCM process. The TCM process is a systematic approach designed to promote a unified, structured vision of the common purpose for the many cost engineering practices. It is also designed to be industry and asset generic in that it applies to any enterprise, program, facility, project, product or service.

The Value of the TCM Framework for Industry

Companies are continually looking for ways to tie everything they do to their strategic missions and objectives. As they strive for better strategic performance, they are frequently re-engineering their organizations. To find efficiencies and improve quality, they are documenting, benchmarking, analyzing and improving business and work processes. For the many enterprises seeking ISO certification a process focus is required.[2] TCM provides a strategic model that can help an organization design its own processes related to cost management.

Likewise, re-engineering increases the challenges for individual professionals as employers break down functional silos and increasingly expect staff and leaders to be competent in many different practices, while also being more knowledgeable of business processes. For individuals, the *TCM Framework* provides a "map" to help them understand all the practice areas while also helping guide their career planning.

In the academic arena, the *TCM Framework* provides a model for developing cost engineering education and training products and curricula that will serve those individuals and enterprises in need of a broader, more integrated perspective.

How to Use the TCM Framework

Because the *TCM Framework* process is based on broadly accepted "first principles" (i.e., the Deming/Shewhart cycle), it applies to all industries. It can be used by all levels of practitioners and in all business, academic, and institutional environments (customers, subcontractors, government, prime contractors, construction managers, design-build, etc.) worldwide. It also applies to the entire life cycle of asset and project portfolios.

It is a *generic reference* process model or guideline. It is not intended to be used directly "out-of-the-box" in any specific application. Managers, practitioners, educators, and others will need to build their own processes and improve practices in the context of their business, assets, organization, culture, project systems, and so on. As a generic reference model, the *TCM Framework* has already been successfully tested in reengineering consulting and training.

The *TCM Framework* can be read and applied section-by-section at a sub-process or functional level. However, optimal effectiveness of a sub-process requires that it be developed in the context of and relationship to associated sub-processes that share common strategies and objectives. In that respect, all readers with limited interest or time should understand the *Part 1* overview sections before focusing on the sections and sub-processes of interest.

---

[1] Sik-Wah Fung, Patrick, and Dodo Ka-Yan Ip, "Cost Engineering as an Academic Discipline," AACE International Transactions, 1998.
[2] International Organization for Standardization ISO 9000 and its family of related standards is focused on an enterprise having, maintaining, and following documented process and procedures.

AACE International and the TCM Process

AACE International assumes responsibility for the advancement and promotion of scientific principles and techniques in the practice areas of business and program planning; cost estimating; economic and financial analysis; cost engineering; program and project management; planning and scheduling; and cost and schedule performance measurement and change control. However, an effective process must also ensure that the skills and knowledge of cost engineering are advanced in a way that promotes and is consistent with best business and program cost management practices. Therefore, the *TCM Framework* includes practice areas for which AACE International is not the primary caretaker, but which interact extensively with cost engineering practices and cost management (e.g., cost accounting). For these areas, the intent is to demonstrate their integration with cost engineering, not take technical ownership of them. AACE will monitor advancements in allied fields to ensure that each supports an effective business and cost management process. Likewise, AACE International educational and certification products will focus on the *core* skill and knowledge areas while ensuring that professional cost engineers have a solid grounding in the business and program planning context in which these skills and knowledge are applied.

The Development of and Contributors to the Publication

The *TCM Framework* had its beginnings in 1994 as an effort to develop a professional handbook to be called *AACE International's Total Cost Management Guide for the 21st Century* with Wes Querns as the editor. A significant and successful effort was made to enlist recognized leading professionals in their respective fields as contributing authors and a publisher was lined up.[3] However, as the *Guide's* scope was defined, it became apparent that a book with independent experts covering the traditional cost engineering topics in their own ways would not provide the required *systematic approach*. Therefore, in 1995, the *Guide* project was re-scoped as the *Framework* project.

1996, the high level TCM process was published in an article in *Cost Engineering* journal entitled "A New Look at Total Cost Management." The Technical Board solicited member comment via a special survey and we drafted the introductory chapters (now Part I). These overview chapters were subjected to considerable review and consensus building (during what may be called phase one) until 2002 when the introductory chapters were formally published.[4]

Completing the remaining 30 sections was not so much a traditional writing process as a process reengineering project for the editor and contributors. The effort consisted of taking common practice knowledge about cost engineering and allied fields, breaking it down into steps, connecting the steps based on a time honored management process model, and finishing it with consistent narrative using a *single voice*. Once again, the support of leading professionals was sought to assist in the development. The novelty and value of the resulting product is in *integration and structure,* not new practices, "how-tos," or narrative. The detailed parts and pieces of the technical content are generally well-trodden material covered by many sources. Every reasonable effort was made to appropriately reference material from other sources per AACE publication guidelines.

The product was then reviewed by AACE's Technical Committees, the main and associate AACE Boards, and other subject matter experts. Comment was sought from related associations as well. All these contributors are acknowledged in the next section. The review and approval process used was the same stringent approach that AACE uses for its Recommended Practices. This multi-stage process requires formal requests for comment, documented comment disposition, and Technical Board approval to help ensure that general consensus is achieved.

---

[3] Many of these experts provided early outlines or draft chapters for the cancelled *Guide*. They are listed in the Acknowledgement section. Some of these experts are also acknowledged as author/key contributors for *Framework*.

[4] Individuals that commented at that time are included among the contributors listed in the Acknowledgement section.

The Next Edition

The *TCM Framework* will be a living document and AACE International plans to update it periodically. As a living document, readers are encouraged to send their comments on the text to tcm@aacei.org. These will be considered by AACE in future revisions of the *Framework*. AACE encourages those that apply the concepts presented in this document to share their experiences through articles, papers, and presentations.

Special Thanks

The editors would like to thank our past employers, Eastman Kodak and Independent Project Analysis Inc. (particularly Mr. Edward W. Merrow, IPA's founder and owner) for their support of the editors' time and effort on this project and for support of employee professional development in general.

Several AACE International members, officers, and Fellows were particularly supportive of this product's development. Richard E. Westney PE, Past President and Fellow, first coined the term Total Cost Management in 1991 as part of the Board of Director's "Vision 21" initiative. Subsequently, Larry G. Medley Sr. ECCC, Past President and Fellow, provided early and continuing support including helping define the TCM concept for inclusion in AACE's Constitution and Bylaws in 1994. Dorothy J. Burton, VP Technical and Fellow helped get the *Framework* off the ground and through its sometimes rocky inception. The late Franklin D. Postula PE CCE, Past President and Fellow, provided much welcome encouragement along the way. Also, the following Technical Board Vice Presidents and Directors since 1995 each had a hand in helping the *Framework* find its way into your hands: these include Dorothy J. Burton (Fellow), Dr. James E. Rowings Jr. PE CCE (Fellow), James G. Zack Jr., Edward D. Hamm PE CCE (Fellow), Jennifer Bates CCE (Fellow), Joseph W. Wallwork PE CCE PSP, and Larry R. Dysert CCC.

Finally, we would like to thank our wonderful wives Cindy Hollmann and Susan Querns for their support and forbearance during this decade long project.

John K. Hollmann, PE CCE Editor Sterling, Virginia	Wesley R. Querns, CCE Editor-Phase 1 Phoenix, Arizona

ACKNOWLEDGEMENTS

Authors/Key Contributors for the TCM Framework

John K. Hollmann, PE CCE edited and contributed to all sections.[5] The Technical Board would like to express its gratitude to the following individuals who provided original text, ideas, or otherwise contributed to or helped technically validate the contents (listed in their order of contribution by section).

Author/Key Contributor	TCM Framework Section
Wesley R. Querns, CCE *PMO Director, Perot Systems Corporation* wesley.querns@chw.edu.	Preface Chapter 1 Introduction Chapter 2 The Total Cost Management Process 9.1 Project Cost Accounting 9.2 Progress and Performance Measurement 10.1 Project Performance Assessment
Gregory D. Githens *Catalyst Management Consulting, LLC* gdg@catalystpm.com	3.1 Requirements Elicitation and Analysis 3.2 Asset Planning
John R. Schuyler, PE CCE *Instructor/Consultant, PetroSkills-OGCI* john@maxvalue.com	3.2 Asset Planning 3.3 Investment Decision Making
Larry R. Dysert, CCC *Managing Partner, Conquest Consulting Group* ldysert@ccg-estimating.com	4.1 Project Implementation
Susan G. Seber, CCE *Director, Lean Manufacturing, Eastman Kodak* susan.seber@kodak.com	4.1 Project Implementation
Gary Cokins *Strategist, SAS Institute Inc.* gary.cokins@sas.com	5.1 Asset Cost Accounting 5.2 Asset Performance Measurement 6.1 Asset Performance Assessment 11.4 Quality and Quality Management
Stephen M. Jacobson, CCC *Director, Project Mgmt, Hilton Hotels Corp.* stephen_jacobson@hilton.com	6.3 Asset Historical Database Management 10.2 Forecasting 10.3 Change Management 10.4 Project Historical Database Management 11.5 Value and Value Improving Practices
Paul E. Makris, PE PSP	6.4 Forensic Performance Assessment
James G. Zack, Jr. *Exec. Director, Corporate Claims Mgmt, Fluor* jim.zack@fluor.com	6.4 Forensic Performance Assessment
Earl T. Glenwright, Jr. PE PSP *Partner, Koevsky-Glenwright Associates* earl_csss@yahoo.com	7.1 Project Scope & Execution Strategy Dev. 7.2 Schedule Planning and Development 8.1 Project Control Plan Implementation
Donald F. McDonald, Jr. PE CCE PSP Fellow *Fluor Enterprises, Inc.*	7.2 Schedule Planning and Development
Bernard A. Pietlock, CCC	7.3 Cost Estimating and Budgeting
Douglas W. Leo, CCC *Sr. Project Estimator, Eastman Kodak* doug.leo@censeo.us	7.3 Cost Estimating and Budgeting
Sarwar A. Samad, CCE *Program Manager, Federal Aviation Admin.* ssamad786@hotmail.com	7.4 Resource Planning 7.7 Procurement Planning

---

[5] *John K. Hollmann, PE CCE, President, Validation Estimating LLC; jhollmann@validest.com*

Author/Key Contributor	TCM Framework Section
Donald E. Parker, PE CCE *Consultant* *d@dparker.com*	7.5 Value Analysis and Engineering
Michael W. Curran *President and CEO, Decision Sciences Corp.* *mcurran@uncertain.com*	7.6 Risk Management
Kevin M. Curran *Exec. Vice President, Decision Sciences Corp.* *kcurran@uncertain.com*	7.6 Risk Management
Bonnie L. Halkett	11.1 The Enterprise in Society 11.4 Quality and Quality Management
Robert E. Templeton, PE CCE Fellow	11.1 The Enterprise in Society 11.4 Quality and Quality Management
Dr. Carl Wolf, CCE Fellow	11.1 The Enterprise in Society 11.4 Quality and Quality Management
Dr. Ginger Levin *Proj. Mgmt. Consultant and Lecturer, Univ. of Wisconsin-Platteville* *ginlevin@aol.com*	11.2 People and Performance Management
Keith Watson	11.3 Information Management
Donald J. Cass, CCE EVP Fellow	11.6 Environment, Health, and Safety
Dr. Neil L. Drobny, PE *Consultant* *nld268@rrohio.com*	11.6 Environment, Health, and Safety
Richard A. Selg, CCE Fellow *Principal Project Controls Engineer, Parsons* *richard.selg@parsons.com*	11.6 Environment, Health, and Safety

Contributing Authors of the Draft Guide to Total Cost Management (1995/96)

The following individuals submitted draft outlines or chapters for this cancelled precursor handbook text for which Wesley R. Querns, CCE was the editor. The Technical Board would like to express its gratitude for their previously unrecognized contribution.

Dr. Neil L. Drobny, PE
Gregory D. Githens
Dr. Deborah J. Fisher, PE
Murray W. Janzen
Harvey A. Levine
Dr. Anthony K. Mason, ECCE
Gary Nelson
Nghi M. Nguyen, PE
Dr. James T. O'Connor, PE
Neil D. Opfer, CCE
Dr. Joseph J. Orczyk, PE CCE

Sarwar A. Samad, CCE
John R. Schuyler, PE CCE
Jon E. Seidel
Sam L. Shafer
M. Larry Shillito
R. Gary Stillman, PE CCE
Henry C. Thorne, ECCE Fellow
George C. Tlamsa
Keith Watson
Roy L. Wilson, PE CCE
Andrew Young

Commentors

The Technical Board would like to express its gratitude to the following individuals and groups who made formal comments during the various technical reviews. Inclusion in these lists does not imply full or partial endorsement of the contents of this text as published.

Part I (Published 2002)

Rodney B. Adams, CCE
Vittorio Alby, PE CCE
Jennifer Bates, CCE Fellow
James A. Bent, ECCC
Nelson E. Bonilla, CCE
Dorothy J. Burton, Fellow
Mary Beth Cionek, CCC
Michael J. Davis, CCE
Larry R. Dysert, CCC
Jack F. Enrico, ECCE Fellow
Clive D. Francis, CCC Fellow
Peter W. Griesmyer
Laura Ann Guidice
Allen C. Hamilton, CCE
Kurt G. R. Heinze, ECCE Fellow
John K. Hollmann, PE CCE
Wieslaw J. Jurkiewicz
Dinesh R. Kansara, CCE
Dr. Deborah S. Kezsbom
Dr. Richard E. Larew, PE CCE
Bryan R. McConachy, P ENG

Donald F. McDonald, Jr. PE CCE PSP Fellow
Larry G. Medley, Sr. ECCC Fellow
Yuri Minkovski, CCE
Stephen E. Mueller, CCE
Dr. James M. Neil, PE Fellow
Anghel Patrascu, ECCE
Jean-Paul Prentice, CCE
Charles Poulton, PE ECCE Fellow
Franklin D. Postula, PE CCE Fellow
Wesley R. Querns, CCE
Dwight E. Ray
Rafael Angel Rodriguez, CCE
Dr. James E. Rowings, Jr. PE CCE Fellow
Richard A. Selg, CCE Fellow
Bruce Alan Spence
Walter J. Strutt, PE CCE Fellow
Dr. George Stukhart, PE Fellow
George R. Stumpf, PE
Kul B. Uppal, PE
James G. Zack, Jr.

Section 7.2 (2002 Preliminary Review)

Edward E. Douglas, III CCC PSP Fellow
Stephen M. Jacobson, CCC
Murray W. Janzen

Paul D. Lubell
Dick Van Steenbergh

Section 7.3 (Published 2002)

A. Larry Aaron, CCE
Rodney B. Adams, CCE
Dr. Deepak Bajaj, PE
Dallas R. Lee, CCE
Kelly M. Burke
Guy J. Dixon
Jack F. Enrico, ECCE Fellow
Anthony L. Huxley

Young H. Kwak
Dr. Anthony K. Mason, ECCE
Yuri Minkovski, CCE
Jonathan Moss, CCC
Charles Poulton, PE ECCE Fellow
John R. Schuyler, PE CCE
Max M. Shoura, PE
Joseph W. Wallwork, PE CCE PSP

Section 7.4 (2002 Preliminary Review)

Stephen W. Essig, PE CCE
Charles R. McDuff, PE CCE
Lawrence D. Miles Value Foundation

Franklin D. Postula, PE CCE Fellow
Del L. Younker, CCC
Value Management Working Group—
  Dutch Association of Cost Engineers (DACE)

Section 7.6 (2002 Preliminary Review)
    Kevin M. Curran
    Paul D. Lubell
    Bruce R. Mulholland, PE
    Donald E. Parker, PE CCE
    Franklin D. Postula, PE CCE Fellow
    R. Eugene Reed, Jr. PE CCE
    Jon E. Seidel
    Sam L. Shafer, PE

2005 Reviews-Full Text
    Alistair J. Bowden
    Timothy T. Calvey, PE PSP
    Edward E. Douglas, III CCC PSP Fellow
    Paul D. Giammalvo, CCE
    Earl T. Glenwright, Jr. PE PSP
    Eugene L. Grumer
    Dr. Kenneth K. Humphreys, PE CCE Fellow
    Walter M. Jazwa
    Donald F. McDonald, Jr. PE CCE PSP Fellow
    Alexia A. Nalewaik, CCE
    David A. Norfleet, CCC
    Andy Padilla, CCE
    Saleh El Shobokshy
    Gregory C. Sillak
    Ronald M. Winter, PSP

I. INTRODUCTION TO TOTAL COST MANAGEMENT

CHAPTER 1

INTRODUCTION

1.1 Definition of Total Cost Management

1.1.1 Total Cost Management and Related Terminology

The Constitution of AACE International provides the following definition of total cost management:

"Total Cost Management is the effective application of professional and technical expertise to plan and control resources, costs, profitability and risks. Simply stated, it is a systematic approach to managing cost throughout the life cycle of any enterprise, program, facility, project, product, or service. This is accomplished through the application of cost engineering and cost management principles, proven methodologies and the latest technology in support of the management process."

Put another way, Total Cost Management (TCM) is the sum of the practices and processes that an enterprise uses to manage the total life cycle cost investment in its portfolio of strategic assets.

For example, a real estate developer may build, maintain, renovate, and then demolish an office building during its life cycle—at each phase of the building life cycle the developer makes significant investments. To manage these investments, the building developer monitors building operating costs and profitability; evaluates alternative investment opportunities; and initiates, plans, and controls improvement projects. These activities are all within the scope of the TCM process.

Costs in TCM include any investment of resources in the enterprise's assets including time, monetary, human, and physical resources. *Total* refers to TCM's comprehensive approach to managing the total resource investment during the life cycle of the enterprise's strategic assets. The *enterprise* can be any endeavor, business, government, group, individual, or other entity that owns, controls, or operates strategic assets.

Strategic asset is shorthand for any unique physical or intellectual property that is of long term or ongoing value to the enterprise. For most cost engineers, strategic assets equate to "capital assets"; however, the term *strategic asset* is more inclusive (e.g., may include things that are considered expenses). The asset may be a building, an industrial plant, a software program, or a stage production. Strategic asset investments are made through the execution of projects or programs. Projects are temporary endeavors for creating, modifying, maintaining, or retiring strategic assets. Products and services may be considered strategic assets in that before a product can be made or a service performed, many investments must be made through the execution of projects for research, development, design, and so on.

As an example of where TCM fits within a company's undertakings, consider a company that designs and manufactures integrated circuits. The chip's design is a strategic asset of the company created through the execution of research and design projects. In order to fabricate a new chip, the company develops a unique manufacturing process or layout—that process design or layout is also a strategic asset developed through the execution of projects. Next, a project is performed to design, procure, and build the plant for fabricating the microchips—the physical plant is another strategic asset. Finally, workers are hired and trained to operate the plant. Worker skill and knowledge are strategic assets and their initial training and plant start-up are executed as projects. The new plant must be maintained and eventually decommissioned. Each component of the chip maker's strategic asset portfolio requires investments realized through the execution of projects whose cost must be managed. Each component of the company's asset portfolio has its own life cycle with cost investments to integrate over time. The complex interaction of the asset portfolio component costs over their various life cycles and during operations calls for a total cost management process.

One way that TCM adds value to the body of cost engineering knowledge is that it integrates areas of cost management that are too often treated as separate entities or fields. While AACE is not the caretaker or custodian of all this is covered in the *TCM Framework*, it is important that cost engineers understand the relationships between the various fields of practice with which they are likely to interact or in which they may be expected to perform.[6]

1.1.2 Total Cost Management's Relationship to Other Fields

TCM is an integrating process that not only maps the fields of practice of cost engineering, but it also provides links to the fields of project management, resource management, and management accounting practice.[7] TCM provides a unique technical perspective that is often missing from financially focused approaches (hence the term cost "engineering"). Figure 1.1-1 illustrates how TCM, with roots and emphasis in project management and project control, has a balanced focus on product and capital costs, project and operational work processes, and resources of all types. In other words, it covers the "total costs" of the business.

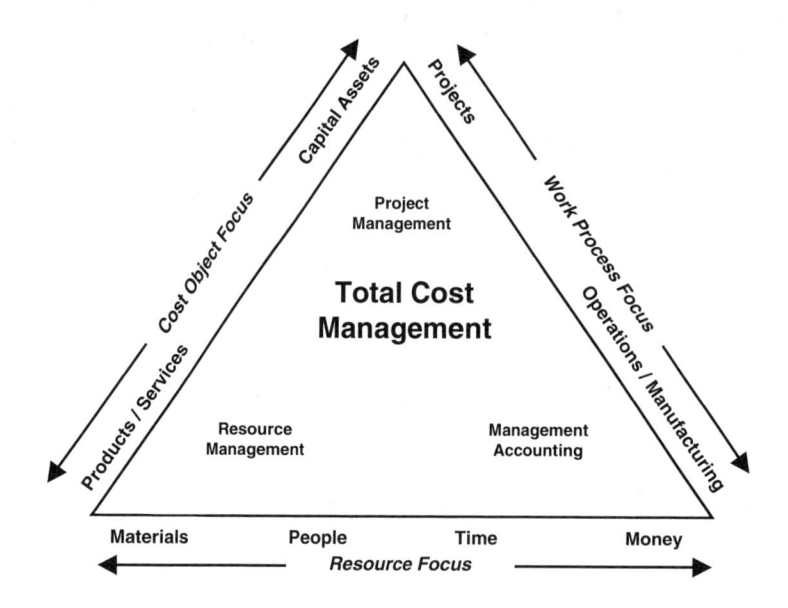

Figure 1.1-1 TCM's Place in the Cost Management Spectrum

Recently, project management models have been enhanced to better address pre-project processes, project portfolios, and consideration of overall business organization strategies. An example is the Project Management Institute's Organizational Project Management Maturity Model (OPM3). However, these models still do not cover production and operation management and costs to the extent addressed by TCM.

Product and operations costs have been the focus of the resource management and management accounting fields. Resource management's developments in enterprise resource management (ERP) and management accounting's developments in activity-based-costing (ABC) are significant advancements that are incorporated in TCM. However, unlike TCM, those fields have focused on product costs and typically address capital project costs as an incidental cost (i.e., depreciation) as it affects products.

In summary, TCM is unique in that it integrates the best approaches from all the major fields that have cost management interests while emphasizing cost engineering's practices and major role in them all.

---

[6] AACE's website provides links to organizations related to cost engineering and TCM (www.aacei.org or www.cost.org).
[7] See the Further Reading and Sources section for references to the organizations that are primary caretakers for the project management, resource management, and management accounting bodies of knowledge.

1.2 Purpose and Uses of the TCM Framework

The purpose of the *TCM Framework* is to provide an integrated and theoretically sound structure upon which AACE recommended practices (RPs) can be developed for those areas of TCM for which AACE is the primary caretaker.[8] The *Framework* achieves this objective by establishing an integrated process map of TCM. The process map helps ensure that RP products are consistent with each other and free of unnecessary duplication. As the structure for RP products, the *Framework,* by extension, also provides a technical framework that all AACE International educational and certification products and services can use.

Having achieved its primary purposes, there are many other possible uses of the *Framework*. For example, the *Framework* defines key concepts[9] and provides illustrations that can aid communication between cost engineering practitioners. This is particularly important because cost management is practiced in a myriad of enterprises such as construction, manufacturing, software development, real estate development, healthcare delivery, and so on. Also, practitioners striving for functional excellence may lose sight of overall cost management objectives.

In addition, students and newcomers to the cost management field can gain a broad understanding of the field from the *Framework*. For educators, the *Framework* can provide the structure for a course that can be enhanced with selected readings. Companies and skilled cost engineering practitioners that are looking for better ways to tie their disparate cost functions and asset management into an effective system will find that the *Framework* adds structure and value to their efforts. The *Framework* also provides a conceptual process model on which professionals can benchmark or pattern cost management work processes and practices within their enterprises.

---

[8] AACE's Constitution defines the areas of association focus as follows: "Total Cost Management is that area of engineering practice where engineering judgment and experience are utilized in the application of scientific principles and techniques to problems of business and program planning; cost estimating; economic and financial analysis; cost engineering; program and project management; planning and scheduling; and cost and schedule performance measurement and change control." Furthermore, AACE's Recommended Practice 11R-88, "Required Skills and Knowledge of a Cost Engineer" specifies cost engineering knowledge that is "core" (i.e., recommended that professional cost engineers know) and identifies skills that are recommended for individuals to put that core knowledge into practice. Recommended Practice 11R-88 is included in the Appendix.

[9] Where concept definitions are provided, they are consistent with AACE's primary terminology reference: Recommended Standard 10S90, "Standard Cost Engineering Terminology."

1.3 Organization of the TCM Framework

1.3.1 The TCM Framework Uses Process Management Conventions

Total cost management is a quality driven process model. As such, the *Framework* employs process management conventions. A process consists of a flow of inputs and outputs with mechanisms that transform the inputs to outputs. The *Framework* maps the process flows of TCM. The transforming mechanisms or activities are referred to as tools, techniques, or sub-processes. The inputs and outputs of TCM consist primarily of data and information.

1.3.2 The TCM Framework Uses a Standard Organization Structure

The *Framework* is organized into parts, chapters, and sections. The chapters correspond to the process elements (i.e., blocks) in the high level TCM process map that is illustrated and described later in Section 2.2. Figure 1.3-1 below illustrates how the chapters and key sections can be grouped by basic or overarching processes, functional or working processes, and enabling and supporting processes.

The TCM Framework

Basic Processes of Total Cost Management
- 1 Introduction
- 2 The TCM Process Maps
  - 2.1 Basis
  - 2.2 Total Cost Management
  - 2.3 Strategic Asset Management
  - 2.4 Project Control

Functional Processes for Strategic Asset Management
- 3 Strategic Asset Planning
- 4 Project Implementation
- 5 Strategic Asset Performance Measurement
- 6 Strategic Asset Performance Assessment

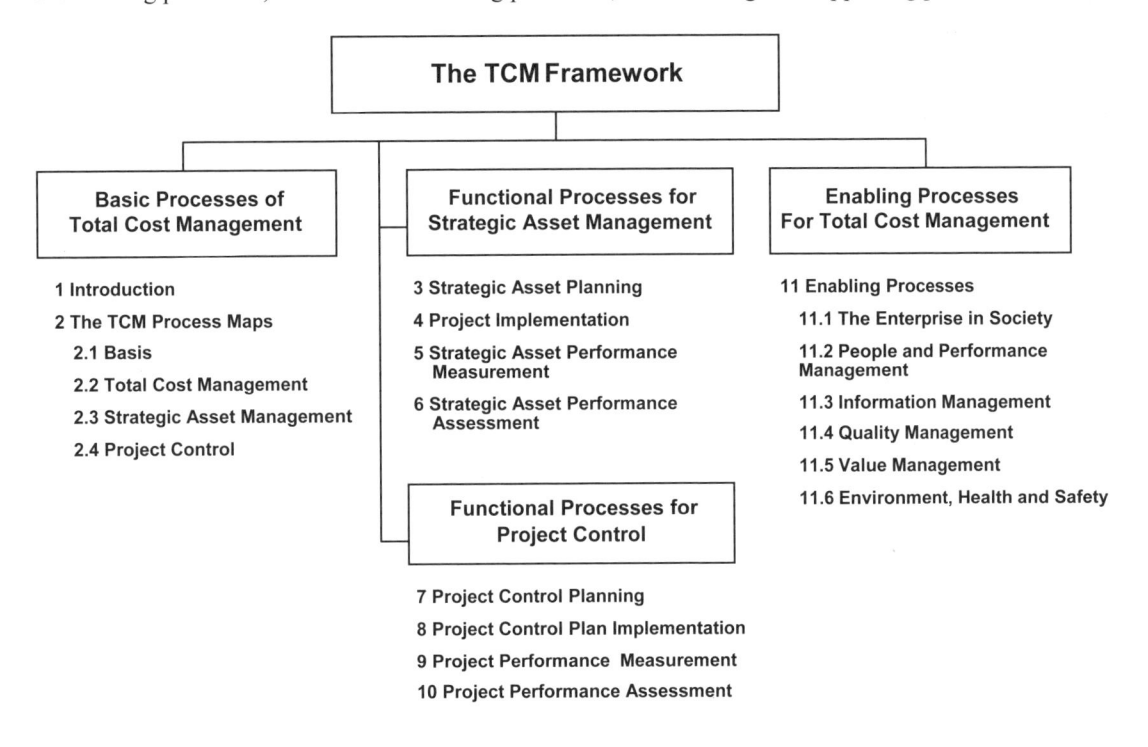

Functional Processes for Project Control
- 7 Project Control Planning
- 8 Project Control Plan Implementation
- 9 Project Performance Measurement
- 10 Project Performance Assessment

Enabling Processes For Total Cost Management
- 11 Enabling Processes
  - 11.1 The Enterprise in Society
  - 11.2 People and Performance Management
  - 11.3 Information Management
  - 11.4 Quality Management
  - 11.5 Value Management
  - 11.6 Environment, Health and Safety

Figure 1.3-1 The Structure of the Framework's Parts and Chapters

The "sections" in each chapter correspond to the functional level process steps that are illustrated and described later in Sections 2.3 and 2.4. The process sections are organized as follows (for the "enabling" processes, maps, inputs, and outputs are not applicable and are excluded):

    x.x.1 Description of the Process
    x.x.2 Process Map
    x.x.3 Inputs to the Process
    x.x.4 Outputs of the Process
    x.x.5 Key Concepts for the Process

Each section also includes a list of further readings and sources. These are included because the *Framework* is very conceptual in nature and readers are likely to want to learn more about specific topics.

These readings and sources were suggested by the editors and contributors and may not have been referred to in development of the *Framework* (i.e., the listed materials may be at odds in some cases). AACE International is not endorsing these sources as anything other than products of general interest.

1.4 Key Introductory Concepts for Total Cost Management

.1 *Total Cost Management.* The sum of the practices and processes that an enterprise uses to manage the total life cycle cost investment in its portfolio of strategic assets. Describes the process employed in the profession of cost engineering.

.2 *Resource Management.* (1) The effective planning, scheduling, execution, and control of all organizational resources to produce a good or a service that provides customer satisfaction and supports the organization's competitive edge and, ultimately, organizational goals. (2) An emerging field of study emphasizing the systems perspective, encompassing both the product and process life cycles, and focusing on the integration of organizational resources toward the effective realization of organizational goals. Resources include materials; maintenance, repair, and operating supplies; production and supporting equipment; facilities; direct and indirect employees; and capital.[10]

.3 *Project Management.* The methodical application of management knowledge, skills, and practices to project activities in order to meet project objectives.

.4 *Management Accounting.* The process of identification, measurement, accumulation, analysis, preparation, interpretation, and communication of financial information used by management to plan, evaluate, and control within an organization and to assure appropriate use of and accountability of its resources.

.5 *Costs and Resources.* Any investment of time, money, human effort, or physical objects in the enterprise's products, services, and assets.

.6 *Strategic Asset.* Any unique physical or intellectual property of some scope that is of long term or ongoing value to the enterprise.

.7 *Enterprise.* Any endeavor, business, government entity, group, or individual that owns or controls strategic assets.

.8 *Process.* A flow of inputs and outputs with mechanisms that transform the inputs to outputs.

.9 *Projects.* A temporary endeavor to conceive, create, modify, or terminate a strategic asset.

.10 *Operations.* Ongoing endeavors that use strategic assets.

.11 *Life Cycle.* Describes the stages or phases that occur during the lifetime of an object or endeavor. A life cycle presumes a beginning and an end. The asset life cycle describes the stages of an asset's existence, and the project life cycle describes the phases of a project's endeavors.

.12 *Life Cycle; Asset.* Describes the stages of asset existence from ideation through termination during the lifetime of an asset.

.13 *Life Cycle; Project.* Describes the stages of project progress from ideation through closure during the lifetime of the project.

Further Readings and Sources

The TCM process is a new concept and the *Framework* is the original defining text. However, the following are sources of general information about the practice areas that are involved in or associated with the TCM process.

Cost Engineering and Total Cost Management
AACE International, the Association for the Advancement of Cost Engineering, www.aacei.org
- *Cost Engineers Notebook* (current revision)
- *Recommended Practices* (current revisions)
- *Professional Practice Guides* (current editions)
- *Skills and Knowledge of Cost Engineering*, 5th ed. Editor Scott J. Amos, 2004.
- *Certification Study Guide*, 3rd ed., 2005.

Management Accounting and ABC
Institute of Management Accounting (IMA), www.imanet.org
- Cokins, Gary. *Activity Based Cost Management: An Executive Guide.* New York: John Wiley & Sons, 2001.

---

[10] *APICS Dictionary*, 9th ed., James F. Cox and John H. Blackstone (www.apics.org).

- Player, Steve and David E. Keys. *Activity-Based Management*. New York: MasterMedia Limited, 1995.

Project Management

Project Management Institute (PMI), www.pmi.org
- *A Guide to the Project Management Body of Knowledge (PMBOK® Guide)*, 3rd ed. Upper Darby, PA: PMI, 2004.
- *An Executive's Guide to OPM3: A Guide to Strategic Success, Business Improvement and Competitive Advantage*, Upper Darby, PA: PMI, 2004.

Resource Management and ERP

APICS, the Association for Operations Management, www.apics.org
- Langenwalter, Gary A., *Enterprise Resources Planning and Beyond*. Boca Raton, FL: St. Lucie Press, 2000.

CHAPTER 2

THE TOTAL COST MANAGEMENT PROCESS MAP

2.1 Basis of Total Cost Management Processes

This section describes the fundamental basis or foundation of the TCM process and defines the process mapping conventions used in the *Framework*. Sections 2.2, 2.3, and 2.4 further describe the respective processes of TCM, Strategic Asset Management, and Project Control.

2.1.1 TCM Is Based on Process Management Principles

The pursuit of increased productivity and quality has been a driving force of worldwide business management for decades. Process management and process reengineering emphasize the need for enterprises to identify their work processes and continually improve them. At the same time, global mergers, acquisitions, and reorganizations in the digital age have created continual disruption, deconstruction, and re-birth in the economy. This seeming chaos demands speed and flexibility while putting a premium on innovation and leadership. Effective processes are needed to support continuous quality improvement while nurturing innovation and change without chaos.

TCM as described in the *Framework* is a process map that supports continuous process improvement while being flexible. It is not intended to be a set of rigid rules or work procedures. While each of the sub-process maps of TCM may look rigid when set on paper, users may chose to emphasize those process steps that are most critical to their situation. Steps can be skipped when they are not applicable and information flows can be modified to suit the needs of the enterprise. If the enterprise or market is growing, the emphasis can be placed on asset creation and scheduling aspects. On the other hand, if the enterprise or market is mature, the emphasis may be put on asset maintenance and cost aspects. In practice, the processes are quite flexible.

In addition, TCM supports cross-functional integration and multi-skilling. Few enterprises in a dynamic environment can afford to have cadres of functional specialists. However, multi-skilling may come at the price of having less experience, skill, and knowledge than desired in any one function. Weaknesses in individual skill and knowledge place a premium on having reliable, integrated processes like TCM.

2.1.2 The Basic TCM Process Model—Plan, Do, Check, and Assess (PDCA)

The TCM process model is based upon the "PDCA" management or control cycle, which is also known as the Deming or Shewhart cycle. The PDCA cycle is a generally accepted, quality driven, continuous improvement management model. PDCA stands for plan, do, check, and assess, with the word *check* being generally synonymous with *measure*. The word *assess* is sometimes substituted with *act* as in *to take corrective action*. The PDCA cycle is the framework for TCM because (1) it is time-proven and widely accepted as a valid management model, (2) it is quality driven, and (3) it is highly applicable to cost management processes, which are cyclical by nature.

The PDCA cycle in TCM includes the following steps:

- **Plan** - plan asset solutions or project activities
- **Do** (i.e., execute) - initiate and perform the project or project activities in accordance with the plan
- **Check** (i.e., measure) - making measurements of asset, project, or activity performance, and
- **Assess** (i.e., act) - assessing performance variances from the plan and taking action to correct or improve performance to bring it in line with the plan or to improve the plan.

These steps are repeated as activities and time progress until such time as the asset or project life cycle is complete. Figure 2.1-1 illustrates the PDCA process steps.

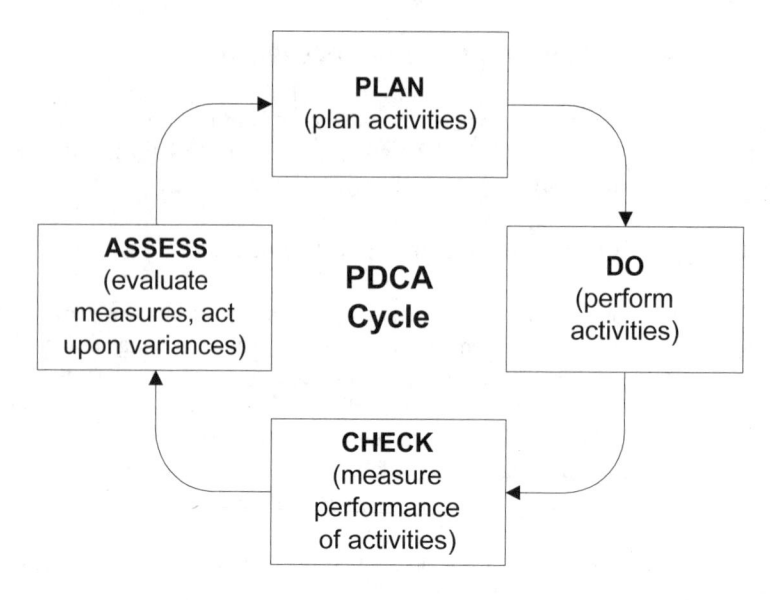

```
                    PLAN
                (plan activities)

    ASSESS          PDCA            DO
   (evaluate        Cycle        (perform
 measures, act                   activities)
 upon variances)

                    CHECK
                   (measure
                  performance
                  of activities)
```

Figure 2.1-1 The Plan, Do, Check, Assess Cycle

Two underlying tenets of the PDCA process cycle and process management in general are that:

- you can't manage what you can't measure
- whatever you measure tends to improve

Measurement is a key element that is often lacking in management systems that focus on planning. However, use caution in what and how you measure—"playing for score" is not the way to achieve the desired improved outcomes.

A cyclical process model is useful because strategic assets and the projects that create them each have an inherent life cycle. With each stage or phase of the asset or project life cycle, successive iterations of the cost management process are required. Each iteration of the cycle achieves a new or improved level of performance or progress for the asset or project.

2.1.3 The Asset Life Cycle

The PDCA control process takes place within the context of the asset and project life cycles. The *life cycle* describes the stages or phases that occur during the lifetime of an object or endeavor. The stages or phases are sequential groupings of processes that result in an intermediate deliverable or progress milestone.

While the life cycle for a given asset has a defined beginning and end, the process actions are not a straight line—an asset is usually modified and recycled many times with ongoing ideation leading to changes and improvements. The life cycle of a strategic asset can be summarized in five stages as follows:

1) **Ideation** - recognize an opportunity or need for a new or improved asset; evaluate, research, develop, and define optional asset solutions that address the opportunity; and select an optimum asset solution.
2) **Creation** - create or otherwise implement the asset solution through execution of a project or program.
3) **Operation** - deploy or put the new or modified asset into service, function, production, operation, or other use.
4) **Modification** - improve, modify, or otherwise change or recycle the asset through execution of a project or program.

5) **Termination** - decommission, close, retire, demolish, remove, dispose, or otherwise terminate the asset from the enterprise's portfolio (often through execution of a project or program).

Resource investments are made via the execution of projects during the asset ideation, creation, operation, modification, and termination phases. Figure 2.1-2 illustrates the asset life cycle of a factory as it passes through time.

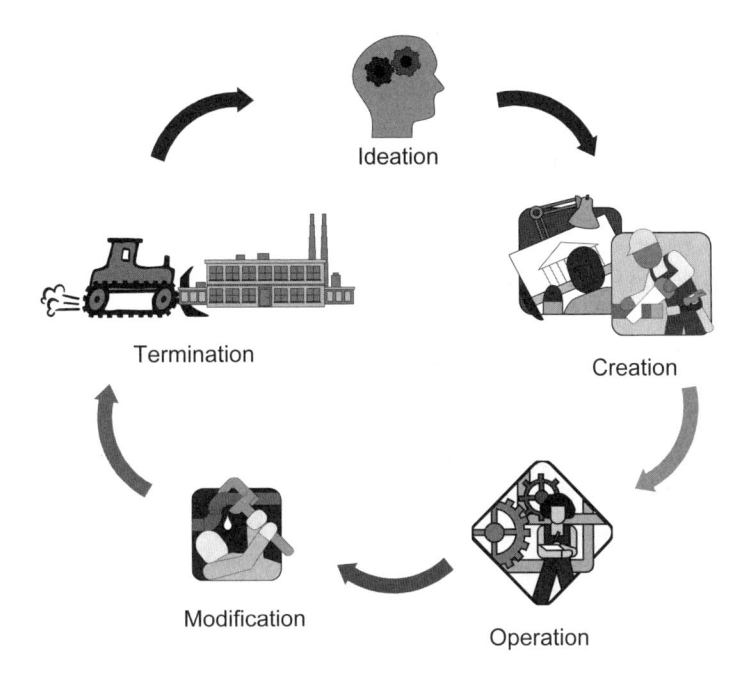

Figure 2.1-2 Asset Life Cycle of a Factory

2.1.4 The Project Life Cycle

Within the life cycle of an asset, projects are temporary endeavors for the ideation, creation, modification, or termination of assets. Projects have a defined beginning and end. In the asset life cycle, only operation is not generally considered a project endeavor. However, there may be many projects within the operation phase of an asset to maintain, relocate, modify, repair, enhance, or otherwise improve the utility of the asset. The elements of the project life cycle are often referred to as *phases*. Each phase yields one or more deliverables or outputs that become resources or inputs for the following phase. The deliverable may be a requirements document, a plan, a design document, a model, and so on. The life cycle of most projects can be summarized in four sequential phases as follows:

1) **Ideation** - given overall requirements of the project, the project team assesses alternative concepts for performing the project and selects an optimal performance strategy. Strategic performance requirements for the project are established.
2) **Planning -** project plans are developed that address the strategic requirements and selected performance strategy.
3) **Execution** - the plans are implemented through the execution of planned project activities.
4) **Closure** - the asset or deliverable is reviewed, tested, verified, validated, and turned over to the customer. Learnings for future use in ideation are documented.

These phases are recursive; this means that each phase may be a project in itself that produces a deliverable but not the final asset. For instance, the ideation phase has a life cycle including planning for ideation, executing the ideation process, and closure of the ideation phase (e.g., completion of a requirements document). At this recursive level, the closure of a phase usually represents a hand-off of a deliverable and achievement of a project milestone, decision point, or gate. If the deliverable does not pass the phase gate review, it is returned for correction or the project may be killed or terminated.

While the project phases discussed above are performed sequentially, they usually overlap to some extent. Fast tracking, concurrent engineering, and similar terms refer to project strategies that have highly overlapping phases to achieve faster cycle times.

2.1.5 Continuous Improvement During a Life Cycle

The two-dimensional PDCA cycle and traditional asset and project life cycle illustrations, such as Figures 2.2-1 and 2.2-2, do not adequately illustrate the concept of progress through time or continuous improvement. Two-dimensional illustrations infer that one is always returning to the starting point, or that work follows a sequential line from beginning to end. In fact, with each iteration of the PDCA cycle, the asset portfolio or project performance or state is continually improved—it does not return to its original state. An asset's life cycle may include scores of projects to modify the asset. Likewise, a project may go through many iterations of design. In addition, innovation may lead to discontinuous leaps in performance or progress.

There are many ways to illustrate the concept of continuous improvement or progress through time including cyclones, spirals, wheel and axle, and other diagrams. In each of these diagrams, the circular motion aspect illustrates some cyclical process (e.g., PDCA) while the axis or axle represents progress through time or phases. Figure 2.1-3 illustrates the TCM concept for a project life cycle with PDCA shown as a spiral. The axis represents the life cycle phases of a project from ideation through closure. The spiral attempts to show that the plan-do-check-assess process is employed continually to achieve various milestones or deliverables at each phase of the project life cycle. The asset life cycle can be represented in the same way by substituting the asset life cycle phases along the axis.

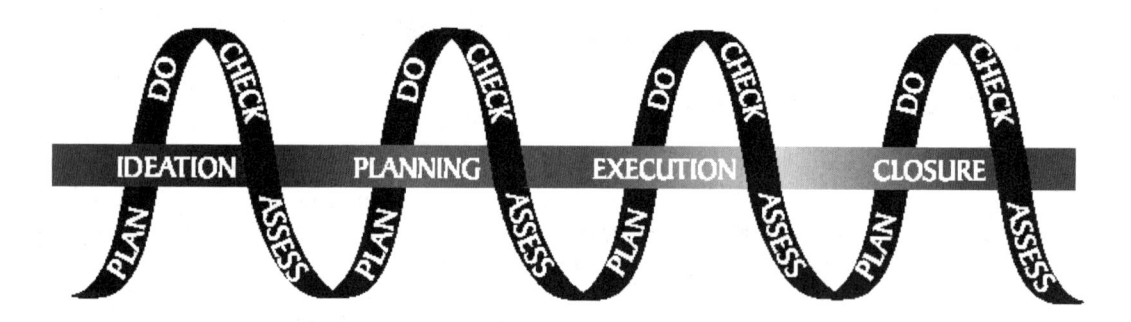

Figure 2.1-3 TCM Applies the PDCA Concept Throughout the Project or Asset Life Cycle

2.1.6 General Process Mapping and Diagramming

As was discussed previously, TCM is a quality driven process. Processes represent real work with which to create and deliver value to customers. A process consists of inputs, outputs, and mechanisms that transform the input to meaningful outputs. Outputs of one process may be inputs to another. The transforming mechanisms are referred to in the *Framework* as tools, techniques, or sub-processes.

These processes are illustrated in the *Framework* with block diagrams (i.e., blocks connected with arrows). The blocks represent a transforming mechanism or tool, technique, or sub-process. The TCM processes are "governing" or directing processes that deal with information rather than physical objects; therefore, the arrows represent the input and output flow of information or information products rather than physical objects. The arrows may be double headed indicating two-way flow or feedback. Groups of blocks surrounded by a dashed outline indicate alternative tools, techniques, or sub-processes or those performed in conjunction with each other using the same inputs and outputs. Input and output arrows that tie to separate diagrams are labeled with the related *Framework* chapter or section numbers that they tie to. Figure 2.1-4 illustrates the basic diagramming conventions used in the *Framework*.

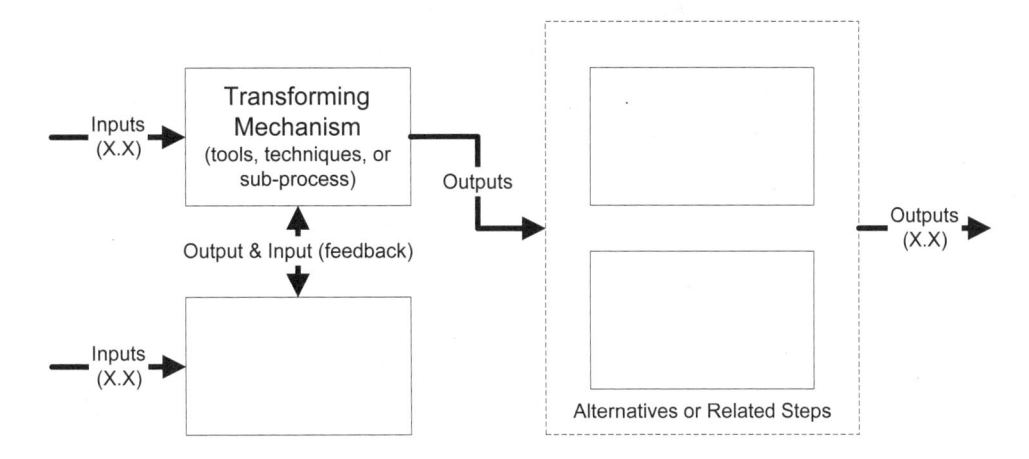

Figure 2.1-4 Process Map Representations as used in the TCM Framework

The *Framework* includes high-level, integrative process "maps" showing basic inter-relationships and sequencing of processes, and a rudimentary flow of information. The processes are mapped or diagrammed to the highest meaningful level of abstraction. These maps are not intended to be detailed data-flow, flow chart, procedural, logic, or other type of work definition diagrams. A process map does not show the way work is done—it attempts to balance the requirements of communication and content. A single block in a diagram may represent a complex process that would require an entire text to fully explain and document, and a single arrow may represent a large volume and variety of information and data products.

2.1.7 Key Concepts for Processes

The following concepts and terminology described in this and other sections are particularly important to understanding the process and life cycle basis of TCM:

.1 *Process.* A series of actions bringing about a result.
.2 *Business Processes.* There are various types of business processes including governing, asset creating, value adding, and enabling. *TCM is a "governing" process.* Governing processes direct or control other processes. A project is an "asset creating" process in that its output is an asset. Value adding processes are those that provide enhanced outputs to the external customer. Enabling processes are those that establish or provide capabilities for the other processes.
.3 *Process Map.* A diagram of a process that illustrates high level groupings of sub-processes and their interrelationships. A process map does not illustrate the way work is done at a detailed level.
.4 *PDCA Cycle (Shewhart or Deming cycle).* A basic management process first described in the 1930s. It is conducive to process management and control by inherently incorporating continuous improvement and measurement.
.5 *Recursive Process.* A process model that repeats itself when one of the steps of the process is described at a lower level of detail. As described in Section 2.2, the project control sub-process of TCM is a recursive application of the PDCA process model.
.6 *Inputs and Outputs.* The inputs to projects are resources and the outputs are assets. An asset may be a resource to a downstream process. Internal to the process maps, inputs and outputs are information and information products that are produced or utilized by tools, techniques, and sub-processes.
.7 *Tools, Techniques, and Sub-processes.* These are the transforming mechanisms and technologies that convert the inputs to outputs.

Further Readings and Sources

PDCA Cycles and Processes
Juran, Joseph M. and A. Blanton Godfrey. *Juran's Quality Handbook*, 5th ed. New York: McGraw-Hill, 1999.

Process Illustration
Fosberg, Kevin, Hal Mooz, and Howard Cotterman. *Visualizing Project Management.* New York: John Wiley & Sons, Inc., 2000.

Process Mapping
Galloway, Dianne. *Mapping Work Processes*. MilwaukeeASQ Quality Press, 1994.

2.2 Total Cost Management Process Map

2.2.1 Description

.1 Total Cost Management

This section builds on the information provided in the previous section by illustrating how the generic Plan-Do-Check-Assess (PDCA) model is implemented in the total cost management process map.

As defined earlier, total cost management is the sum of the practices and processes that an enterprise uses to manage the total life cycle cost investment of resources in its portfolio of strategic assets. Furthermore, the maximum value of TCM can only be realized when the enterprises' practices are applied logically in an integrated process. The TCM process map is a generic outline of that integrated process.

Figure 2.2-1 shows the TCM process map (the numbers in parenthesis correspond to chapters and sections of the *Framework* that cover each step). The figure shows how the PDCA model is applied recursively (i.e., in a nested manner) in TCM—the basic process is applied for each asset and group or portfolio of assets, and then again for each project being performed to create, modify, maintain, or retire those assets.

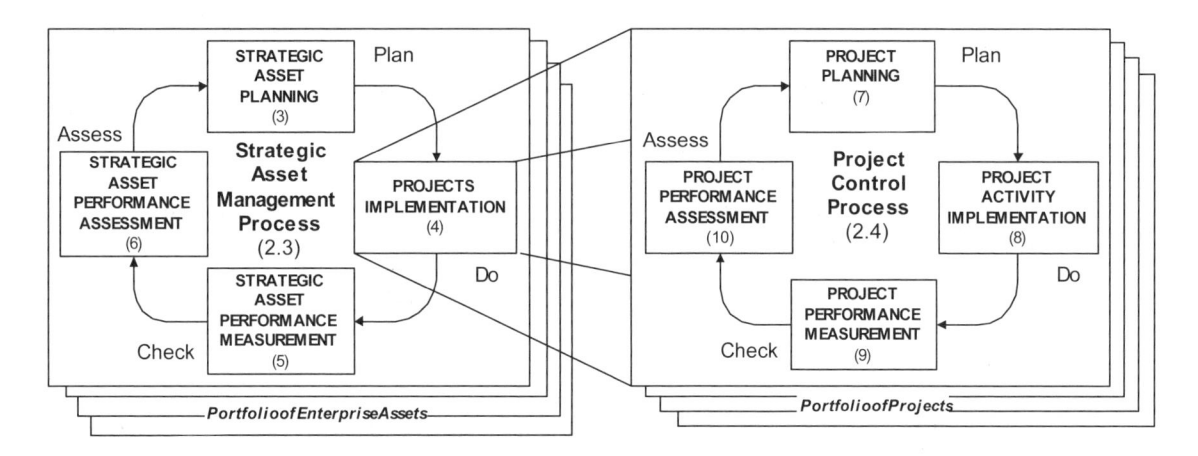

Figure 2.2-1 Total Cost Management Process Map

The two levels of the TCM process in Figure 2.2-1 are referred to respectively as the Strategic Asset Management and Project Control processes. Project Control is a recursive process nested within the "do" or project implementation step of the strategic asset management process. An enterprise will have a portfolio of assets in various stages of their life cycles, and during each asset's life cycle, many projects will be performed to create, modify, or terminate that asset.

.2 The Strategic Asset Management Process Cycle

Strategic Asset Management (SAM) refers to the macro process of managing the total life cycle cost investment of resources in an enterprise's portfolio of strategic assets. The portfolio will contain many assets in various stages of their life cycles (including those assets that are nothing more than ideas). Although investments are made in an asset through the performance of a project or program, SAM is not concerned with day-to-day project tasks; SAM focuses instead on initiating and managing the overall portfolio of projects in a way that addresses the strategic objectives of the enterprise.

The PDCA steps of the strategic asset management process cycle include:

1) Strategic asset planning - converts asset portfolio improvement ideas into plans for investing resources in assets.
2) Project implementation - asset investment plans and requirements are communicated to and executed by project teams. Project teams request resources as needed and report on their performance.
3) Strategic asset performance measurement - includes measurement of both operational asset and project performance.
4) Strategic asset performance assessment – performance measurements are compared to the plan, and corrective, mitigating, or improvement actions are taken as may be determined.

Section 2.3 further defines the SAM process map and the specific steps in its process cycle.

.3 The Project Control Process Cycle

Project Control is the recursive process cycle nested within the "do" step of the Strategic Asset Management process cycle. A project is a temporary endeavor an enterprise undertakes to create, modify, maintain, or retire an asset. During the life of a project, various resources are invested in the asset by the project team. Ultimately, a usable or operational asset is returned to the enterprise's asset portfolio at the completion of the project.

The PDCA steps of the project control process cycle include:

1) Project planning - converts project requirements or corrective action ideas into plans for investing resources in project activities.
2) Project activity implementation – project plans and requirements are communicated to and executed by project team members.
3) Project performance measurement - includes measurement of project activity progress and performance.
4) Project performance assessment – performance measurements are compared to the plan, and corrective, mitigating, or improvement actions are taken as may be determined.

Section 2.4 further defines the project control process map and the specific steps in its process cycle.

.4 Parallels Between Strategic Asset Management and Project Control Process Cycles

Strategic Asset Management and Project Control are both recursive PDCA processes. Many of their sub-processes are the same as will be described in Sections 2.3 and 2.4. For example, cost estimating is a planning sub-process in strategic asset management with an emphasis on stochastic estimating methods, while in project control, cost estimating emphasizes deterministic methods. Decision analysis, value analysis and engineering, risk analysis, and resource planning are some other sub-processes that are practiced in both the strategic asset management and project control process cycles. In the *Framework*, these parallel sub-processes are described only one time for brevity (e.g., the value engineering process is grouped with Project Control processes).

.5 Enterprise Organization for Total Cost Management

There is no one best organizational approach to achieve successful TCM implementation. Organizational approaches will be as varied as the strategic objectives of enterprises. However, all organizations should be focused on customer needs and on the entire life cycle of strategic assets rather than on short term functional considerations.

People are every enterprise's most important strategic asset. Organizational or human resource development can be viewed as a portfolio of projects undertaken to continually improve the work life and performance of each person in the enterprise. Narrow functional task training alone does not address the needs of TCM. For instance, a person who understands both stochastic strategic asset management cost estimating methods and deterministic project control estimating methods will be a more valuable asset than a person who understands only one type of cost estimating approach.

2.2.2 Process Maps for Total Cost Management

The process map for Total Cost Management was shown previously in Figure 2.2-1. At a more practical level, TCM is a combination of the process maps for Strategic Asset Management and Project Control as described in Sections 2.3 and 2.4.

2.2.3 Inputs to Total Cost Management

.1 *Investment of Costs or Resources.* Costs refer to any investment of resources in the enterprise's strategic assets. Resources may include time, monetary, human, and physical resources. An alternate definition of costs is economic resources used in achieving an objective.

.2 *Strategic Objectives and Requirements for Asset and Project Investments.* The TCM process takes place within the overarching context of the enterprise. Enterprise management establishes objectives and performance requirements for its assets and processes. TCM is concerned with the deployment of business strategy, not its formulation.

.3 *Working Environment Considerations.* (See Chapter 11.) TCM processes are enabled or constrained by technologies such as information and communication management and organizational development management. Also, the enterprise exists and processes take place within society where concerns for culture, environment, health and safety must be addressed.

2.2.4 Outputs from Total Cost Management

.1 *Managed Asset Portfolio.* The end products of the TCM process are new, modified, maintained, or retired assets that achieve the enterprise's strategic performance objectives and requirements.

.2 *Managed Project Portfolio.* For larger enterprises, projects will be in progress at all times. While individual projects have a beginning and end, the enterprise must consistently manage the project process to assure that all projects achieve the enterprise's objectives and requirements.

2.2.5 Key Concepts for Total Cost Management

The following key concepts and terminology are described in this section:

.1 *Strategic Asset Management.* (further described in Section 2.3) Refers to the TCM process as applied at an enterprise wide level to manage costs of the enterprise's entire strategic asset portfolio.

.2 *Project Control.* (further described in Section 2.4) Refers to the TCM process as applied at an individual project level to manage costs of creating, modifying, maintaining, or retiring individual strategic assets.

2.3 Strategic Asset Management Process Map

2.3.1 Description

.1 Definition of Strategic Asset Management (SAM)

Strategic Asset Management refers to the macro process of managing the total life cycle cost investment of resources in an enterprise's portfolio of strategic assets. The portfolio will contain many assets in various stages of their life cycles (including those assets that are nothing more than ideas). Although investments are made in an asset through the performance of a project or program, SAM is not concerned with day-to-day project tasks; SAM focuses instead on initiating and managing the overall portfolio of projects in a way that addresses the strategic objectives of the enterprise.[11] To paraphrase an old saying, the SAM process is more concerned with doing the right projects than with doing the projects right.

The main financial objective of many enterprises is to maximize the total long-term economic return or profit from its asset investments.[12] The economic performance of existing and proposed assets is often difficult to measure, yet the pressure to improve performance is relentless. Resources available to invest in assets are often limited or scarce while various parts of the enterprise may be in competition for those resources. In addition, the business environment is dynamic and uncertain. The SAM process therefore attempts to balance opportunities and risks against demand and supply for resources in such a way that the enterprise's objectives are met.

As discussed in Section 2.1, SAM is built on the PDCA cycle steps of (1) plan—establishing resource investment plans in assets, (2) do—making measurements of asset and project performance, (3) check—comparing the measurements against the plan, and (4) assess/act—taking corrective, mitigating, or improvement action as may be determined. This section translates those overall steps into sub-processes that will be more generally recognizable by practitioners.

.2 The Strategic Asset Management Process Cycle

Figure 2.3-1 in this section illustrates strategic asset management as a process. Each step or sub-process in the figure is covered in a section in the *Framework*. The SAM process starts with the established enterprise business strategy, goals, and objectives. From there, the needs and desires of customers and stakeholders are elicited, analyzed, and translated into asset performance requirements (Section 3.1). Considering the requirements and opportunities from performance assessment, asset investment options are identified and developed (Section 3.2), and then evaluated and decided upon (Section 3.3).[13] Asset investment plans and requirements are communicated to and executed by project teams (Section 4.1).

Asset performance is then measured, including cost accounting measurements (Section 5.1) and non-cost performance measurements such as quality (Section 5.2). Asset performance assessment (Section 6.1) includes techniques for determining if the profitability, cost of quality, and other parameters vary from established plans and benchmarks. Also, adverse or positive trends or changes in performance are evaluated. Benchmarking and other means are used to identify improvement opportunities for new or existing asset performance. If everything is according to plan, the process continues. If there are performance deviations noted in assessments, action should be taken to correct or improve the asset performance trend. If performance corrections or improvements will affect asset portfolio investment plans, or changes to stakeholder needs, requirements, or resource availability occur, then these changes must be managed using a change management process (Section 6.2). Finally, asset and project

---

[11] The SAM process assumes that the enterprise has developed its strategic objectives through a strategy formation process that is not part of TCM. TCM is focused on business strategy *deployment* in respect to cost management of its assets.
[12] Return on assets (ROA) or return on net assets (RONA) are common financial measures.
[13] Asset planning and investment decision making employ the planning processes covered in Chapter 7.

performance, history, and lessons learned are captured in a historical database for use in future asset management (Section 6.3).

.3 Organization for Strategic Asset Management

In smaller enterprises that have few and/or low value assets, the strategic asset management process may be managed by whoever controls or operates the asset, be it the proprietor, the facility operation manager, the financial manager, or so on. In larger enterprises, there may be a dedicated asset management organization that includes managers, strategic planners, cost estimators, financial and budget analysts, value specialists, cost accountants, and other specialists. In large enterprises, there may be a tiered organizational approach where major investments are managed centrally by a dedicated organization while minor investments are taken care of by the operators of the asset.

The asset management organization may also be responsible for development of project management personnel, processes, and procedures for the enterprise. This organization may also manage relationships with key resource providers.

2.3.2 Process Map for Strategic Asset Management

Figure 2.3-1 below maps the major steps or sub-processes of Strategic Asset Management.

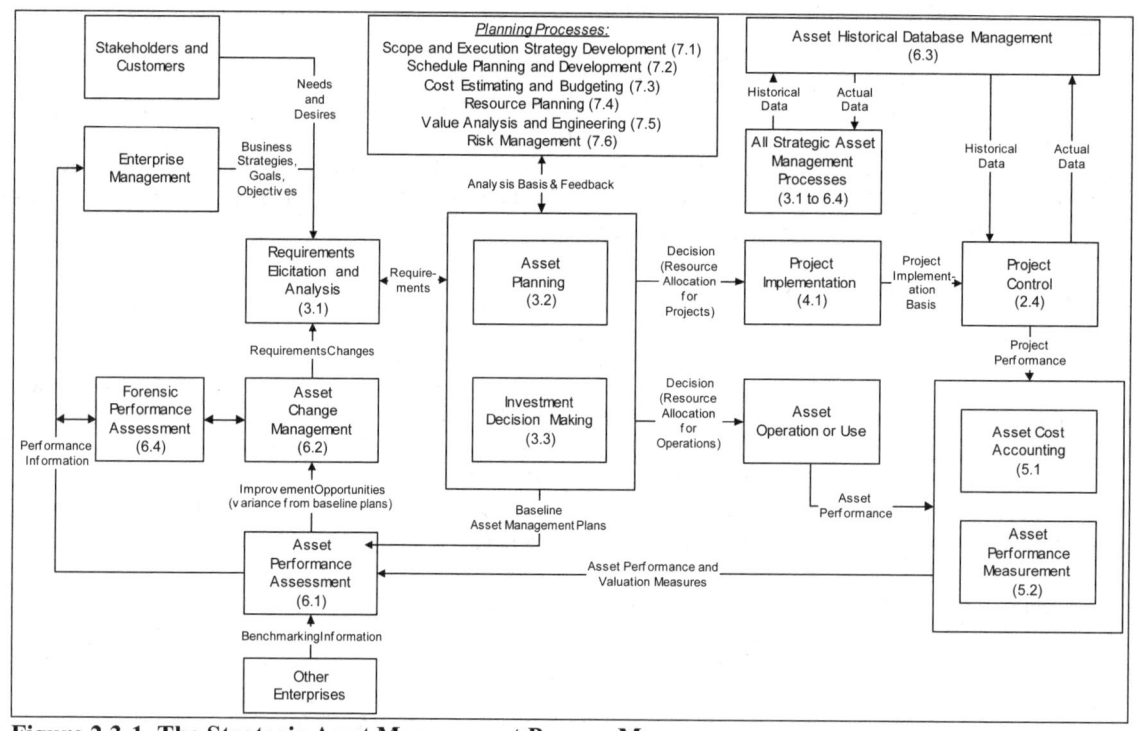

Figure 2.3-1. The Strategic Asset Management Process Map

The processes mapped conceptually above have each been diagrammed at a detail level in the sections noted. Those detail diagrams have also been combined into an integrated process diagram for strategic asset management, which is included in the Appendix.

2.3.3 Inputs to Strategic Asset Management

.1 *Business Strategies, Goals, and Objectives.* Guiding information, directives, and imposed requirements are elicited for analysis and translation to asset requirements.
.2 *Stakeholder and Customer Needs and Desires.* Information is elicited for analysis and translation to asset requirements.
.3 *Asset and Project Performance.* Relevant physical and performance characteristics and behavior of each asset and project are described in a timely manner in sufficient detail to support strategic asset management.
.4 *External Benchmarking Information.* Performance improvement ideas may be obtained through the benchmarking of practices and results for external enterprises and their assets and projects.
.5 *Project Actual Data.* Information and data from projects are captured for use in future asset planning.

2.3.4 Outputs from Strategic Asset Management

.1 *Project Implementation Basis.* The scope of asset solutions to be implemented in a project or program is described in sufficient detail to provide a basis for project scope and execution strategy development (Section 7.1). The asset performance requirements (Section 3.1) are also conveyed so that the project team may address them in its project control planning. Cost, schedule, and resource requirements such as target costs, capital and maintenance budgets, schedule milestones, enterprise resource constraints, and other information is included.
.2 *Non-Project Decisions.* The investment decision may select a non-project solution (change to operation practice, expense, etc.) for implementation by the asset operator or user.
.3 *Performance Information.* The performance of the enterprise's asset and project portfolio is reported to enterprise management for its consideration in business strategy formulation.
.4 *Asset Historical Data.* Information and data from asset management may be used for project control purposes.

2.3.5 Key Concepts for Strategic Asset Management

The following concepts and terminology described in this and other sections are particularly important to understanding the strategic asset management process of TCM:

.1 *Benchmarking.* A process that compares the processes and performance of an enterprise's endeavors to the processes and performance of the endeavors of a set of peers or competitors selected because they are considered to be the best in whatever endeavor is being assessed.
.2 *Planning.* A management or control sub-process that consists of defining scope and establishing baselines or targets against which work performance can be measured. In strategic asset management, integrated asset project plans for cost, schedule, and resourcing are established. All plans should address risks.
.3 *Economic Evaluation.* A set of financial analysis techniques that considers all the relevant income and costs associated with an asset or project investment during all or part of the asset or project life-cycle.
.4 *Profitability.* A financial measure of the excess income over expenditure during a period of time. In terms of asset management, it is the net economic benefit resulting from an investment in an asset or a project.
.5 *Decision Analysis.* A set of analysis techniques that considers all relevant performance and requirements data about a set of asset investment options and produces a decision to pursue or not pursue one or more of the options evaluated.
.6 *Resource Allocation.* In terms of asset management, resource allocation is the end result of a decision when actions are taken to invest resources (human, time, or monetary) in an asset investment option to be realized through performance of a project.

Further Readings and Sources

The concept of strategic asset management as presented in the *Framework* as an integrated process is not well covered in industry literature. Most literature focuses on product and project planning and investment decision making practices. Less attention is given to following up on the decisions with asset performance measurement and assessment. To find sources on the various sub-processes of strategic asset management, readers should refer to each section's readings and sources list. The following references provide a broader context:

- Consortium for Advanced Manufacturing International (CAM-I). Programs include Cost Management Systems (CMS) and Process Based Management (PBM). www.cam-i.org.
- Cokins, Gary. *Performance Management (Finding the Missing Pieces to Close the Intelligence Gap)*. New York: John Wiley & Sons, 2004.
- Department of Energy. *Life Cycle Asset Management Good Practices Guides.* Department of Energy, Office of Science, DOE Order 430.1A (available at www.sc.doe.gov/sc-80/sc-82/430-1.shtml).
- Klammer, Thomas P. *Managing Strategic and Capital Investment Decisions*. Burr Ridge, IL: Irwin Professional Publishing, 1993.
- Pietlock, Bernard A. "Cost Engineering Taking on Capital Management," *Cost Engineering*, AACE International, January 2002.
- Rapp, Randy R., Editor. *Professional Practice Guide (PPG) #14: Business and Program Planning*. Morgantown, WV: AACE International, 2002.

2.4 Project Control Process Map

2.4.1 Description

.1 Definition of Project Control

Project Control is a process for controlling the investment of resources in an asset. In TCM, project control is the recursive process cycle that is nested within the "do" step of the strategic asset management process cycle. A project is a temporary endeavor an enterprise undertakes to create, modify, maintain, or retire a unique asset. Being a temporary and therefore unique endeavor, projects are by nature uncertain and that element of risk puts a premium on control and discipline.

As discussed in Section 2.1, project control (or control of any process for that matter) is built on the PDCA cycle steps of (1) plan—establish a plan, (2) do—make measurements of performance, (3) check—compare the measurements against the plan, and (4) assess/act—take corrective, mitigating, or improvement action as may be determined. As a cycle, steps 2 through 4 are repeated periodically until the project is complete.

.2 The Project Control Process Cycle

Figure 2.4-1 illustrates project control as a process. Each step or sub-process in the figure is covered in a section in the *Framework*. A project starts with project scope and execution strategy development, which translates the project implementation basis (i.e., asset scope, objectives, constraints, and assumptions from Section 4.1) into controllable project scope definition and an execution strategy (Section 7.1). From the work breakdown structure (WBS) and execution strategy, integrated plans for cost, schedule, and resource management are developed (Sections 7.2 to 7.4). The plans are time-phased baselines against which performance is measured. Value analysis and engineering (Section 7.5) ensures that the scope and plans consider functional importance of scope relative to costs. Risk management (Section 7.6) ensures that the scope and plans address uncertainty at that point in time. Procurement planning ensures that information about resources (e.g., labor, material, etc.) as required for project control is identified for, incorporated in, and obtained through the procurement process.

The project control plans are communicated to and implemented by the performing parties (Section 8.1). For work in progress, performance measurements include accounting for cost expenditures and commitments, as well as physical progressing, which includes measures of the work and resource quantities that have been completed (Sections 9.1 and 9.2.)

Performance assessment includes evaluative techniques for determining if the expenditures and progress vary from the plans (Section 10.1). If everything is according to plan, the control process continues on with more measurements. If there are performance deviations or trends noted in assessments, action should be taken to correct or improve the performance trend. Forecasting techniques (scheduling, estimating, and resource planning) are used to determine if corrective actions will achieve plan targets (Section 10.2). If performance corrections will affect the project scope, or changes to the requirements or scope are initiated by the strategic asset or other stakeholder, the project baseline plans must be managed to incorporate the changes (Section 10.3). Finally, project performance, history, and lessons learned are captured in a historical database for use in future asset management and project control (Section 10.4).

.3 Relationship of Project Control to Other Processes

Project control is essentially equivalent to the project management process stripped of its facilitating sub-processes for safety, quality, organizational, behavioral, and communications management. Project control may be considered the quantitative resource control subset of the project management process (or as the AACE International constitution states, where "…engineering judgment and experience are utilized").

Project control is also roughly analogous to the processes of manufacturing and enterprise resource planning (MRP/ERP) with the difference being that MRP/ERP is focused on ongoing operations rather than projects. The enterprise has a portfolio of operations, and MRP/ERP is a recursive process of controlling the investment of resources within those ongoing operations. MRP/ERP and project control processes share many of the same tools and techniques.

As was discussed in Section 2.2, many of the sub-processes in project controls are the same as in strategic asset management.

.4 Organization for Project Control

On smaller projects or those with limited types and quantity of resources, the project control process may be managed by the project leader be they a project manager, engineer, architect, systems analyst, cost engineer, or whoever. On larger projects, with many resources to deal with (such as major construction projects), there may be planners, schedulers, estimators, cost/schedule controllers, value specialists, cost accountants, and other specialists involved. Project control on large teams may be coordinated by a lead cost/schedule or resource manager, quantity surveyor, project controls manager, or project manager. For certain techniques, the individual performing the project tasks (i.e., turning the wrench) may be responsible for control tasks such as progress measurement.

A central project management organization may be responsible for development of project personnel, processes, and procedures for all projects in an enterprise (i.e., a project system). That organization may also manage relationships with project resource providers. All of the project control steps require experience and skills in which an enterprise should develop organizational excellence.

2.4.2 Process Map for Project Control

Figure 2.4-1 below maps the major steps or sub-processes of Project Control.

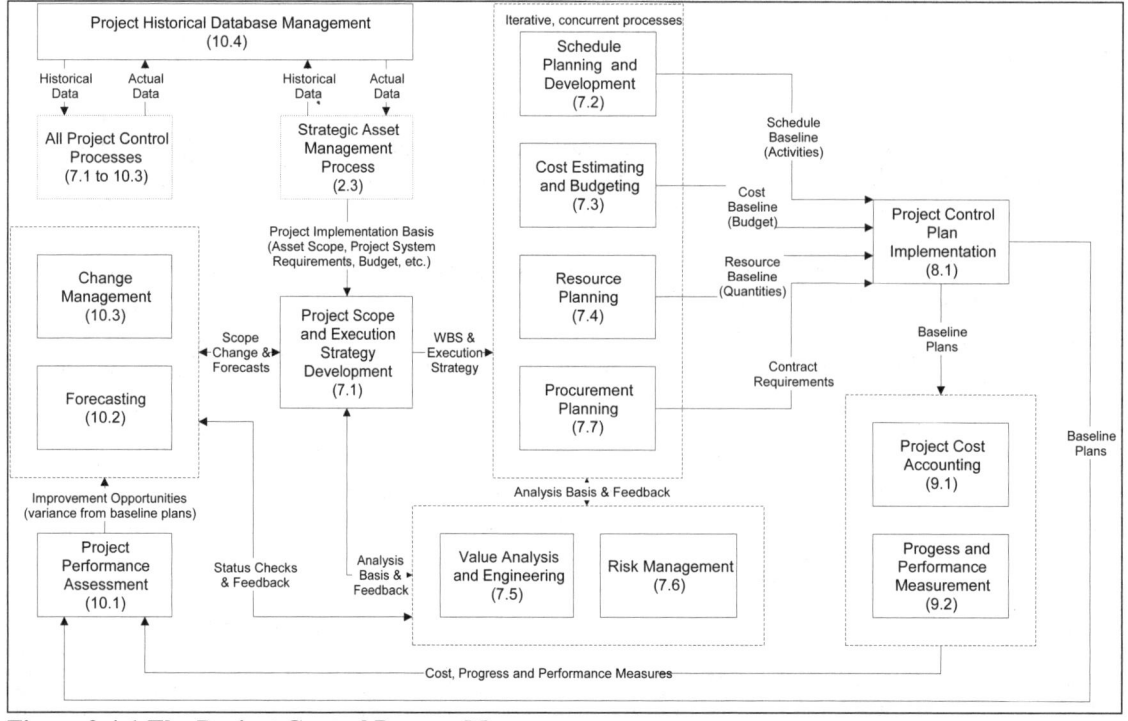

Figure 2.4-1 The Project Control Process Map

The process blocks or steps mapped above have each been diagrammed at a detailed level in the sections noted. Those detailed diagrams have also been combined into an integrated process diagram for project control, which is included in the Appendix.

2.4.3 Inputs to Project Control

.1 *Project Implementation Basis.* The basis includes objectives, constraints, and assumptions to be addressed in project control planning. The enterprise may establish requirements for schedule planning and development such as completion milestones, constraints, or limitations on the use of resources, and other criteria (see Section 4.1). The basis also includes the scope description of the asset solution in sufficient detail to provide a basis for planning.

.2 *Asset Historical Data.* Information and data from strategic asset management (e.g., relevant asset performance metrics) may be useful for project control planning purposes.

2.4.4 Outputs from Project Control

.1 *Asset.* The end product of the project process (of which project control is a subset) is the new, modified, maintained, or retired asset along with any information products defining or related to the asset. The overall output of project control is information needed for Strategic Asset Management.

.2 *Project Performance Information.* Project performance information is conveyed to the enterprise level for strategic assessment and financial analysis and reporting.

.3 *Project Actual Data.* Information and data from projects may be used in strategic asset management.

2.4.5 Key Concepts for Project Control

The following concepts and terminology described in this and other sections are particularly important to understanding the project control process of TCM:

.1 *Project.* A temporary endeavor undertaken to create, modify, maintain, or retire a unique asset (product or service). Control of ongoing endeavors producing non-unique assets (e.g., factories) is not covered by project controls but is covered by processes such as *manufacturing resource planning*. Given their temporary nature, an important characteristic of projects to address is risk and uncertainty.

.2 *Planning.* The management or control sub-process of defining scope and establishing baselines or targets against which work performance can be measured. For project control, integrated plans for cost, schedule, and resourcing are established (some refer to *planning* as the activity definition and sequencing steps in the scheduling process). All plans should address risks.

.3 *Control.* A process to ensure that an endeavor produces a desired end result. The process includes identification of the desired end result, measurements and assessment of intermediate results, and identification of actions needed to ensure that the end result is achieved. *Project controls* then is a control process applied to a project to ensure a desired asset investment result.

.4 *Requirements.* An established requisite characteristic of an asset, product, process, or service.

.5 *Scope.* The sum or end result of all resources and activities to be invested in an asset or project. *Scope definition* is a process to decompose the scope into manageable elements.

.6 *Scheduling.* A predictive process of estimating and assigning the duration of activities based on available resources and planned means and methods and iteratively refining the planned activity logic in a way that achieves asset investment and project time objectives. A *schedule* is the output of the planning and scheduling process that documents planned activities and their start and finish times in a way that is logically sequenced; achieves asset investment, operation, project or other time objectives; and addresses available resources, investment objectives, and constraints. A schedule may be used for projects, operations, maintenance, business planning, and other purposes.

.7 *Estimating.* A process to predict or approximate the cost of or price for scope. Estimating quantification techniques are also used to predict or approximate resource quantities and schedule durations.

- .8 *Budgeting.* A process to develop a cost plan by allocating estimated costs or prices to controllable *cost accounts* or activities and time phasing the cost in accordance with the schedule.
- .9 *Resource Planning.* A process of defining resource types and quantities needed to achieve the scope and time phasing the resourcing in accordance with the schedule.
- .10 *Cost Accounting.* A process of measuring and reporting actual costs for financial reporting and project control purposes. For control, costs are collected in *cost accounts* that correspond to the budget accounts.
- .11 *Baseline.* A plan or target against which performance is measured. Analogous to baseline targets in statistical process control.
- .12 *Value Analysis and Engineering.* A process to analyze the functional value of a process, asset, product, or service where *value* is defined as the ratio of importance to cost. Increasing value is not synonymous with decreasing cost because value takes into consideration measures of functional importance.
- .13 *Risk Management.* A process to identify, quantify, manage, and communicate risks or uncertainties that may impact an asset investment or project. Also includes steps to find ways to mitigate risk factors; to continuously monitor the project or asset for the occurrence of risk factors; and to continue to identify, quantify, manage, and close out risks throughout the life cycle of the project or asset.

Further Readings and Sources

The following sources provide basic information related to project control. There are many references for project control principles in various industries. Because project control is a major subset of project management, texts on project management are also good general references.

Cost Engineering and Project Control

AACE International, the Association for the Advancement of Cost Engineering, www.aacei.org

- *AACE International's Cost Engineers Notebook.* Morgantown, WV: AACE International (current revision).
- *AACE International's Recommended Practices.* Morgantown, WV: AACE International (current revisions).
- Amos, Scott J., Editor. *Skills and Knowledge of Cost Engineering*, 5th ed. Morgantown, WV: AACE International, 2004.
- Clark, Forrest and A.B. Lorenzoni. *Applied Cost Engineering*, 3rd ed. New York: Marcel Dekker, 1996.
- Gransberg, Douglas D. and James E. Koch, Editors. *Professional Practice Guide (PPG) #12: Construction Project Controls.* Morgantown, WV: AACE International, 2002.
- Hackney, John (Editor: Kenneth Humphreys). *Control and Management of Capital Projects*, 2nd ed. Morgantown, WV: AACE International, 1997.
- Humphreys, Kenneth, Editor. *Jelen's Cost and Optimization Engineering.* New York: McGraw-Hill, 1995.
- Humphreys, Kenneth, Editor. *Project and Cost Engineer's Handbook*, 4th ed. New York: Marcel Dekker, Inc., 2005.
- Humphries, Kenneth and Paul Wellmann. *Basic Cost Engineering*, 3rd ed. New York: Marcel Dekker, 1996.
- O'Brien, James J. and Fredric L. Plotnick. *CPM in Construction Management,* 6th ed. New York: McGraw-Hill, 2005.
- Pritchett, Michael B., Editor. *AACE International's Certification Study Guide*, 3rd ed. Morgantown, WV: AACE International, 2006.
- Stumpf, George R., Editor. *Professional Practice Guide (PPG) #5: Earned Value.* Morgantown, WV: AACE International, 1999.
- Ward, Sol. *Cost Engineering for Effective Project Control.* New York: John Wiley & Sons, 1992.

Project Management and Project Control
Project Management Institute, www.pmi.org
- *A Guide to the Project Management Body of Knowledge (PMBOK® Guide)*, 3rd ed. Newton Square, PA: PMI, 2004.
- Bent, James and Kenneth Humphreys, Editors. *Effective Project Management Through Applied Cost and Schedule Control*. New York: Marcel Dekker, Inc., 1996.
- Kerzner, Harold. *Project Management*, 7th ed. New York: John Wiley & Sons, 2000.
- Murch, Richard. *Project Management: Best Practices for IT Professionals*. New Jersey: Prentice Hall, 2000.
- O'Brien, James J. and Robert G. Zilly. *Contractor's Management Handbook,* 2nd ed. New York: McGraw-Hill, 1991.

II. STRATEGIC ASSET MANAGEMENT PROCESS

CHAPTER 3

STRATEGIC ASSET PLANNING

3.1 Requirements Elicitation and Analysis

3.1.1 Description

Requirements elicitation and analysis is the entry process to TCM and the first of the strategic asset planning processes. It is a process of identifying stakeholders and their needs, wants, and expectations; probing deeper into them; and documenting them in a form that supports planning, communication, implementation, measurement, and assessment. The goal of requirements elicitation and analysis is to understand the problem or opportunity and state what will be required of any solution. A design team will consider the requirements and formulate alternate solutions that will be decided upon for implementation. Asset performance assessment and change management identify the business performance issues (problems and opportunities) for the existing asset and project portfolio (Sections 6.1 and 6.2).

Generally speaking, requirements deal with what users or customers need to accomplish, and not how the solution or assets (i.e., facilities, products, systems, etc.) will achieve the desired result. The asset planning process (Section 3.2) determines and specifies the scope of asset alternatives and how they will function, and the project implementation process (see Section 4.1) sets in motion the processes to determine how the selected asset alternative will be implemented. The alternatives may be a project to create or modify a capital asset or product, or a non-project maintenance or operational *corrective action* to an existing asset or product.

In as much as the project process or system is also an asset of the enterprise, requirements for solutions to project problems and opportunities, in general or in respect to a particular project, are elicited, analyzed, and specified as well.

.1 Requirements

Requirements originate from the user, customer, or other stakeholder's perceptions of problems or opportunities that stimulate a request to address it.[14] A *user* requirement is a condition or capability that particular users communicate and agree any solution must have to address their perceived problem or opportunity. *Requirement specifications* however are derived by *eliciting and analyzing* all stakeholder input. Specified requirements that result from the analysis process are sometimes called *derived* requirements because, unlike *user* requirements, they are not expressed directly by the stakeholder. This distinction is important because if the elicitation and analysis process is done poorly, the final derived requirement specifications may diverge from what the stakeholders want or need.

In TCM, requirements are sometimes *imposed* (e.g., as a business or government mandate, a condition of a contract, etc.) by or upon the business. These requirements may be directly documented as a requirement specification and may influence the derivation of other requirements. The TCM process does not include business strategy development during which many of these more "strategic" requirements are established. The process described in this section is most applicable to *derived* requirements.

It is important to recognize that needs, wants, and expectations are not requirements until they have been elicited, analyzed, and documented through a requirements elicitation and analysis process. The desired characteristics of a requirement include the following:

- *Solution free or technology independent.* Multiple design options may satisfy a requirement. The term "design constraint" is often used when there is only one feasible solution that can meet the requirement. It should define what the asset will do, and not how it will do it or how it will be implemented. The "hows" are defined in the asset planning process (Section 3.2).
- *Organized.* A hierarchical structure is preferred. The structure should ensure that the

---

[14] Texts on product design tend to focus on users or customers; this section uses the term "stakeholders" to represent all users, customers, and others affected by a problem or its potential solution (which may include society at large).

requirements are complete, readily locatable, sorted by type, and integrated without conflicting with each other.
- *Clear.* Short, simple, unambiguous requirement statements are preferable; however, any qualifications regarding the requirements should be noted.
- *Prioritized.* The value of each stakeholder requirement may be ranked.
- *Traceable.* Each requirement should be specific to a stakeholder or other origin. This facilitates the change management process (Section 6.2).

Requirements can generally be categorized as either a *functional* requirement (i.e., what the solution has to do), or a *constraint* or *non-functional* requirement (i.e., qualities or attributes that a solution must have). A functional requirement is usually a verb-noun description of what the solution needs to be able to do (e.g., it must *pump water*). A constraint is usually an adjective description (e.g., it must be *reliable* and *profitable*).

Some might add *business* requirements (i.e., enterprise or operations missions, goals, or drivers) as a category, but, in general, these can often be categorized as *constraints*. For example, the main business objective of a corporate enterprise may be to maximize the total long-term economic return of or profit from its asset investments (see Sections 2.3 and 3.3); the need for profit can then be expressed as a constraint for an investment.

TCM and other quality-driven processes rely on measurement. Therefore, the description of each functional requirement and constraint must also include a measurable performance quantity or statement. The quantified aspect of a functional requirement or constraint is called a *performance* requirement. For example, the requirement to "pump water" could be expanded to specify "...at X capacity." Likewise, the required attributes of being "reliable and profitable" could additionally specify "...with downtime less than X percent and return on investment of at least Y percent."

The overall document of requirements, and output of this process, is a *requirements specification* (not to be confused with the more common "design specification"). A requirement specification can be a conceptual or broad representation of the customer wants and needs for an overall solution, or detailed and specific enough to support the design and procurement of individual solution components.

.2 Business Strategy and Requirements

The business strategy development process must align with the strategic asset management (i.e., strategy deployment) process.[15] *Balanced scorecard* is a common methodology that aligns these processes. Balanced scorecard seeks to ensure that business strategy development and deployment look at performance from a "balanced" perspective, measuring business drivers in addition to traditional financial metrics. Most balanced scorecard implementations focus on four perspectives in the asset planning, measurement, and assessment processes: *financial, customer, business process*, and *learning and growth*. For each perspective, the business identifies strategic objectives (e.g., "exceed shareholder expectations" from a financial perspective or "faster order process" from a business process perspective). In some cases, the objectives may be expressed in the form of a requirement (i.e., an imposed business requirement or constraint such as a return on investment measure). In other cases, the requirements elicitation and analysis process is used to translate the objectives to quantified requirements.

The number of requirements established, and hence asset performance measures to capture and assess, can be quite large. Therefore, most enterprises that used a balanced scorecard approach focus on a few key requirements or performance indicators (KPI) that are measures believed to most directly correlate with successful achievement of business objectives.

---

[15] The business strategy *development* process, which covers all aspects of business management, is not included in the TCM Framework. However, in regard to asset investments, business strategy implementation or deployment uses the strategic asset management process to plan assets and implement projects, and to measure and assess the performance of the enterprise's asset portfolio.

Addressing "balanced" objectives from many perspectives adds several challenges to requirements elicitation and analysis: stakeholders may be difficult to identify and communicate with; their individual priorities and goals may differ and conflict; their awareness and understanding of their needs (let alone business strategy) is sometimes unclear or difficult to articulate; and their needs may differ depending on shifting conditions in the environment in which the enterprise exists. In addition, requirements may change (e.g., by refining or clarifying details, by stakeholders changing their mind, etc.) during the life cycle of the asset. Therefore, considering balanced perspective during requirements elicitation and analysis puts a premium on having an effective established process such as TCM.[16]

.3 Cost Management and Requirements

A balanced requirements perspective also includes the early consideration of costs. Traditionally, the primary cost management concern during the requirements elicitation and analysis process has been business requirements regarding profitability. Functional requirements were usually determined initially with little regard for cost and it was not until a solution alternative was designed and estimated that costs were considered. This often resulted in costly, time-consuming design rework when the alternatives were found to be too costly and/or unprofitable.

However, *target costing* methods (includes design-to-cost [DTC] and cost as an independent variable [CAIV])[17] are being used more frequently. In these concepts, cost is an imposed or derived constraint (or preference), and the costs of meeting functional requirements are considered from the very start of strategic asset planning. Quality function deployment (QFD), which has traditionally been focused on "deployment" of functional requirements, is also evolving to consider cost as a requirement. If the QFD variation called *cost deployment* is going to be used in strategic asset planning, then cost constraints will also need to be considered in requirements elicitation and analysis.

---

[16] See Section 11.1 concerning societal values and ethics and 11.6 concerning the environment, health, safety, and security for which identifying stakeholders and eliciting and analyzing their wants and needs is particularly challenging.

[17] While the goals of these concepts are similar, the specifics of each methodology differ. Target costing has generally been applied in commercial industry while DTC and CAIV have been applied in government programs. The term "target costs or costing" is used here generically to apply to all methods in which costs are established as a requirement.

3.1.2 Process Map for Requirements Elicitation and Analysis

Figure 3.1-1 illustrates the process map for requirements elicitation and analysis. The input is customer requests and information about performance problems and opportunities and the output is improved, actionable knowledge in the form of a requirement specification.

While the map is shown as a sequential process, the elicitation, analysis, and review steps are likely to be more concurrent and iterative in practice. For example, at a detailed requirements interview with a given stakeholder or team (for a problem of limited scope), an analyst or planner may simultaneously elicit, analyze and review information, and specify a requirement that addresses that stakeholder's needs. As the analysts elicit information, they are constantly and simultaneously evaluating to test if the stakeholders are saying what they mean, and assuring that the stakeholders agree with a specified requirement.

A complex problem will have many stakeholders, often with conflicting needs. There may be separate interviews as described above, followed by analysis and review steps to resolve conflicts. This is to assure a balanced perspective, and to test whether, after negotiation and compromise, the specified requirements are still addressing everyone's perceptions of the problem or opportunity. Also, the process is applied iteratively with asset planning (see Section 3.2) in a phased manner as understanding of the problem and planning of the solution is progressively elaborated.[18]

These variations need to be kept in mind while considering the illustrated process and the process step discussions that follow.

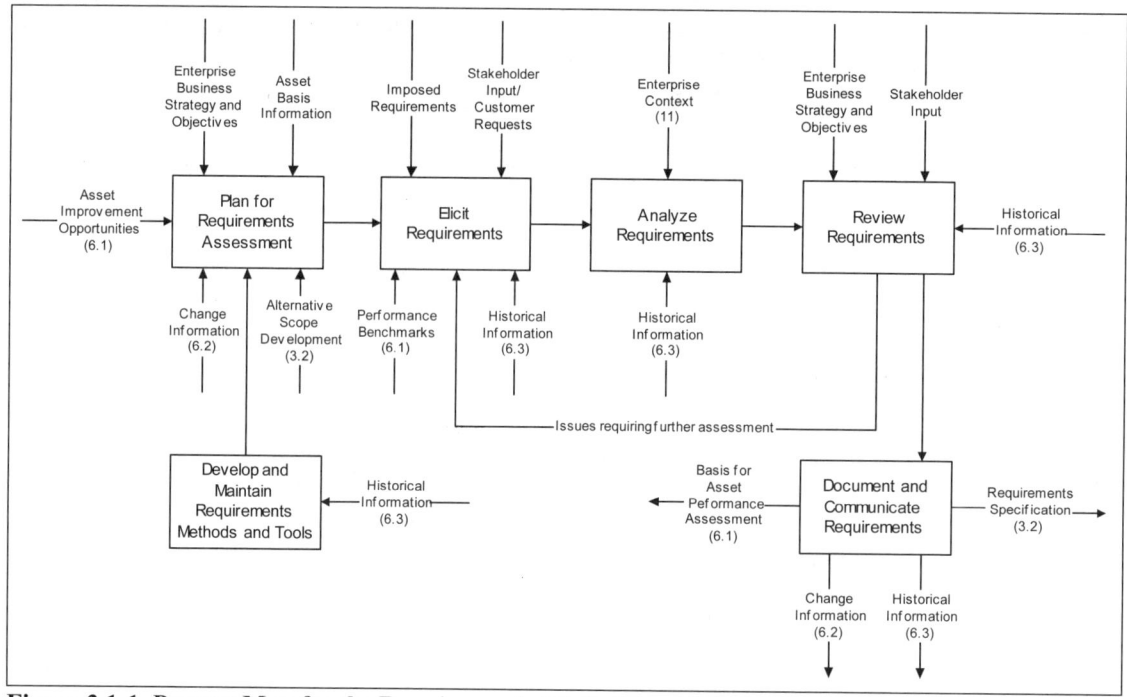

Figure 3.1-1. Process Map for the Requirements Elicitation and Analysis

The following sections briefly describe the steps (i.e., sub-processes) in the requirements elicitation and analysis process.

---

[18] See Sections 4.1 and 7.1 regarding phased project scope development.

.1 Plan for Requirements Elicitation and Analysis (and Asset Planning)

The requirements elicitation and analysis process is performed throughout the life cycle of an asset or project. Discrete or periodic efforts may occur as part of a regular capital or operating budgeting or asset management cycle. Requirements are also reconsidered regularly during change management, and prior to conducting a forensic performance assessment (Sections 6.2 and 6.4, respectively). In any case, the process requires that leadership for the assessment process be established. Process leadership, working with the client or sponsor (i.e., generally a business manager or management team for whoever is investing in and/or will own the asset), must first define the general nature and boundaries of the business problem that must be solved. These boundaries include the scope of the asset portfolio components affected (e.g., facilities, products, etc.) and where they fit in the business environment (i.e., the context). The process leadership must then select or develop appropriate methods and tools for the process. Because strategic asset planning processes (requirements elicitation and analysis, asset planning, and investment decision making) and methods (e.g., target costing, QFD, etc.) are generally integrated, planning for the process should address the effort as a continuum.

The process leadership then identifies and obtains the resources required to perform the study process (i.e., the feasibility study or product development team). The team then gathers or identifies sources of applicable information relative to the subject asset and context and appropriate to the methodology.

Basic inputs to requirements elicitation and analysis planning include the business strategy and objectives relative to the study scope. Enterprises generally have strategic planning and business modeling processes that help identify and frame market and other improvement opportunities. For existing assets, improvement opportunities are identified by the asset performance assessment process (Section 6.1), and the need for changes in requirements is identified in the asset change management process (Section 6.2).

Historical data regarding the performance of existing assets in relation to their requirements provide lessons as to past challenges and successful approaches (Section 6.3). However, changing organizations, business environments, and markets call for periodically refreshing requirements.

Finally, a key planning task is to identify stakeholders. It is their needs, wants, or expectations that are assessed by this process. Stakeholders are persons and organizations such as shareholders, customers, sponsors, performing organizations, and the public who may obtain, own, and/or use the asset as well as those whose interests may be otherwise affected by the existence or use the asset. They also include those who may be actively involved in associated projects, or whose interests may be affected by execution or completion of the projects. They may exert influence over the management and use of assets and/or the project and its deliverables.

.2 Elicit Requirements

As was defined earlier, some requirements may already be documented and imposed (e.g., existing standards or specifications) and these need to be identified. Other requirements must be drawn out of or elicited from the stakeholders. There are many techniques for eliciting requirements. The most basic methods include questionnaires, surveys, interviews, checklists, and group brainstorming sessions. As the business problems, systems, and requirements become more complex and uncertain, prototyping, modeling, and other techniques may be applied.

Individuals are often poor proxies for organizations, constituencies, or systems. Stakeholders may be difficult to identify and communicate with, their awareness and understanding of their needs is sometimes unclear or difficult to articulate, and their needs may differ depending on shifting conditions in the environment in which the enterprise exists. Other stakeholders may be inappropriately certain as to what the requirements and/or scope of the asset alternative are. Or their awareness and understanding of the requirements may be incomplete. These factors may require that a variety of elicitation techniques be used with the various stakeholders, and that modeling be used. Historical requirements elicitation and analysis information is also useful as it may identify requirements otherwise overlooked.

In QFD and other processes, technical performance metrics (i.e., performance constraints) are identified in this step. Competitive benchmarks (see Section 6.1) for performance metrics may also be identified for consideration in the analysis step.

Elicitation is an iterative process with asset planning (Section 3.2). All requirements are not elicited at once; requirements are progressively elaborated and become more detailed, moving from defining overall business requirements (e.g., translated from goals such as maximized return on investment) to functional requirements for components of an asset as its scope is elaborated in the asset planning process.

As was noted, elicited needs, wants, or expectations of the stakeholders are not requirements until they have been analyzed, validated, and documented. In many cases, various needs will conflict, will not be quantified, or otherwise will not yet form a basis for strategic asset management.

.3 Analyze Requirements

The goal of analysis is to take the generally unstructured input from the elicitation step and make it suitable as a basis for asset planning and performance assessment. Section 3.1.1.1 describes the characteristics of a good requirement for performance assessment. Analysis techniques may vary from an analyst simultaneously eliciting, analyzing and reviewing information and specifying requirements that address stakeholder needs on the spot, to a workshop held by a study team, to elaborate requirements modeling. Modeling can help describe or simulate the interaction of a system, its stakeholders, the enterprise, and the context within which they all exist. That context includes society, politics, the environment, and so on (see Chapter 11). The purpose of modeling is to ensure that all the requirements are identified and that their interaction and conflicts are identified over the course of the life cycle of the requirements application.

If target costing methodologies are being used, the identified "wants" of the market must be translated to a target price for the asset and subsequently to a cost requirement. For example, if the business problem (or opportunity) is a need for more electrical power, and the market price for power is a certain cost per kilowatt-hour, then any planned alternative solution must provide the power at some cost that allows for the desired investment rate of return. Methodologies that consider life cycle costs are generally preferred.

Regardless of whether costs are considered in requirements elicitation and analysis, effective requirements documentation should include the priorities or value placed on the requirements by the stakeholders. This information will be an important input to later asset planning and decision making. The QFD process specifically calls for requirements to be prioritized and rank ordered.

While requirements do not cover the "hows," which are specifically defined later in the asset planning process, it is not uncommon that ideas for asset solutions to the business problem begin to emerge during the requirements elicitation and analysis steps. These ideas and options should be captured for later consideration. At the end of the analysis step, the requirements are documented for review and communicated to the appropriate stakeholders who will participate in the review.

.4 Review Requirements

Requirements must be reviewed and tested to determine if they are:

- *Valid*. The requirements accurately describe the need for a solution to a problem. For example, a productivity measurement shows that a manufacturing line is producing X units per hour less than planned. The plant manager concludes that there is a need is for a new training program because the equipment operators are incompetent, when in fact the need is to reduce the downtime of the equipment and there is no problem with operator skills.

- *Complete.* The requirements address all needs. In the previous example, if there was really a need for both better training and less downtime and only one is addressed, then the problem will persist.
- *Consistent.* The requirements are not contradictory.
- *Balanced.* Requirements of all the stakeholders are fairly captured. When there are disagreements among stakeholders, they must be negotiated or otherwise resolved.

The review should also ensure that the requirements elicitation and analysis process is still working on the right business problem by considering any changes in the enterprise's situation. This and other issues identified during the review may require recycling through the requirements elicitation and analysis process.

As with analysis, techniques may vary from an analyst simultaneously eliciting, analyzing, and reviewing information and specifying requirements that address stakeholder needs on the spot, to a workshop(s) held by a study team. Review and testing may use techniques such as intuition, checklists, models (see previous section), comparison to historical assessments, group reviews, and so on.

Negotiating conflicts usually involves prioritizing each stakeholder's requirements and trying to include each stakeholder's most important requirements, while compromising on those that are less important. When testing if requirements are valid, the performance measurements and assessments may need to be challenged (e.g., is the plant manager in the prior example effectively measuring operability and downtime).

.5 Document and Communicate Requirements

The final step of the requirements elicitation and analysis process is to document and communicate the validated requirements. The requirements documentation (often called a *requirements statement or specification*) identifies and characterizes the requirements as described in Section 3.1.1.4. The requirements are then communicated to those who will be responsible for asset planning (Section 3.2) and asset performance assessment (see Section 6.1) and are entered in a database as appropriate (Section 6.3).

In a project environment, to ensure that the asset planning team (e.g., feasibility study team, product development team, etc.) understands the requirements, kick-off or alignment meetings may be held at the start of requirements elicitation and analysis work and then again as asset planning begins. As was mentioned, the requirements elicitation and analysis and asset planning processes are iterative and are generally managed as an integrated process.

The requirements specification is a living deliverable that is a representation or notation of the requirements; not the requirement itself. The stakeholders change and, in a dynamic enterprise, market, and social environment, their needs and desires change constantly. The requirement specification is also likely to change as asset planning is progressively elaborated. In any case, as was mentioned, change must be managed through the asset change management process (Section 6.2).

3.1.3 Inputs to Requirements Elicitation and Analysis

.1 Stakeholder Input/Customer Requests. Stakeholder needs, wants, or expectations are elicited. A need is something that is required for the system to function; a want is a demand or motivation by the customer; a request is not necessarily a requirement.

.2 Imposed Requirement. Some requirements (typically constraints) are already documented and imposed on the system. These may be a matter of enterprise policy (e.g., decision policy in Section 3.3).

.3 Enterprise Business Strategy and Objectives. Business strategy and objectives are described in sufficient detail to provide a basis for strategic requirements elicitation and analysis and to support review (i.e., to ensure that objectives are achieved).

.4 *Asset Basis Information.* The scope of the asset portfolio components affected by the business problem (e.g., facilities, products, etc.) is described to provide a basis for strategic requirements elicitation and analysis.

.5 *Asset Improvement Opportunities.* Asset performance assessment (see Section 6.1) identifies problems and potential improvements to asset performance.

.6 *Alternative Scope Development.* Asset planning (see Section 3.2) progressively elaborates the scope of the asset alternative solutions for which requirements will need to be elaborated as well.

.7 *Asset Change Information.* Changes to or new problems with business and/or asset performance may require that requirements be reassessed and changed (see Section 6.2).

.8 *Performance Benchmarks.* Performance metrics for competitors (see Section 6.1) are sometimes considered requirements (i.e., potential constraints).

.9 *Enterprise Context.* The requirements are analyzed in part to determine if they address the needs of or interaction with society, politics, the environment, and so on (see Chapter 11).

.10 *Historical Information.* Historical information supports each step of the assessment process by providing lessons learned, examples, and so on from past approaches (see Section 6.3).

3.1.4 Outputs from Requirements Elicitation and Analysis

.1 *Requirement Specification or Statement.* (See Section 3.2.) The asset planning process progressively elaborates the scope of the asset solution for which requirements need to be elaborated and become more detailed.

.2 *Basis for Strategic Performance Assessment.* The requirements establish quantitative measures against which the performance of the asset portfolio can be assessed (see Section 6.1).

.3 *Asset Change Information.* The documented requirements establish a basis against which potential changes can be assessed (see Section 6.2).

.4 *Historical Information.* The documented requirements and other deliverables from the process are information captured in a database to support future requirements elicitation and analysis (see Section 6.3).

3.1.5 Key Concepts and Terminology for Requirements Elicitation and Analysis

The following concepts and terminology described in this chapter are particularly important to understanding the requirements elicitation and analysis process:

.1 *Needs, wants, or expectations of stakeholders.* (See Section 3.1.1.1).
.2 *Requirements (including user vs. derived, functional vs. constraint, and performance).* (See Section 3.1.1.1).
.3 *Stakeholders/Customers.* (See Sections 3.1.1.1 and 3.1.2.1).
.4 *Balanced Scorecard.* (See Section 3.1.1.2).
.5 *Target Costing.* (See Section 3.1.1.3).
.6 *Requirements Statement or Specification.* (See Section 3.1.2.5).

Further Readings and Sources

Requirements elicitation and analysis is a key concept in various practice areas such as systems engineering, requirements engineering, configuration management, quality management, and product development. Government acquisition and software engineering fields have been leading sources of development in practices. The following references provide basic information and will lead to more detailed treatments.

- Burman, Deepak. "The Design to Cost (DTC) Approach to Product Development," *AACE International Transactions*. Morgantown, WV: AACE International, 1998.
- Cokins, Gary. *Performance Management (Finding the Missing Pieces to Close the Intelligence Gap)*. New York: John Wiley & Sons, 2005.

- Nuseibeh, Bashar and Steve Easterbrook. "Requirements Engineering: A Roadmap," *Proceedings of the International Conference on Software Engineering*. New York: ACM Press, 2000.
- Poortinga, Herman C. "From Business Opportunity to Cost Target," *AACE International Transactions*. Morgantown, WV: AACE International, 1999.
- Project Management Institute. *The Guide to the Project Management Body of Knowledge*, 3rd ed. Upper Darby, PA: Project Management Institute, 2004.
- Robertson, James and Suzanne Robertson. *Mastering the Requirements Process,* 2nd ed. New York: Addison-Wesley Professional, 2006.
- Wollover, David R. "Quality Function Deployment as a Tool for Implementing Cost as an Independent Variable," *Acquisition Review Journal*. Defense Acquisition University, 1997.

3.2 Asset Planning

3.2.1 Description

Asset planning is a process to identify, define, analyze, and specify the scope of alternative asset solutions that satisfy requirements. A good requirement is one that is "solution free" and describes the problem or opportunity as perceived by the customer and user. Thus, requirements are an input to this process. The outputs of asset planning are documents describing alternative asset solutions for further analysis in the investment decision making process (i.e., asset scope description). The asset planning process is sometimes referred to as a feasibility or appraisal study process.

Asset scope description defines the purpose or role, functions, specifications, and other attributes of the asset solution (e.g., features, appearance, etc.). For tangible assets, physical attributes tend to be most important. For services, processes, and other intangible assets, the important attributes tend to be more experiential in nature. The scope description also includes the cost, schedule, and resource requirements as well as risk and value attributes for consideration during the investment decision making process (see Section 3.3). In asset planning, the asset specification or product definition is only elaborated to the extent or level needed (i.e., feasibility level) to serve as a basis for effective investment decisions. Further definition (i.e., detail or production design) is usually an output of the project scope and execution strategy development process that takes place as a project is implemented (see Section 4.1).

There are two key steps in asset planning: identifying asset solution alternatives, and then analyzing their feasibility. The identification step applies the project scope development process (see Section 7.1) at a conceptual level of detail. Similarly, the feasibility analysis step applies the processes of schedule planning and development, cost estimating, resource planning, value analysis/engineering, and risk management to the scope definition at a conceptual level of detail. These planning processes, which are included in the *TCM Framework* project planning sections (7.2 through 7.6), also apply to asset planning. Further analysis of the alternatives in regard to decision making criteria (e.g., net present value) is done later in the investment decision making process (see Section 3.3).

Asset planning and project control planning can be viewed as related processes with differing purposes. Asset planning establishes a basis for deciding to implement an asset solution (i.e., either through a project per Section 4.1 or through some direct change to asset performance). Project control planning establishes a basis for implementing project control (i.e., the project control plan implementation process per Section 8.1).

The asset planning process is iterative with requirements elicitation and analysis (see Section 3.1) and investment decision making (Section 3.3), and these are generally managed as integrated processes. Such integrated processes have been described in the literature and are used most commonly in product development, software engineering, and government acquisitions (particularly for complex or new technology). Some common integrated methodologies used in these industries (introduced in Section 3.1) include target costing, design to cost (DTC), cost as an independent variable (CAIV), quality function deployment (QFD), and activity-based cost management (ABC/M). If a balanced scorecard strategy development and deployment approach is used, the associated key performance indicators (KPIs) or measures will also be considered in asset planning and investment decision making.

While the processes are generally integrated, the goal of requirements elicitation and analysis (which is business problem or opportunity understanding and communication) differs from the goal of asset planning and investment decision making (which is optimizing solutions). Requirements define "what" an asset solution has to do while asset planning defines "how" the requirements will be met. The investment decision making process then acts as a gate, through which an alternative is either approved and passes through for project implementation or is recycled for further elaboration of requirements or planning or other disposition as appropriate. As an iterative, cyclical process (i.e., see the spiral model in Figure 2.1-3), the requirements and asset scope definition are progressively elaborated, with asset requirements moving from defining overall business requirements (e.g., goals such as desired economic value added or return on investment) to functional requirements for components of the asset solution scope.

Enterprises may also use the asset planning process to address a business requirement to update a long term capital budget as part of their business strategy development process.[19] This process attempts to plan capital investments 2 to 10 years in advance. The scope definition of asset alternatives when they first appear in a long term capital budget is usually highly conceptual. Capital budgeting, which allocates funds to enterprise investments, including projects, is distinct from project control budgeting as covered in Section 7.3.

Unfortunately, the early cost estimates included in long term plans tend to become management expectations or *de facto* cost requirements. That is, succeeding updates of asset planning and capital budgeting have been anchored on prior long term plans regardless of how relevant prior plans are to the current requirements. This is an inappropriate method of target costing, which instead must start in each budget cycle with requirements (including cost) that address the current business problem.

The strategic asset planning process is generally sponsored by a business lead (i.e., the client who is investing in and/or will own the strategic asset), though much of the work is performed by the technical and planning organizations of the enterprise. In any case, the process is most effective when all the principal stakeholders with established requirements participate. Depending on the industry, the planning process work may be facilitated or led by product developers, design engineers, manufacturing engineers, or others. Cost and value engineers often play a key role and may lead the feasibility analysis step of the process, which tends to focus on cost and value issues.

Cost engineers may play a significant role in the planning process when target costing processes are used for requirements assessment and asset planning (includes DTC, CAIV, cost deployment, etc.). Using these concepts, cost is a requirement (specifically a constraint). As was discussed in Section 3.1, functional requirements and early design have traditionally been defined with little regard for cost; cost estimation was saved until alternative design completion. Using target costing type methods, the asset planning process considers the costs of meeting functional requirements as asset solution functions are elaborated and defined. In any case, cost engineers may be heavily involved in the estimating aspects of analyzing the feasibility of alternatives, particularly when ABC/M methods are used rather than simplistic (and inappropriate) cost allocations.

A key asset planning challenge is bringing creativity to the identification of alternate solutions. Soft requirements (i.e., resulting from social, cultural, political, and similar problems) can be particularly difficult to address. In some cases, conceptual prototyping and piloting are useful; these efforts can be projects in their own right and add complexity to the planning cycle. However, traditional bottoms-up, detailed planning processes and tools can stifle creativity and/or yield analysis paralysis. Therefore, a key asset planning concept is *modeling* (i.e., of asset performance, cost, risk, etc.), which can greatly facilitate creative solution identification and effective feasibility analysis.

3.2.2 Process Map for Asset Planning

Figure 3.2-1 illustrates the process map for asset planning. As mentioned, there are two key steps in asset planning: identifying asset scope solution alternatives, and then analyzing their feasibility. These steps generally apply the project planning processes covered in Chapter 7 to the scope definition at a conceptual level of detail (or the level necessary to make an investment decision). In addition, operations or production planning processes are also applied.

---

[19] The business strategy development process, which covers all aspects of business management, is not included in the TCM Framework. However, in regard to asset investments, that process uses the strategic asset management process to plan assets and implement projects, and to measure and assess the performance of the enterprise's asset portfolio.

While the map is shown as a sequential process, the steps are typically iterative in practice. This is indicated on the map by the "concept improvements" loop. Furthermore, issues raised during asset planning may lead to recycle for requirements elaboration (Section 3.1). Likewise, issues raised during the investment decision making process (Section 3.3) may lead to recycle for further definition and feasibility analysis.

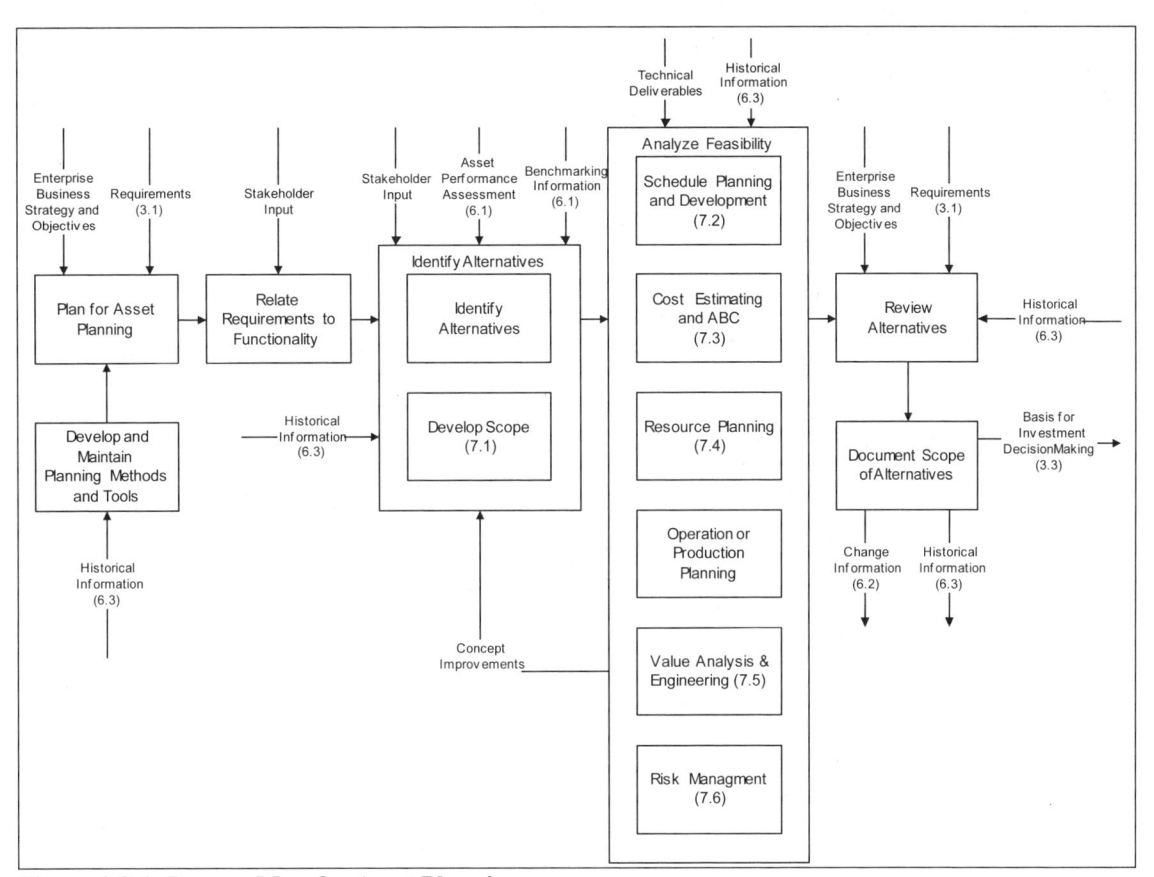

Figure 3.2-1. Process Map for Asset Planning

The following sections briefly describe the steps in the asset planning process.

.1 Plan for Asset Planning

As was discussed, requirements elicitation and analysis and asset planning are generally managed as integrated processes. Therefore, the planning for asset planning step is generally covered in Section 3.1 (i.e., integrated processes such as target costing and QFD address the processes as a continuum). However, as any phase of requirements assessment is completed and asset planning begins, plans for the effort should be revisited, reviewed, updated, and elaborated as appropriate.

The documented requirements (i.e., typically a requirements statement or specification) are the key inputs to planning for asset planning. Based on an assessment of these documents, the asset planning team (e.g., product development team, etc.) further identifies activities, resources, and tools for asset planning and plans for the effort accordingly. As was mentioned, many technical and planning skills and knowledge are applied during the asset planning process, and some of these resources may have to be acquired from outside of the enterprise (see procurement planning in Section 7.7). Also, modeling tools for asset planning may need to be created or modified, which may require significant resources and time. The asset planning team must also establish the general criteria and measures that will be used to rate, rank, or decide upon the feasibility of alternatives ideas during the performance of feasibility analysis.

As was mentioned, if significant prototyping and piloting are involved, these will require planning and project implementation decisions in their own right. However, if the business only requires an appraisal of the existing asset status or value, the asset planning process is simplified and may start with the analysis step.

The output of the planning step is documentation of the scope of the asset planning study effort, as reviewed and agreed to by the asset planning team and business leadership as appropriate. The scope describes the basis of the study (e.g., objective, methods, measures, assumptions, constraints, etc.) and defines what is or is not included in the study. To ensure that the asset planning team understands the requirements, kick-off meetings may be held as asset planning begins.

.2 Relate Requirements to Functionality

Documented requirements are an important input to asset planning. As described in Section 3.1, requirements define what assets (i.e., products, systems, etc.) are to do and not how they will do it. Requirements define specific and measurable asset performance requirements that can generally be categorized as business requirements (i.e., enterprise goals or drivers), functional requirements (i.e., what the asset has to do), and constraints (i.e., qualities or attributes that the asset must have).

Asset planning generally begins with the team examining each documented functional requirement (i.e., what the asset has to do), and describing the behaviors (i.e., functionality), features, or technical characteristics of any asset alternative (i.e., product, system, etc.) that might meet the functional requirements (i.e., how it must perform). Various methodologies have been developed that help teams relate the "whats" to the "hows." For example, QFD methodology uses a tool called the "house of quality," which is a matrix with requirements listed on the left, technical performance characteristics across the top, and the strength of the relationship between each requirement and characteristic rated within matrix cells. A characteristic that positively addresses one requirement might negatively impact another. The method allows for ranking the requirements and characteristics as well. This and similar methods help planners and developers ensure that the performance of alternative asset solutions (whether measured in terms of quality, cost, technology, or other measures) optimally addresses the requirements. In this step, the specific design of the solution is not developed, but its functionality and characteristics are framed.

As was mentioned in Section 3.1, all requirements are not elicited at once. Requirements are progressively elaborated, moving from defining overall business requirements (e.g., goals such as desired return on investment) to functional requirements for components of an asset as its scope is elaborated. Progressively breaking down functional requirements and functionality—from the highest level, to system, to unit, and so on—is called functional decomposition. Functional decomposition is similar to work breakdown (see Section 7.1), but it is focused on asset functionality rather than project work.

When target costing processes are used (i.e., DTC, CAIV, cost deployment, etc.), costs, as a constraint type of requirement, can also be matrixed by or allocated to functionality to help guide effective alternative asset solution identification. ABC/M methods similarly align cost with activities, although costs for activities may or may not be requirements or targets at this stage.

An advantage of functional decomposition for complex problems is that it is a useful starting point for developing rational models that can be used to identify, analyze, and validate the performance of alternative solutions. For simpler problems, for which off-the-shelf or historical approaches may effectively apply, formally relating requirements to functionality may not add much value, but the issues must still be considered. Also, as was mentioned, if the business requirement only requires the appraisal of an existing asset's status or value, the requirements and functionality assessment step may not be needed and the process can begin with the analysis step.

Having described the functionality, features, and technical characteristics of any asset alternative that might meet the functional requirements, the next step is to describe specific asset concepts (and their components as applicable) that provide the functional performance and features identified.

.3 Identify Alternatives and Develop Their Asset Scope

Two closely related steps are covered here: (a) identifying asset alternatives and (b) defining their scope to a level of detail sufficient to support feasibility analysis. The process of scope development is covered fully in Section 7.1. The step for identifying alternative asset solutions is usually led by the technical community (e.g., engineering, design, manufacturing, etc.). To bring creativity to the identification of alternate solutions, it helps to have multiple disciplines represented on the team.

The first information to obtain for this step, if applicable, is the status and performance capability of any part of the asset portfolio associated with the current business problem. This information is an output of the performance assessment process (see Section 6.1). It is possible that the capabilities of existing assets might be able to meet some or all of the strategic requirements. With this information in hand, there are many different methods that the team can use to identify alternative solutions. First, as was mentioned in Section 3.1, it is not uncommon for asset solution ideas to emerge spontaneously during the requirements elicitation and analysis steps. If these ideas are recorded, they are a useful starting point.

From there, methods include, but are not limited to, various problem-solving techniques such as: brainstorming, process analysis, benchmarking, research of historical designs or design patterns, and identifying off-the-shelf technology. For complex and/or risky concepts, prototyping or piloting may be justified (i.e., to test manufacturability, operability, constructability, etc.). The QFD process specifically highlights benchmarking competitive approaches.

No matter what method is used or who participates, there is a tendency to recycle proven ideas; however, in most cases, repeating past approaches is unlikely to lead to improved competitive performance of the enterprise's asset portfolio. However, historical or off-the-shelf solutions are often appropriate, especially for sub-components of the asset that are not a source of competitive advantage for the overall asset, or where the risk of using a particular new approach is unacceptable.

The output of the concept identification step is the documented scope of potential alternative asset solutions. As was discussed, the scope description defines the purpose or role, functions, specifications, and other attributes of the asset solution (e.g., features, appearance, etc.). The scope description must be detailed enough to support feasibility analysis.

.4 Analyze Alternative Feasibility

The analysis of alternative asset solution feasibility may be conducted by a team led by the planning community (e.g., cost engineers, value engineers, etc.) or technical specialists with experience in planning methods. In the feasibility analysis step, the team applies the project planning processes included in the *TCM Framework* project planning sections (Sections 7.2 through 7.6). While the analysis process steps are the same for asset and project control planning, asset planning is usually based on a conceptual level of asset and project scope definition.

In addition, the team must perform conceptual operation or production planning, which includes scheduling, cost estimating, and resource planning processes from an operations perspective (i.e., ongoing work) rather than a project perspective (work with a defined beginning and end).

An asset life-cycle model is often the basis for the feasibility analysis and later for investment decision making (Section 3.3). Such a model involves *forecasting* investment, revenues, and costs. Industry, economy, and other external factors are also part of the model.

The following sections briefly summarize each of the planning processes and discuss special considerations and/or provide examples for applying them in the asset planning process. In general, for each process, modeling is more likely to be used in feasibility analysis than in project control planning. This is because of the need to examine many alternatives, cases, and scenarios, and the limited resources and time available for analysis. When modeling is used, the team will require specialized tools and skills, including an understanding of systems analysis, operation processes, accounting, economics, probability, and statistics.

Schedule Planning and Development (see Section 7.2):

Schedule planning and development are the processes for the planning of work over time in consideration of the costs and resources for that work. Schedule planning and schedule development are separate but related sub-processes that call for different skills and knowledge emphasis. Schedule planning translates work package scope (see Section 7.1) into manageable activities and determines the manner and sequence (i.e., logic) in which these activities are best performed. Starting with the initial schedule model from schedule planning, schedule development allocates the available resources (e.g., cost, labor, etc.) to activities in the schedule model in accordance with cost and resource planning and alternative allocation criteria while respecting project constraints affecting the schedule (e.g., milestone dates). Schedule development generally includes iteratively refining the schedule planning (i.e., planned durations, means and methods, workflow sequence, or preferential logic) in a way that optimally achieves project objectives for time (e.g., milestones), cost (e.g., cash flow), and others.

For feasibility analysis, the work package scope is not well defined. The level of definition available may support only a simple bar chart schedule showing overall activities such as scope development, engineering, procurement, and construction of a facility or development and manufacturing of a product. Schedule development at this summary level may be done by using a simple model of estimated duration versus cost. Such a schedule will support very rudimentary cash flow and resource loading analysis and provide reasonable assurance that milestone date requirements can be met.

Cost Estimating and Budgeting (see Section 7.3):

Cost estimating is the predictive process used to quantify, cost, and price the resources required by the scope of an investment option, activity, or project. Budgeting is a sub-process within estimating used for allocating the estimated cost of resources into cost accounts (i.e., the budget) against which asset cost performance will be measured and assessed.

The cost estimating process is generally applied during each phase of the asset or project life cycle as asset or project scope is defined, modified, and refined. As the level of scope definition increases, the estimating methods become more definitive and produce estimates with increasingly narrow cost probability distributions. Stochastic and deterministic parametric cost models, factoring, and other estimating methods and tools are most widely used in asset planning.

With limited scope definition, the cost estimate will have very little detail. For example, only the building area and general features of the space (the payload, speed and key functions for a vehicular asset, etc.) may be defined for a building asset. Therefore, the estimate may consist only of the total cost of the building, vehicle, and so on with very limited breakdown. Estimating at this summary level may be done using a simple parametric model of estimated cost versus the identified parameters (e.g., area, speed, etc.), adjusted for major defined features.

One estimating concept that supports effective investment decision making is called activity based costing (ABC; see Section 7.3). Using ABC, costs are attributed or budgeted to the item or activity causing or driving the expenditure rather than through arbitrary or non-causal allocations. Too often, estimates allocate "overhead" costs to asset alternatives using methods such as pro-rating the overhead costs in accordance with direct costs. In fact, some asset alternatives may be disproportionate drivers of overhead costs. Such misallocation is likely to lead to many poor investment decisions.

If the business requirement is to sell, insure, or to take some other action requiring asset valuation or appraisal, estimating is generally the key (or possibly the only) analysis process applied.

Resource Planning (see Section 7.4):

Resource planning is a process to evaluate and plan the use of physical and human resources in asset investments and project activities. Most activities involve using people (i.e., labor) to perform work tasks. Some tasks involve creating an asset using component physical elements or parts (i.e., materials) as well as other items consumed during creation (i.e., consumables). Other tasks involve creating an asset using only information inputs (e.g. engineering or software design). To perform most tasks, people use tools (e.g., construction equipment, computers, etc.) to help them. In some cases, automated tools may perform the task with little or no human effort. The goal of resource planning during asset planning then is to ensure that labor, materials, tools, and consumables, which are often limited in availability, are invested in assets and projects over time in a way that optimally achieves business objectives and requirements.

As with estimating and scheduling, resource planning during feasibility analysis will not be detailed. However, the enterprise is likely to have multiple assets and projects competing for key resources, and business management must decide on the best allocation of those key (i.e., strategic) resources. Therefore, resource planning for key limited resources must be done as appropriate.

Operation or Production Planning

The preceding discussions primarily focus on scheduling, cost estimating, and resource planning processes from a project perspective (work with a defined beginning and end). However, these same basic processes are also applied for operation or production planning (i.e., ongoing work).

Depending on the nature of the operations (e.g., continuous, batch or repetitive, etc.), scheduling must consider not only work activities in a given production process or step, but the overall alignment of these processes with output capacity scheduling requirements. For feasibility analysis, operations scheduling is most concerned with overall capacity scheduling as it affects cost and revenue cash flows.

Cost estimating for operations is focused on product cost rather than fixed or capital assets. The methods of ABC are of paramount concern for operations and products. That is because operations tend to deal with many products or outputs that share common cost and resource inputs, making it more of a challenge to ascribe costs to each product appropriately. For feasibility analysis and investment decision making, it is critical to assign costs appropriately to the products being evaluated.

Resource planning for operations is heavily concerned with inventory and supply chain management, both for input and outputs of the operation. Enterprise Resource Planning (ERP) information technology has greatly facilitated resource planning for operations and provides a wealth of historical performance information that can be used for feasibility analysis.

Value Analysis and Engineering (see Section 7.5):

Value analysis (VA) and value engineering (VE), when applied as processes, are "the systematic application of recognized techniques which identify the functions of the product or service, establish the worth of those functions, and provide the necessary functions to meet the required performance at the lowest overall cost."[20] Typically, the lowest overall cost refers to the lowest life-cycle cost. VE is focused on the development of new assets and VA on existing assets or projects. We refer to them as VA/VE in this text.

The VA/VE process is most often applied at the initial phases of asset, product, or project planning when scope definition is evolving and changes are least disruptive. VA/VE may be the most important analysis process for asset planning (keeping in mind that VA/VE relies on estimating and the other planning processes), given its focus on the function of assets. Integrated requirements assessment and asset planning processes such as target costing and QFD are often applied in conjunction with VA/VE; they are supportive of each other. For example, in target costing, as an asset's function and components are decomposed, the target costs are decomposed and assigned to the components. This is similar to aspects of the function analysis step of VA/VE.

---

[20] SAVE International, Value Methodology Standard (Glossary), 2003.

VA/VE is one of many *value improving practices* (VIPs), which can be any practice that has a particular strong focus and/or effect on getting the most value from the process and is performed in a way that sets the practice apart from "business as usual." Section 11.5 describes VIPs in more detail.

Risk Management (see Section 7.6):

Risk management is the process of identifying risk factors (risk assessment); analyzing and quantifying the properties of those factors (risk analysis); mitigating the impact of the factors on planned asset or project performance and developing a risk management plan (risk mitigation); and implementing the risk management plan (risk control).[21] For asset planning, the goal of risk management is to improve the value versus risk profile of the asset.

The risk management process is applied in conjunction with the other feasibility analysis processes. For example, when risk management identifies a risk that can be mitigated using an alternative asset solution, the alternative concept is developed using the applicable planning process (e.g., cost estimating, scheduling, etc.). This iterative planning approach of assessing and analyzing risk factors and developing alternative concepts that mitigate the risks is applied until an asset alternative is selected for project implementation. Risk assessment, analysis, and mitigation efforts studies are typically applied in a phased manner consistent with the project scope development phases described in Section 7.1.

Feasibility Analysis Output

In some cases, it will be apparent that an alternative concept is not worthy of further analysis or that changes to the initial scope are needed to make the concept worthy. The planning team may drop or recycle these concepts through the alternative identification step as appropriate. Formal requirements or configuration change management is not applied at this stage as no basis of control has yet been established.

As appropriate to the plans and criteria established for strategic asset planning, the planning team will eventually conclude the feasibility analysis. The output of the feasibility analysis step is the documented scope of potential alternative asset solutions including their cost, schedule, resource, value, and risk attributes. The scope description must be detailed enough to support the investment decision making process (see Section 3.3) during which additional analyses regarding the key decision making criteria (e.g., net present value) are performed.

.5 Review Alternatives

The alternative concepts identified and analyzed need to be reviewed to verify that they meet the requirements as well as any criteria set for the planning process while ensuring that the process is still working on the right business problem. Issues identified during the review may require recycling through the asset planning or requirements elicitation and analysis processes. The review process may use techniques such as checklists, models, comparison to historical analyses, group reviews, and so on.

.6 Document the Scope of Alternatives

As was mentioned, the output of the process is the documented scope of potentially feasible alternative asset solutions including their cost, schedule, resource, value, and risk attributes. The scope description also defines the purpose or role, functions, and specifications of the proposed asset solutions for consideration during the investment decision making process. If an asset life-cycle cost or similar analytical model was developed to support the feasibility analysis, the model(s) should be documented for potential use in the investment decision making process. Finally, the results of and lessons learned from the asset planning process are also captured in a historical database (see Section 6.3) for consideration in future asset planning.

---

[21] These four phases were identified by AACE International's Risk Management Committee and published in the AACE International *Risk Management Dictionary* (Cost Engineering, Vol. 37, No. 10, 1995).

The documented scope will also be the basis of the configuration management process for any asset alternative selected for implementation. Configuration management is defined as a process to "...identify and document the functional and physical characteristics of a product, result, service, or component; control any changes to such characteristics; record and report each change and its implementation status; and support the audit of the products, results, or components to verify conformance to requirements."[22] This methodology is discussed in more detail in the asset change management process (see Section 6.2).

3.2.3 Inputs to Asset Planning

.1 *Enterprise Business Strategy and Objectives.* Business strategy and objectives are considered in planning for strategic asset planning and to support validation (i.e., ensure that objectives are achieved).
.2 *Requirements.* (See Section 3.1) A condition or capability that must be met or possessed by a strategic asset (i.e., system, product, service, result, or component).
.3 *Stakeholder Input.* Stakeholders may be the source of ideas for asset solution alternatives. Stakeholder input is also used to rank the importance of asset functionality, features, and attributes.
.4 *Asset Performance Assessment.* (See Section 6.1) Solutions may lie in the performance capability of the current asset portfolio.
.5 *Benchmarking Information.* (See Section 6.1) Asset solutions used by competitors or others may be considered as a source of alternative ideas.
.6 *Technical Deliverables.* Design information describing alternative asset solutions is developed as needed to support feasibility analysis.
.7 *Historical Asset Management Information.* (see Section 6.3) Historical information supports each major step of the process by providing learnings, examples, and so on from past approaches.

3.2.4 Outputs from Asset Planning

.1 *Basis of Investment Decision Making.* (see Section 3.3) The asset alternative's scope—including its cost, schedule, risk, and value attributes—is detailed to the level needed to make effective investment decisions. Asset life cycle cost models used for planning can also support investment decision making.
.2 *Change Information.* The documented asset scope establishes a basis against which potential changes in requirements, and in the asset configuration, can be assessed (see Section 6.2).
.3 *Historical Asset Management Information.* The documented asset scope and other deliverables from the process are information captured in a database to support future asset planning (see Section 6.3).

3.2.5 Key Concepts and Terminology for Asset Planning

The following concepts and terminology described in this chapter are particularly important to understanding the asset planning process:

.1 *Requirements.* (See Section 3.1).
.2 *Functions.* Attributes of an asset or project that give it a purpose (i.e., allow user/operator to accomplish a task) and make it useful or desirable (i.e., to have value).
.3 *Functional Decomposition.* (See Section 3.2.1.2).
.4 *Stakeholders.* (See Section 3.1).
.5 *Target Costing (including DTC and CAIV).* (See Section 3.1).
.6 *Quality Function Deployment (QFD).* (See Section 3.1).
.7 *Feasibility Analysis or Study.* A study to determine if requirements can be achieved by a proposed alternative asset, project, or course of action.
.8 *Project Control Planning Processes.* (See Section 3.2.2.4 and 7.1 though 7.6).

---

[22] *A Guide to the Project Management Body of Knowledge*, 3rd ed., Project Management Institute, Upper Darby, PA, 2004.

.9 *Operations or Production Planning.* (See Section 3.2.2.4).
.10 *Forecasting.* (See Section 3.2.2.4).
.11 *Activity Based Costing (ABC).* (See Section 3.2.2.4 and 7.3).
.12 *Appraisal (of Value).* To impartially estimate the value or worth of all or part of an asset based on examination of the asset and review of all the factors that would affect its value. This practice is usually performed by appraisers. Appraised value is typically calculated based on cost, income, or market comparisons. Some types of appraised value include fair market, liquidation, savage, scrap, replacement, or reproduction value.
.13 *Modeling.* The creation of a physical representation or mathematical description of an object, system, or problem that reflects the functions or characteristics of the item involved.
.14 *Prototype Modeling (Prototyping).* The creation of an original physical, functional version of an asset for the purpose of testing its feasibility and/or on which to pattern additional assets.
.15 *Configuration Management.* (See Sections 3.2.1.6 and 6.2).
.16 *Value Improving Practices.* (See Sections 3.2.2.4 and 11.5).

Further Readings and Sources

Asset planning is a key concept in various practice areas such as systems engineering, configuration management, quality management, product development, and project management. The following references provide basic information and will lead to more detailed treatments.

- Amos, Scott, J., Editor. *Skills and Knowledge of Cost Engineering*, 5th ed. Morgantown, WV: AACE International, 2004.
- Cokins, Gary. *Activity Based Cost Management: An Executive Guide.* New York: John Wiley & Sons, 2001.
- Klammer, Thomas P. *Managing Strategic and Capital Investment Decisions.* Burr Ridge, IL: Irwin Professional Publishing, 1993.
  Leo, Douglas W., Larry R. Dysert, and Bruce Elliott, Editors. *Professional Practice Guide No. 13: Parametric and Conceptual Estimating.* CD ROM. Morgantown, WV: AACE International, 2002.
- Ostrenga, M., M. Harwood, R. McIlhatten, and T. Ozan, Editors. *Ernst & Young's Guide to Total Cost Management.* New York: John Wiley & Sons, 1992.
- Pietlock, Bernard A. "Cost Engineering Taking on Capital Management," *Cost Engineering*, AACE International, January 2002.
- Player, Steve and David E. Keys. *Activity-Based Management.* New York: MasterMedia Limited, 1995.
- Project Management Institute. *The Guide to the Project Management Body of Knowledge*, 3rd ed. Upper Darby, PA: Project Management Institute, 2004.
- Rapp, Randy R., Editor. *Professional Practice Guide No. 14: Business and Program Planning.* CD ROM. Morgantown, WV: AACE International, 2002.

3.3 Investment Decision Making

3.3.1 Description

In TCM, investment decision making is a process to analyze investment alternatives and determine whether, how, and when to allocate the enterprise's limited resources to them. While this section specifically addresses investment decisions during enterprise planning (e.g., capital planning and budgeting), the general process is applicable to other decisions that may be made in any process described in the *TCM Framework*. The primary input to the decision making process is the scope description for one or more asset solutions that satisfy requirements (see Section 3.2). The output of the decision making process is a defined scope of the selected alternative and the assumptions (i.e., *business decision basis* or *business case*) upon which the investment decision was made. This output information is the basis of the project implementation process (Section 4.1) as well as the basis for asset performance measurement and assessment (Chapters 5 and 6). For non-project alternatives, the output is the basis for implementing asset changes (e.g., a change to process activities, etc.).

This section focuses on for-profit corporations as the enterprise context and on maximizing wealth creation as the dominant objective. Despite this focus, the discussion applies to techniques useful for evaluations in business, not-for-profit organizations, government, and personal lives.

Asset planning, including investment decision making, addresses any of three types of problems: choosing the best alternative; assessing cost or value; and optimization. All three problem types are addressed essentially by the same decision analysis approach: choosing the highest-value (or lowest-cost) alternative. Optimization analyses are among the most interesting to perform, and these include engineering design, competitive bidding, and activity scheduling.

Decision analysis (DA) is the foremost process for helping decision makers choose wisely under uncertainty. DA involves concepts borrowed from probability theory, statistics, psychology, finance, and operations research. The formal discipline is called decision science, a subset of operations research (management science). The essence of DA involves (1) capturing judgments about risks and uncertainty[23] as probability distributions, (2) having a single value measure of the quality of the outcome, and (3) putting these together in expected value calculations. An *expected value* (EV) is the probability-weighted outcome, and this is synonymous with the *mean* statistic.

The core analysis technique in this section, DA, is a type of economic analysis. Decision and economic analysis consider economic costs. Economic costs is a relative view of costs, rather than an absolute measure of money. That is, it recognizes that costs represent opportunities lost (i.e., opportunity costs) and that the value of money is relative to the time, currency, and context (e.g., how it is accounted for and taxed) in which it is expended and the definition of "value" that is applied in the valuation process.

The purpose of the decision process is making good decisions. A good decision is one that is logical and consistent with the strategy and objectives of the enterprise (represented in the organization's decision policy) and consistent with the information available at the time. Because of risks and uncertainties, a good decision does not guarantee a good outcome. However, making good decisions over the long term can be expected to maximize the enterprise's progress toward its objectives.

.1 Decision Policy

The investment decision making process is closely integrated with the requirements elicitation and analysis and asset planning processes (Sections 3.1 and 3.2, respectively). Decisions should always be made in the context of the whole enterprise, including portfolios for assets, resources, and projects. Ideally, all decisions would be optimized in the context of a whole enterprise model. However, it is impractical to solve an all encompassing model for other than the most significant decisions. The practical approach is to

---

[23] Key input variables in a model may be either discrete or have a continuous range of possible values. Most often, discrete variables (especially the binary type) are called *risks* and each outcome is assigned a probability of occurrence. Continuous drivers are most-often called *uncertainties* and judged as continuous probability density functions. However, in TCM, risk is defined as being the same as uncertainty (see Section 7.6).

first optimize parameters of decision policy using the whole enterprise model. The policy, which is practical to use, then guides day-to-day decisions. The decision policy is, in effect, a requirement for the decision making process. The decision policy aligns the investments with the strategic plan and objectives.

Decision policy is customarily decomposed along three dimensions:

- **Objective**. How we measure the progress toward the organization's purpose. In situations where wealth creation is the primary objective, the wealth measure is usually in monetary units. Other objectives and requirements (e.g., environmental, health, safety, and security per Section 11.6) may be more difficult to monetize but the effects on future net cashflows can generally be modeled. Using a single wealth measure as the reflection of the enterprise's objectives is a *monetary-equivalents* decision policy.

  However, having multiple requirements as well as multiple important internal and external stakeholders—with different objectives—sometimes requires an analysis with multiple decision criteria (*multi-criteria decision making*). Optimizing the decision in this case usually requires a multi-criteria value function. In this context, crafting a decision policy is mainly about designing the *objective function*: an algebraic scoring function of the several criteria important to decisions. The objective function (i.e., multi-criteria decision policy) expresses how the organization values and intends to make trade-offs between these often-conflicting criteria.

- **Time value**. How we make trade-offs between costs and benefits realized at different times. Customarily, future values are translated into today's equivalents. This is called *present value* discounting. Most often, time preference is represented by the discount rate used in the present value calculation. With money as the objective measure, the chosen *present value discount rate* typically corresponds to either a *marginal cost of capital* or an *opportunity cost of capital*. For an organization in equilibrium, these two rates are approximately equal.

- **Risk attitude**. Sometimes, an enterprise wants to be conservative in a logical, systematic way (this is relevant mostly for a closely-held company or an individual). This want or need can be translated into a risk policy. *Risk policy* is a guide to making trade-offs between risk and value. A *utility function* is a succinct, measurable way to represent risk policy. This is a transformation function converting an objective value measure (e.g., *NPV*) into utility (value) units. Using this transformation ahead of the expected value calculation, in effect, applies a risk attitude adjustment to the outcome values. Then the expected value utility may be translated to real money equivalence by using the inverse utility function. The *certainty equivalent* is the cash-in-hand equivalent to the uncertain investment (assuming, again, that we measure the success of the outcome in monetary units).

In most circumstances, the outcome quality can be measured in monetary equivalents and risk attitude adjustments are unimportant.[24] In most economic evaluations, the outcome measure is *net present value* (*NPV*) of the future net cashflow stream. When the project model incorporates judgments about risks and uncertainties, the single-point forecast is the expected value *NPV*. In a maximization problem (usually involving revenues), the expected value is called the *expected monetary value* (*EMV* = EV *NPV*). In a cost minimization problem, the single-point forecast is *expected value cost* (abbreviated *EV cost*).[25] Though usually implicit, the cost should be a present value cost. In best practice, NPV analysis is supplemented by efforts to forecast company bottom-line net cashflow impact, including inflation and tax effects.

The oft-cited "three pillars" of project management are cost, schedule, and quality. Decision makers must make trade-offs between these criteria and other requirements. Consistent investment decisions require either (a) a multi-criteria decision policy or (b) monetary-equivalents decision policy (i.e., putting schedule and quality into cost terms). Most practitioners find the monetary-equivalents approach more workable. This applies both to the investment decision and to project management decisions. This is because (1) it uses the familiar time value of money concept to reflect time preference, and (2) the asset

---

[24] Risk adjustments per risk policy are not the same as uncertainty weightings for alternatives in a decision tree or similar analysis. These weightings are generally important to decision analysis.

[25] Simply calling this "expected cost" invites misinterpretation as "the cost we expect." This implies an exaggerated precision in forecasting ability. It is important to ensure that the information recipient understands there is a range of possible outcomes and *expected value* refers to the probability-weighting calculation.

life-cycle analysis that was used to approve the investment is the basis for assessing cost-equivalents for project schedule and quality changes.

In many enterprises, other decision making criteria may be used to supplement or substitute for *EMV* or *NPV*. These other criteria or measures include *payout (PO)*, payback period, *internal rate of return (IRR)*, *discounted return on investment (DROI or ROI)* and others. For logical, consistent decisions, these should not be the basis of the enterprise's decision policy because they do not work well with probabilities or measure value. However, these other criteria may be useful in helping the decision maker better understand the investment. ROI-like measures are especially useful in enterprises operating under a capital constraint assumption.

.2 Model-Centric Analysis

Forecasting is a critical process within strategic asset planning. Central to almost any planning and assessment analysis is the forecasting model. Models help structure thinking, handle much more detail than possible with the unaided human brain, and help avoid the biases so common in judgment.

A company's value is based upon the expectation that it can generate free cashflow available to distribute to investors or attractively reinvest in the enterprise. Forecasting future net cashflow is therefore central to investment economic evaluations. The appropriate model detail depends upon the decisions to be made at various stages of the asset's life cycle. More modeling effort is suitable when any of these factors is present: high investment, high risks and uncertainties, design to be optimized, and competing good alternatives.

An asset life-cycle model is the basis for the feasibility analysis (see Section 3.2). This involves forecasting investment, revenues, and costs. Physical operations drive the business, such as production from a factory or an oil reservoir. Industry, economy, and other external factors are also part of the model. Important uncertain input variables to the model can be described as probability distributions. The model is then solved in a way that propagates probability distributions through the calculations. The workhorse methods in decision analysis (DA) are decision trees and Monte Carlo simulation. With probability distributions for some inputs, the output of the models used in these methods is a distribution. Most often, the primary output is a distribution of *NPV*, and the mean of this distribution is *expected monetary value (EMV)*.

Evaluation models in DA are called *probabilistic* or *stochastic* models. In addition to representing the range of possible outcomes, the stochastic model provides a more accurate value assessment. Because of the way probability distributions propagate through the calculations, there is often a substantial improvement in accuracy. Sometimes, both decision tree analysis and Monte Carlo simulation are used in the same analysis. Decision trees are better suited for problems with low probabilities or subsequent decision points (value of information problems). Monte Carlo simulation is better when there are continuous probability distributions (and there are lots of them in typical project models and design optimization problems).

Most often, the project model used during project execution will be much more detailed than the feasibility analysis model. In project management decisions, including value analysis and engineering, the asset model is the source of trade-off values. As examples:

- The asset model helps with: What is the value of this performance improvement? What is the value impact of completion delay?

- The project model has the detail to answer: When will the predecessors be complete for this activity? What is the probability this activity is on the critical path (the *criticality index*)?

Project risk management (see Section 7.6) addresses uncertainty in both the asset life-cycle and project execution. *Threats* and *opportunities*, once identified, should be the basis for brainstorming candidate actions. An action (singly or in combination) is usually appropriate when the expected value cost improvement is greater than the cost of the action. The typical risk is modeled as a binary event (it either happens or not), with a distribution of impact (schedule or cost) if the event happens. Most often, these risk events are embedded as simple tree logic in the Monte Carlo simulation project model.

For very large projects, there is often a need to plan in greater detail than is suitable for a stochastic project model. A detailed work breakdown structure for a large project might contain hundreds or thousands of activities. In this situation, two project models might be the best approach: a stochastic project model (e.g., 50-100 input variables) used for important project decisions and high-level project risk management; and a deterministic project model (e.g., 500+ input variables) for detailed project planning and management.

After project completion, the feasibility model remains part of the full company model, perhaps moving from an investment or project portfolio to an asset portfolio. The model should be maintained though the remaining life and is used for budgeting, and strategic planning. The model will be useful for decisions about reinvestments and ultimate abandonment, disposition, or conversion.

3.3.2 Process Map for Investment Decision Making

Figure 3.3-1 illustrates the process map for investment decision making. As was mentioned, the process centers on decision analysis or evaluation that is based on a decision model. The investment decision making process acts as a gate, through which an alternative from asset planning is either approved and passes through for implementation or is recycled for further elaboration of requirements or planning or other disposition as appropriate.

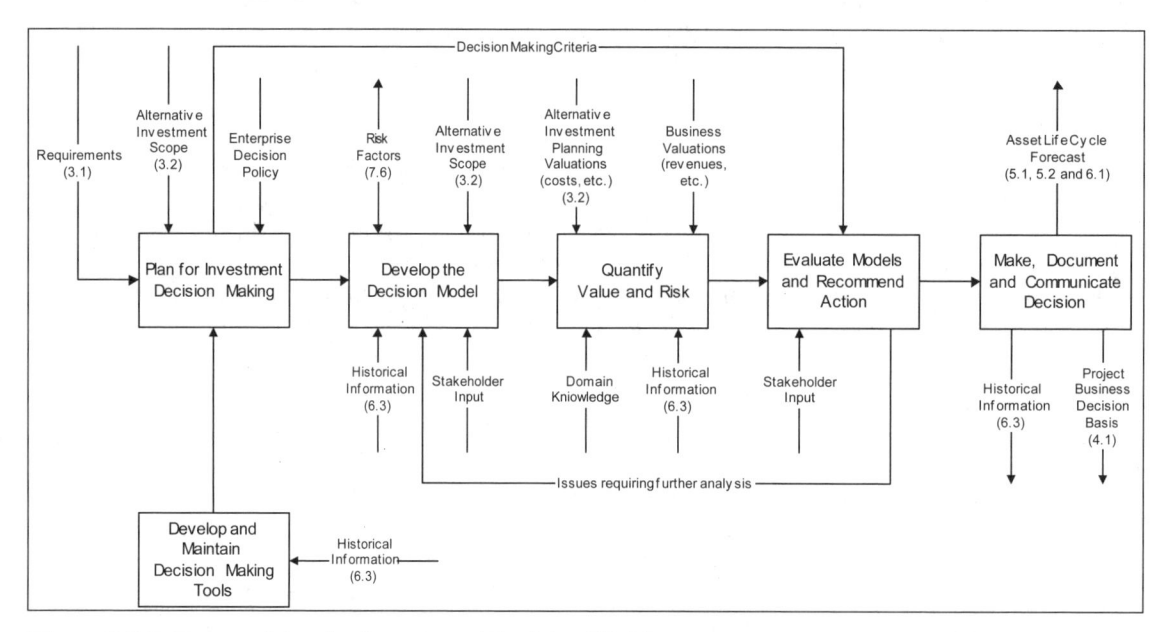

Figure 3.3-1. Process Map for Investment Decision Making

The following sections briefly describe the steps or sub-processes in the investment decision making process.

.1 Plan for Investment Decision Making

Strategic asset planning (requirements elicitation and analysis, asset planning, and investment decision making) should be planned as an integrated process. For example, the asset planning or evaluation team (see Section 3.2) may be the same team that conducts the decision analysis, and the resources for this effort may have been planned well before any investment decisions need to be made.

The key inputs to planning for investment decision making are the scope description of one or more asset solutions that satisfy requirements, the business strategy and objectives, and the business decision making policy of the enterprise.

Based on an assessment of the process inputs and the decision criteria established, the planning team further identifies specific activities, resources, and tools for the effort at hand. Specialized analysis skills are applied during decision analysis; some of these skills may have to be acquired from outside of the enterprise. Often, existing models are suited to the present project and may be reused. If the project requires a custom model, the modeling effort is usually considerable. Learning new software tools and developing the model(s) may require significant resources and time that need to be planned for.

The output of the planning step is documentation of the scope of the decision analysis effort, as reviewed and agreed to by the planning team and business leadership as appropriate. The scope describes the basis of the decision analysis (e.g., objective, criteria, methods, assumptions, etc.); any special concerns about stakeholder interests, strategy, resources, or other issues that are not addressed by the company's decision policy; and what is or is not included in the analysis and what the team is or is not able to control or change.

The planning activities may be fairly routine for asset investments for which the company has well established practices. It may be clear to the team that the best decision is based upon experience. If so, the process can proceed quickly to making, documenting, and communicating the decision. Decision analysis only adds value to the process if it has the potential to alter what the decision maker is otherwise going to do (however, if the decision policy is not clear, what might alter the decision maker's actions may not be clear).

.2 Develop the Decision Model

A decision model is the central framework for the evaluation team's assessment of the project alternatives. This is based around a deterministic cashflow projection model. Key inputs to the model are risks or uncertainties that will be judged as probabilities or probability distributions. Including probabilities in the model converts it to a stochastic model: If just one input to the model is a distribution, the outcome (e.g., *NPV*) will be a distribution.

The decision model is most often developed as a graphic representation of the key elements in the evaluation process. In particular, chance variables (e.g., sales will be low, medium, or high) and decision alternatives (e.g., build, rent, or do nothing) are organized in sequence. Decision trees, influence diagrams, and flow diagrams are the most popular formats for decision modeling. A script outline is an alternative, and some software programs use a structured word syntax.

The most important part of the decision analysis is developing a well-formed decision model. Once the evaluation team agrees on the model, this is a good basis for reviewing the assessment approach with the decision maker. Once the decision model is approved, the rest of the evaluation process is fairly routine. Although the initial decision model may hold up, it is common for new project insights to initiate model revisions.

While best practice is to a use single well-formed decision policy based on optimizing an expected value, a reality is that there will often be lack of consensus. Sensitivity analysis, forecasting supplemental criteria, and testing alternative decision policies may be useful. A multi-criteria value function provides a visible way to combine different criteria and weights. In the monetary-equivalents policy approach, decision makers can adjust the trade-off values.

.3 Quantify Value and Risk

The decision model describes possible scenarios (realizations) for alternative investment outcomes, as combinations of chance variable outcomes and decision alternatives. Every path in a decision tree represents a unique scenario, and the analysis needs a corresponding net cash flow projection to calculate *NPV* (assuming this is the relevant value measure). There are infinite possible outcomes with continuous variables.

Often, investment alternatives are supported by well-established cashflow models. In other cases, a custom cashflow model is required and this represents a substantial part of the analysis effort. Usually the physical processes are modeled first, including project execution or development. Then revenues and costs are added in. Conservation concepts familiar to engineers have analogs in modeling: conservation of physical quantities, cash, and account balancing. Model definition, documentation, review walk-through, and validation methods are especially important with custom models. Embellishing the scope definition for each alternative becomes part of the model documentation.

The deterministic cashflow model will be used to produce many investment alternative realizations (outcome scenarios). Its inputs will include the outcomes of every relevant chance variable and decision variable. A *robust model* is one that produces valid projections for all reasonable combinations of input variables. Many decision analysis tools will interface with cashflow models in existing spreadsheets. Care must be taken in developing the cashflow model so that the input value cells are well segregated and so that the model is robust. After meeting these requirements, only a few minutes are required to convert the traditional deterministic spreadsheet model into a stochastic decision analysis model.

Sensitivity analysis is an important way to ensure that the evaluation team focuses on the drivers of outcome value uncertainty. The traditional methods change one variable at a time, holding all other variables at their base case values. Spider and tornado diagrams are popular presentation formats. When a Monte Carlo simulation model is available, a popular sensitivity method is to compute *correlation coefficients* between the stochastic (input) variables and the outcome value; prioritization is usually displayed by ranking correlation coefficient magnitudes in a tornado diagram.

For those uncertain input values found to be most important, the evaluation team asks experts to provide their experienced judgments. Judgments will be expressed as probability distributions that are best elicited through an interview process. Usually the best available expert is chosen to provide a judgment. This often requires going outside the evaluation team or even outside the enterprise. *Risk analysis* is a term often used for the process of assessing a probability distribution. Although the *TCM Framework* describes risk management as a separate process (see Section 7.6), working with risks and uncertainties is pervasive in the modeling and evaluation effort.

We only need to model in detail sufficient to make an informed decision. If doubting whether additional analysis or information is worth the cost, a value of imperfect information analysis can evaluate the option of additional data collection and evaluation effort.

The models used for decision analysis are not static. For projects using phased planning, the level of detail in the decision model changes during the project life cycle. An asset life-cycle model is the basis of the feasibility analysis. In this model, the project development is represented at a high level. Upon approval, typically, a detailed stochastic project model forms the basis for decisions during project execution (e.g., change management per Section 10.3). Detailed project planning will often result in updates to the asset life-cycle model. After project completion, the asset life-cycle model is again updated to reflect the asset in service through the end of its life.

.4 Evaluate the Decision Model and Recommend Action

Once the life-cycle cashflow model is ready and the evaluation team has the judgments about uncertain inputs, the team is ready to calculate the *expected monetary value* (*EMV*) for each alternative. Payoff tables work well for very simple problems. Decision trees are usually best when there are subsequent decision points. Monte Carlo simulation is usually required for optimization and for problems having many *stochastic variables*.

Before recommending the apparent best alternative, the evaluation team should review the analysis. In particular, new insights might suggest other investment alternatives. Would acquiring additional information provide an *EMV* improvement? Are there cost-effective actions, not previously considered, to mitigate threats or exploit opportunities? The team should perform any analysis rework as needed.

The evaluation team then prepares and communicates the recommendation for the alternative that maximizes value (usually *EMV*). Many enterprises have standard procedures and tools for documenting the basis and results of the decision analysis (i.e., the "business case") and summarizing the investment recommendation. The business case describes the investment scope considered, the decision analysis methods used, constraints and assumptions, and then summarizes the decision analysis results and the recommendation for action. If the decision policy is working, the evaluation team will be confident its recommendation will be accepted by the decision makers.

.6 Make, Document, and Communicate Decision

Upon receiving the recommended action, the decision making authorities should verify that the recommended investment meets the documented requirements, including the decision policy, while ensuring that the asset planning process is still working on the right business problem. Generally, the decision makers meet with the key evaluation team members to ensure that everyone has a good understanding of the business case and recommendation.

Sometimes the decision analysis result (e.g., *EMV*) is marginal, and a strong case cannot be made for either implementing or dropping. Management may then decide based upon strategic and portfolio concerns. Management might also direct the evaluation team to rework the analysis with a different scope context (e.g., bringing in a partner) or modified alternatives (e.g., delaying or stretching the project timeline).

If the investment is not approved and marginal, it remains a candidate and the updated scope remains in the pool of investment candidates to revisit another time. The asset management team will generally reexamine the various portfolios each budget cycle and when the business environment or company circumstances change significantly.

In some cases, particularly for major capital investments, there may be multiple tiers of analysis, review, and decision making. For example, as part of a capital budgeting process, each organization in the enterprise may decide which strategic investments best address its objectives. Then, on an overall portfolio basis, enterprise management analyzes, reviews, and decides on the competing recommendations from the various organizations. Optimally, the organizations are working within a strategic asset management framework. A common decision policy ensures that they are all working toward the same business objectives and making consistent decisions.

Making timely decisions can be a challenge because of indecisiveness (e.g., always wanting more information or analysis paralysis), busy decision maker schedules, or conflicts between stakeholders or organizations. Generally, asset planning or project teams are resourced and ready to begin the next phase of scope development, and if decision making is not timely, resources may have to be reassigned, greatly disrupting progress and detracting from performance. Well defined and managed processes and decision policy and thorough analysis help address this challenge.

The final output is a well documented business decision basis or business case. This is the basis for implementing projects (see Section 4.1), implementing non-project asset changes (e.g., a change to process activities, etc.), or further asset planning elaboration. The cost attributes of the selected alternative are also inputs to the business capital and non-capital control budgets. The business case and budgets, as well as key performance indicators (KPIs) and other targets, are inputs to the performance measurement and assessment processes (Chapters 5 and 6, respectively) in which measures such ROI are assessed on an ongoing basis.

If a project is implemented, it is common to have a kick-off meeting that helps ensure that the project leadership team understands the decision analysis and basis of decision. The asset life-cycle model remains relevant and is the basis for making tradeoffs among cost, schedule, and performance during project execution.

Finally, the analysis is documented for organizational learning and captured in a historical database (see Section 6.3). The team should organize the information and documents in way that will be easily retrievable for post-project review and for consideration in future strategic asset planning.

3.3.3 Inputs to Investment Decision Making

.1 *Enterprise Decision Policy*. This incorporates considerations about business strategy and objectives. For day-to-day decisions, portfolio considerations (such as any capital constraint) are embedded in the parameters of decision policy.

.2 *Requirements* (see Section 3.1). Establishes the conditions or capabilities that must be met or possessed by a strategic asset (i.e., product, process, etc.) and may include requirements for the decision making process itself (*decision policy* is a particular type of requirement).

.3 *Alternative Investment Scope* (see Section 3.2). The initial scope definition to be used by the asset planning or decision evaluation team in developing and appraising alternatives.

.4 *Risk Factors* (see Section 7.6). Effective decision models identify risk factors (i.e., chance events) for which methods from the risk management process apply.

.5 *Alternative Investment Planning Valuations* (see Section 3.2). The asset alternative's cost, schedule, risk, and value attributes (generally in terms of cash flows) are used to quantify value and uncertainty in the decision model(s).

.6 *Business Valuations*. Decision models require information about revenues. Non-financial criteria or measures are also considered (and are usually monetized).

.7 *Stakeholder Input*. While requirements should reflect stakeholder needs and wants, their further input may be needed to support review when there are unresolved conflicts or marginal analysis.

.8 *Historical Information* (see Section 6.3). A data and knowledge base of historical information supports tools development, model building, and so on. Prior investment evaluations may provide data sources, models, risk lists, and other pertinent information.

.9 *Domain Knowledge*. Experience among evaluation team members and other persons tapped for their special expertise. Usually the best available expert is asked to judge probabilities for chance variables. Custom cashflow modeling should be performed by someone experienced in that area.

3.3.4 Outputs from Investment Decision Making

.1 *Project Business Decision Basis*. A decision as to whether, when, and how to do the project is communicated to the project team (see Section 4.1). The basis includes the *updated scope definition and a description of the decision model,* including the assumptions upon which the investment decision was made. Embedded in this model is a high-level scheduling and cost model for project execution. The model will be useful for risk and assumption monitoring through project execution.

.2 *Asset Life-Cycle Forecast*. The cost and other information used in asset planning and decision making are the basis for performance measurement and assessment. (see Sections 5.1, 5.2, and 6.1).

.3 *Historical Information*. The project evaluation itself is a learning process. The lessons learned here should be available as part of the enterprise's knowledge base (see Section 6.3). Historical data are also used for post-implementation review of performance.

3.3.5 Key Concepts and Terminology for Investment Decision Making

The following concepts and terminology described in this chapter are particularly important to understanding the investment decision making process:

.1 *Economic Analysis* (sometimes referred to as *profitability analysis*). (See Section 3.3.1).
.2 *Economic Costs*. (See Section 3.3.1).
.3 *Expected Value*. (See Section 3.3.1.1).
.4 *Decision Policy*. (See Section 3.3.1.1).
.5 *Decision Criteria*. (See Section 3.3.1.1).
.6 *Multi-Criteria Decision Making*. (See Section 3.3.1.1).
.7 *Expected Monetary Value (EMV)*. (See Section 3.3.1.1).
.8 *Monetary Equivalents*. (See Section 3.3.1.1).
.9 *Profitability*. (See Section 6.1).
.10 *Decision Modeling*. (See Section 3.3.1.2).

.11 Feasibility Analysis. (See Sections 3.2 and 3.3.1.2).
.12 Decision Tree. (See Section 3.3.1.2).
.13 Sensitivity Analysis and Monte Carlo Simulation. (See Section 3.3.1.2).
.14 Value. (See Sections 7.5 and 3.3.2.3).
.15 Uncertainty and Risk. (See Sections 7.6 and 3.3.2.3).
.16 Risk Policy. (See Section 3.3.1.1).
.17 Net Present Value (NPV). (See Section 3.3.1.1).
.18 Rate of Return. (See Section 3.3.1.1).
.19 Business Decision Basis or Business Case. (See Section 3.3.2.5).
.20 Capital Budgeting. (See Section 3.3.2.6).
.21 Portfolio Management. (See Section 3.3.2.6).

Further Readings and Sources

Decision making is a concept applicable to many areas of practice beyond asset and project management. From a TCM perspective, texts that cover decision making related to capital investment planning and budgeting are most applicable. Increasingly, the economic analysis is done in the context of decision analysis. The following references provide basic information and lead to more detailed treatments.

- Amos, Scott J., Editor. *Skills and Knowledge of Cost Engineering* (sections on economic analysis and engineering economics), 5th ed. Morgantown, WV: AACE International, 2004.
- Bierman, Harold and Seymour Smidt. *The Capital Budgeting Decision: Economic Analysis of Investment Projects*. 8th ed. New York: MacMillan, 1993.
- Clemen, Robert T, and Terence Reilly *Making Hard Decisions with DecisionTools*, 2nd ed. Belmont, CA: Duxbury Press, 2001.
- Goodwin, Paul, and George Wright. *Decision Analysis for Management Judgment*, 3rd ed. New York: John Wiley & Sons, 2004.
- Hertz, David B. "Risk Analysis in Capital Investment," *Harvard Business Review*, vol. 57, no. 5 (1979): pp. 169-181.
- Keeney, Ralph L. *Value-Focused Thinking: A Path to Creative Decision Making*. Cambridge, MA: Harvard University Press, 1992.
- Klammer, Thomas P. *Managing Strategic and Capital Investment Decisions*. Burr Ridge, IL: Irwin Professional Publishing, 1993.
- Samson, Danny. *Managerial Decision Analysis*. Homewood, IL: Richard D. Irwin, Inc., 1988.
- Schuyler, John R. *Risk and Decision Analysis in Projects*, 2nd ed. Upper Darby, PA: Project Management Institute, 2001.
- Thorne, Henry C. and Julian A. Piekarski. *Techniques for Capital Expenditure Analysis*. New York: Marcel Dekker, 1995.
- United States General Accounting Office, Accounting and Information Management Division. *Executive Guide: Leading Practices in Capital Decision-Making* (US GAO/AIMD-99-32). United States General Accounting Office, 1999.
- Wang, John X. *What Every Engineer Should Know About Decision Making Under Uncertainty*. New York: Marcel Dekker, 2002.

CHAPTER 4
PROJECT IMPLEMENTATION

4.1 Project Implementation

4.1.1 Description

The project implementation process governs the project control process by putting into effect the decisions and will of the enterprise in respect to its projects. The decisions of the strategic asset management team that initiate the first phase of project scope development are implemented by establishing project team leadership and then, working together, developing initial project direction and guiding documents including a description of the asset scope (product of the project that addresses a business problem or opportunity), project objectives, constraints, and assumptions.[26] These outputs of the process are referred to as the "project implementation basis."[27] Initial inputs to the project implementation process include information about the physical and functional characteristics (i.e., design basis) of the selected asset investment option, and the business constraints and assumptions (i.e., business decision basis, business case, or justification) upon which the asset investment decision was made (Section 3.3).

In addition, the enterprise maintains a project system (i.e., a process and attendant set of capabilities and tools) that supports project team's efforts to manage and control its projects. At project initiation, the system and other enterprise capabilities and resources are made available to the project team to use as appropriate or as required. The project team, using the project system capabilities, then develops the project implementation deliverables into a controllable project scope definition.

Typically, the implementation process is reviewed as the project scope and execution strategy development process (Section 7.1) progresses through proscribed or controlled phases (i.e., phases and gates process). A gate review at the end of each phase results in updated direction (i.e., a decision to proceed to the next phase, a request for additional work or information, or a halt to the project) and resource authorizations (i.e., phased project funding). A project system with scope development phases and gates ensures that the project scope definition and project plans are always aligned with the asset scope and the enterprise's objectives and constraints. When project scope development and control planning reach a level of definition such that baseline project control plans are unlikely to change significantly during project execution, then final directions are given to the project team and full project funds are authorized.

After full funds are authorized, the project team proceeds with the full project control process, while the strategic asset management team measures and tracks the project performance as one project investment in its project portfolio (Sections 5.1 and 5.2) and typically only intervenes in the project management to the extent required by the project change management process (Section 10.3). When all or parts of the project scope are complete and ready for turnover from control of the project team, the project implementation process is used to formally review and accept that scope and initiate management of the asset.

4.1.2 Process Map for Project Implementation

The project implementation process centers on steps that help ensure that good investment decisions (Section 3.3) become good projects. The primary output is the basis for project control planning (Chapter 7). Figure 4.1-1 is a process map for project implementation.

---

[26] The term *requirements* is sometimes considered synonymous with objectives plus constraints, but the term is most often used in reference to products (as in Section 3.1: Requirements Elicitation and Analysis) and not projects.

[27] The Project Management Institute (PMI) refers to this as the *project scope statement*. The phrase *project implementation basis* is used here to recognize that the deliverables of this process (including objectives, constraints, and assumptions, and other guidance) are more than *project scope* that PMI defines as the "work that must be performed to deliver a product, service, or result…" At initial implementation, the project scope has not been developed, only the asset investment option physical and functional scope.

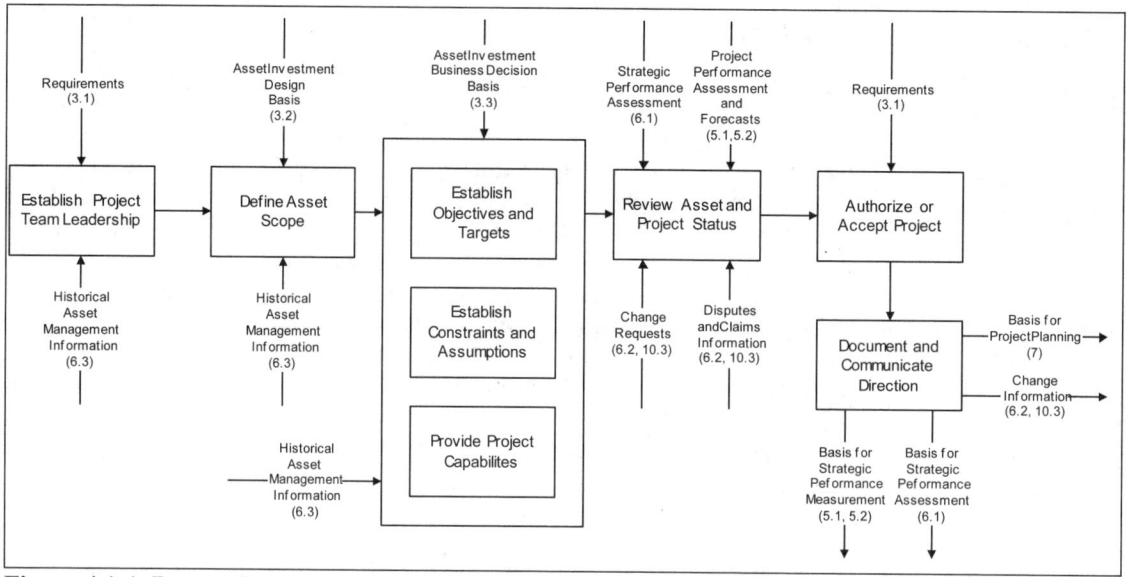

Figure 4.1-1. Process Map for the Project Implementation Process

The following sections briefly describe the steps in the project implementation process.

.1 Establish Project Team Leadership

At initiation, a project leadership team is formed including both strategic (i.e., business) representatives and project leads to ensure that the entire team understands the asset scope and design and the business decision basis. The business representative must be knowledgeable of the strategic asset management process work that led to project implementation. That representative must also be familiar with the project system and have authority to make project implementation decisions, or to otherwise ensure that informed decisions are made effectively and in a timely manner. The team should also include representatives of those responsible for running, using, operating, maintaining, or otherwise dealing with the asset or product that will result from the project. Again, it is important that these individuals have the authority to make project decisions in an effective and timely manner.

The leadership team will also include a project manager, and depending on the level of project scope development and planning required for a specific gate review, may also include (but will not be limited to) leads of the project control functions (e.g., estimating, scheduling, cost control, etc.), technical or creative functions (e.g., engineering, systems analysis, etc.), procurement and contracting functions, project execution functions (e.g., construction, programming, etc.), and the quality and safety functions. Suppliers or contractors may be part of the team to the extent that they have a leadership role at that phase. At these critical reviews, it is important to get the full core team representation, understanding, and commitment to the project because this is the where the stage is set for project success.

.2 Define Asset Scope

As was mentioned, an initial input to the project implementation process is information about the physical, functional, and quality characteristics or design basis of the selected asset investment (see Section 3.2). The leadership team crafts this information into a concise asset scope description (i.e., statement, list, etc.) that forms the basis for project scope development (Section 7.1) and provides the project team with a clear understanding of the requirements (Section 3.1) that the asset scope will address. The stakeholders in the asset (i.e., those whose needs are reflected in the requirements) must also be identified.

As the definition of the asset scope is further developed into project scope, gate reviews ensure that the project scope is still aligned with the project implementation basis. Any changes to the project implementation basis must be managed through the change management process (Section 10.3).

.3 Establish Objectives and Targets

Objectives are measures of project success. The measures are primarily investment decision making criteria (Section 3.3). The core project team crafts these criteria into a concise set of measures that are well understood and agreed upon. The measures should also be prioritized in a way that the team understands how to evaluate and make project decisions when one objective must be balanced against another (e.g., cost-schedule tradeoff).

Typical measures include but are not limited to the following:

- scope (i.e., the project scope must deliver the required physical scope of the asset or product)
- operability (i.e., the project scope must deliver the required functionality or usability of the asset or product)
- cost (i.e., budget and cash flow for the financial investment)
- schedule (i.e., start, finish, and milestone dates)
- resources (i.e., conservation of materials, use of local or disadvantaged labor, etc.)
- profitability (i.e., return on investment)
- quality (i.e., of the asset and outputs resulting from the asset function)
- environmental, health, and safety (i.e., project effects on people and the environment)
- satisfaction (i.e., qualitative perceptions of success from the viewpoint of various stakeholders)

Intermediate or sub-objectives may be established for each scope development phase (e.g., budget and completion date for the phase) and for different parts of the project scope as appropriate.

Objectives usually reflect the general success criteria of the asset owner and/or whoever is funding the investment. In some cases, targets may also be established. Targets are established by the project team as measures of its success in achieving project team (or project system) objectives such as achieving best-in-class cost performance as identified through competitive benchmarking. "Stretch goal" targets can also be used to foster project success. Stretch goals are targets intended to motivate the team, in a positive way, to the limits of what is reasonably achievable. Negative motivation (i.e., punishing those that fail to achieve targets) will in the long run motivate teams to bias or distort the asset management processes to result in easily achieved and generally non-competitive targets.

.4 Establish Constraints and Assumptions

Constraints are restrictions, limits, or rules on the project's use of resources and/or activities. They may quantitative in nature (e.g., when work will be done) or qualitative (e.g., how work will be done). A common constraint is that the project must use the enterprise's project system. The required use of pre-approved or alliance suppliers and/or contractors is also a common constraint. A project is generally not considered a success unless it meets its objectives within the stated constraints. For example, if a constraint required that a union labor to be used, and the project kept its cost under budget by using a non-union supplier, the project would not be considered successful, and the project team's performance would be viewed unfavorably.

Assumptions, in regards to project implementation, are not rules or restrictions, but are documented asset and project factors, conditions, characteristics, and other information that the project leadership used and relied upon as a basis of understanding at the time of project initiation or at a gate review. A project can be a success if assumptions are not met or do not occur; however, some explanation may be in order, and it may affect perceptions of the degree of success. For example, if an assumption was that weather would always be difficult and rainy all during construction, and the project kept its cost at budget but the weather was always excellent, the project would be considered a cost success, but the project team's performance may not be viewed favorably.

.5 Provide Capabilities (i.e., Project System)

As mentioned above, a common constraint is that the project must use the enterprise's project system. The project system is a process with a set of capabilities and tools that enables effective and efficient project execution (i.e., better considered an enabler than a constraint). Typical capabilities made available to project teams include procedures and tools (e.g., forms, templates, websites, etc.) for the phases and gates process of scope development (Section 7.1), the project historical database (Section 10.4), project change management (Section 10.3), schedule planning and development systems, cost estimating systems, cost/schedule control systems, financial and accounting systems, information technology, and so on.

In larger enterprises, an organization that is responsible for developing and maintaining project system capabilities is sometimes referred to as a project or capital office. In smaller enterprises that have few or low-value assets, the need for established project system capabilities may be minimal. In any case, even if the enterprise's personnel do not perform many project activities themselves, it is their responsibility to maintain fit-for-use project system capabilities to ensure that the enterprise's requirements are effectively addressed by suppliers and contractors performing project activities.

A key challenge in managing project system capabilities is to avoid bureaucratic approaches that impose needless constraints on project performance. The goal of the project system is to facilitate effective project management and control. The asset and process performance measurement and assessment processes (Sections 5.2 and 6.1, respectively) will help ensure that project system capabilities are monitored and continually improved.

.6 Review Asset and Project Status

Having completed all the steps above, the project team reviews the information to ensure that it provides a suitable basis for project implementation (i.e., basis for authorizing funds and guiding further scope development). For projects at intermediate phases of scope development, the status of scope development must also be assessed in terms of the performance of the work completed to date. Both project performance and strategic asset performance assessments must be reviewed to ensure continued alignment of the project work with the project implementation basis, and alignment of the project implementation basis with current asset performance (e.g., if the current asset production rate is deteriorating faster than expected, the project schedule objectives may have to be reconsidered).

The status review will also identify any special circumstances that might affect the authorization of further resources (e.g., change requests, claims, etc.). These circumstances may require additional strategic asset planning (Chapter 3) or forensic performance assessment (6.4) before implementation approval.

.7 Authorize and Accept Project

After the project leadership team determines that the basis for project implementation is appropriate, the project scope, objectives, targets, constraints, assumptions, and other information are documented to the extent and in the format needed to support the authorization step (e.g., the funding or authorization request). The asset owner and/or whoever is funding the investment reviews the request, and if found satisfactory, authorizes the project team to advance the scope development to the next phase, or to complete project execution. They also make whatever decisions and authorizations are needed for the project team to access the approved funds, resources, and capabilities. If the authorization request is not approved, the authorities must direct the project team on what steps it must take (if any) to obtain approval, or to close out work in progress if the project is cancelled. Typically, the authority to approve major investments resides with multiple people in upper management. It can often be a challenge to obtain authorization within a planned timeframe; delays in approvals often delay project progress and these delay risks should be communicated in detail.

When the project is complete, the project implementation process is used to formally accept the completed asset solution and initiate management of that asset. After the final review and acceptance, the project team and other resources are available for other enterprise projects or uses.

.8 Document and Communicate Project Implementation Basis

Either before or just after the work is authorized, the scope, objectives, targets, criteria, and assumptions are documented by the project leadership team in a manner that will support understanding and buy-in by all participants in the project. These documents form the basis for project planning (Chapter 7).[28] In essence, the project implementation basis can be viewed as a quasi-contract between the asset owner and the project team. To ensure that the entire team understands this basis, many projects start the scope development phases or project execution with kick-off or alignment meetings or workshops in which all key project team members participate. In addition, team building exercises can be used to reinforce common understanding as well as to build motivation, encourage teamwork, set the stage for optimum project success, and so on.

4.1.3 Inputs to Project Implementation

.1 *Requirements.* Requirements (Section 3.1) play a part in project team selection (as they did to strategic asset planning [Chapter 3]). They are also inputs to the asset and project status review.

.2 *Asset Investment Design Basis.* Information about the physical and functional characteristics of the selected asset investment option or product of the project (Section 3.2).

.3 *Asset Investment Business Decision Basis or Business Case.* The investment decision and information about the business constraints and assumptions upon which the asset investment option decision was made (Section 3.3).

.4 *Project Performance Assessments and Forecasts.* For projects at intermediate phases of scope development, the status of scope development must be assessed in terms of the performance of the work completed to date and forecasts for remaining work, and the continued alignment of that work with the current asset scope, cost and schedule objectives, and so on (see Sections 10.1 and 10.2).

.5 *Strategic Performance Assessments.* For projects at intermediate phases of scope development, the status of the asset performance (Section 6.1) must be reviewed to ensure that the project planning basis is still appropriate.

.6 *Change Requests.* Changes to the approved project basis usually require approval (see Section 10.3).

.7 *Disputes and Claims Information.* In the course of the project, disputes and/or claims may occur that require a management implementation decision, or other special effort (e.g., forensic performance assessment) by the enterprise to analyze and resolve (see Sections 6.3, 6.4, and 10.3).

.8 *Historical Asset Management Information.* Historical project system performance information supports selection of the project team and establishment of the project planning basis (See Section 6.3).

4.1.4 Outputs from Project Implementation

.1 *Project Implementation Basis.* The asset scope definition, objectives, constraints, assumptions, and other guidance are inputs to the project control planning processes (see Chapter 7).

.2 *Basis for Strategic Performance Measurement and Assessment.* (Sections 5.1, 5.2, and 6.1, respectively). The asset scope, objectives, constraints, and so on are inputs to the processes in which project and project system success are measured and assessed.

.3 *Change Information.* (Section 10.3). Authorization or other guidance (e.g., constraints, etc.) regarding change requests, or disputes and claims are communicated to the project team.

4.1.5 Key Concepts and Terminology for Project Implementation

---

[28] Again, *project implementation* goes by many names such as the project charter, project scope statement, project scope, and objectives statement, and so on. If the party managing the project is a supplier or contractor, the documentation may actually be part of a legal contract.

The following concepts and terminology described in this chapter are particularly important to understanding the project implementation process:

.1 *Project Implementation Basis.* (see Section 4.1.4.1) Synonym: Project Scope Statement.
.2 *Phases and Gates Process.* A project system procedure in which the project implementation process is re-visited (i.e., gate reviews) as the project scope definition process progresses through proscribed phases (i.e., phases). Each gate review results in updated direction (i.e., proceed to the next gate review) and resource authorizations (i.e., phased project funding). The process ensures that the project scope and project plans are always aligned with the asset scope and the enterprise's objectives and constraints.
.3 *Project or Capital Office.* An organization whose responsibility is to establish and maintain project system capabilities.
.4 *Asset Scope.* The physical, functional, and quality characteristics or design basis of the selected asset investment.
.5 *Objectives.* Measures of project success.
.6 *Constraints.* Restrictions, limits, or rules on the project's use of resources, and/or performance of activities.
.7 *Assumptions.* Documented asset and project factors, conditions, characteristics, and other information that the project team uses and relies on as a basis of understanding at the time of project initiation or at a gate review.
.8 *Authorization.* Approvals granted by the asset owner and/or whoever is funding the investment for the project team to proceed with work and to expend or use funds, resources, and capabilities as appropriate.
.9 *Acceptance.* Agreement by the asset owner and/or whoever is funding the investment that all or part of the project work, as defined by the project planning basis, is complete.

Further Readings and Sources

Project implementation is a basic step of project management that is covered by most general project management texts. The following references provide basic information and will lead to more detailed treatments.

- Amos, Scott J., Editor. *Skills and Knowledge of Cost Engineering* (section on planning), 5th ed. Morgantown, WV: AACE International, 2004.
- Rapp, Randy R., Editor. *Professional Practice Guide No. 14: Business and Program Planning.* CD ROM. Morgantown, WV: AACE International, 2002.
- Project Management Institute. *A Guide to the Project Management Body of Knowledge*, 3rd ed. Upper Darby, PA: Project Management Institute, 2004.

CHAPTER 5

STRATEGIC ASSET PERFORMANCE MEASUREMENT

5.1 Asset Cost Accounting

5.1.1 Description

Asset cost accounting refers to the process of measuring and reporting the commitment and expenditure of money on the enterprise's strategic assets such as products or equipment. The output of the process is cost data for assessing the asset portfolio's performance relative to established business objectives and requirements. The inputs to the process include the basis against which asset portfolio performance is assessed (quantified requirements per Section 3.1 and cost budgets per Section 3.2) and expense data from ongoing asset operation during the asset life cycle. The TCM process map does not explicitly include the cost accounting process; it only addresses the strategic asset management interface with cost accounting.[29]

The "accounting" process excludes the performance measurement process (Section 6.2) that covers the measurement of asset or process functional performance (e.g., operability, quality, achievement of schedule milestones, etc.). Together, accounting and performance measurement provide the information needed for business control and planning, just as project cost accounting and performance measurement provide the measures for project control (Sections 9.1 and 9.2). In terms of information technology (IT), the distinction between cost accounting and performance measurement is increasingly less distinct as materials or enterprise resource planning (MRP and ERP) systems increasingly encompass the measurement of all resource usage and performance data for both asset management and project control. However, disregarding IT integration, cost accounting practice remains a unique function in itself.

The most significant cost accounting technique of interest to cost engineering and strategic asset management is activity-based cost management (ABC/M) which improves upon traditional cost accounting by assigning costs to the work activities and then to the assets that drive the workload. This superior costing method based on cause-and-effect relationships is in contrast to simply capturing the spending expenses in cost centers and making somewhat arbitrary guesses or using broad averages (e.g., number of units produced) as to the relationship of the costs to the assets that are uniquely consuming the various types of costs. Traditional cost allocations leads to simultaneous over-costing and under-costing of outputs relative to their actual costs. As was mentioned in Section 3.2, ABC/M also supports asset planning. As asset design is elaborated, understanding the cost by work activity (by worker or by equipment) allows more effective assets to be developed.

.1 The Importance of Cost Measurements to Strategic Asset Management

As discussed in Section 3.1, requirements are a condition or capability that a problem solution must have to address their perceived problem or opportunity The first characteristic of a good requirement is that it defines what the asset will do. The next is that it be quantified to serve as a basis of performance measurement. For example, performance against a requirement such as "must have good reliability" cannot be measured; a statement such as "must have less than 1 percent downtime" is better.

As further discussed in Sections 2.3 and 3.3, the most important business requirement for most enterprises, and the basis for their asset investment decisions where applicable, is a measure of economic return on investment; a single measure that expresses in monetary terms the value of the investment over its life cycle to the enterprise.[30] Allowing for the time value of money, return on investment improves with greater and/or sooner income and less and/or later costs incurred. In decision and investment analysis, income and costs may include non-monetary benefit and cost factors expressed in monetary terms.

---

[29] IMA, the Institute of Management Accounting, is a key resource for accounting process knowledge, which extends to general practices in the areas of business or financial planning, measurement, and control.

[30] It is important because an investment that does not meet a return on investment requirement will rarely be considered a success. However, if the investment fails to meet some other requirements (e.g., functional, quality, etc.) but still has an excellent return, it may still be considered a success.

An asset's return on investment is determined through assessment (see Sections 6.1); however, the financial view of assessment is based on measured income, benefits, and costs that comes from multi-period accounting (i.e., capital budgeting). The assessment is based on measured income, benefits, and costs. Revenue, the most common benefit, is usually unambiguous and easy to account for by asset. For example, when an enterprise sells a known number of products for a known price, it knows the origin, amount, and timing of income for each product. In other words, revenue measures (and many functional performance measures such as production rates) are inherently asset-based (i.e., unit or product price). Some costs are also unambiguous and easy to account for by asset. Typically, these costs include direct labor expenses for workers on the frontline who do repeated work directly on the asset, and the expense for material used directly in the asset.

However, many costs cannot be directly accounted for by asset because the resources (e.g., people, equipment, supplies) invested in it are also shared in work on other assets or they are invested indirectly in systems, processes, services, and so on that support other assets. An example of the former is a worker partly running a machine and partly sorting component parts. An example of the latter is maintenance workers repairing various machines or plant office personnel supporting the production of many products in a plant. The expense (e.g., their salary or wage) for their services cannot be directly traced and accounted to any particular product (i.e., their costs are typically accounted to a cost center such as plant management expense or "overhead"). However, the time period for their various types of work can be measured.

Therefore, the enterprise's assessment of return on any given asset investment (and decisions regarding the investment) are significantly affected by which assets the indirect expenses are assigned to. If the assignment is arbitrary, without being based on causality, then success of the investment, and the enterprise, will be uncertain. Therefore, this section focuses on methods that result in asset-based cost accounting, specifically ABC/M.

.2 Traditional and ABC/M Accounting

In cost accounting, actual monetary transactions are entered in a financial bookkeeping ledger per a chart of accounts that is generally organized by resource type. Resources are sources of work or expense such as labor salaries, electrical power, supplies, and so on. Accounting then translates the expenses (i.e., "what was spent") to costs for various cost centers (i.e., "what it was spent doing") so that the expenditures can be compared to the budgets established for the cost centers. An analogy to describe absorption costing is that the cost centers are sponges that absorb the work activities of the expenses captured in the ledger's spending buckets. Note that costs are calculated in absorption costing, not directly measured. In traditional accounting, the calculation assigns indirect expenses from the cost centers into the assets per established cost allocation methods such as proration in accordance with direct expenses, output volumes, or some other simple means with broad averages. In many cases, the cost centers and control budgets are established by organization (i.e., more "where" or "by whom," as opposed to "what" it was spent for). In that case, there is very little visibility as to the cost of assets, processes, or anything else that crosses organizational bounds.

As was mentioned, ABC/M improves upon traditional cost accounting by assigning or tracing indirect costs to the activities that drive them. These activities are work performed on or for a particular cost object or asset (e.g., products or standard service-lines). One way resource expenses are traced is to use the time that people or equipment spend performing certain activities. Figure 6.1-1 illustrates an ABC/M cost re-assignment network.

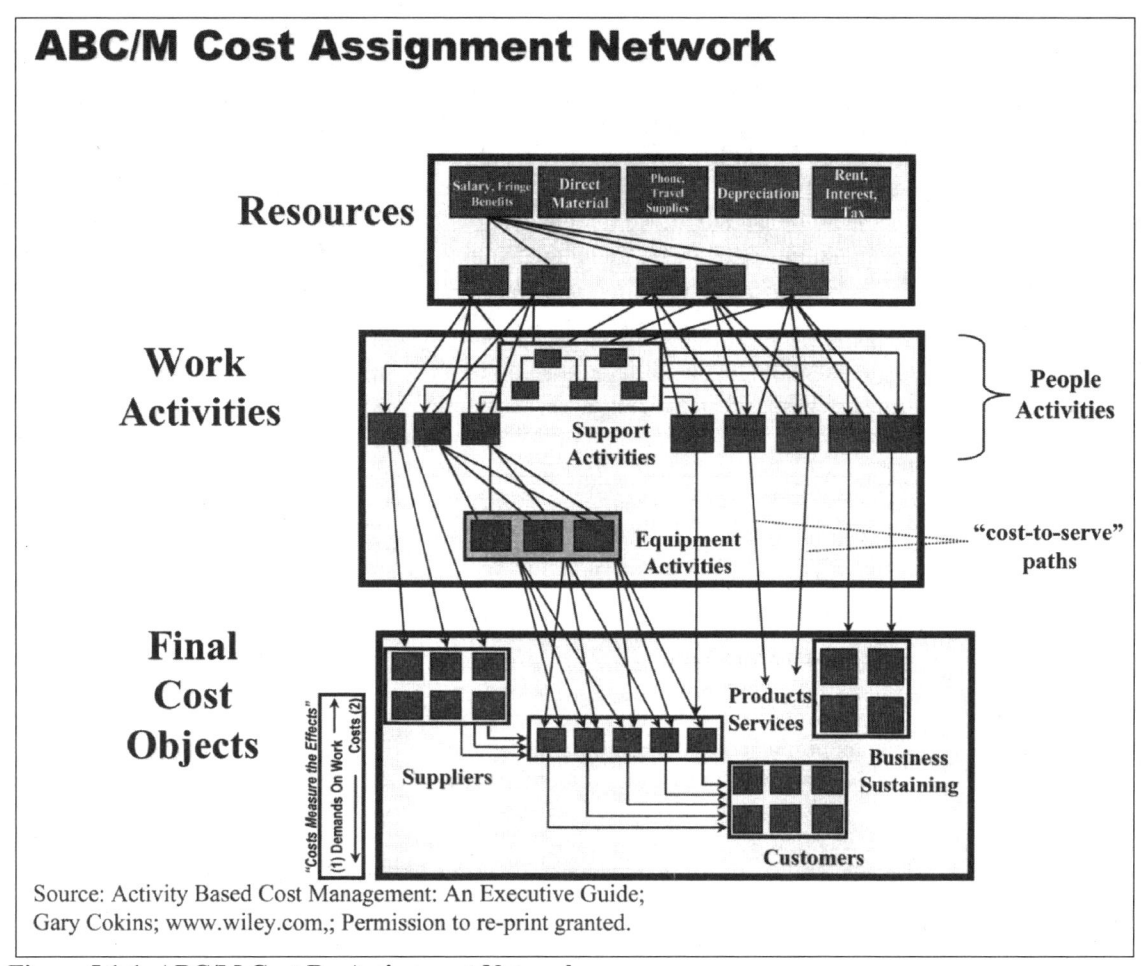

Figure 5.1-1. ABC/M Cost Re-Assignment Network

The activity tracing method is more complex than simple prorations, but it is the only accounting method that consistently and reliably supports the enterprise objective of improving the return on assets. ABC/M has increased the role of cost engineers in the asset cost accounting process because the method requires a greater knowledge of the work activities that belong to various processes than do traditional cost allocation accounting methods that conveniently use broad averages rather than reflect how the assets uniquely consume different work activities. The complexity of the process has been mitigated in recent years by integrated ABC/M software that allows enterprises to use the approach efficiently and consistently with automated data collection from transactional systems, such as an enterprise resource planning (ERP) system.

Most industry discussions of ABC/M methods, and software developed for the methods, center on cost management of recurring operational costs for non-capital assets such as products, process, and services (and in some cases also types of sales/distribution channels and types of customers). Industry discussions of project cost accounting, which usually center on the control of capital expenditures (CAPEX), do not often describe ABC/M accounting methods. However, if the methods used for project cost accounting are based on a work breakdown (i.e., activity-based), they inherently apply ABC/M principles. Indirect costs in a project environment where the direct costs are non-recurring, but the indirect costs are relatively more repetitive, can blend the ABC/M traced costs with the project accounting of the direct costs to view all of the enterprise's costs.

.3 Accounting and CAPEX

The previous discussions focused on accounting for current expenses that are recorded in the general ledger and can be immediately deducted from income during the time period (e.g., month, quarter) when determining profit. However, CAPEX investments are amortized over time periods typically beyond a year. Before those expenses can be amortized, the absorption process first must assign the expenses to a work activity cost center, and then causally trace each activity cost to an asset cost object (i.e., an item in the asset ledger). Then, when the asset or some component of it is put in use (e.g., commonly at or near the end of a project), depreciation of these assigned costs begins (i.e., some portion of the cost is expensed each time period in accordance with established rules for that asset or industry class in that taxation jurisdiction).

ABC/M methods are applied at two phases for CAPEX. First, at the close of a project (see Section 9.1) ABC/M techniques help ensure that indirect project expenses are properly assigned to either the direct project work or to the appropriate capital asset, which is a cost object in its own right (i.e., capitalization). However, that asset (e.g., a factory) may be a resource in support of producing other assets (e.g., a product produced by that factory). In that case, ABC/M methods are used to help ensure that the depreciation expenses are properly assigned to the appropriate cost objects (e.g., products).

The first step (i.e., asset capitalization cost assignment) has been a traditional role of cost engineers because of their knowledge of asset and project costs. Cost engineers have long used ABC/M principles in capital cost assignment based on causal relationships, in part because ABC/M principles are inherent to activity-based project control, and projects are the process through which most CAPEX is expended.

As discussed in Section 9.1, it is common for the enterprise financial functions to be more concerned with capitalization (i.e., how they must deal with the expenses) than project control (where the resource expenses originated). The result is that enterprise accounting systems are often set up to support asset accounts, but not project control accounts. Therefore, cost engineers and project control practitioners often find themselves heavily involved in helping to change and improve accounting systems as more companies add ERP and project management capabilities.

5.1.2 Process Map for Asset Cost Accounting

The asset cost accounting process illustrated in Figure 5.1-2 includes not only the measurement of costs, but the review, classification, and accounting of them for asset management purposes. The process is integrated with performance measurement (see Section 5.2). The measured costs are inputs to the asset performance assessment process (Section 6.1)

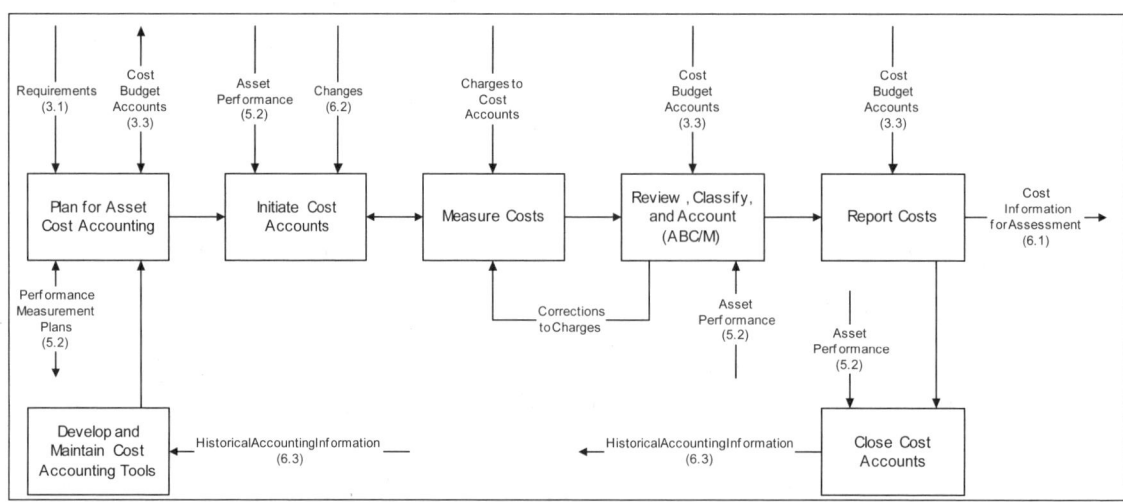

Figure 5.1-2. Process Map for Asset Cost Accounting

The following sections briefly describe the steps in the asset cost accounting process.

.1 Planning for Strategic Asset Cost Accounting

The process for asset cost accounting starts with planning for cost accounting. Initial planning starts during the requirements elicitation and analysis process (see Section 3.1) and continues through development of cost budgets in support of investment decision making (see Section 3.3). Business control is facilitated when the cost accounting process reports costs using the same coding structure or chart of accounts as the control or budget accounts. However, general ledger accounting systems were never designed to support cost allocations, including ABC/M (i.e., they lack cost assignment network capabilities). Therefore, the interface (i.e., cost assignment) between cost accounting and asset-based business control systems must be designed and planned. As was mentioned, ABC/M methods also apply to asset planning (see Section 3.2), so planning must begin early.

Planning ensures that the managerial accounting system cost accounts are either consistent with the control accounts, or that processes and procedures are in place to assign the accounting system cost data to the control accounts in the cost control system. The cost assignment network (i.e., cost absorption mapping) may be automated or facilitated by commercial software or it may involve manual translation and reentry of data (e.g., spreadsheets). In addition, the interaction/interface of owner, supplier, and contractor accounting systems, if any, must be considered and addressed in cost accounting plans.

.2 Initiate Cost Accounts

After cost accounting has been planned, cost accounts are opened or initiated in the cost accounting system or ledgers in accordance with the applicable chart of accounts. If ABC/M is used, the accounts for ABC/M purposes will be based on activity-based principles of cause-and-effect with an action verb-adjective-noun naming convention for the work activities (e.g., process customer orders) that are consumed by the cost objects. For recurring expenses, the cost accounts may always be open. However, accounts in the asset ledger, in which CAPEX will be assigned at project closeout, are opened as projects are implemented and closed out upon completion. The accounting plan will establish who may enter, change, delete, view, or otherwise use data and information in or from the system. To avoid mischarges, cost accounts are generally opened only as needed, not all at once.

.3 Measure, Review, Classify and Account Costs

Once accounts are opened, payments made by the enterprise for resource expenses (e.g., payroll, suppliers, contractors, etc.) are recorded by the accounting process against the appropriate resource cost account. Payments may also be made from one internal cost account to another within an enterprise. In any case, the cost account ledgers are charged (debited) to reflect the dispersal of funds.

The accounting function regularly checks that the costs recorded by the accounting process are appropriate. Cost data are commonly miscoded, misfiled, improperly invoiced, or otherwise mischarged. In addition, work may have been completed or materials received, but not yet invoiced; accounting must review progress measurements (Section 5.2) to determine if a commitment has been made.

As was discussed, indirect or overhead costs are assigned by the accounting process to other cost centers. Indirect or overhead costs may be apportioned using a percentage markup on the direct costs method ignoring causality and introducing some cost inaccuracy or the ABC/M method may be used to assure higher accuracy and visibility to individual indirect cost elements and their drivers. The accounting process periodically evaluates the cost assignment method used to ensure that the costs incurred are in balance with allocations. Cost engineers may be involved with establishing or reviewing the basis of assigning expenses to cost centers and how each cost center is consumed by its activity driver into the enterprise's cost objects.

The accounting process may charge to a cost account (i.e., book a debit to the ledger) on a cash or accrual basis. Cost accounting is on a cash basis when a check is cut and the expense is recorded as expended during the same time period, such as the month recorded. In accrual accounting, the payment may occur in a different time period than the period when the profit and loss expense is recognized. For example, costs may be booked before the check is cut in recognition that while an actual payment has not been made, a commitment or liability to make that payment has been incurred. It may also be booked after the check is cut in recognition that while an actual payment has been made, the work or resource for which payment has been made has not yet occurred or been received. Cost accounting reports both accrued (i.e., committed) and cash (i.e., actual) expenditures. This helps business understand the enterprise's liabilities and supports forecasts of remaining costs.

.4 Report Project Costs

The cost accounting system reports expenses as they are debited and credited to the various expense accounts in the ledgers. As was discussed, if the accounting system cost accounts are inconsistent with the control accounts, the accounting process must transfer the expenses to the cost control system.

.5 Close Cost Accounts

Cost accounts are closed to accepting charges when no longer needed. For recurring expenses, the cost accounts may always be open. However, accounts in the asset ledger, in which CAPEX has been assigned at project closeout, are closed after the asset is fully depreciated.

5.1.3 Inputs to Asset Cost Accounting

.1 *Requirements.* (see Section 3.1) Establishes the conditions or capabilities that must be met or possessed by an asset (i.e., system, product, service, result, or component). Requirements often include cost targets. The methods to be used to measure and account for costs and performance are often established as requirements.
.2 *Cost Budget Accounts.* The investment decision making process (see Section 3.3) establishes cost budgets for the selected asset solutions. The budgets should follow a chart of accounts that aligns with the way costs will be measured and assessed; plans must address how expenses will be assigned to the appropriate cost accounts (e.g., ABC/M).
.3 *Performance Measurement Plans.* Plans for measuring asset performance (Section 5.2) should be aligned with cost accounting plans as appropriate. Alignment may consider the frequency of measurements, alignment with control accounts, etc.
.4 *Asset Performance.* (Section 5.2) The time of initiation and closing of cost accounts is partly dependent on activity start and completion dates. Also, activity performance is compared to payments made to identify committed costs.
.5 *Changes.* During project execution, changes to requirements and asset planning are identified in the change management process (Section 6.2). Change may result in changes to asset cost accounting.
.6 *Charges to Cost Accounts.* In the accounting process (steps of which are not part of the TCM process map), the disbursal of funds is recorded by the accounting process against the appropriate cost account.
.7 *Historical Accounting Information.* Successful past asset cost accounting approaches are commonly used as future planning references.

5.1.4 Outputs from Asset Cost Accounting

.1 *Cost Budget Accounts.* Asset cost accounting planning may identify improvements to the basis of investment decision making (Section 3.3).
.2 *Performance Measurement Plans.* Asset cost accounting planning may identify improvements in plans for measuring performance (Section 5.2).

.3 *Cost Information for Assessment.* Cost information is used in asset performance assessment (Section 6.1).
.4 *Historical Accounting Information.* The enterprise cost accounting approaches are captured for use as a future planning reference. Asset cost data are also captured in the project historical database (Section 6.3).

5.1.5 Key Concepts for Asset Cost Accounting

The following concepts and terminology described in this and other chapters are particularly important to understanding the asset cost accounting process of TCM:

.1 *Cost Accounts.* Charts of accounts for capturing expenditure and cost information.
.2 *Expenditures/Expenses.* An expense that is charged to a ledger account when a payment or disbursement is made. Expenses differ from reported costs because costs (e.g., a process cost, activity cost, product cost, or customer cost) are always calculated.
.3 *Commitments.* The sum of all financial obligations made, including expenditures as well as obligations, which will not be performed or received until later. May also be referred to as an "accrued expenditure."
.4 *Cost Allocation or Assignment (overhead, markups, etc.).* The process of representing and reflecting how outputs of work (or the work itself) consumes and draws on resources by transferring costs from one account to another so that calculated and reported costs are consistent with the basis for the cost included in the cost control budget.
.5 *Cash and Accrual Accounting.* In cash accounting, costs are accounted for when expended (i.e., payments are made or cash disbursed). In accrual accounting, costs are accounted for when an obligation to make an expenditure is incurred, even if cash will not be expended or disbursed until a later time.
.6 *Capitalization and Depreciation.* Some costs are charged (i.e., expensed) as immediate or current expenses. However, capital expenses (CAPEX) are held in suspense as work-in-progress (i.e., a suspense account), until the capital asset is put in service. Prior to being put in service, the capital project costs are assigned to items in the capital asset ledger and balance sheet (i.e., capitalized), and these costs are then charged or recognized over time in the profit statement as a depreciation expense. Capital and expense designations and depreciation rules are usually defined by government tax authorities. Cost engineers often assist the finance function in making the cost allocations.
.7 *Activity-Based Costing/Management (ABC/M).* A superior method to causally trace and assign resource expenses into costs (rather than allocate costs) in a way that the costs budgeted and charged to an account truly represent all the resources consumed by the activity or item represented in the account (i.e., the allocation is not arbitrarily based on broad averages without causality, but reflects what events drive the cost).

Further Readings and Sources

The interface of asset management with cost accounting is generally covered in business management and accounting texts. The following references provide basic information and will lead to more detailed treatments.

- AACE International. *Skills and Knowledge of Cost Engineering*, 5th ed. (chapter on Activity-Based Cost Management). Morgantown, WV: AACE International, 2004.
- Cokins, Gary. *Activity Based Cost Management: An Executive Guide.* New York: John Wiley & Sons, 2001.
- Humphreys, Kenneth, Editor. *Project and Cost Engineer's Handbook*, 4th ed. New York: Marcel Dekker, Inc., 2005.
- Klammer, Thomas P. *Managing Strategic and Capital Investment Decisions.* Burr Ridge, IL: Irwin Professional Publishing, 1993.

- Ostrenga, M., M. Harwood, R. McIlhatten, and T. Ozan, Editors. *Ernst & Young's Guide to Total Cost Management*. New York: John Wiley & Sons, 1992.
- Piekarski, Julian A. "Advanced Managerial Costing in Industry," *AACE International Transactions*. Morgantown, WV: AACE International, 1994.
- Player, Steve and David E. Keys. *Activity-Based Management*. New York: MasterMedia Limited, 1995.

5.2 Asset Performance Measurement

5.2.1 Description

Asset performance measurement refers to the process of measuring and reporting the non-monetary performance of the enterprise's strategic asset portfolio including its use of non-monetary resources. The output of the process is performance data for assessing the asset portfolios performance relative to established business objectives and requirements (Section 3.1). The inputs to the process include the basis against which asset portfolio performance is assessed (quantified requirements per Section 3.1 and the investment decision basis per Section 3.3) and performance and resource data from ongoing asset operation during the asset life cycle.

Together with asset cost accounting measures (Section 5.1), performance measures are the basis for asset performance assessment. The asset performance measurement and assessment processes are part of a continuous effort to evaluate and improve investment decisions so that the enterprise's business objectives are more successfully achieved. Performance assessment methods such as benchmarking and investment analysis are covered in Section 6.1. The TCM process map does not explicitly include the performance measurement process (e.g., industrial engineering, etc.); it only addresses the strategic asset management interface with these processes.[31]

In terms of information technology (IT), the distinction between cost accounting and performance measurement is increasingly less distinct as materials or enterprise resource planning (MRP and ERP) and business intelligence (BI) data mining systems increasingly encompass the measurement of all resource and calculating performance data (scores, ratios, indices, etc.) for both asset management and project control.

.1 Requirements and the Investment Decision Basis Establish What to Measure

As discussed in Section 3.1, requirements are a condition or capability that a problem solution must have to address their perceived problem or opportunity. The first characteristic of a good requirement is that it defines what the asset will do. The next is that it be quantified to serve as a basis of performance measurement. For example, performance against a requirement such as "must have good reliability" cannot be measured; a statement such as "must have less than 1 percent downtime" is better. In this example, the enterprise would measure percentage downtime for this asset.

As further discussed in Sections 2.3 and 3.3, the most important business requirement for most enterprises, and the basis for their asset investment decisions where applicable, is a measure of economic return on investment (ROI); ROI is a single measure that expresses in monetary terms the value of the investment over its life cycle to the enterprise.[32] Allowing for the time value of money, return on investment improves with greater income and less costs. In decision and investment analysis, income and costs may include non-monetary benefit and cost factors expressed in monetary terms. For example, if a reliability or quality requirement for the asset investment was "must have less than 1 percent downtime," the downtime would be measured and the cost or detrimental effects of more or less downtime would need to be monetized in investment analysis as a measure of lost revenue and increased indirect cost per unit of production.[33]

Investment alternative solution planning and decisions are based on requirements, but also on various performance assumptions and constraints. A common example is resource assumptions and constraints.

---

[31] APICS, the Association for Operations Management (www.apics.org), is a key resource for asset performance measurement knowledge.
[32] It is important because an investment that does not meet a return on investment requirement will rarely be considered a success. However, if the investment fails to meet some other requirements (e.g., functional, quality, etc.) but still has an excellent return, it may still be considered a success.
[33] For many assets and processes, cycle time (and its components) is often one of the most important performance measures driving ROI.

These may relate to assumed attributes or performance of a supply chain, or availability of key personal with special skills, and so on. The use and performance of these resources would need to be measured if they were part of the basis of the investment decision.

The number of requirements established, and hence measures to capture, can be quite large. Therefore, most enterprises focus on only a few high level key performance indicators (KPIs) that are the measures believed to most directly correlate with successful achievement of the executive team's strategic business objectives. Gradually and later more KPIs can be cascaded down into the core business processes, but it is still a good practice to restrict the number of KPIs for each employee team to the vital few (recommended at about three) rather than the trivial many for which measures become outside the team's influence and control. KPIs can be established at the enterprise level as a strategy for the overall portfolio of asset investments, or for individual asset investments at the time the investment decision is made. An important KPI is usually return on investment, so priority should be placed on measures that drive ROI.

If a process requirement is that activity-based costing/management (ABC/M) methods be used (see Section 5.1), costs are accounted for and will be assessed by the work activities that belong to the business processes, and are then subsequently causally traced to the intermediate outputs, products, channels, and customers (i.e., cost objects) that consume the work. Therefore, the performance of work activities, both employees and equipment, must be measured (or reasonably estimated) as well as the quantity of the activity driver (e.g., the number of purchase orders to calculate "the unit cost per purchase order"). For example, if an ABC/M cost assignment network traces resource expenses to activities using the time that people spend performing a certain activity, that time or percentage of their week must be measured (or estimated) as well as the quantity of the activity driver that traces the activity cost into its cost object. The measure is generally a proxy (i.e., an activity measurement factor) that is assumed to represent the performance of the activity.

5.2.2 Process Map for Strategic Asset Performance Measurement

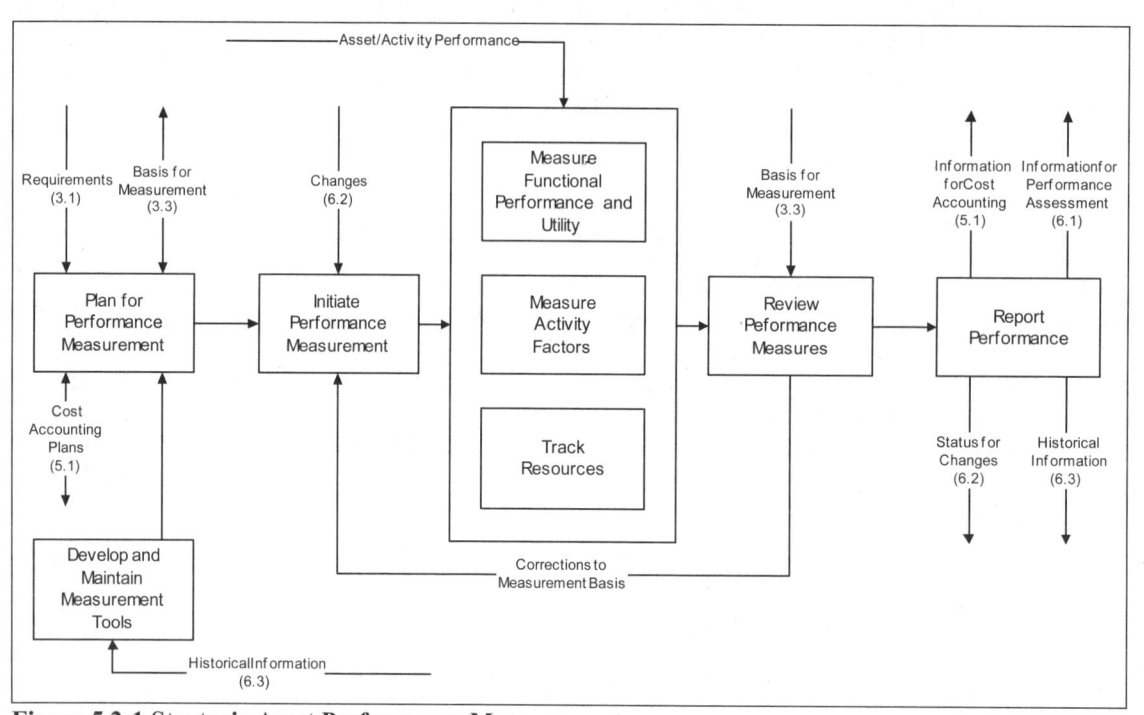

Figure 5.2-1 Strategic Asset Performance Measurement

The following sections briefly describe the steps in the asset performance measurement process.

.1 Planning for Asset Performance Measurement

The process for performance measurement starts with planning for the measurements. As an integrated process, initial planning starts with development of the requirements (Section 3.1) and continues through development of the investment decision basis or business case (Section 3.3). As was discussed, requirements must be quantified and measurable. Because the measurements are done to support the assessment methods that will be used, planning for measurement and assessment must be done together as well.

One aspect of planning includes assigning specific roles and responsibilities for measuring the performance of each asset investment. Much of the measurement work is the responsibility of ongoing operations and functional management (or equivalent) and may require little planning. The role of cost engineers may be limited to helping plan the measurement process, communicate requirements, and review measures to ensure they meet the needs of performance assessment.

Another aspect to plan is the interface (i.e., data transfer) between transactional systems (e.g., ERP systems, etc.) where base metrics reside and the business intelligence (BI) data mining systems used to store data from disparate data sources into common database platforms for performance assessment. Business intelligence systems provide not only a common database for all measures, but the capability to analyze and assess these measures against established performance criteria (e.g., balanced scorecards, "KPI dashboards," etc.), as well as predict and forecast. Enterprise performance management (EPM) systems operate on and draw data from enterprise information platforms (EIP).

Planning ensures that the measures captured in and reported by various systems are either consistent with the assessment tools (e.g., ABC/M, Quality Function Deployment, etc.), or that processes and procedures are in place to obtain measures and/or translate them to the assessment basis. This may involve manual measurement (e.g., audits or inspections), translation, and entry of data. In addition, the interaction/interface of owner, supplier, and contractor reporting systems, if any, must be considered and addressed in performance measurement plans.

After performance measurement has been planned, measurement processes or systems are initiated for each resource type for which consumption or status is to be measured and each asset activity factor or function that will be measured. The performance measurement plan will establish who may enter, change, delete, view, or otherwise use data and information in or from each system.

.2 Measuring Performance

It is difficult to summarize the possible measures that may be captured regarding an asset's performance. Some are measured on a continuous basis in ERP systems, process control systems, and business intelligence (BI) systems. Others may be obtained on an as needed or spot basis through audits, inspections, special studies, or surveys (for more qualitative measures). In general, however, there are three main types of measures obtained as described in the paragraphs that follow.

Functional Performance and Utility

Functional requirements and functionality measures capture what an asset does and how it does it. These measures may include such performance attributes as production rates, operability (e.g., percentage downtime), maintainability, usability, and so on. They may also include quality control attributes such as reliability, defect rates, and so on. Another common functionality measure is cycle time (i.e., economic costs are in large part driven by timing). These are generally highly objective, physical measures.

Utility measures capture user or customer perceptions of how well the asset meets their wants and needs. These should be quantified as requirements, but measurements may indicate that the requirements elicitation and analysis process (see Section 3.1) missed the mark. These measures often reflect "soft" or experiential requirements and the measurements tend to be more subjective in nature. Methods such as surveys may be used to capture performance information.

Measure Activity Factors

As discussed in Section 5.2.1.1, if ABC/M methods are used, cost assignment network tracing ties expenses to activities whose performance must be measured; and then into output costs, product costs, and so on (i.e., cost objects). Resource measurements, as discussed below, are often used as proxies for activity (i.e., activity factors).

Track Resources

The purpose of investment decision making is to make good decisions as to how to invest or allocate the enterprise's resources. The use of resources in or by an asset must be measured as applicable, including labor, materials, and so on. ERP systems are one source for this measurement as well as work order systems in project-oriented environments. Emphasis will often be focused on scarce or otherwise critical resources.

.3 Review Performance Measures

The asset management function (e.g., strategic or capital planning, etc.) regularly checks that the basis of performance measurement is appropriate and in alignment with the asset management plans and the investment decision and performance assessment basis. Measures are also reviewed to ensure timeliness and accuracy. Most measurements are not made directly by those responsible for the performance assessment. Much of the data will be obtained from ERP systems. However, those with performance assessment responsibility should spot check the work progress and performance measurements to some extent (i.e., audits, inspections, questioning operations management, etc.) to ensure that the data being received and reviewed are reliable, appropriate, and understood.

.4 Report Performance Measures

After review, measurement information is reported to the performance assessment process (Section 3.1). Also, measurement data are used in the evaluation of changes in the change management process (Section 3.2). Performance information may also be used in the cost accounting process (Section 6.1) to identify when cost accounts should be initiated or closed.

Finally, historical performance information is captured (see Section 3.3). The information is used to help improve measurement tools such as software, forms, checklist, procedures, and so on. Measurement data, including experiences and lessons learned about past measurement practices, are used for planning future asset investments.

5.2.3 Inputs to Strategic Asset Performance Measurement

.1 *Requirements.* Quantified requirements define some performance measures (Section 3.1) as well as methods to be used for the process.
.2 *Basis for Measurement.* Planning assumptions and constraints incorporated in the basis of the investment decision (Section 3.3) define some performance measurements.
.3 *Asset/Activity Performance.* Measurements of asset performance are obtained from operating or project processes.
.4 *Changes.* Changes to the baseline requirements and asset plans are identified in the change management process (see Section 6.2). Requirement changes may result in changes to performance measurement.
.5 *Historical Information.* Successful past performance measurement approaches are commonly used as future planning references. Historical performance data are also captured.

5.2.4 Outputs from Strategic Asset Performance Measurement

.1 *Basis for Measurement.* Measurement planning may identify improvements to investment decision making (Section 3.3).

.2 *Asset Cost Accounting Plans.* Performance measurement planning may identify improvements in plans for cost accounting (Section 5.1)

.3 *Corrections to Measurement Basis.* Review of performance measurements may identify corrections that need to be made in the measurement process (e.g., timeliness, quality of measures, etc.).

.4 *Measurement Information for Cost Accounting.* Measures of asset/activity performance are reported to the cost accounting process (Section 5.1) to support the initiation and closing of accounts. Also, the tracking of resource expenditures identifies cost obligations (i.e., commitments).

.5 *Measurement Information for Performance Assessment.* Measurement information supports performance assessment (Section 6.1).

.6 *Status Information for Change Management.* Measurement data are used in the evaluation of requirements and planning changes (Section 6.2). In order to evaluate the effect of a change, it is necessary to know how the asset is functioning, etc.

.7 *Historical Project Information.* The performance measurement approaches used are captured in a database (Section 6.3) for use as future planning references. Measurement data are captured as well.

5.2.5 Key Concepts for Strategic Asset Performance Measurement

The following concepts and terminology described in this and other chapters are particularly important to understanding the strategic asset performance measurement process of TCM:

.1 *Requirements.* (Sections 5.2.1.1 and 3.1).
.2 *Return on Investment (ROI)* (Section 5.2.1.1 and Section 3.3).
.3 *Benefits and Costs* (Section 5.2.1.1 and Section 3.3).
.4 *Investment Decision Basis/Business Case.* (Section 3.3).
.5 *Asset Cost Accounting.* (Section 5.1).
.6 *Enterprise Resource Planning (ERP).* (Section 5.2.1).
.7 *Business Intelligence (BI).* (Section 5.2.1).
.8 *Enterprise Performance Management (EPM).* (Section 5.2.1.2).
.9 *Key Performance Indicators (KPIs).* (See Section 5.2.1.1).

Further Readings and Sources

The strategic asset performance measurement process is generally covered in business and strategic management texts, including those that cover decision making, ERP systems, ABC/M methods, business intelligence, and so on. The following references provide basic information and will lead to more detailed treatments.

- Cokins, Gary. *Activity Based Cost Management: An Executive Guide.* New York: John Wiley & Sons, 2001.
- Cokins, Gary. *Performance Management (Finding the Missing Pieces to Close the Intelligence Gap).* New York: John Wiley & Sons, 2004.
- Klammer, Thomas P. *Managing Strategic and Capital Investment Decisions.* Burr Ridge, IL: Irwin Professional Publishing, 1993.
- Ostrenga, M., M. Harwood, R. McIlhatten, and T. Ozan, Editors. *Ernst & Young's Guide to Total Cost Management.* New York: John Wiley & Sons, 1992.
- Player, Steve and David E. Keys. *Activity-Based Management.* New York: MasterMedia Limited, 1995.
- Schuyler, John R. *Risk and Decision Analysis in Projects*, 2nd ed. Upper Darby, PA: Project Management Institute, 2001.

CHAPTER 6

STRATEGIC ASSET PERFORMANCE ASSESSMENT

6.1 Asset Performance Assessment

6.1.1 Description

The asset performance assessment process analyzes cost accounting and performance measurement data to identify asset performance problems, opportunities, and risks for which the requirements for a solution can be assessed. Performance problems with existing assets (which are also improvement opportunities) are generally identified by analyzing variances between planned and actual performance. Through internal and external benchmarking and intelligence gathering, the assessment process also identifies new business opportunities. Identified asset portfolio performance improvement opportunities and risks are assessed and managed through the requirements elicitation and analysis and asset change management processes (Section 3.1 and Chapter 6.2, respectively), which close the strategic asset management cycle loop. Findings and experiences from the performance assessment process are captured in the asset historical database (Section 6.3) for use in future asset management.

The primary inputs to the process are internal asset cost accounting and performance measurement data (see Sections 5.1 and 5.2, respectively). The quantitative measurement data are analyzed for variances against the asset performance requirements (Section 3.1) and the investment decision basis (Section 3.3). Measurements of the attributes and performance of other enterprises' assets are another basis of comparison; these are generally obtained through benchmarking methods. Root cause analysis and lessons learned methods identify improvement opportunities and risks (generally from a more qualitative perspective) for immediate assessment and for future requirements assessment when captured in a historical database.

The asset performance measurement and assessment processes are part of a continuous effort to evaluate and improve investment decisions so that the enterprise's business objectives, as reflected in requirements, are more successfully achieved (i.e., business problems are solved).

.1 Requirements and the Investment Decision Basis Establish What to Assess

Requirements are conditions or capabilities that must be met or possessed by an asset to solve a business problem. They are the basic unit of communication that links the needs of the customer to the design of the solution. When a realized asset meets requirements, we have a solid basis for evaluating the strategic success of that asset. As discussed in Section 3.1, asset requirements can generally be categorized as either a *functional* requirement (i.e., what the solution has to do), or a *constraint* or *non-functional* requirement (i.e., qualities or attributes that a solution must have).

Some might add *business* requirements (i.e., enterprise or operations missions, goals, or drivers) as a category, but in general, these can often be categorized as *constraints*. Another requirement to assess is whether the requirements themselves are solving the business problem as intended. Asset performance is unlikely to be considered successful if either the requirements are not met or requirements are not adequately addressing the business problem or opportunity.

Profitability analysis is the key method for assessing performance against general business requirements. It recognizes that the most important business requirement for most enterprises and the basis for their asset investment decisions, where applicable (see Section 3.3), is a measure of economic return on investment (ROI) or equivalent; ROI is a single measure that expresses in monetary terms the value of the investment over its life cycle to the enterprise.

Cost of quality analysis is the key method for assessing performance against functional requirements and constraints. Cost of quality refers to the cost of error-free, conforming, and not conforming (i.e., at variance) with these requirements. Costs of quality are generally analyzed in the following five categories: error-free, prevention-related, appraisal-related, internal failure, and external failure. Prevention and appraisal costs, such as employee training or product testing, are essentially designed into the asset or process during asset planning (i.e., costs of conformance that are fixed or controllable by design), so performance assessment tends to focus on the "resultant" cost of failure or variance during the asset's use (i.e., costs of nonconformance are more variable by nature).

A business strategy map and its companion balanced scorecard is another popular methodology used to first communicate the executive team's strategy to employees, second align the organization's work and priorities with the relevant measures (referred to as key performance indicators or KPIs) that will achieve the strategy, and then assess performance variance between the actual and target for each KPI. Balanced scorecard seeks to ensure that business strategy and deployment look at performance from a "balanced" perspective of non-financial measures (such as on-time delivery performance) measured *during* a period that ultimately contribute to the financial measures reported at the *end* of the period (when it is too late to act). Specifically it recommends that metrics from multiple perspectives be considered, such as a financial, customer, business process, and learning and growth perspective. Some organizations add additional perspectives such as environment or safety or prefer to use the seven core value and concept elements of the Malcolm Baldrige National Quality Award.[34]

The important point is to apply metrics in a linked framework that reflects the strategic intent of the executive team. After KPIs are cascaded from executive and middle manager levels into the core processes, then the number of requirements established, and hence to "score," can be quite large. Therefore, enterprises ideally focus on the vital few (rather than the trivial many) key performance indicators that are measures believed to most directly correlate with successful achievement of business objectives within the inter-related perspectives. A most important KPI from a financial or cost perspective is ROI (or its equivalent) as assessed using profitability analysis. Other key indicators may include target costs and so on. However, elements or drivers of cost of quality that focus on the customer and business process perspectives can be used as KPIs.

6.1.2 Process Map for Asset Performance Assessment

As was discussed, the asset performance assessment process analyzes measurement data to identify asset performance problems, opportunities, and risks for which the requirements for a solution can be assessed. As shown in Figure 6.1-1, the process centers on steps that analyze performance variances from a cost perspective and identify performance improvement opportunities and risks.

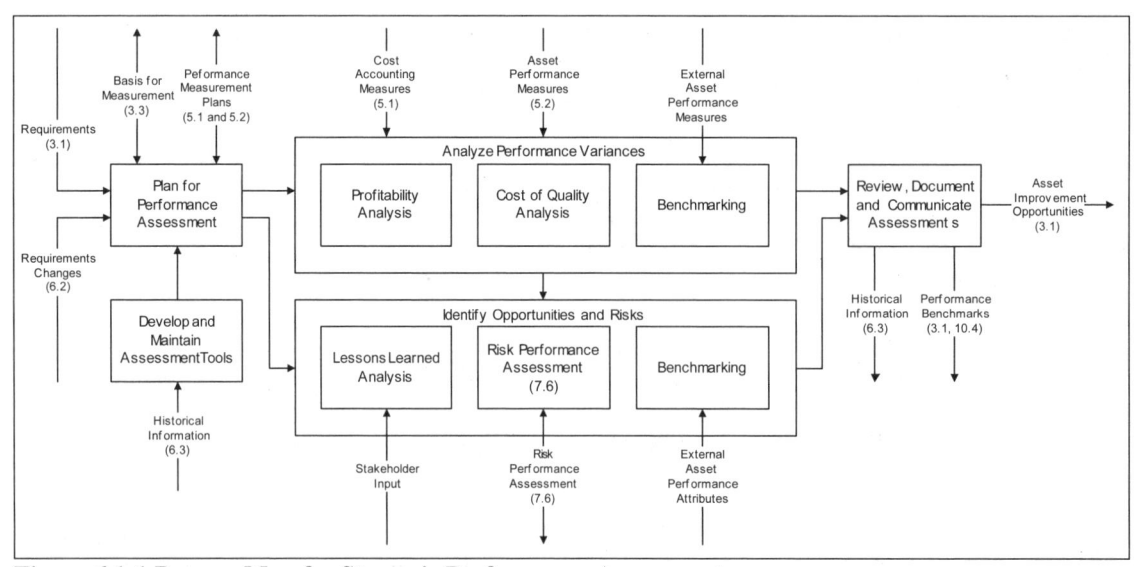

Figure 6.1-1 Process Map for Strategic Performance Assessment

---

[34] Baldridge National Quality Program, *Criteria for Performance Excellence*. Gaithersburg, MD: National Institute of Standards and Technology, 2006.

The following sections briefly describe the steps in the strategic performance assessment process.

.1 Plan for Performance Assessment

The process for performance measurement starts with planning for the assessment. Strategic asset management is an integrated process, so initial planning starts with development of the requirements (Section 3.1) and continues through development of the investment decision basis or business case (Section 3.3). As the basis for assessment, the requirements and investment decision basis are the key inputs for the planning step. If only a few KPIs will be measured and assessed, these need to be identified when planning the process. Also, because performance measurements are done to support the assessment methods, planning for measurement (Sections 5.1 and 5.2) and assessment must be done together.

Much of the performance assessment work will be ongoing and may be somewhat automated as part of the enterprise business reporting cycle. This ongoing effort may require little planning. However, profitability analysis of products, service-lines, types of channels, and types of customers (preferably calculated with ABC/M principles), cost of quality, benchmarking, and lessons learned may be routinely reported from a repeatable computer system or optionally undertaken on a special study or cyclical basis. These methods typically rely on analytical software modeling tools and data that must be managed to support the process.

Specific roles and responsibilities for assessment need to be planned. Some of the assessment work (e.g., operations analysis) is the responsibility of ongoing operations and functional management or equivalent and may require little planning. The role of cost engineers is most significant for performing cost-based assessments on a special study basis such as ROI and ABC/M analyses.

Another aspect to plan is the use of information technology for assessment. Enterprise performance management systems expand on enterprise resource planning (ERP) systems by constructing an enterprise information platform (EIP), which is a common database from multiple disparate data sources for all performance measures. This platform, commonly referred to as a data warehouse provides the capability to assess measures against established performance criteria (e.g., balanced scorecards, "KPI dashboards," etc.) as well as extract, transform, and analyze information for decision support. This is the growing field of "business intelligence" (BI).

Planning ensures that the measures captured in and reported by various measurement systems are either consistent with the assessment tools (e.g., ABC/M), or that processes and procedures are in place to translate measures to the assessment basis. In addition, the interaction/interface of various reporting systems within the enterprise or with external suppliers, if any, must be considered and addressed in performance assessment plans.

.2 Analyze Performance Variances

With the assessment basis established and assessment plans in place, performance assessment begins with analyzing quantitative performance variances. The methods used for analyzing asset performance generally mirror the methods used for asset planning and investment decision making.

Investment Return and Profitability Analysis

As discussed in Section 3.3, the most common economic valuation method used to support decision making is net present value (NPV). NPV calculations convert cash flows to a lump sum (i.e., single point) equivalent financial value at the present time by discounting future cash flows assuming a cost of capital rate that recognizes the time value of money. Most analysis problems examine the financial return for an investment for which there are both cash inflows (i.e., revenue or benefits) and outflows (costs). The alternative with the highest positive NPV is usually the one selected. The ROI for an investment alternative is that interest rate for which the NPV is zero.

At the time of assessment, the ROI or other profitability metric is updated with actual revenue and expense cash flows instead of estimates depending on where the asset is in its life cycle. The initial actual expense is generally the cost invested in the project to create the asset. The longer the asset has been in use, the greater the confidence in the investment return and profitability analysis.

Profitability will generally be assessed for each asset investment as well as for all or parts of the enterprise (e.g., by organization, programs, portfolios, etc.). To appropriately determine the ROI on a particular asset or cost object (e.g., facility, product, product line, sales channel, distribution channel, customer, process, etc.), profitability analysis may apply activity-based costing/management (ABC/M) accounting and analysis methods (see Section 5.1) since different work activities are first consumed by different cost objects. These cost objects in turn consume each other, such as customers purchase a basket mix of products as well as consuming non-product-related costs-to-serve.

An enterprise's project system is an asset and process for which performance is assessed as well. Requirements for project system performance usually focus on project cost and schedule performance. These measures are usually assessed project by project (see Section 10.4) and are reported to the asset management system for portfolio analysis.[35] However, the ultimate success of a project (i.e., investment) is its profitability and this cannot be assessed with confidence until some time after the project has been completed.

Cost of Quality (COQ) Analysis

As was mentioned, cost of quality highlights the location in a business process and magnitude of the costs of not conforming with requirements. It also sheds light on prevention and appraisal costs, such as testing, to avoid non-conformance costs. Cost of quality analysis is nevertheless a cost separate from simply processing outputs the first time error-free. Figure 6.1-2 illustrates the cost of quality concept with costs varying with the degree of quality attainment. The typical cost of quality categories are prevention, appraisal, and failure (internal and external failures are summed in the figure).

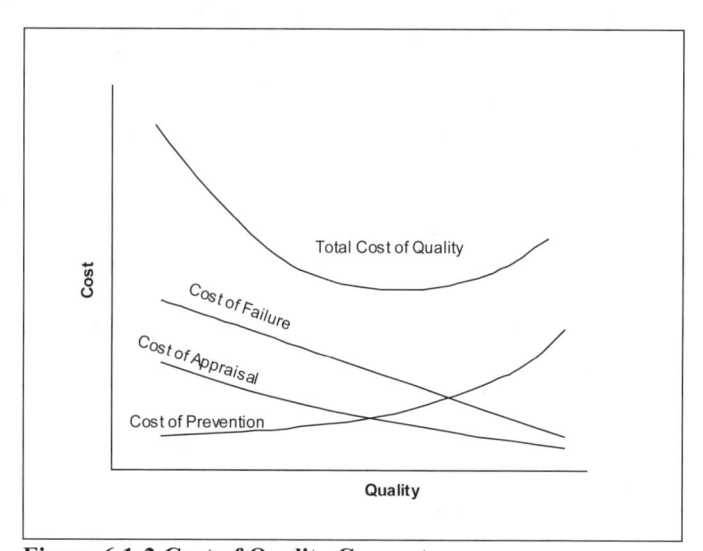

Figure 6.1-2 Cost of Quality Concept

The cost of prevention, which is usually a function of asset planning, will tend to increase as more physical and/or process "perfection" is built into the design. The cost of appraisal tends to decrease as the need for inspection and monitoring is reduced. Finally, the cost of failure tends to decrease as the need for rework decreases and customer satisfaction increases.

---

[35] When assessing project system performance, ABC/M methods can be used to assign indirect enterprise project system capability management costs to the projects depending on which projects are driving these costs (i.e., each project is an activity in the project system). As is true for any activity, assigning project system indirect costs to projects on an arbitrary basis (e.g., flat percentage) contributes to poor decisions.

Performance assessment tends to focus on the cost of varying from requirements (i.e., cost of nonconformance or "failure"). Failure costs are usually sub-categorized as internal or external. Internal costs tend to relate to process nonconformance and include items such as scrap materials, additional labor (poor productivity), and rework. External costs tend to relate to physical nonconformance and include items such as warranties, returns, and lost sales, as well as difficult to measure costs such as customer dissatisfaction or lost goodwill.

Cost of quality variance analysis consists of comparing planned failure costs (which should be minimal) versus actual costs for the asset in question and relating the variances to the requirements that were not conformed to. The requirement nonconformances that have the most cost effect are then given priority as opportunities for improvement.

The cost of internal failures is easiest to measure and assess (e.g., labor, material, etc.). Much of an organization's COQ is "hidden costs" beyond the obvious and easily trackable costs of an inspection department or person or scrap or reworked material. Various parts of a worker's day involve testing or reacting to unplanned mistakes. ABC/M is an ideal method used to "unhide" these costs because it not only assigns and traces (rather than allocates) indirect costs effectively, but also allows all activity costs to be classified by the five COQ categories (and optionally indented deeper). That is, nonconformance work activities often originate from the performance of non-value adding activities in a process that can be studied with ABC/M.[36] (Scoring and tagging each work activity cost by its COQ classification using ABC/M "attributes" is referred to as an additional dimension of cost—the "color of money"). Some external costs are also easy to measure (e.g., returns), but others such as customer dissatisfaction must be estimated.

While the cost assessment focus is generally on the failures, the total cost of quality must also be assessed to determine if the planned balance of prevention, appraisal, and failure cost was achieved.

If the assessment finds that the requirements were met, but external failure costs are still high or increasing (e.g., the customer is dissatisfied), then the requirements need to be reassessed in the asset change management process (see Section 6.2) because they may not be addressing the customer needs or wants.

<u>Benchmarking</u>
Benchmarking is a measurement and analysis process that compares practices, processes, and relevant measures to those of a selected basis of comparison (i.e., the benchmark) with the goal of improving performance. The comparison basis includes internal or external competitive or best practices, processes, or measures. As Watson states, "the process of benchmarking results in two types of output: benchmarks, or measures of comparative performance, and enablers (i.e., practices that lead to exceptional performance)."[37] Therefore, though benchmarking is one process, Figure 6.1-1 shows benchmarking twice to reflect its use in performance variance analysis ("benchmarks") and identifying improvement opportunities ("enablers).

The benchmarking process has four basic steps that follow the Shewhart or Deming "plan, do, check, and act" PDCA cycle (i.e., the basis of the TCM process as a whole) as follows:

1. plan the study
2. collect the data
3. analyze the data
4. adapt and implement practices

---

[36] Philip Crosby estimates that it is common for 80 percent of the cost of quality to originate with the process (Crosby, Philip B., *Quality Is Still Free*, McGraw Hill, 1996).
[37] Watson, Gregory H., *Strategic Benchmarking*, John Wiley and Sons, Inc., 1993.

In the first step, the asset or process to be studied is defined, performance measures are identified, and the external enterprises or internal organizations to include in the study are determined (i.e., what and whom should be benchmarked). In the second step, data are collected from applicable sources (e.g., direct contact, questionnaires, public data, etc.). In the third step, performance measures of the enterprises are compared and the enablers (i.e., improvement opportunities) that facilitated the best performance are identified. The last step, which is included in the strategic asset planning process in TCM, is to adapt the enablers to the enterprise's situation and implement the practices as appropriate.[38]

In terms of analyzing performance variances, benchmarking's role is to provide an external basis of comparison to supplement the enterprise's internal basis. Its role in identifying improvement opportunities is covered in the following section.

.3 Identify Opportunities and Risks

In many cases, findings from quantitative performance variance analysis can be used to immediately correct asset or process function or operation when the cause of the variation is obvious and readily corrected. However, long term and continuous performance improvement for the asset portfolio generally requires further analysis of opportunities and risks.

As shown in Figure 6.1-1, the step for identifying opportunities and risks is shown both in parallel to and receiving input from the variance analysis step. This is intended to reflect the fact that while the steps serve different purposes and can be performed somewhat independently, they are best done together in an integrated way.

Lessons Learned

Lessons learned is qualitative information that describes what was learned during the performance of a process, method, or tool. Lessons learned are typically elicited through the use of subjective surveys, narrative descriptions, interviews, or formal lessons learned workshops. Lessons learned are captured in a database to support ongoing development or improvement of processes, methods, and tools. Lessons learned activities are focused on increasing the asset or project management team's understanding of asset or project performance.

Lessons learned are a subset of the evolving field of knowledge management, which seeks to create and share knowledge in an organizational or social context to support making the right decisions. While shown in Figure 6.1-1 as taking place after the asset planning and performance measurement processes, lessons should be captured as they are learned. Once captured, the lessons can be reviewed by the asset or project management team, usually in group settings, and analyzed to identify and document potential asset or process improvement opportunities or risks. Lessons learned assessment and analysis tend to be subjective in nature.

Root Cause Analysis

A more objective method of assessment is *root cause analysis*. As generally practiced in a quality management process, root cause analysis investigates and identifies the most basic reasons for non-conformance with requirements. Methods such as cause and effect diagrams are used to identify and classify causes so that corrective actions can be identified.

Risk Performance Assessment

Each of the performance assessment methods described above may identify imminent or occurring risk factors, as anticipated in risk management planning (see Section 7.6) or otherwise. The risk management plan includes plans for monitoring anticipated risk factors. Risk assessments are considered in the requirements change management and assessment processes as appropriate.

---

[38] Adapted from Watson.

Benchmarking

As discussed in Section 6.1.2, the benchmarking process identifies not only "benchmarks," but also "enablers," which are practices that facilitate best, or at least improved, performance. It is important that organizations follow a common definition of items, resources, or costs when benchmarking to assure comparability and avoid flawed conclusions from "apples-and-oranges" comparisons. Along with market research and general business intelligence gathering, benchmarking also identifies asset concepts, qualities, attributes, or plans that the enterprise may consider in its own requirements assessment and asset planning.

.4 Review, Document, and Communicate Performance Assessments

The asset management function (e.g., strategic or capital planning, etc.) regularly checks that the basis of performance measurement and assessment is appropriate and in alignment with the current requirements assessment, asset management planning, and performance measurement basis. Assessments are also reviewed to ensure timeliness and accuracy. Most performance measurements are not made directly by those responsible for the performance assessment; therefore, those with performance assessment responsibility should spot check the performance measurements to some extent (i.e., audits, inspections, questioning operations management, etc.) to ensure that the data being received and assessed are reliable, appropriate, and understood.

After review, asset improvement opportunities and benchmarks are documented and communicated to those responsible for the requirements elicitation and analysis process (Section 3.1) for consideration in ongoing management of the asset portfolio. Also, any assessment findings that the requirements are not appropriately addressing business problems or opportunities are communicated to those responsible for the asset change management process (Section 6.2).

Finally, performance assessment information is captured in a historical database (Section 6.3). The information is used to help improve assessment tools such as software, models, procedures, and so on. Assessment data, particularly lessons learned, are used for planning future asset investments.

6.1.3 Inputs to Strategic Performance Assessment

.1 *Requirements.* Quantified requirements define some performance measures to be assessed (Section 3.1) as well as methods to be used for the assessment process.
.2 *Requirements Changes.* Changes to the baseline requirements and asset plans are identified in the change management process (see Section 6.2). Requirements changes may result in changes to performance assessment.
.3 *Basis for Measurement.* Planning assumptions and constraints incorporated in the basis of the investment decision (Section 3.3) define some performance measurements to be assessed.
.4 *Performance Measurement Plans.* The measurement and assessment processes are usually planned together.
.5 *Cost Accounting and Asset Performance Measures.* These measures are the basis against which quantitative variances will be analyzed.
.6 *Stakeholder Input.* Lessons learned are captured from all applicable parties that have a role in managing the asset.
.7 *Risk Performance Assessment.* The risk management process (see Section 7.6) identifies potential risk factors to track and assess.
.8 *Other Asset Performance Attributes and Measures.* Internal or external asset performance measures and practices information is gathered for benchmarking.
.9 *Historical Information.* Successful past performance assessment approaches are commonly used as future references. Historical performance data and lessons learned are also captured.

6.1.4 Outputs from Strategic Performance Assessment

.1 *Asset Improvement Opportunities.* Asset performance problems, opportunities and risks are identified so that requirements for a solution can be assessed (see Section 3.1).
.2 *Performance Benchmarks.* Internal and external measures obtained from benchmarking may be used in requirements assessment and project planning (e.g., competitive targets).
.3 *Information for Change Management.* Assessment findings that a requirement is no longer addressing the business problem are reported to the change management process (see Section 6.2).
.4 *Historical Information.* The performance assessment approaches used are captured in a database (Section 6.3) for use as future planning references. Assessment findings, particularly lessons learned, data are captured as well.

6.1.5 Key Concepts for Strategic Performance Assessment

The following concepts and terminology described in this and other chapters are particularly important to understanding the strategic asset performance measurement process of TCM:

.1 *Requirements.* (Section 6.1.1.1 and 3.1).
.2 *Investment Decision Basis/Business Case.* (Sections 6.1.1.1 and 3.3).
.3 *Balanced Scorecard.* (Sections 6.1.1.1, 3.1, and 5.2).
.4 *Key Performance Indicator (KPI).* (Sections 6.1.1.1, 3.1, and 5.2).
.5 *Investment Return and Profitability.* (Section 6.1.2.2 and 3.3).
.6 *Cost of Quality.* (Section 6.1.2.2).
.7 *Benchmarking.* (Section 6.1.2.2).
.8 *Lessons Learned.* (Section 6.1.2.3).

Further Readings and Sources

The strategic performance assessment process is generally covered in business and strategic management texts, including those that cover quality management and benchmarking methods. The following references provide basic information and will lead to more detailed treatments.

- Amos, Scott J., Editor. *Skills and Knowledge of Cost Engineering* (section by Gary Cokins on quality management), 5th ed. Morgantown, WV: AACE International, 2004.
- Cokins, Gary. *Performance Management (Finding the Missing Pieces to Close the Intelligence Gap).* New York: John Wiley & Sons, 2004.
- Crosby, Philip B. *Quality Is Still Free.* New York: McGraw Hill, 1996.
- Czarnecki, Mark T. *Managing by Measuring.* New York: AMACOM Books, 1999.
- Klammer, Thomas P. *Managing Strategic and Capital Investment Decisions.* Burr Ridge, IL: Irwin Professional Publishing, 1993.
- Watson, Gregory H. *Strategic Benchmarking.* New York: John Wiley and Sons, Inc., 1993.

6.2 Asset Change Management

6.2.1 Description

Asset change management refers to the process of managing any change to documented information defining the scope of an asset or the basis of measuring and assessing its performance over its life cycle. The process maintains consistency between the physical or functioning asset and the documented information that defines it while ensuring that information leads and the asset follows.

In other words, the process goal is to ensure that no change is made to the physical asset or its function until the requirements assessment and asset planning processes define, document, and decide on the change. This improves strategic asset planning by ensuring that the information that forms the basis of planning (i.e., basis documents) reflects the asset as it actually exists. If the basis documents are not consistent (i.e., someone has unbeknownst changed the asset), then it is more likely that the wrong investment decisions will be made, projects will be less cost effective (e.g., rework to address poor scope information), asset performance assessments will be somewhat meaningless, and costly corrective actions will have to be made to the asset.

The asset and project change management processes (see Section 10.3) are similar. Both include steps for the identification, definition, categorization, recording, tracking, analyzing, disposition (i.e., approval or disapproval for incorporation into requirements and plans), and reporting of changes. The difference is the emphasis on the scope of "work" in project control and the scope of the "asset" (or information defining it) in strategic asset management. In both processes, change management imposes the required structure and discipline in their respective overall processes by protecting the integrity of the control basis (i.e., it represents a plan in alignment with objectives and requirements) for performance measurement. The process objective is not to limit or promote change, but to manage and report it. Change can be good or bad, but it must always be carefully evaluated, approved, or rejected, and upon approval, methodically incorporated into the revised baseline plan.

The process described in this section deals with managing changes to the asset portfolio performance control basis, but does not include processes that might lead to a change request. For example, business process reengineering (BPR) is a common method used to improve and change processes of all types. BPR itself is not included in TCM, but because the definition of the new or revised process resulting from BPR is a type of asset, TCM ensures that the changed documented process definition is a suitable basis for measuring and assessing the future performance of that business process.

.1 Asset Change Management and Configuration Management

Asset change management also shares the same goals and framework as the configuration management (CM) process. The section title of "asset change management" is used because the process is not identical to those promulgated by the Institute of Configuration Management (ICM)[39] or contained in published standards.[40] CM traditionally was focused on engineering documentation, but has evolved in recent years to encompass the entire business process infrastructure and include any information that could impact safety, quality, schedule, cost, profit or the environment. In other words, CM is coming closer to asset change management which recognizes that all these impacts have cost management implications.

CM, as with other strategic asset management methods (e.g., QFD, ABC/M, etc.) has been used most frequently in the software, product development, and military program arenas. Many enterprises in these arenas have established functional organizations for CM. However, the asset change management process is equally applicable to any designed environment (i.e., any asset).

---

[39] The Institute of Configuration Management (www.icmhq.com) offers a certification program referred to as CMII.
[40] The current primary standard for configuration management is ANSI/EIA-649-1998.

.2 Information Ownership and Change Management Authority

Each asset has its own unique set of defining information or documentation. Changes to the documents are managed; the physical assets must then conform. The documents specify, define, or describe the requirements, asset planning or design documents, processes, and so on. Rules of the CM process specify that each document be co-owned by its creator or author and one or more of its users. The co-owners are responsible for its integrity and have the authority, together, to make changes as needed.[41] Co-ownership of the documents ensures that the process maintains consistency between the physical or functioning asset and the information that defines it while ensuring that information leads and the asset follows.

In the case of new or modified assets created by a project, design or other basis documents are validated at project closeout and turned over by the project "creators" to asset management and the new "users." Document control procedures establish how documents will be managed during the project and how ownership will be transitioned.

6.2.2 Process Map for Asset Change Management

Figure 6.2-1 illustrates the process map for asset change management. As was mentioned, the change management process closes the strategic asset management loop. It is largely a governing process that is characterized by extensive interaction between the performance assessment (Section 6.1) and requirements elicitation and analysis and asset planning processes (Sections 3.1 and 3.2, respectively).

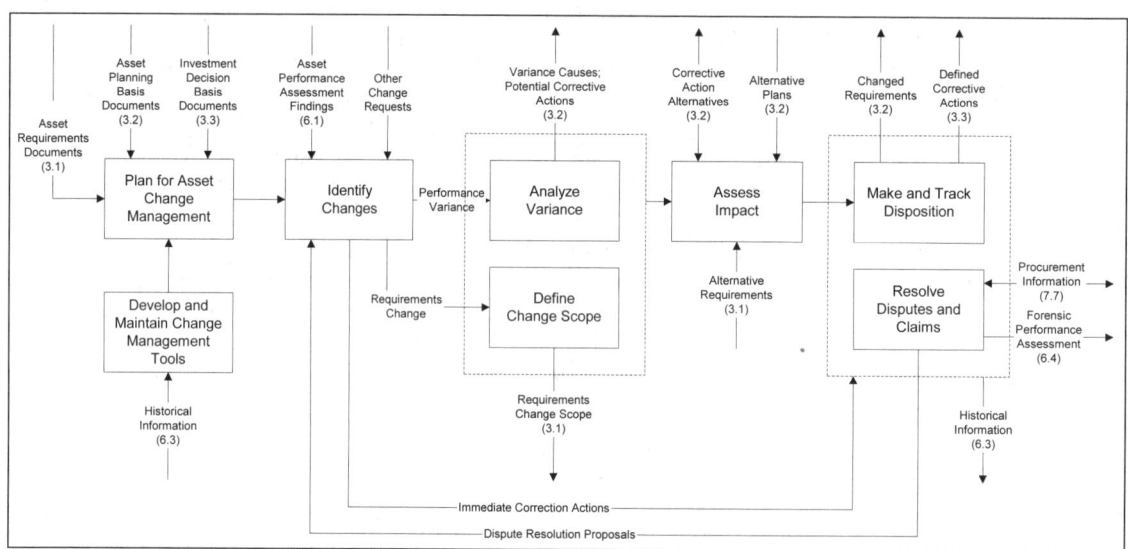

Figure 6.2-1 Process Map for Asset Change Management

The following sections briefly describe the steps in the asset change management process.

.1 Plan for Asset Change Management

Asset change management starts with planning. Initial planning starts with requirements elicitation and analysis (Section 3.1) and continues through the investment decision making process (Section 3.3). It is critical that the basis of asset planning and design and decision making be thoroughly documented because all changes are assessed relative to that documented basis. The asset change management plan itself should describe specific systems and approaches to be used in change management in alignment with the other planning, measurement, and assessment processes.

---

[41] This section is based on the following paper: Institute of Configuration Management, "CMII—Model for Configuration Management (White Paper-Revision B)," 2003.

Successful change management starts with good strategic asset planning. Even the best planned and executed change management or CM processes and systems have been known to collapse under the burden of the avalanche of change requests that result if initial requirements assessment and asset planning is poor.

Planning also assigns specific roles and responsibilities for asset change management. Some enterprises may employ CM specialists to facilitate the process. As was mentioned, each basis document should be co-owned by its creator and one or more of its users and they should be identified during planning. The co-owners are responsible for its integrity and have the authority, together, to make changes as needed. Cost engineers are often responsible for change assessment work. However, those responsible for the documents and assets affected by change will be included in assessments as appropriate; this creates a significant communication challenge.

Another aspect to plan is the use of tools and systems for asset change management (e.g., CM software, forms, etc.). In addition, the interaction/interface of the owner, suppliers, and contractors in asset change management must be addressed in change management plans.

.2 Identify Performance Variances and Requirements Change

The asset change management process depends on the co-owners of basis documentation actively watching for potential or actual changes to requirements. In addition, the performance assessment process (Section 6.1) identifies and notifies whoever is responsible for the change management process of asset performance variances.

The initial notification should be immediate (e.g., verbal, email, etc.), allowing asset management to make immediate disposition (e.g., reject, direct an action, etc.) as appropriate. Immediate disposition may be appropriate if the correction action clearly has no significant impact on basis documentation or the performance of other activities. However, if the issue cannot be disposed of without further analysis of its nature and consequences, the notification is done in writing, usually using a previously established notification form. Notification forms have many names (e.g., design change requests, etc.) but all have the same purpose of providing asset management with a basic description of the nature of the change, a quick assessment of its cause and general impact, and basic descriptive data (e.g., name, date, scope, etc.).

Once notified, asset management records and begins tracking the change requests (i.e., using a change log or logs) to ensure that the process addresses each one appropriately. Notices should be categorized in the logs by source (e.g., engineering, operations, maintenance, etc.), cause (e.g., safety, environmental, operability, etc.), and so on, so that management can better understand the change drivers. Applying greater levels of definition and categorization to notices during the logging process allows for improved analyses later in the process when root causes for change drivers are being sought and lessons learned are being determined. For suppliers, the contract will establish mechanisms for handling change requests.

Notification of performance variances is typically part of the normal assessment and report cycle. As with change requests, immediate disposition may be appropriate if the performance correction action clearly has no significant impacts.

For those change requests and variances for which disposition is not immediate, further definition and analysis is required before corrective actions can be taken.

.3 Analyze Variance

Variance analysis is a process to determine if a variation is a trend or a random occurrence and whether the variation is acceptable (it is argued by many that no variation should be acceptable). If the variation is not acceptable, variance analysis also determines the most likely cause of the variation (whether it is a trend or random) and identifies potential corrective actions that address the cause. Corrective action alternative development is integrated with the asset planning process (Section 3.2).

.4 Define Change Scope

The scope of requirements change requests for which disposition is not immediate must be defined. The cause must also be assessed (e.g., requirement not meeting some specific customer need). The individual notification should include a basic description of the nature of the change, a quick assessment of its cause and general impact, and basic descriptive data (e.g., name, date, etc.).

After notification, it is usually the CM specialist's (or equivalent) responsibility to further define the scope as needed to assess the change impact on requirements and planning. This scope definition step is integrated with the requirements elicitation and analysis process (Section 3.1). At the same time, the most likely cause (e.g., failed to assess this specific customer's needs) must be determined so that corrective actions can be developed that will both address the cause and mitigate impacts.

.5 Assess Impact

Having defined the nature and cause of trends and the scope and cause of requirements changes, corrective action alternatives are developed and assessed using the asset planning process (Section 3.2). The asset change management process may initially identify alternative actions to implement requirements changes and to correct performance trends (including process improvements).

6. Make and Track Disposition

Based on the impact assessment, a correction action is decided upon and implemented as appropriate. Management records and tracks the change requests to ensure that the asset change management process addresses each one appropriately.

7. Resolve Disputes and Claims

Managing contract change is a part of the change management process. The interactions/interfaces of the owner, suppliers, and contractors in change management are addressed in contract documents and change management plans. Disputes and claims may arise in contracts related to either asset management or project control; the general discussion in Section 10.3.2.8 is applicable to both situations.

.8 Revise Measurement and Assessment Basis

The asset change management process, in integration with the requirements assessment and asset planning processes, results in a revised basis for investment decision making and, if implemented, a revised basis against which performance will be measured and assessed for the remaining life cycle of the asset. It is a project control responsibility to keep those responsible for work packages apprised of the approved control baselines.

At the close of the asset change management process, historical information, including experiences and lessons learned about change management practices, is used to improve change management tools such as notification forms, logs, procedures, etc.

6.2.3 Inputs to Asset Change Management

.1 *Requirement Documents.* (see Section 3.1). Requirements specifications against which variances and changes should be analyzed.
.2 *Asset Planning Basis Documents.* (see Section 3.2) Documents from planning and design against which variances and changes should be analyzed.
.3 *Investment Decision Basis Documents* (see Section 3.3). Documents regarding decision analysis assumptions and constraints against which performance variances should be analyzed.

.4 *Other Change Requests.* Any notification to asset management of a potential or actual change.
.5 *Asset Performance Assessment Findings.* Performance assessment (Section 6.1) identifies differences between actual and planned performance for variance analysis in the change management process.
.6 *Corrective Action Alternatives.* Alternative designs, specifications, and so on are identified in concert with the asset planning process (Section 3.2).
.7 *Alternative Requirements and Plans.* Requirements elicitation and analysis (Section 3.1) and asset planning (Section 3.2) provide basis information for alternate corrective actions and designs.
.8 *Historical Information.* Successful asset change management approaches are captured and applied as future planning references and to help improve change management methods and tools.

6.2.4 Outputs from Asset Change Management

.1 *Performance Variance Causes and Potential Correction Actions.* Variance causes and possible corrective actions are further assessed in the asset planning process (Section 3.2).
.2 *Requirements Change Scope.* After identification of a requirements change, the requirements elicitation and analysis process (Section 3.1) is used to further analyze it.
.3 *Corrective Action Alternatives.* In interaction with asset planning, the assessment of impact may identify additional corrective action alternatives.
.4 *Changed Requirements.* Approved requirements are defined in the asset change management process and are inputs to the asset planning process (Section 3.2).
.5 *Defined Corrective Actions.* Approved corrective actions are defined in the asset change management process and are decided upon in the investment decision making process (Section 3.3).
.6 *Information for Forensic Performance Assessment.* (See Section 6.4).
.7 *Historical Information.* Asset change management approaches are captured and applied as future planning references and to help improve asset change management methods and tools.

6.2.5 Key Concepts for Asset Change Management

The following concepts and terminology described in this and other chapters are particularly important to understanding the asset change management process of TCM:

.1 *Asset Change Management.* (See Section 6.2.1).
.2 *Change.* (See Section 6.2.1).
.3 *Requirements.* (See Sections 3.1 and 6.2.1).
.4 *Basis Documentation.* (See Section 6.2.1).
.5 *Configuration Management (CM).* (See Section 6.2.1.1).
.6 *Document Control.* (See Section 6.2.1.2).
.7 *Corrective Action.* (See Section 6.2.1). Also referred to as *improvement action*.
.8 *Variance.* (See Section 6.2.2.3).
.9 *Variance Analysis.* (See Section 6.2.2.3).

Further Readings and Sources

The asset change management process is primarily covered in configuration management, document control, and general quality management texts. The following references provide basic information and will lead to more detailed treatments.

- Guess, Vincent C. *CMII for Business Process Infrastructure.* Scottsdale, AZ: Holly Publishing, 2002.
- Harrington, H. J., Daryl Conner, and Nicholas L. Horney. *Project Change Management.* New York: McGraw-Hill, 1999.
- Institute of Configuration Management. *CMII—Model for Configuration Management (White Paper-Revision B).* ICM, 2003. (see www.icmhq.org)
- National Consensus Standard for Configuration Management, ANSI/EIA-649-1998.

- Watts, F.B. *Engineering Documentation Control Handbook,* 2nd ed. New Jersey: William Andrew Publishing/Noyes, 2000.

6.3 Asset Historical Database Management

6.3.1 Description

Asset historical database management is a process for collecting, maintaining, and analyzing asset historical information so that it is ready for use by the other strategic asset management processes and for project control. Empirical information is the most fundamental asset planning resource available, and it is manifested in the form of quantified and documented historical data and information. The historical database management process captures empirical information and retains this experience within the institutional memory to support the development of continually improving asset management plans as well as improved methods and tools. The purpose of the process is not to repeat history, but to learn from it (i.e., to enable continuous improvement in the asset management system).

To illustrate historical data's importance, Figure 6.3-1 provides a simplified block flow diagram of the information flow in the strategic asset management process. Each block represents an asset management process that incorporates data manipulation methods or tools (e.g., investment decision analysis models). The interconnecting lines show the general flow of data and information products among the processes. Clearly, if you remove the historical block from the diagram, there is no closure in the information flow. Without the historical data process, asset planning methods and tools have no other basis other than the personal knowledge of the asset planning team members; no institutional memory is developed and no opportunity for a learning organization exists.

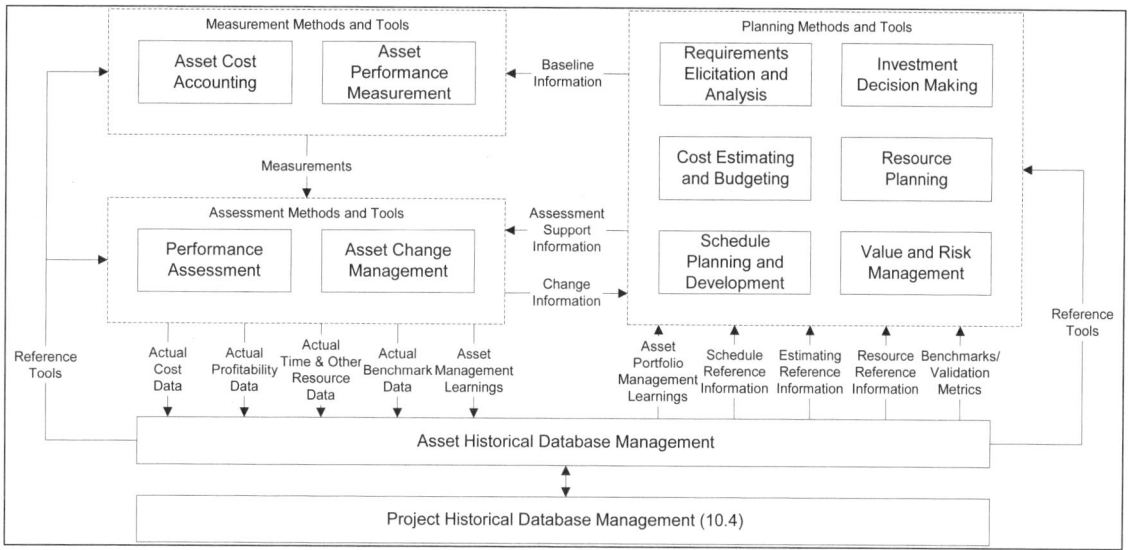

Figure 6.3-1 Strategic Asset Management Process Information Flow

For asset management, historical data take on even greater importance because asset planning and decision making are highly dependent on cost and economic modeling and risk analysis that use stochastic, probabilistic methods. Without empirical data, the quality of output of these types of methods is greatly diminished and it is much more likely that inappropriate investment decisions will be made.

.1 Asset Management and Project Control Database Integration

Figure 6.3-1 is essentially the same as Figure 10.4-1 (Section 10.4) for the project historical database management process. While the figures show separate blocks for the asset and project processes, the distinction between them is somewhat artificial. Both processes have similar needs for performance benchmarks, cost references, and other information. If an enterprise's project system is viewed as a strategic asset of the enterprise, the asset database can be viewed as the master. In any case, through a relational database structure or some other means, the databases should be integrated, allowing users to access life cycle information about the asset and project portfolios.

Where the distinction between the databases is real is in the data sources (more apt to be external for projects), end users (e.g., teams or organizations), and processes they support. In terms of end users, project teams may use a closely integrated project information system or more or less independent systems. Assets may be owned and operated by various business units that may have centralized or decentralized databases.

Increasingly, enterprises are using enterprise resource planning (ERP) and business intelligence (BI) systems that use one software platform and database to support most of the enterprise's business functions such as finance, manufacturing, human resources, warehousing, and so on. These systems have evolved to include the project management/control function as well. ERP systems are complex and are a major asset of any enterprise that uses them. Projects to implement and maintain ERP and similar systems are often among the enterprise's most significant asset investments.

.2 Other Systems Integration

Strategic asset management uses data for planning, assessing, and reporting performance from multiple perspectives such as investment decision making (Section 3.3), profitability analysis, and target costing (Section 3.1). Sometimes the data structure or characteristics required from one analytical perspective may conflict with another. For example, data for financial reporting that is in accordance with Generally Accepted Accounting Principles (GAAP) often does not readily support product costing using ABC/M methods (e.g., when costs are recognized, how they are allocated, etc.). Attempts to fully integrate databases and systems (e.g., ERP) can lead to sacrifices in the quality or timeliness of information from one or more perspectives. Figure 6.3-2 illustrates an example of a modular approach that uses legacy accounting systems and specialized ABC/M systems to feed a common data repository that in turn supports customized planning and assessment toolboxes (or workbenches).[42] Many enterprises with ERP systems have not implemented the available project management modules because of perceived problems or tradeoffs with full integration.

---

[42] Player, Steve and David E. Keys, Editors, "Activity-Based Management: Arthur Anderson's Lessons from the ABM Battlefield," MasterMedia Limited, 1995.

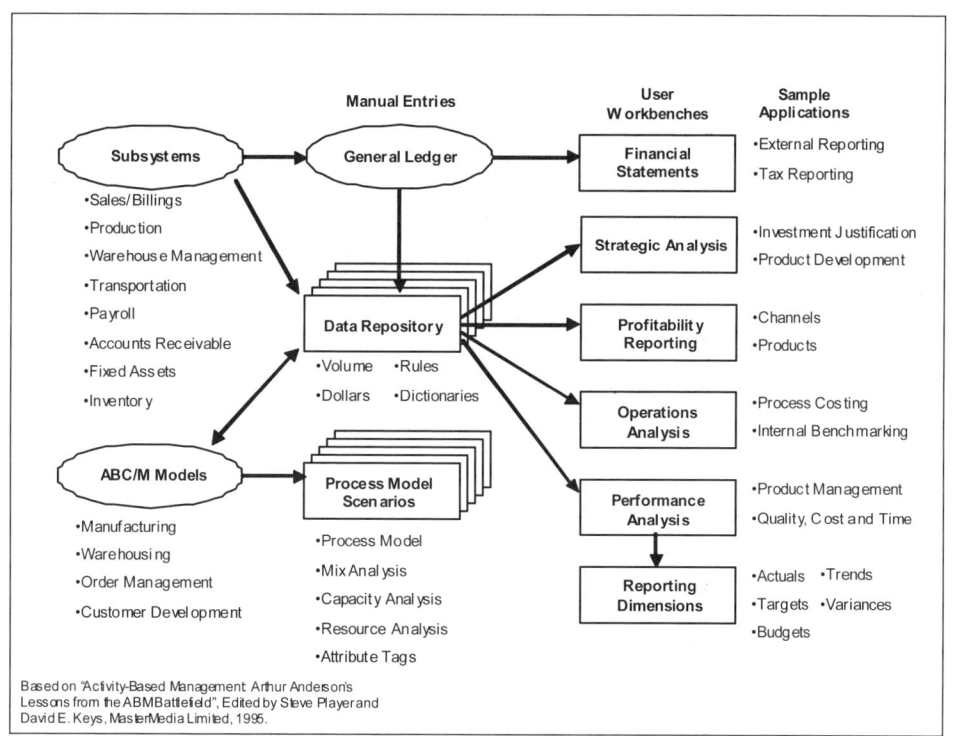

Figure 6.3-2 Illustration of an Overall Analytical Database and Reporting Vision

Data for specialized end uses are often manually entered in the data repository. However, ERP and Enterprise Performance Management (EPM) system developers are increasingly attempting to provide systems that integrate all the functions so that data are only entered once and can be broadly accessed. However, it is likely that there will always be specialized analysis models, tools, and data that will reside outside of the ERP scope.

6.3.2 Process Map for Asset Historical Database Management

Figure 6.3-3 illustrates the process map for asset historical database management. The two main steps of the process include collecting data of various types and processing it into useful information products.

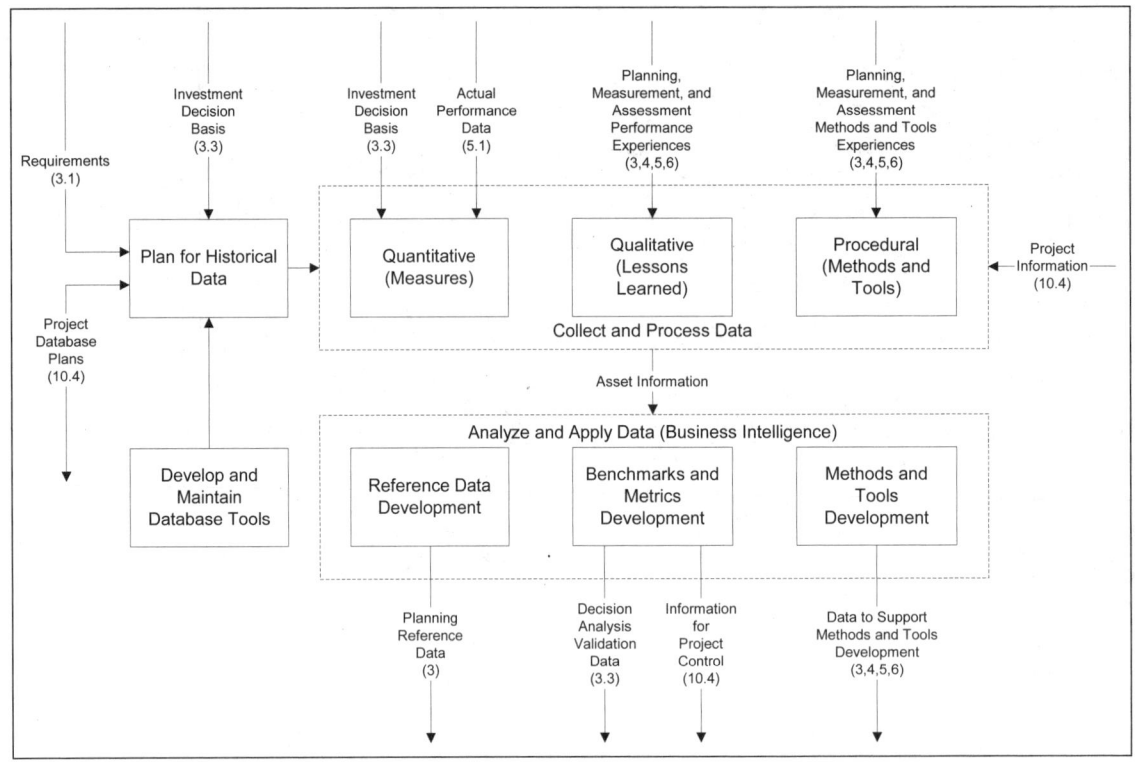

Figure 6.3-3 Process Map for Asset Historical Database Management

The following sections briefly describe the steps in the asset historical database management process. These steps are very similar to those in the project historical database management process (see Section 10.4).

.1 Plan for Asset Historical Database Management

Asset historical database management starts with planning. As discussed, the asset and project databases should be integrated; therefore, planning must first consider the interface/interaction of the project data inputs and outputs with the asset management database. For example, are project data captured in real time, at some reporting time interval, or only during the project closeout process?, what data formats and level of granularity should be used?, and so on.

The asset historical database management inputs include planned and actual quantitative data and qualitative information about the performance of assets and asset management methods and tools. Data from the project system, which are an asset of the enterprise, are an input to the asset database management process. The quantitative data (e.g., cost estimates, actual costs, schedules, etc.) must be processed. Processing includes cleaning, organizing, and normalizing the data as required for inclusion in the master database(s) for continued use. The qualitative information (e.g., lessons learned, etc.) must be cleaned, organized, and standardized as required for inclusion as well. These collection and processing activities, some of which are done on an ongoing basis, and others periodically or as a specific effort, must be planned and resources allocated for their performance.

The processed quantitative data are then used for the development and maintenance of reference databases for planning (e.g., cost estimating model databases), metrics for plan validation (e.g., check estimate competitiveness), and tools development (e.g., estimating algorithm development, templates, etc.). The processed information, including lessons learned, helps guide the effective application of the data in the development and maintenance tasks, but also serve as direct references to aid asset planning.

The plan for asset historical database management must address the collection and processing work. Planning topics may include, but are not limited to the following:

- roles and responsibilities
- allocated resources
- collection methods (throughout the asset life cycle)
- data structure and format (asset registers, cost code structure, etc.)
- level of detail and comprehensiveness of records
- data and record quality
- storage and maintenance (tools and systems)
- access and retrieval (methods and access rights)
- analysis methods (where applicable)
- information product quality (data validation)
- legal issues (retention, claims issues, etc.)

Databases capture both electronic and hard-copy information; each type of data has specific considerations. In whatever form it is captured, the goal is to store the data in a way that is easy to find, retrieve, update, and use. There may also be multiple databases that support specific purposes that each must be considered. Finally, some enterprises have limits or restrictions on retaining original data and records that must be adhered to as a matter of policy and must be addressed (e.g., use the raw data to create metrics, then discard the original data).

For projects, data collection and processing activities may be a responsibility of cost engineers in a project control role supporting the project manager. For assets, data collection and processing responsibilities tend to be the more dispersed among finance, operations, maintenance, and other organizations. However, database analysis and development for strategic asset management purposes may be supported by a cost engineer. Another aspect to plan for is the interaction/interface of suppliers and contractors with the owner's databases and vice versa. Given the many participants or users of an asset historical database, it is important to give prior consideration to the available data format and granularity to ease data integration into the database or facilitate the data's later use and to ensure that responsibilities are clearly defined.

.2 Collect and Process Data

Quantitative (Measures)
The database inputs include estimated, planned, and actual quantitative data about the performance of assets including the project system. The quantitative data (cost, revenues, performance rates, etc.) must be collected and processed. Data collection for assets is usually done in real time or at regular reporting intervals. As illustrated in Figure 6.3-2, much of the data also supports the enterprise's financial reporting system (increasingly supported by an ERP system database), which will have established data needs and reporting requirements.

Data processing includes cleaning, organizing, and normalizing the data as appropriate to incorporate into the master database(s) for continued use. Data cleaning refers to ensuring that the data are complete and acceptably accurate for database purposes, which may differ from accounting, finance, and operations purposes. Organizing data refers to making sure the data are coded in accordance with the structures used by the database and are otherwise identifiable (e.g., meaningful account titles, category descriptions, etc.).

It should be noted that cost data as reported directly from cost accounting systems are useful, but are usually neither clean nor organized in a manner that best supports asset planning, methods, and tools development, and so on.

Normalizing data is a more complex step that involves translating the data so that it is on a standard or "normal" basis in terms of time, location, and currency. After processing, the data may then be entered in an electronic database and/or kept in hard-copy form.

Qualitative Data (Process Lessons Learned)

Database inputs also include qualitative information about the performance of the strategic asset management processes or systems. This information may include assessments of how successful the asset portfolio is in achieving its objectives, and what factors contributed to the success or failure. Subjective information may be captured through the use of surveys, narrative descriptions, interviews, formal lessons learned workshops, or forensic performance assessment (Section 6.4). More objective information can be obtained by benchmarking (see Section 6.1), which involves comparing asset management and project system practices and performance to that of other enterprises that used the best practices and achieved the best performance.

The qualitative information must also be cleaned, edited, and organized as required for incorporation into master database(s). After processing, the data may then be entered in an electronic database and/or kept in hard-copy form. The goal is to capture qualitative information that will allow the next investment decision to be made based on successful approaches, avoid repeating unsuccessful ones, and provide context for assessing quantitative data.

Procedural (Methods and Tools Lessons Learned)

In an extension of the above methods, additional qualitative information is captured about the performance of asset management methods and tools. For asset management, models are central to many of the processes (e.g., decision analysis, ABC/M, etc.), so lessons learned about model development and use will be most useful.

.3 Analyze and Process Data

Reference Data Development

Many planning and assessment methods and tools rely on reference databases of some sort. For example, the reference database for a conceptual cost estimating system may contain many parameters and adjustment factors. The reference data provide an empirical basis for planning.

The reference data should be consistent, reliable, and competitive with a well defined basis (e.g., assumptions, conditions, etc.) such that any asset planning effort can determine how its requirements and basis conditions differ from the reference and adjust accordingly. The quality of a reference database is not judged by how correct or accurate its entries are in terms of representing the absolute cost or duration of any given item or activity on any given project. Rather, it is judged by how reliable a planning "base" it is in terms of competitiveness and consistency, with consistency meaning that the basis is known and is consistent between similar items and does not change over time unless the change is has been justified by analysis.

Reference data are typically normalized to a standard basis (i.e., in terms of time, location, currency, conditions, etc.). Established reference databases generally do not require constant updating; annual updates are common. At the time of review and update, the data from the asset portfolio collected over the period are analyzed to determine if the existing data are still good references. If new reference data are developed, the basis must be consistent and well documented.

Benchmarks and Metrics Development

Benchmarks and metrics are a form of reference data, but the purpose is primarily to support the validation of asset planning (See Section 3.2). Benchmarking metrics are also useful references for stochastic (i.e., top-down or conceptual) planning methods and tools, including models. Benchmarking is a process that compares practices, processes, and relevant measures to those of a selected basis of comparison (i.e., the benchmark) with the goal of improving performance. The comparison basis includes internal or external competitive or best practices, processes, or measures. Validation is a form of benchmarking applied specifically to plans to assess whether the plan results are competitive and achieve the performance objectives.

Methods and Tools Development

Each of the strategic asset management processes includes a step for methods and tools development (e.g., new or updated models, forms, systems, etc.). Each of these processes has historical information as an input for development of methods and tools. This information typically includes examples of methods and tools used on other assets and lessons learned from their use. Also, quantitative data can be used to support the development of planning algorithms and models (e.g., regression analysis of inputs and outputs to develop a parametric estimating model).

6.3.3 Inputs to Asset Historical Database Management

.1 *Requirements.* The requirements elicitation and analysis process (see Section 3.1) will establish requirements for the historical databases, which are assets of the enterprise.
.2 *Investment Decision Basis.* Asset investment plans (see Section 3.3) may describe specific systems and approaches for asset historical database management. Also, the historical database captures plan data as well as actual performance data.
.3 *Project Database Plans.* Asset and project historical database management (see Section 10.4) should be planned together.
.4 *Actual Performance Data.* Asset performance assessment (see Section 6.1) feeds actual performance data to the historical database management process.
.5 *Performance and Methods and Tools Experiences.* Qualitative lessons learned are collected from all strategic asset management processes (Chapters 3, 4, 5, and 6).
.6 *Project Information.* The project historical database management process (Section 10.4) provides project data as needed to manage the enterprise's project system.

6.3.4 Outputs from Asset Historical Database Management

.1 *Asset Database Plans.* Asset and project historical database management (see Section 10.4) should be planned together.
.2 *Planning Reference Data.* Many asset planning methods and tools (Chapter 3) rely on historically based reference data. This is particularly true for the stochastic, probabilistic methods (e.g., models, risk analysis, etc.) used in asset planning.
.3 *Planning Validation Data.* Benchmarking and validation methods rely on historically based benchmarks and metrics.
.4 *Data to Support Methods and Tools Development.* Each of the strategic asset management processes (Chapters 3, 4, 5, and 6) includes a step for methods and tools development, and each of these steps has historical project information (e.g., examples, lessons learned, model parameters, etc.) as an input.
.5 *Information for Project Control.* Some asset and project system performance benchmarks and metrics may be used for project control purposes.

6.3.5 Key Concepts for Asset Historical Database Management

The key following concepts and terminology described in this and other chapters are particularly important to understanding both the asset and historical database management processes of TCM (also refer to section 10.4.5 for further elaboration on these concepts):

.1 *Database.* (See Sections 6.3.1 and 11.3).
.2 *Continuous Improvement.* (See Section 6.3.1).
.3 *Basis.* (See Section 6.3.1).
.4 *Enterprise Resource Planning (ERP).* (See Section 6.3.1.1).
.5 *Enterprise Performance Management (EPM).* (See Section 6.3.1.1).
.6 *Normalization.* (See Section 6.3.2.2).

.7   Lessons Learned. (See Section 6.3.2.2).
.8   Reference Data. (See Section 6.3.2.3).
.9   Metric. (See Section 6.3.2.3).
.10 Benchmark and Benchmarking. (See Section 6.3.2.3).
.11 Validation. (See Section 6.3.2.3).

Further Readings and Sources

Sources on ERP/EPM and business intelligence systems provide most of the literature regarding databases to support strategic asset management processes. Much of the discussion is centered on financial, operational, and perspectives other than asset investment and management. The following references provide basic information and will lead to more detailed treatments.

- Cokins, Gary. *Performance Management (Finding the Missing Pieces to Close the Intelligence Gap)*. New York: John Wiley & Sons, 2004.
- Langenwalter, Gary A. *Enterprise Resources Planning and Beyond.* Boca Raton, FL: CRC Press, 1999.
- Player, Steve and David E. Keys, Editors. *Activity-Based Management: Arthur Anderson's Lessons from the ABM Battlefield.* New York: MasterMedia Limited, 1995.

6.4 Forensic Performance Assessment

6.4.1 Description

The forensic performance assessment process is conducted outside of, or as an extension to, cost and schedule control processes. The forensic study process is usually applied when performance variances, trends, deviations, or changes result in disputes or claims (see Sections 6.2, 9.2, and 10.3), or at *project close-out* to support *lessons learned* development. While the adjective *forensic* is usually associated with work in a legal context, the process and methods are not limited to legal matters.

The primary goal of performance assessment in the *control* mode (see Sections 6.1 and 10.1) is to assess the need for, identify, and take timely corrective actions to keep performance on plan and avoid damages. In the *forensic* mode, the perceived damage has occurred, and the primary goal of performance assessment is then to determine causation, damages, and liability (i.e., responsibility and entitlement). Forensic performance assessment is also used to resolve disputes in a legal context and/or to gain knowledge to support long term performance improvement (i.e., reduce risk of future failure) of an asset or project system. It is also used in loss and damages valuation and in analyzing the cost of mitigating and/or remediating the effects of failures or defects.

This process is a branch of *forensic science*. Related practices include *forensic engineering*, which involves the analysis of physical and safety failures while *forensic accounting* focuses on economic crime, fraud, and business valuation. Cost engineering, with forensic specialization (i.e., claims and dispute resolution), generally involves the analysis of asset and project cost and schedule performance failures.[43]

The forensic performance assessment process is usually initiated during the asset or project life cycle when a change order remains unresolved, a claim is made, or some other disputes arises (see Sections 6.2 and 10.3). However, the process may continue for some considerable amount of time after the asset or project life cycle; it is not an asset or project control function. Often, the process becomes a separate project in its own right, with its own business or legal goals and objectives. In some cases, particularly when the situation is highly contentious, those project personnel involved in a claim may not be the best to lead the study effort (e.g., operations or project management) because of potential bias, conflicts of interest, and/or distraction from ongoing management and technical responsibilities.

The following sections highlight the two primary reasons that forensic performance assessments are conducted (i.e., claims and lessons learned), and the key role that good information has in either case.

.1 Claims and Dispute Resolution

The interactions/interfaces of the owner, architect, suppliers, subcontractors, and contractors in change management are addressed in contract documents and change management plans (Section 7.7). However, performance variances, failures, or changes sometimes result in disputes and claims if the parties cannot agree on some aspect of the performance or change in relation to contract agreements (i.e., scope, compensation, time, relief, damages, delay, etc.). Generally, disputes are best resolved by the operations or project team using the established contract mechanisms (i.e., changes and dispute clauses); these mechanisms may include mediation, arbitration, or litigation.

However, if the dispute cannot be resolved, a claim may result. A claim is a written statement by one of the contracting parties seeking adjustment (e.g., additional time and/or money) or interpretation of an existing contract because of acts or omissions during the preparation of or performance of the contract. Unresolved claims are submitted to mediation or arbitration or filed with the courts and from there the legal

---

[43] In TCM, an equivalent *forensic cost engineering* field, if so named, would effectively apply professional and technical expertise to investigate resource, cost, and schedule performance failures and problems with assets or projects.

claims resolution or litigation process (which varies widely depending on the nature of the claim, contract provisions, jurisdiction, etc.) takes over.

Claims also arise in the context of insurance, letters of credit, and performance and payment bonds and other third party financial risk mitigation mechanisms. If a party suffers damages or loss due to a physical or performance failure or failure to pay, a claim for cost recovery may be filed. This claim needs to be assessed by both the claimant and the insurer or surety (the company that issued the bond).

.2 Lessons Learned

It is a good practice for asset and project management to assess and capture how successful its assets or projects are in achieving their objectives, and what root cause factors contributed to success or failure. As discussed in Section 6.1, lessons learned information is typically elicited through the use of subjective surveys, narrative descriptions, interviews, or formal lessons learned workshops to identify all contributing causes, analyze for root cause, and identify new or improved work processes. When performance is successful, subjective approaches work well because the team is generally willing to share information. However, with performance failures, when stakeholders are not so willing to share information, a more in-depth, objective forensic analysis may be the only way to identify root causes and responsibility for contract variances.

.3 The Role of Information

The success of forensic performance assessment in properly relating causation to performance degradation and then determining responsibility generally depends on having or obtaining good information about the planning, performance measurement, and assessment of the work in question. A goal of forensic analysis is to replace supposition ("project myths") with persuasive factual evidence. Poor or unsubstantiated information works against that goal. In a legal situation, the best preparation for or defense against a claim is using best practices and maintaining thorough, accurate, and complete records of all communications, plans, actual cost and schedule performance data, and so on.

A disciplined process like TCM helps avoid failures, claims, and the need for forensic studies, but when needed, helps support a successful effort or resolution. Most experts agree that sharing accurate planning and performance measurement information about a project during its performance helps avoid disputes and facilitates their resolution. The potential for claims and forensic assessment is a key consideration in the procurement process (Section 7.7); that is, the team must include requirements for good information and records as part of the contract, in addition to considerations for dispute resolution.

6.4.2 Process Map for Forensic Performance Assessment

The basic forensic performance assessment process illustrated in Figure 6.4-1 is common to processes that involve the investigation of performance variances or failure (e.g., forensic engineering, accounting, failure analysis, or root cause analysis). The main work of the process begins with information gathering and background research. This step is not found in control assessment, which relies on regular performance measurement data. Much of the work in the process takes place in the analysis step, which takes the information and applies cost engineering skills and knowledge (e.g., scheduling, cost estimating, etc.) to tie causation and responsibility to performance. The results of the analysis are then reported and communicated as needed for legal action (e.g., mediation, trial, etc.) and/or performance improvement or corrective action of an asset or project system.

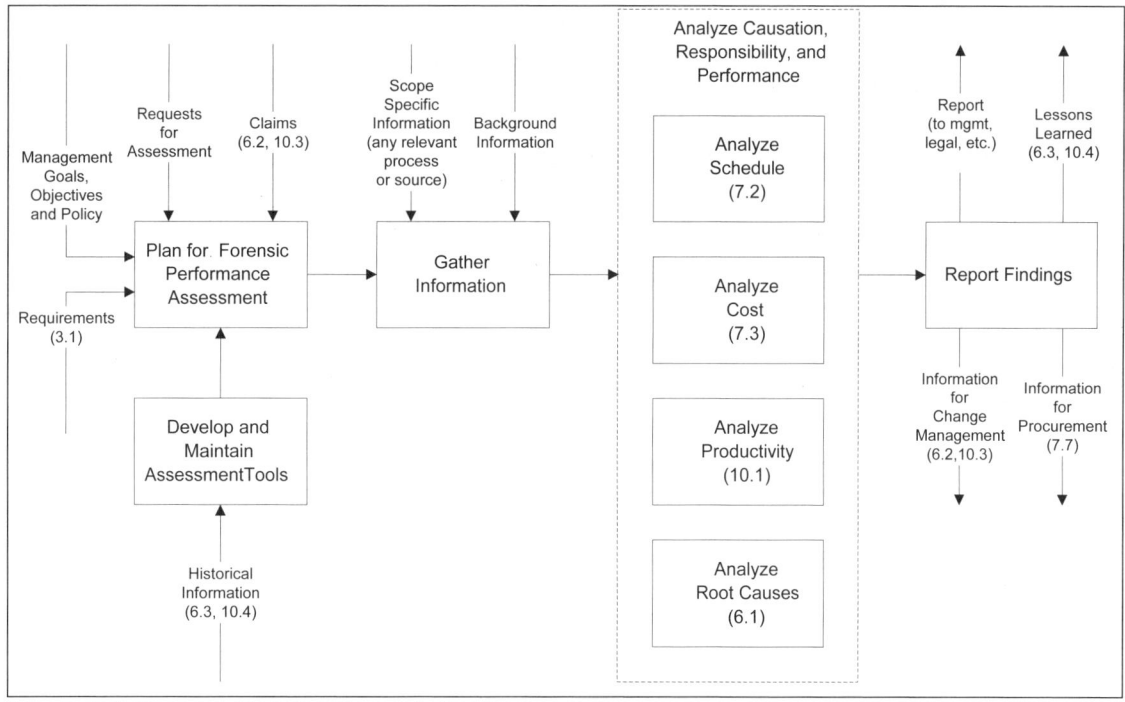

Figure 6.4-1 Process Map for Forensic Performance Assessment

The following sections briefly describe the steps in the forensic performance assessment process.

.1 Plan the Study

At the start of a forensic assessment, study leadership is established (by the project team, business unit, or legal management as applicable) with responsibility to plan and prepare for the study effort. The general study goals and objectives, study scope, and plan for study activities are established, with a study team whose roles, responsibilities, and milestones are identified and assigned.

It is important to identify a clearly understood objective (e.g., recover or avoid costs, defend a principle, etc.). The team should also understand what is at risk (e.g., long term relationship, performance of other ongoing work, financial loss, etc.). The team may determine early that the potential benefit of the effort does not justify the cost and/or risk.

The study team then begins to define the failure or problem scope (i.e., effect) and further define the bounds of the study (e.g., the scope of the affected asset or project, affected or involved parties or stakeholders, locations, time frames, etc.). Legal requirements, issues, and risks (if any) must be identified to help guide remaining work.

Initial hypotheses as to mode and mechanisms of the variance or failure may be established early so as to identify likely information, resources, models, and tools that may be required for the study.

The study scope and plan are revisited as information and analysis indicate need for revision.

.2 Gather Information

As was mentioned, good information (contemporaneous documentation suitable for evidentiary purposes) almost always drives success of the study. Information is gathered regarding liability, causation, responsibility, performance impacts, and damages as appropriate to the goal of the study. Information gathering usually includes locating and collecting contracts and records related to the failure. It is common to have standard checklists to assist in identifying records. It may also involve questioning and interviewing those involved, site visits, and inspections as needed to provide facts and understanding that hard documents cannot convey. In a legal situation, information gathering usually involves a discovery process, including document production, interrogatories, and depositions.

Background research is also done to obtain information about comparable situations and their failures or successes. The study leadership may also obtain or build models of cost, schedule, and other attributes as appropriate for the study.

Technical and programmatic information about the asset or project is also gathered as needed to support analysis. For example, if the analysis effort required a cost estimate of damages to a building, information about the design and construction of the building and its repair will be required for the estimating analysis process.

The key to analysis and settlement of claims and disputes is proper documentation. Facts of the matter are proved or disproved based on contemporaneous documentation. The law that governs a particular matter is tied to a specific fact pattern and legal precedent. If the facts change, the outcome may change. Therefore, establishing the facts accurately is of paramount importance. To increase the probability of capturing events correctly, procedures for documenting events need to be established prior to project commencement.

As information is gathered, plans are revised for the remainder of the study effort.

.3 Analyze Performance Degradation, Causation, and Responsibility

As mentioned, analysis applies cost engineering skills and knowledge (e.g., scope definition, planning and scheduling, cost estimating, resource planning, etc.) to tie performance degradation to causation and responsibility. Some studies such as financial damage valuation may apply deterministic cost estimating. Other studies such as schedule delay impacts may apply more stochastic modeling and event reconstruction techniques, which are particularly useful to study and demonstrate likely causation and determine responsibility.

Analytic methodologies vary widely depending on the type of study and failure. Forensic cost engineering studies tend to evaluate cost, schedule, and/or productivity issues as follows.

Schedule Impacts (Delay, Acceleration, etc.)
Schedule analysis seeks to evaluate impacts and answer questions such as: Was a schedule extension justified? Was the contractor accelerated and what was the result? Was the contractor's original project plan reasonable and capable of implementation? Schedule analysis may apply conventional schedule planning and development processes and methods as covered in Section 7.2. However, the starting point for forensic analysis is often a schedule model that resulted from that process, and/or the statused schedule resulting from the progress measurement process (Section 9.2). The following methods are those most commonly used when working with Critical Path Method (CPM) schedules:

- Retrospective Analysis – This is analysis of schedule impacts from the date the delaying event is overcome or from the project completion date back to the beginning of the event or the project to determine the impact of events on the overall project. Retrospective analytical techniques include:

    1. Contemporaneous Period Analysis (sometimes referred to as the Observational Method) –This is the analysis of each periodic update to determine schedule slippage (if any) and assessment of responsibility and liability for the slippage determined.

2. As-Built vs. As-Planned Analysis–This is a comparison of the as-planned schedule with the as-built schedule to determine the total amount of delay encountered and, from this, assessment of the causation and liability for such delay.[44]
3. Collapsed As-Built or But For Analysis–This is an analysis of the as-built schedule to determine which activities drove the increased time and who was responsible for those activities. Once liability for the delaying activities is determined, the analyst removes only one party's delays from the as-built schedule to determine when the schedule would have been completed "but for" the actions of the other party.
4. Impacted As-Planned Analysis–This is an analysis of the project to determine delays caused by one party to the contract and then addition of these delaying events to the as-planned schedule to show the impact of the events on the overall schedule.
5. Windows Analysis (also referred to as the Snapshot Technique or the Periodic Analysis Technique)–This is an analysis of each periodic update to the schedule to determine which events were delayed in that "schedule window" (or time period) and, based on that analysis, to determine responsibility for each event.[45] It is similar to but somewhat different from the Contemporaneous Period Analysis mentioned above.
6. Global Impact Analysis–This method is used when a project changed so much from that which was bid and the contractor never had an opportunity to perform in accordance with its project plan.
7. Bar Chart Analysis–This method uses a simple format that shows the sequence and timing of activities. To be effective in a forensic analysis, logical relationships between activities would be required. The result is called a "fenced" bar chart.
8. Resource Profile Analysis—This method is used to show the effect of changes in sequence and timing of activities on resource requirements. The project's as-planned resource requirements are compared to actual or impacted requirements.

- Prospective Analysis–This is analysis of schedule impacts from the date of the event forward to determine what is the likely impact of an event on the remainder of the project. A key prospective analytical technique is *Time Impact Analysis*. This technique starts with the latest accepted or approved schedule update and impacts this schedule by the addition of events. Once the events are input to the schedule, the schedule is recalculated to determine whether a delay has occurred. If a delay is demonstrated then the event is, by definition, the cause of the delay and responsibility is assigned to the party causing the event.

Productivity Impacts (Disruption, Inefficiency, etc.)

Productivity analysis may apply the conventional assessment methods as covered in Section 10.1. However, the starting point for forensic analysis is often progress measurement (e.g., time card records and physical progress measures) and performance assessment reports and forecasts (Sections 9.1, 10.1, and 10.2). These records are analyzed to link the productivity losses to causes such as schedule changes, delays, or acceleration.[46]

Cost Impacts (Loss, Damage, or Defect Quantification and/or Valuation)

Cost analysis may apply the conventional cost estimating process and methods as covered in Section 7.3. However, the starting point for forensic analysis is often the statused cost report resulting from the cost accounting process (Section 9.1) rather than historical costs or costs from an estimating database.

Monsey[47] explains the difference between conventional and forensic claims estimating as follows: "A cost estimate for a new project has as an objective the formulation and quantification of projected financial

---

[44] If the schedule consists of only bar charts or Gantt charts, this is the only technique that can be utilized for schedule delay analysis purposes.
[45] AACEI's Claims and Dispute Resolution Committee is preparing a Recommended Practice on Forensic Schedule Analysis, which contains a more detailed description of each technique and the differences among them.
[46] See AACEI's Recommended Practice (RP) 25R-03, which discusses the myriad ways to perform a productivity loss or impact analysis in a forensic situation.
[47] Monsey, Arthur, "Estimating Construction Claims-A Different Problem," 1993 AACE International Transactions.

considerations for the purposes of establishing a reasonable budget and/or profit. A computation of costs associated with a claim has the general objective of determining the scope of financial damage perceived by one party, recovery costs believed to be unpaid by a party; or an amount of money that will make a party 'whole' from actions, non-actions; or wrong actions undertaken by another party."

Forensic cost estimates also must deal with categories of costs that may not be significant or considered at all in a conventional estimate such as the following:
- penalty or liquidated damage costs;
- storage;
- time related and ripple-effect costs;
- unearned profits;
- lost productivity;
- cost to repair defective or non-conforming work;
- unabsorbed overhead;
- medical costs;
- attorney fees and claim preparations;
- acceleration costs;
- consequential damages;
- consultants and expert witness costs;
- attorney fees and claim preparations.

It is common to use special models to estimate or simulate cost impacts; however, it is reported that there are "no universally accepted methods."[48] Most models require a large dose of judgment regarding input values, calculation methods, and result interpretation.

In forensic estimating, once costs are estimated, there remains the issue of what portion of the cost the claimant is entitled to recover. Much of this depends on what risk the contract and other documentation indicates each party agreed to bear (entitlement), and then relating the causes of the failure (risk event) to their impact. There may also be the need to allocate the costs among responsible parties such as design professionals, contractors, and the various subcontractors based on their contribution or participation in the failure. This allocation may take the form of a subrogation action if insurers or sureties are involved in the claim.

Root Cause Analysis

The study may apply conventional root cause methods as covered in Section 6.1. The team performing the analysis must drill down below the surface of the situation to determine the true root cause of the situation being examined. This is especially true in claims situations because the purpose of root cause analysis is to determine responsibility and liability for each situation under the terms of the contract or controlling case law where the contract is silent or in conflict. The analyst must establish the root cause of any costs that the claimant expects to recover and demonstrate not only that the claimant is not responsible for the cost variance but also that the added cost can be linked to the actions or inactions of the responsible party.

For example, labor disruptions often occur when a project schedule is re-sequenced due to delays or changes. This situation may call for incorporating the contractor's labor cost distribution system into its schedule to determine the labor impact caused by the schedule changes. Protocols such as *measured mile*, industry studies, expert evaluation, modified total cost, and jury verdict method may be applicable, depending on the factual circumstances and available data.

.4 Report Findings

The results of analysis and findings are reported as appropriate to the intended purpose of the study. The report may include or be supplemented by various illustrations, models, displays, and so on. Records

---

[48] Heather, Paul R., and Michael D. Summers, "Consequential Cost Effects," 1996 AACE International Transactions.

management, with careful consideration of confidentiality issues, is particular important in legal situations. Lessons learned are captured in a database.

If not too late for the asset or project in question, initiate corrective actions through the change management process (6.2 and 10.3) to improve performance as appropriate. Often, corrective actions are taken to improve the asset or project system management strategies, policies, organization, processes, or practices as needed to avoid or mitigate the risks of future failures.

6.4.3 Inputs to Forensic Performance Assessment

.1 *Management Goals, Objectives, and Policy.* At the start of the process, management must communicate its objectives from the forensic performance assessment (e.g., recover or avoid costs, defend a principle, preserve a relationship, and so on).

.2 *Requirements.* At the start of the process, any management requirements (or constraints) applicable to planning of the forensic assessment (legal or otherwise) must be identified and communicated to the assessment team (e.g., adhere to certain procedures or rules, etc.).

.3 *Claims.* Contractors submit affirmative claims to recover damages incurred during performance of the work. Damages may include cost of labor losses caused by delay or disruption, additional labor costs for changed work, costs of repair, remission of improperly held liquidated damages, acceleration costs, and improper back charges. A project owner is obligated to evaluate and resolve the issues using a dispute resolution mechanism, or prepare to defend its position in litigation. Owners may assess liquidated damages and back charges. Contractors, if they want to recover those funds, will evaluate the matter and submit proof of entitlement. Sureties who receive a notice of default and claim for payment upon the payment or performance bond are obliged to investigate the matter and, in accordance with the terms of the bond, render performance, payment, or assert various defenses.

.4 *Requests for Assessment.* In some cases, a forensic assessment may not be initiated by a claim but by management.

.5 *Scope Specific Information* (including technical and programmatic information). Information such as progress reports, drawings, estimates, schedules, contract documents, material or process submittals, and applicable building and safety codes are gathered as needed to support the analysis. Technical expertise is required to identify and evaluate issues such as document completeness and accuracy.

.6 *Background Information.* In addition to information specific to the scope and contract, general information about the economy, markets, and other factors that may affect the analysis is gathered from appropriate sources.

6.4.4 Outputs from Forensic Performance Assessment

.1 *Report* (including basis documentation). Reports need to communicate findings in a clear and understandable format. Reports should document the process followed during the analysis, assumptions relied upon, and the results of the analysis. If the report is to support civil litigation, it must conform to the applicable jurisdictional rules. Most importantly, the forensic report developed in support of litigation is not a tool of advocacy. It is an objective expert analysis, following ethical principles, reasoned in its approach and conforming to engineering and forensic principles customarily followed by the industry.

.2 *Lessons Learned.* Contractors or owners may elect to take the information gathered, which is an evaluation of the causes of performance variances, and investigate what management practices require modification, implementation, or additional training. As a result, long term performance improvement (i.e., reduced risk of future failure) of an asset will be gained and future variances will thereby be reduced as the new procedure and training become routine management practices.

.3 *Information for Change Management* (Initiate Correction Actions). See 6.4.4.2.

.4 *Information for Procurement* (Contract Management). Lessons learned can be used to improve processes or procedures. For example, procedures for contracting may include provisions for bilateral liquidated damages, incorporating labor inefficiency formulae in change order pricing, or incorporating appropriate key intermediate milestones into project schedule requirements. An example for contractors includes implementing labor production monitoring and commodity installation tracking systems or schedule update mechanisms to capture accurate actual project progress as well as to track events that disrupt or delay progress.

6.4.5 Key Concepts for Forensic Performance Assessment

The following concepts and terminology described in this and other chapters are particularly important to understanding the forensic performance assessment process of TCM:

.1 *Forensic Performance Assessment.*
.2 *Claims.*
.3 *Damages.*
.4 *Dispute Resolution*
.5 *Cause and Causation.*
.6 *Documentation.*
.7 *Supposition vs. Fact.*
.8 *Root Cause Analysis.*
.9 *Responsibility and Entitlement.*

Further Readings and Sources

The forensic performance measurement and assessment process is covered in a variety of sources. The following references provide basic information and will lead to more detailed treatments.

- AACE International. *Recommended Practice No. 25R-03: Estimating Lost Labor Productivity in Construction Claims.* Morgantown, WV: AACE International, 2003.
- Zack, James G., Editor. *Professional Practice Guide No. 1: Contracts and Claims*, 3rd ed. CD ROM. Morgantown, WV: AACE International, 2000.

III. PROJECT CONTROL PROCESS

CHAPTER 7

PROJECT CONTROL PLANNING

7.1 Project Scope and Execution Strategy Development

7.1.1 Description

The project scope and execution strategy development process translates the project implementation basis (i.e., asset scope, objectives, constraints, and assumptions) into controllable project scope definition and an execution strategy. The project scope defines what the work is (i.e., the work that must be performed to deliver a product, service, or result with the specified features and functions[49]). The execution strategy establishes criteria for how the work will be implemented (i.e., the general approaches through which the work will be performed).

Project scope and execution strategy development provides the basis for the integrated project control planning process, which also encompasses schedule planning and development, cost estimating and budgeting, resource planning, value analysis and engineering, risk management, and procurement planning (i.e., the other sections of Chapter 7).

Project scope and execution strategy development is preceded by the project implementation process in which a project leadership team is established and the project implementation basis is developed. Project control planning is typically a phased process in which the project implementation process (see Section 4.1) is revisited to obtain incremental authorization and funding at the completion of each phase. The primary outputs of the project scope and execution strategy development process include a defined and documented work breakdown structure (WBS), work packages, and execution strategy. During the project, these outputs are updated as needed to address phased development and changes resulting from the project change management process (see Section 10.3).

The project scope and execution strategy development process is also applied in asset planning (see Section 3.2) where it is used to develop the scope of potential alternative asset solutions. However, for asset planning, the work to deliver the asset is only defined to the level needed to support the feasibility analysis (i.e., the first level or two of a WBS).

7.1.2 Process Map for Project Scope and Execution Strategy Development

Figure 7.1-1 illustrates the process map for project scope and execution plan development. The simplicity of the process map belies its importance as this process sets the stage for all the other project control planning processes. The process map illustrates a single phase; however, the process is repeated as the project scope and execution strategy are progressively elaborated. Also, the double headed arrows indicate a fair amount of concurrent development that is likely to take place in actual practice.

---

[49] *A Guide to the Project Management Body of Knowledge*, 3rd ed., Project Management Institute, Upper Darby, PA, 2004.

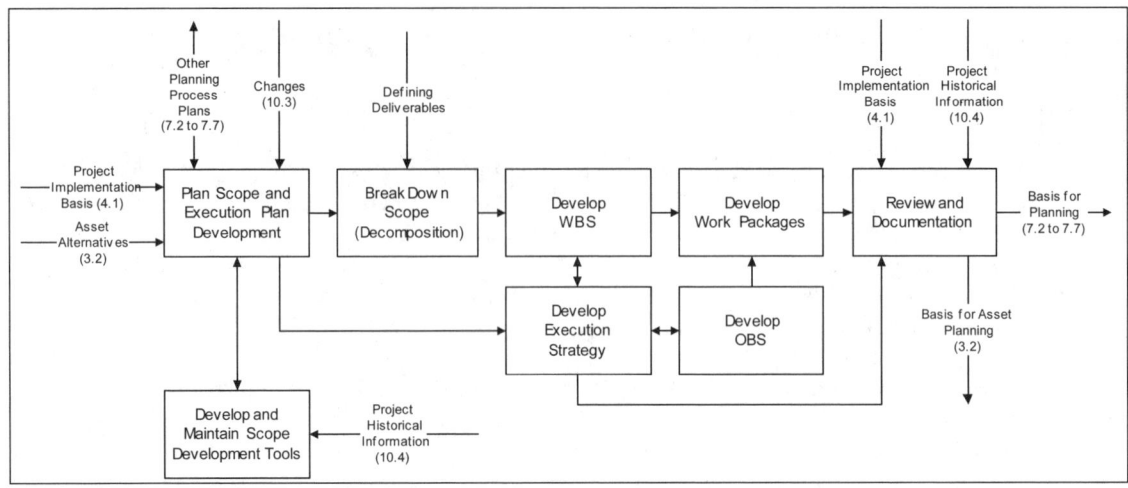

Figure 7.1-1 Process Map for Project Scope and Execution Strategy Development

The following sections briefly describe the steps in the project scope and work breakdown development process.

.1 Plan Project Scope and Execution Strategy Development

The work and resources required to perform the project scope and execution strategy development process need to be planned. These plans must consider the plans for the other project control planning processes (Sections 7.2 to 7.7) as well. These plans must consider that project control planning is typically a phased process in which the project implementation process is revisited to obtain incremental authorization and funding at the completion of each phase.

In the initial phase, a project team is formed and identifies specific asset alternatives that they consider most likely to deliver the general asset scope while achieving the project's objectives within the constraints established by the project implementation basis. The team then defines the conceptual project scope and execution strategy for each alternative using the process covered in this Section. Based on this, the team develops conceptual plans (i.e., estimates and schedules) to the extent needed to reliably analyze and recommend a best alternative project scope (see Sections 7.2 to 7.7). As the initial phase, this conceptual planning work is likely the only work that was authorized and funded by the project implementation process. The project team then documents the conceptual planning work done in this phase (see Section 8.1) and requests that the leadership team authorize additional funds and resources so the project team can perform the next phase of scope development work (see Section 4.1). In the final phase, the project team finishes defining the project scope of the selected alternative such that baseline project control plans for execution of the remaining project scope can be developed.

For example, consider a case in which project leadership requires, as documented in the project implementation basis, that by a certain milestone date, the project team deliver a warehouse facility with capacity to store 30 days supply of a particular product within one day's delivery to anywhere in a given market region. The project team then identifies two alternatives: remodeling an already owned existing warehouse or building a new one. The project scopes of the alternatives are then defined, including the building area (with layout sketches), conditions of the existing facilities and new sites (based on site assessments), transportation, permit and tax situations, and so on. The team then prepares conceptual estimates and schedules for each alternative, and, based on economic cost evaluations, the new building at a given location is recommended for further scope development. The project leadership then reviews the project scope definition status and deliverables, and authorizes the project team to proceed with further project scope and execution strategy development and project planning for the selected alternative.

.2 Break Down Scope (Decomposition) and Develop WBS

During project scope development, creative personnel (depending on the industry, they may be architects, engineers, systems analysts, etc.), under project leadership, translate the asset scope (the ultimate deliverable or product of the project) into component deliverables (intermediate products required to effect the asset scope). These component deliverables may include sketches, diagrams, layout drawings, system architecture, equipment lists, specifications, and so on. These deliverables physically describe the new or modified asset as an entirety that will result from the project; however, not in a way that supports planning and controlling the work (i.e., the effort) to create or modify the asset. For planning, the physical description as defined by various component deliverables must be translated into another deliverable called the "work breakdown structure" (WBS). The translation process, called decomposition, breaks down the entirety of the asset physical scope into discrete components for which work can be planned and controlled effectively. The premise of the WBS is that work is not performed on the entirety of the asset, but piece-by-piece, eventually, and cumulatively resulting in a whole asset.

For example, the warehouse facility from the previous case is broken down into site, foundation, superstructure, wall cladding, electrical and other mechanical systems, and other physical components. These components are still not manageable pieces, so the foundation is further broken down into such pieces that in this case include grade walls and concrete spread footers. This breakdown, when organized in a logical hierarchical manner such as illustrated by the warehouse-foundation-footer example, is called the WBS. Once the WBS is developed, estimators can determine the cost and resources needed for each lower tier item in the WBS (Section 7.3), and planners or schedulers can determine the specific work activities, and activity sequencing, needed to build or execute these items (see Section 7.2). Project control is most effective when each planning process (i.e., estimating, planning and scheduling, etc.) is based on and integrated by a common WBS.

Sometimes a project is part of a *program* or set of related projects. A program can be viewed as the top level on the WBS with the next level including the projects within the program. The basic project control concepts apply to a program with the added complication of integrating its projects.

Scope breakdown and WBS development are team efforts. The team generally includes the project manager or leader, project control personnel (e.g., planners, schedulers, estimators, etc.), and creative, technical, and execution personnel (e.g., engineers, construction managers, etc.). While project managers lead the process with close support from planners, there is generally no one specialist whose primary role is scope breakdown development.

.3 Break Down Organization and Develop Execution Strategy

As was mentioned, the basis for project control planning includes not only defining what the work is, but establishing the general approaches for how the work will be performed. The project implementation process (see Section 4.1) provides the asset scope, objectives, constraints, and assumptions basis for the project as well as authorizing funds and resources. WBS development is focused on further defining the asset scope in consideration of project objectives. Organizational breakdown and execution strategy development then are focused on further translating the constraints, assumptions, and resource provisions into general approaches for how the work will be performed, and by whom, in consideration of the project's objectives and the WBS.

The execution strategy is a general plan (or set of plans) that defines a framework for how the defined work will be implemented. The strategy does not define activities (see Section 7.2) and it is not a baseline control plan; it defines the general approaches through which activities will be performed. For example, using the warehouse facility case, the execution strategy developed for the new warehouse may require that design-build contracting be used, but the owner will procure the loading and material handling equipment. As with the physical scope, the execution strategy is refined as project control planning progresses.

The execution strategy is established in conjunction with developing the organizational responsibility for the project scope. This is because the execution strategy typically includes the contracting strategy, which influences the project organization. In some cases, the execution strategy may also include plans for modularization (e.g., components of project scope aggregated into a single deliverable) or other approaches to the work that might influence the WBS.

Similar to the WBS, organizational responsibilities can be broken down in a logical, hierarchical manner resulting in an organization breakdown structure (OBS). For example, the warehouse project team may be broken down into owner project management and procurement, contractor engineering, and subcontractor construction organizations. Furthermore, the contractor engineering organization may include disciplines such as civil, mechanical, and electrical.

As with project scope development, organizational breakdown and execution strategy development is a team effort. However, for these steps, there is an emphasis on input from those who will manage the execution (e.g., engineering and construction managers) and/or those who will require and acquire resources and services (e.g., procurement and contracting managers).

.4 Develop Work Packages

As shown in Figure 7.1-2., the WBS and OBS can then be integrated via a matrix such that the intersection of each WBS component with an OBS component comprises a work package that can be effectively planned and managed. A work package is a deliverable at the lowest level of the work breakdown structure for which both the work scope and responsibility are defined. Schedule planning and development (see Section 7.2) later identifies activities required to accomplish the work package.

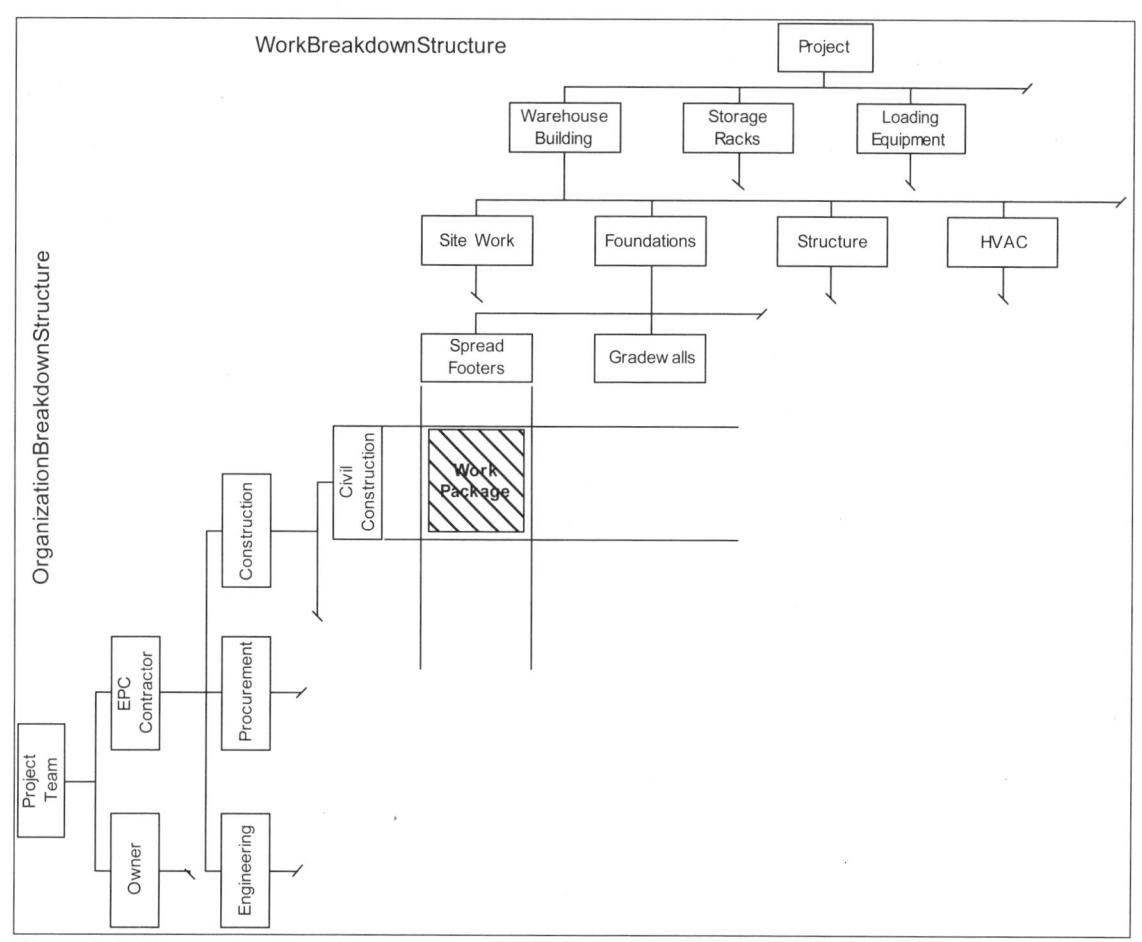

Figure 7.1-2 Example of the WBS, OBS, and Work Package Concept

.5 Review and Documentation

Upon completion of the project scope development phase, the WBS structure, work packages, and execution strategy are reviewed by the project team to determine whether they are complete and suitable as a basis for project control planning (see Sections 7.2 to 7.7), and whether they are in alignment with the project implementation basis.

Project scope and execution strategy development and the review of its outputs are facilitated by having a database of historical WBSs, OBSs, and execution strategies as references (see Section 10.4).

.6 Develop and Maintain Methods and Tools

The enterprise may chose to standardize WBS and OBS development. In particular, basic OBS components (e.g., civil engineering) are often predetermined for the enterprise and are reflected in standard organization structure. Standard WBS templates may be developed for repetitive types of projects (or components of them).

7.1.3 Inputs to Project Scope and Execution Strategy Development

.1 Project Implementation Basis. The project implementation process (see Section 4.1) provides the asset scope, objectives, constraints, and assumptions basis for the project, as well as authorizing funds and resources.

.2 *Asset Alternatives.* The asset planning process (see Section 3.2) identifies the asset scope of alternatives for feasibility analysis.

.3 *Change Information.* During project execution, changes to the project planning basis may be identified in the change management process (see Section 10.3).

.4 *Defining Deliverables.* These component deliverables physically describe the new or modified asset that will result from the project (i.e., intermediate products required to effect the asset scope).

.5 *Historical Project Information.* Successful past project WBSs and execution strategies are useful as references for development and review (see Section 10.4).

.6 *Planning Process Plans.* Project control planning includes a set of integrated processes (Sections 7.1 to 7.7). Plans for conducting each process must consider the others as appropriate to the phase of development.

7.1.4 Outputs from Project Scope and Execution Strategy Development

.1 *Basis for Planning.* The WBS, work packages, and execution strategy provide a common framework of the project work to be incorporated into project control baseline plans (i.e., cost control budgets, schedules, etc).

.2 *Basis for Asset Planning.* When the process is applied in asset planning (see Section 3.2), the work and execution strategy to deliver the asset is only defined to the level needed to support feasibility analysis (i.e., the first level or two of a WBS).

7.1.5 Key Concepts for Project Scope and Execution Strategy Development

The following concepts and terminology described in this and other chapters are particularly important to understanding the scope development process of TCM:

.1 *Project Scope.* (i.e., scope of work). (See Section 7.1.1).
.2 *Project Scope Breakdown (Decomposition).* (See Section 7.1.2.2).
.3 *Work Breakdown Structure (WBS).* (See Section 7.1.2.2).
.4 *Program.* (See Section 7.1.2.2).
.5 *Organization Breakdown Structure (OBS).* (See Section 7.1.2.3).
.6 *Work Package.* (See Section 7.1.2.3).
.7 *Execution Strategy.* (See Section 7.1.2.3).

Further Readings and Sources

There are many references describing project scope and execution strategy development and related practices for various project types in various industries. The topic is generally covered in project management, project control, and project planning and scheduling texts. The following references provide basic information and will lead to more detailed treatments

- Amos, Scott J., Editor. *Skills and Knowledge of Cost Engineering*, 5th ed. Morgantown, WV: AACE International, 2004.
- Gransberg, Douglas D. and Keith Molenaar, Editors. *Professional Practice Guide (PPG) #10: Project Delivery Methods.* CD ROM. Morgantown, WV: AACE International, 2001.
- Haugen, Gregory T. *Effective Work Breakdown Structures.* Vienna, VA: Management Concepts, Inc.; 2001.
- Project Management Institute. *Practice Standard for Work Breakdown Structures.* Upper Darby, PA: Project Management Institute, 2002.

7.2 Schedule Planning and Development

7.2.1 Description

Schedule planning and development are the processes for the planning of work over time in consideration of the costs and resources for that work. Schedule planning and schedule development are separate, but related, sub-processes that call for different skills and knowledge emphasis.[50] Schedule control is covered in Chapters 9 and 10 as part of the performance measurement and assessment processes.

.1 Schedule Planning

Schedule planning starts with translating work package scope (Section 7.1) into manageable activities and determining the manner and sequence (i.e., logic) in which these activities are best performed.[51] The means, methods, and resources used for accomplishing the activities are then identified, alternatives evaluated, and the responsibility and accountability for each activity assigned. Schedule planning concludes with estimating the duration of the sequenced activities based on adequate resources being available and planned means and methods. Planning is a continuously iterative process. The result of schedule planning is a schedule model of a project's execution plan used to monitor and control for successful completion.

Schedule planning puts an emphasis on the practitioner's knowledge of the work, means and methods, and skills with tapping the knowledge and experience of those responsible for performance of that work. Multi-skilled practitioners (often called planners) perform the schedule planning process interactively with the project team members who will actually implement the plan and with whom the best planning knowledge often resides. Effective planning depends not only on the planner having a working knowledge of how each activity is performed, but also on the whole team reaching consensus on what the desired sequence of workflow is. While some "planners" focus only on the work in which they have expertise, other "planners" may have the role of facilitator or coordinator of the work of the more specialized planners or experts.

.2 Schedule Development

Starting with the initial schedule model from schedule planning, schedule development allocates the available resources (e.g., labor, material, equipment, etc.) to activities in the schedule model in accordance with cost and resource planning and alternative allocation criteria while respecting project constraints affecting the schedule (e.g., milestone dates, phasing requirements, etc.). Schedule development generally includes iteratively refining the schedule planning (i.e., planned durations, means and methods, workflow sequence or preferential logic) in a way that realistically, if not optimally, achieves project objectives for time (e.g., milestones), cost (e.g., cash flow), and others (e.g., performance requirements). The primary outcome of the schedule development process is an as-planned schedule model that becomes the schedule control baseline for project control plan implementation (Section 8.1).

As planned schedule models are approximations based upon initial assumptions and interpretations of scope and plans, stakeholders are prone to misunderstanding what an as-planned schedule truly represents. This misunderstanding leads to misuse and errors in performance measurement, assessment, and control. Therefore, at the close of schedule development, the basis of the planned schedule must be thoroughly

---

[50] This section covers *project* schedule planning and development, not production scheduling (i.e., ongoing asset operation). However, project schedule planning and development often must consider production schedule requirements where the project interfaces with operations (e.g., production shutdown and startup).
[51] The topic of this section is often referred to as "planning and scheduling." However, the phrase "schedule planning and development" is used to highlight that "planning" is not referring to the project planning process as a whole. The section topic is also sometimes referred to simply as "scheduling," which inappropriately downplays the steps of schedule planning.

documented and communicated to the project team. The schedule basis is also used in the change management process (Section 10.3) to understand changes, deviations and trends.

Schedule development puts an emphasis on the practitioner's knowledge of the schedule model and skills with scheduling tools. While aspects of the schedule development process and tool usage are mechanistic and conducive to semi-automation, schedule development can not be automated because it is a predictive process working with activity durations affected by uncertain working environments and resource performance. Nor should planners/schedulers rely solely on cloned schedule models; each schedule model must be carefully vetted so that the product truly represents the current project plan. Schedulers must have an understanding of probability concepts to be effective and, as with planners, experience on projects and an understanding of the activities, is of great value.

.3 General Schedule Planning and Development Approaches and Techniques

The schedule model and planned schedule integrate time, cost, resource, and risk planning. Each planned and scheduled activity has defined cost and resource attributes; these attributes are (sometimes formally, but often informally) integrated within the schedule model to form cost and schedule control baselines against which cost and schedule performance can be measured and assessed. Multi-skilled individuals who can do planning, scheduling, estimating, resource, and risk planning are best able to facilitate integration.

Integration is facilitated by performing the schedule planning and schedule development processes concurrently and interactively with the cost estimating and resource planning processes (Sections 7.3 and 7.4, respectively). Concurrent approaches work best because the breakdown of scope into controllable items and activities and the subsequent quantification of time and resource requirements yield the best results when there is lively give-and-take between those performing these various project planning processes. Planned work sequences and time durations can affect costs (e.g., fixed level-of-effort cost accounts such as project management tend to be time-driven) and resources (e.g., a worker's productivity is often affected by the amount of time allowed to perform a given activity).

The general technique used for schedule planning and development is to load work activity and sequencing logic information into a scheduling software package, along with associated cost and resource data. However, well prior to any software tool being used, initial planning should be done in a session (e.g., brainstorming) during which the team dissects the work scope deliverables to create a narrative planning model prior to a logic diagram being developed. For early phases of asset planning, before a project has been implemented (see Section 3.2), narrative planning may be all the planning that is done.

Scheduling software uses algorithms to calculate start and finish dates for each activity and uses graphics tools to illustrate the resultant schedule (e.g., bar charts and logic diagrams). The schedule is a quantitative model that, facilitated by software capabilities, can be readily modified to test alternate criteria, approaches, resource scenarios, and risk factors and events. As such, the schedule model supports value analysis and engineering and risk analysis processes (Sections 7.5 and 7.6, respectively).

The schedule planning and development processes are applied in each phase of the project life cycle as the asset and project scope is defined, modified, and refined. The specific tools and techniques used vary widely depending upon the life cycle phase, the type of project, and the level of definition of scope information available. When there is very limited scope information during strategic asset planning or early project scope development phases, schedule planning and development may be limited to manually developing lists of the major activities and milestones and/or simple bar charts. It is common to have summary activities included early in the schedule. Then, as a specific phase of the project approaches, these activities are expanded into further detail in a type of rolling wave schedule. When scope definition is advanced, and/or there are a great many activities, software tools are almost always used and the schedule planning and development outputs may include extensive activity lists, logic diagrams, time-line graphics and so on, presented in alternate views to suit various needs (e.g., by different levels of the work breakdown structure [WBS], different responsibilities, and reporting requirements). For example, power plant outages often use short interval scheduling (SIS) in which there may be several thousand of activities measured in hours or even fractions of hours.

While planning techniques vary, strategic and project planners should combine historical approaches with team input in ways that stimulate creativity and foster buy-in. As such, the collection of historical schedule information and the analysis, development, and maintenance of creative scheduling tools and algorithms is an imperative in schedule planning and development. Historical schedule information, metrics, and benchmarks also support schedule review and validation. Building on the historical approaches, team input as to best activities, approaches, and investment or work sequencing logic may be obtained through workshops, interviews, "executability" reviews (see Section 11.5), and similar methods.

In some cases, much, if not all, schedule planning and development detail is undertaken by, and is the responsibility of, contractors. In those cases, the contractor's schedule submittals are inputs to the owner's schedule planning and development process in alignment with the execution strategy (Section 7.1) and procurement planning (Section 7.7).

During project execution, schedules are monitored to reflect the performance and progress of activities (Section 9.2) and assessed to determine if there are any significant deviations from planned performance (Section 10.1). Forecasting and the evaluation of schedule deviations, trends, and changes (Sections 10.2 and 10.3, respectively) and the incorporation of their impacts, if any, into an updated schedule use the techniques of and follow the same basic process steps as the development of the original planned schedule and schedule control baseline.

.4 Program and Portfolio Schedules

The preceding discussion takes the perspective of a single project using the project control process. However, projects are sometimes part of a *program* or set of related projects. A program can be viewed as the top level on the WBS with the next level including the projects within the program. The basic project control and schedule planning and development concepts apply to a program with the added complication of integrating its projects.

Each project or program is also part of the enterprise's portfolio of projects. While a portfolio includes a set of projects, the projects are generally not related to each other except that they may be competing for resources, space, and so on. Portfolio scope is often defined by the enterprise organization, plant, or other sub-unit responsible for the assets that the projects affect. In respect to projects, the strategic asset management process can be considered a project *portfolio management* process. The asset planning process (see Section 3.2) may use the schedule planning and development process for a portfolio of projects to determine if the project schedules are in alignment with the enterprise's requirements for each and with overall business strategy. Investment decision making (see Section 3.3) must allocate resources effectively among the projects in the enterprise's portfolios.

7.2.2 Process Map for Schedule Planning and Development

Schedule planning and development involve the translation of technical and programmatic information about an asset or project into an output schedule (i.e., time phased, logically sequenced, resource loaded activities). The outputs of schedule planning and schedule development are used as inputs for asset planning and project cost and schedule control. The process is supported by tools and data that are created and maintained to support the various types of schedules that need to be prepared during the life cycle of the asset or project. Figure 7.2-1 illustrates the process map for schedule planning and development.

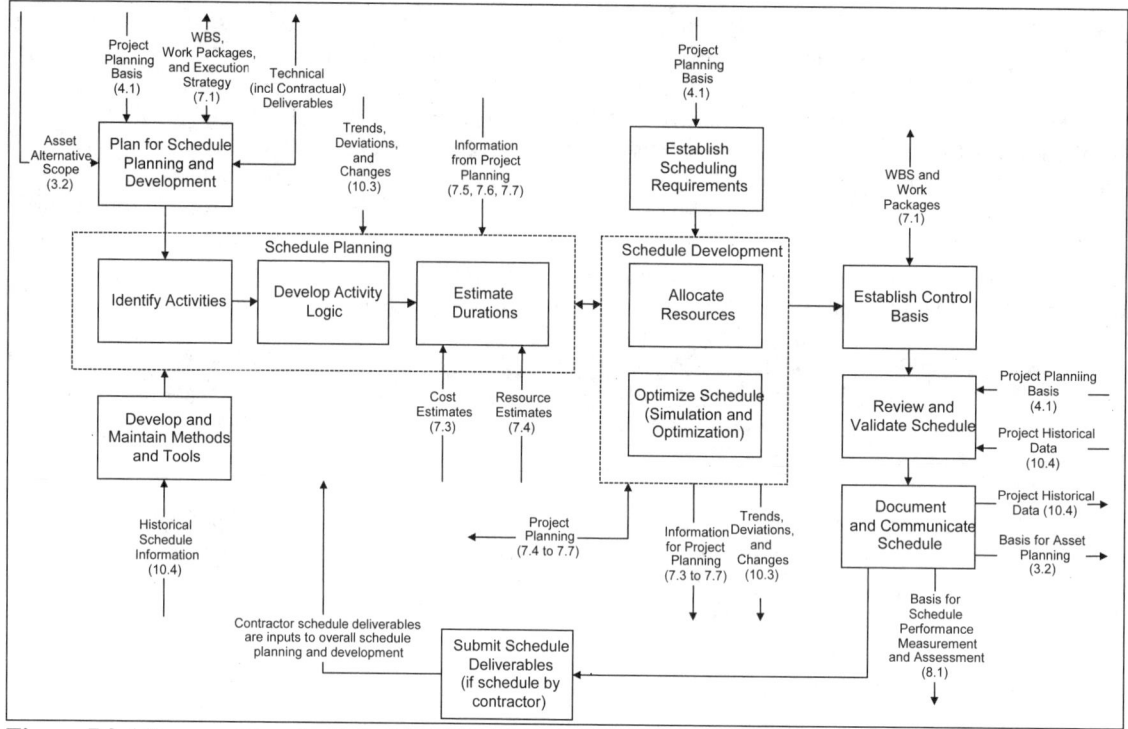

Figure 7.2-1 Process Map for Schedule Planning and Development

The following sections briefly describe the steps in the schedule planning and development process.

.1 Plan for Schedule Planning and Development

Initial planning for this process should be integrated with planning for all the other project control planning processes (Sections 7.1 to 7.7). Project control planning is typically a phased process during which the project implementation process (see Section 4.1) is revisited to obtain incremental authorization and funding at the completion of each phase. Plans for the process must consider the time, costs, resources, tools, and methods required for performance during each phase. Roles and responsibilities for each step and transitions between each phase should be well defined.

At the start of any phase, the current documented scope basis and defining technical (including contractual) deliverables are the key inputs. Based on an assessment of these inputs, the project team further identifies activities, resources, and tools needed.

.2 Identify Activities

To prepare schedules, information from the documents that define the scope must first be translated into identifiable, manageable activities and tasks. For example, the physical asset scope may include a length of pipeline; installing that pipeline may require designing, procuring, cutting, welding, erecting, testing, and inspection activities. Similarly, software code development may require the performance or various logic assessment, coding, and testing activities. The scope definition of an investment or a project is generally described in various planning and technical documents, databases, or other documents. If the scope changes during a project, the added, deleted, or changed activities must be identified in this step.

Activities may represent varying levels of detail depending upon the stage of planning or schedule statusing and/or reporting needs. Using the pipeline example, "installing" the pipeline may be the only activity identified at an early planning phase. In later planning phases, sub-activities of the "installing" activity may be identified such as designing, procuring, cutting, welding, erecting, testing, and inspection.

.3 Develop Activity Logic

Once a set of activities is identified, they must be sequenced logically. The logic reflects the dependencies or relationships between activities. For example, before a concrete foundation can be placed, the formwork must be erected and the reinforcement must be placed. Similarly, software code must be developed before it can be tested. Planning logic methods include Gantt charts, arrow diagramming, or precedence diagramming methods. Logic addresses sequential dependencies between activities, and similar issues such as programmatic, procedural and physical requirements and constraints, and preferential sequencing in consideration of cost or resources.

.4 Estimate Durations

The duration of planned activities is estimated to calculate estimated start and finish dates based on the defined scope of work, estimates of required resources and their availability, and the expected performance (or consumption) rate of those resources. As with any estimate, duration estimating methods are typically probabilistic in nature and therefore must consider the range of possible outcomes. Historical experience from similar projects or processes can assist in determining that the resulting time duration is reasonable and rational. Initially, the activity durations are estimated without adjustment for scheduler bias as to risks and productivity factors. If the duration of the plan does not achieve milestone or other (e.g., funding) requirements, the planned activity's means and methods and/or preferential logic may be revised as needed (e.g., adjusting the schedule). At output of this step is a schedule model to be used for schedule development.

.5 Establish Schedule Requirements

At the start of schedule development, it is necessary to establish the project or contract time limitation requirements and the date constraints within the plan. Business and contract time objectives are often expressed as "milestones." A milestone is a point in time (event) that an activity or asset component is required to be started and/or completed (e.g., a power generating facility contract that requires a power plant to be operational by January 1). Milestones are often established by business needs without having a good understanding of what work must be done or how long it will take based on historical experience.

.6 Allocate Resources

Each activity consumes resources. By assigning (i.e., loading) resources for each activity, available resources can be scheduled in accordance with resource consumption limitations (i.e., money, labor hours, etc.) by resource leveling or balancing. A construction project example is when only a few workers can work in a confined space at any one time. Similarly, a software project may need to consider that only a few specialists are available who know a certain software language. During the schedule optimization phase, the duration of activities will change to keep resource usage or expenditure rates within planned limits or budget constraints.

.7 Optimize Schedule (Simulation and Optimization)

The factors and parameters in a scheduling model algorithm may have a range of possible values that could occur, or that could be selected from within the scope. Simulation refers to methods used to apply alternate factor and parameter combinations in the algorithm; these methods result in a distribution of possible outcomes.

Optimization refers to simulation methods that have a goal of finding an optimum output. These techniques are beneficial for value analysis and engineering (see Section 7.5) to optimize scope decisions in terms of cost and schedule. It is also used for evaluating risk (see in Section 7.6.). This process step may be a manual exercise wherein the scheduler, based on his or her cost engineering judgment and team input and feedback, iteratively modifies the plan and schedule inputs until the most satisfactory schedule is obtained. It may also be a structured Monte Carlo simulation to determine a quantitative evaluation of the probability of achieving the schedule.

One method of schedule optimization is referred to as *schedule crashing*. Typically, schedule crashing is an attempt to shorten the duration of the critical path by adding more resources to selected critical activities while considering cost/schedule tradeoffs.

.8 Establish Schedule Control Basis

With an integrated control process, schedule activities are coded in accordance with the WBS levels, which facilitates schedule performance measurement and assessment (see Sections 9.2 and 10.1). Also, the schedule is resource loaded when cost and schedule control are fully integrated. One of the outputs of the scheduling process is the basis for schedule performance measurement and assessment. Deliverables provided for review and validation and project control plan implementation (see Section 8.1) include the following:

- *The Plan*. The plan includes a list and description of the activities with their planned milestone date information (e.g., start and finish dates).
- *Schedule Control Baseline*. A time-phased, logically linked, resource loaded, detailed interpretation of the plan based on an aggregation of a common attribute of all activities to be measured and assessed (see Section 9.2).
- *Planned Schedule*. The planned schedule includes a list of activities with their planned date information (e.g., early and late start and finish dates) that is usually illustrated as a bar chart.
- *Schedule Basis*. Includes a description of the activities and resources covered, included methodologies, standards, references and defined deliverables, assumptions, inclusions and exclusions made, key milestones and constraints, calendars, and some indication of the level of risk and uncertainty used to establish schedule contingency
- *Schedule Control Plan*. The schedule basis should also include a description of how project performance will be measured and assessed in respect to the schedule including rules for earning progress and the procedures for evaluating progress and forecasting remaining durations.

.9 Review and Validate Schedule

Schedules are typically complex compilations of input from multiple stakeholders. Schedule review seeks to ensure that the schedule reflects the defined scope, is suitable for control purposes, meets the stakeholders' milestone requirements, and that all parties agree on and understand its content, including its probabilistic nature in relation to various agreements made and contractual requirements (i.e., risks). Finally, the schedule should be *benchmarked or validated* against or compared to internal and external schedule metrics to assess its appropriateness, competitiveness, areas of risk, and to identify improvement opportunities.

.10 Document and Communicate Schedule

Requirements for communicating the schedule should be considered in planning for the process. There is often more than one type or version of the same schedule reported. Stakeholders and different members of the team require different levels of detail and types of information from the schedule. Business clients are likely to be most interested in milestone and final completion metrics that they will monitor. Contractors may be most interested in monitoring and controlling their labor and equipment effort at a more detailed level and will be monitoring and controlling their resources at an intermediate schedule level. Subcontractors and vendors may monitor and control their own work at a micro-level, but they also need to interface with the prime contractor and other subcontractors or vendors.

The planned baseline schedule and its documented basis (including assumptions on how project performance will be measured and assessed) need to be communicated to and understood by all appropriate business and project parties. The primary output from the schedule planning and schedule development process is the basis for schedule performance measurement and assessment. The deliverables provided for project control plan implementation (see Section 8.1) were described in Section 7.2.2.8.

.11 Submit Schedule Deliverables

If the contractor develops the schedule, the product of the contractor's schedule planning and development process is often a submission of the requested (in a bid or tender) or contracted schedule deliverables to another contractor and/or to the owner as appropriate with procurement planning (see Section 7.7) and contracting practices in the subject industry. The deliverable typically includes a planned schedule for activities within the contractor's scope of work. The contractor's schedule is generally an input to the overall or master schedule developed and maintained by the general contractor and project owner and can be subject to negotiation.

.12 Develop and Maintain Methods and Tools

The schedule planning and development process typically uses a number of special methods and tools. Estimation of schedule durations can be done using algorithms that translate scope and resource information into time durations. Algorithms used at the early phases of scope development may be based on statistical analyses of historical cost and time duration information (e.g., regression modeling of time duration versus costs). Scheduling software incorporates basic algorithms for schedule development.

7.2.3 Inputs to Schedule Planning and Development

.1 *Project Planning Basis (Objectives, Constraints, and Assumptions)*. The enterprise may establish requirements for schedule planning and development such as completion milestones, constraints or limitations on the use of resources, and other criteria (see Section 4.1).

.2 *WBS, Work Packages, and Execution Strategy* (see Section 7.1). The project work package scope is defined with enough information to support decisions and appropriate control basis development. The WBS provides the overall organization of asset investments or project work to be planned and scheduled. The execution strategy identifies general approaches for planning consideration.

.3 *Technical Deliverables*. The work package scope definition is supplemented with documents, databases, and other detailed technical information to support identification of work activities. These deliverables are the output of work defining processes (e.g., engineering, programming, etc.) that are outside of the TCM process maps (however, there is considerable interaction of TCM with those processes). These deliverables include contractual deliverables as appropriate and other inputs such as memos, meeting minutes, punchlists, photos, and so on.

.4 *Asset Alternative Scope*. If the process is being used in support of strategic asset planning (see Section 3.2), the scope (usually conceptual) of the investment alternative is the primary process input.

.5 *Historical Schedule Information* (see Section 10.4). Information about schedule performance and methods and tools used on prior projects is used to support schedule planning and development. Schedule metrics and benchmarks are used to support the review and validation step.

.6 *Trends, Deviations, and Changes* (see Section 10.3). During a project, trends, deviations, and changes may be noted during the change management process. The definitions of these trends, deviations, or changes are inputs to the schedule planning and development processes in which the trend, deviation, or change will be evaluated and incorporated as appropriate into the schedule control baseline.

.7 *Estimated Costs* (see Section 7.3). Cost from the estimating and budgeting process in alignment with the work package activities.

.8 *Resource Quantities* (see Section 7.4.). Estimated labor hours, material quantities, tools needed to perform the work, and other resources needed for each work package activity from the resource planning process.

.9 *Information from Project Planning*. Resource planning, value analysis and engineering, risk analysis and management, and procurement planning (see Sections 7.4, 7.5, 7.6, and 7.7, respectively) all may provide information to be considered and assessed in the schedule planning and schedule development processes.

.10 *Schedule Submittals.* If a contractor develops part of the schedule, that contractor's schedule planning and development output becomes an input to the overall project schedule planning development process.

7.2.4 Outputs from Schedule Planning and Development

.1 *Refined Scope Development.* Results from the schedule planning and development processes may lead to modifications and refinements to the WBS, work package definitions, and execution strategy (see Section 7.1.)
.2 *Information for Project Planning.* Results from the schedule planning and development processes may lead to modifications and refinements in the cost estimates and cash flow analysis (see Section 7.3), resource plans (see Section 7.4), value engineering analyses (see Section 7.5), risk analyses (see Section 7.6), and procurement planning (see Section 7.7).
.3 *Trends, Deviations, and Changes.* The results of trend, deviation, or change evaluations are inputs to the change management process (see Section 10.3).
.4 *Basis for Schedule Performance Measurement and Assessment.* Deliverables provided for project control plan implementation (see Section 8.1).
.5 *Basis for Asset Planning.* If the process is being used in support of strategic asset planning (see Section 3.2), the schedule (usually conceptual) is used to support feasibility analysis.
.6 *Schedule Submittals.* Often, contractors are responsible for the detailed schedule planning and development of the activities within their contract scope. If so, their schedule deliverables, as required by the contract, are their process outputs (and an input to the overall or master schedule developed and maintained by the asset or project owner).
.7 *Historical Schedule Information.* The planned schedule, schedule control baseline, schedule basis, and other plan information are inputs to project historical database management (see Section 10.4).

7.2.5 Key Concepts and Terminology for Schedule Planning and Development

The following concepts and terminology described in this and other chapters are particularly important to understanding the schedule planning and development process of TCM:

.1 *Schedule Planning.* (See Section 7.2.1.1).
.2 *Schedule Development.* (See Section 7.2.1.2).
.3 *Schedule Model.* (See Section 7.2.1.2).
.4 *Activities.* (See Section 7.2.2.2).
.5 *Activity Logic.* (See Section 7.2.2.3).
.6 *Activity Duration.* (See Section 7.2.2.4).
.7 *Critical Path.* A sequence or chain of activities in a schedule for which a delay in any of the activities in the sequence will delay the completion of the project.
.8 *Milestones.* (See Section 7.2.2.5).
.9 *Resource Quantities.* (See Section 7.2.2.6).
.10 *Resource Loading.* (See Section 7.2.2.6).
.11 *Resource Leveling or Balancing.* (See Section 7.2.2.6).
.12 *Schedule Control Baseline.* (See Section 7.2.2.9).
.13 *Planned Schedule.* (See Section 7.2.2.9).
.14 *Schedule Basis.* (See Section 7.2.2.9).
.15 *Scope.* (See Section 7.1). The planned schedule must reflect only the scope of the asset or project.
.16 *Uncertainty.* A schedule is always an approximation of actual events. Therefore, understanding the probabilistic characteristics of the schedule is essential for applying decision making processes (see Section 3.3), risk analysis, and schedule contingency assessment (see Section 7.6). Measures of uncertainty (range, confidence intervals, etc.) are often key determinates of schedule quality.

Further Readings and Sources

There are many references describing schedule planning and development for various asset and project types in various industries. Recognizing that each text has its limitations (i.e., processes and tools are evolving, perceptions of best practices vary, etc.), the following references provide basic information and will lead to more detailed treatments.

- AACE International. *Cost Engineer's Notebook*. Morgantown, WV: AACE International (current revision).
- Amos, Scott J., Editor. *Skills and Knowledge of Cost Engineering*, 5th ed. Morgantown, WV: AACE International, 2004.
- Bent, James A., and K. Humphreys, Editors. *Effective Project Management Through Applied Cost and Schedule Control*. New York: Marcel Dekker, 1996.
- Callahan, Michael T., Daniel G. Quackenbush, and James E. Rowings. *Construction Project Scheduling*. New York: McGraw Hill, 1992.
- Hackney, John W. *Control and Management of Capital Projects*, 2nd ed. Morgantown, WV: AACE International, 1998.
- Humphreys, Kenneth K, Editor. *Project and Cost Engineer's Handbook*, 4th ed. New York: Marcel Dekker, Inc., 2005.
- Kerzner, Harold. *Project Management: A Systems Approach to Planning, Scheduling, and Controlling*, 8th ed. New York: John Wiley and Sons, Inc., 2003.
- Morris, Peter W., and Jeffrey K. Pinto, Editors. *The Wiley Guide to Managing Projects*. New York: John Wiley & Sons, Inc., 2004.
- O'Brien, James, and Frederick Plotnick., *CPM in Construction Management*, 5th ed. New York: McGraw-Hill, 1999.
- Samad, Sarwar A., Editor. *Professional Practice Guide No. 4: Planning and Scheduling*. CD ROM. Morgantown, WV: AACE International, 1999.

7.3 Cost Estimating and Budgeting

7.3.1 Description

Cost estimating is the predictive process used to quantify, cost, and price the resources required by the scope of an investment option, activity, or project. Budgeting is a sub-process within estimating used for allocating the estimated cost of resources into cost accounts (i.e., the budget) against which cost performance will be measured and assessed.[52]

Cost estimating is a process used to predict uncertain future costs. In that regard, a goal of cost estimating is to minimize the uncertainty of the estimate given the level and quality of scope definition. The outcome of cost estimating ideally includes both an expected cost and a probabilistic cost distribution. As a predictive process, historical reference cost data (where applicable) improve the reliability of cost estimating. Cost estimating, by providing the basis for budgets, also shares a goal with cost control of maximizing the probability of the actual cost outcome being the same as predicted.

The cost estimating process is generally applied during each phase of the asset or project life cycle as the asset or project scope is defined, modified, and refined. As the level of scope definition increases, the estimating methods used become more definitive and produce estimates with increasingly narrow probabilistic cost distributions. The specific estimating tools and techniques used vary widely depending upon the life cycle phase, the type of asset or project, and the level of definition of scope information available. The analysis, development, and maintenance of estimating tools and techniques are steps that are considered part of the estimating process.

The cost estimating process is typically performed concurrent to or iteratively with the asset and project planning and evaluation processes described in Chapters 3 and elsewhere in Chapter 7. Because costs are often dependent on time duration, while resource requirements identified in cost estimating may affect the schedule, the estimation of the time duration of activities (see Section 7.2) must be considered concurrently with costs. Iterative approaches are used because outcomes of a cost estimate often lead to changes in scope or plans. In fact, the estimating process can be viewed as part of the scope definition process because iterative trading off between cost and scope intertwine the processes.

While some steps of the cost estimating process are mechanistic and conducive to semi-automation (e.g., determinations of quantities by computer-aided design tools, and so on), estimating is a predictive process for which judgment and experience add value. Effective cost estimating requires an understanding of the work being planned. In some industries, such as engineering and construction, cost estimating is a recognized discipline because of the specialized knowledge required. In all industries, many individuals contribute to the performance of the estimating process.

.1 Classification of Cost Estimates

Given the goals of reducing uncertainty in the estimating process and improving communication of estimate results, it is desirable to establish standard estimate classifications for the enterprise. The classification system will define the specific input information needed to produce a desired estimating outcome quality at each phase of the asset or project life cycle. Classification schemes help define the requirements for scope definition and they will indicate estimating methodologies appropriate to that scope definition (Recommend Practices 17R-97 and 18R-97 provide classification methods recommended by AACE International).

---

[52] This section's definition and discussion of budgeting for project control purposes is distinct from the process of capital budgeting for strategic asset management, which is included in Section 3.2.

7.3.2 Process Map for Cost Estimating and Budgeting

Figure 7.3-1 illustrates the process map for cost estimating and budgeting. At its core, cost estimating involves the application of techniques that convert quantified technical and programmatic information about an asset or project into finance and resource information. The outputs of estimating are used primarily as inputs for business planning, cost analysis, and decisions or for project cost and schedule control processes The process is supported by tools and data that are created and maintained to support the various types of estimates that need to be prepared during the life cycle of the asset or project. The process is illustrated without recycle loops, but in actual practice, findings in any step or at review may require that all or part of the estimate be recycled through any of the preceding steps of the process.

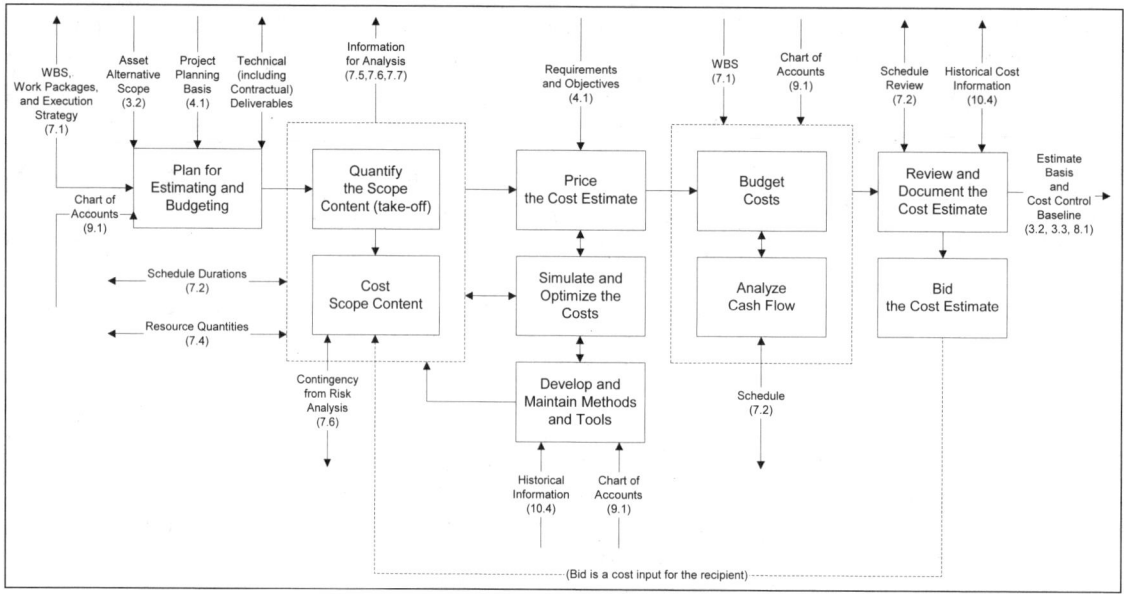

Figure 7.3-1 Process Map for Cost Estimating and Budgeting

The following sections briefly describe the steps in the cost estimating and budgeting process.

.1 Plan for Cost Estimating and Budgeting

Initial planning for this process should be integrated with planning for all the other project control planning processes (Sections 7.1 to 7.7). Project control planning is typically a phased process during which the project implementation process (see Section 4.1) is revisited to obtain incremental authorization and funding at the completion of each phase. Plans for the process must consider the time, costs, resources, tools, and methods for its performance during each phase. Roles and responsibilities for each step and transitions between each phase should be planned as well.

At the start of any phase, the current documented scope basis and defining technical (including contractual) deliverables are the key inputs. Based on an assessment of these inputs, the project team further identifies activities, resources, and tools needed. The output of the planning step is documentation of the scope of the cost estimating and budgeting effort as appropriate to the project size and complexity.

In some cases, much, if not all, the cost estimating detail is undertaken by and is the responsibility of contractors. In those cases, the contractor's schedule submittals are inputs to the owner's process and must be planned in alignment with the execution strategy (Section 7.1) and procurement planning (Section 7.7).

.2 Quantify Scope Content (Take-off)

The scope definition of an investment or a project is generally described in various planning and technical documents, databases, or other deliverables. To cost and price the scope, information in the scope documents must first be quantified in terms or formats required by the estimating algorithms. For example, an algorithm that estimates the cost of developing software programs may require the number of lines of software code as an input. Likewise, a construction estimating algorithm may require the linear meters of pipe as an input. The output of quantification is referred to as a *take-off* when the quantities are derived or developed from a drawing.

.3 Cost the Scope Content

Costing includes a core technique of estimating, which is the translation of quantified technical and programmatic scope planning information into expressions of the resource and financial investment or expenditure required to effect the plan. The translation is done with a mathematical algorithm. Costing does not in itself consider business concerns of how work is to be charged, billed, marked up, or otherwise accounted for by various stakeholders (see pricing and budgeting). *Life cycle costing* is costing applied to the entire life cycle of the asset including creation or modification, operation or use, and decommissioning or retirement to support investment option development and decision making.

Algorithms and Cost Estimating Relationships

The costing step always uses an estimating algorithm or formula. The algorithm transforms project technical and programmatic descriptive information into cost and resource terms. Estimating algorithms are often referred to as *cost estimating relationships (CERs)*. In its simplest form, a CER will appear as:

$$\text{Cost Resource} = \text{Factor} \times \text{Parameter}$$

where: **Cost Resource** = $ (labor, material, total, etc.), or time (labor hours, equipment rental hours, etc.)
Factor = a unit cost factor in terms of cost resource/parameter unit
Parameter = quantification of a scope item

There are a wide variety of CER types. Some CERs are highly probabilistic in nature (i.e., the relationships tend to be highly uncertain). These types of CERs are often called *parametric CERs*. These tend to aggregate a broad chunk of scope and cost into relatively simple algorithms. For example, a parametric CER may estimate the total cost of a building as follows:

Total Building Cost = (Gross Floor Area) x (Cost Per Unit of Floor Area)

Given the wide variety of building types and construction methods, the CER above is unlikely to be an accurate predictor of the cost of most buildings. However, it does not follow that all parametric CERs are highly uncertain. In this example, if the building being estimated was of the same design as all of the buildings upon which the CER was derived, then the CER could be an accurate predictor.

Models are another type of algorithm that tends to be highly probabilistic in nature. Models are complex algorithms (usually a computer program) designed to replicate the performance of a process or system. Models that result in cost outputs are often called cost models. Cost models are particularly well suited for simulation and optimization uses. Models are also the primary costing algorithm used for asset planning (see Section 3.2).

Other CERs tend to be more certain in nature and are often called *definitive, detail unit cost, or line-item CERs*. These CER types tend to disaggregate scope and cost into more clearly defined pieces. For example, a detailed CER may estimate the cost of one item as follows:

Valve type A installation hours = (Number of valves of type A) x (Hours per valve of type A)

An overall detailed estimate then re-aggregates the results of a large number of these types of CERs, and taken together, the overall estimate is likely to be an accurate predictor of the final cost. However, it does not follow that all estimates based on definitive CERs are highly certain. There may be uncertainties in scope definition, in quantification, in cost database quality, or in other areas that result in an inaccurate estimate. Keep in mind that the above examples are somewhat simplistic; CERs can be as complex and varied as mathematics allows.

As successive or phased estimates are prepared over the course of a project's life cycle, the mix of CERs used tends to progress from highly uncertain to highly certain in nature. However, most estimates will use a mix of CER types. In particular, most estimates use probabilistic methods for estimating contingency cost.

Factors and Mark-ups

Basic estimating algorithms are often adjusted by the application of factors to make the result match the current estimate situation. Factors, as drawn from project history or a standard database, almost always reflect conditions from past experience that do not match those in the current estimate situation. The conditions that may vary from the database basis include time differences, escalation and inflation, exchange rates, labor rates, labor productivity, jobsite conditions, material mark-ups, location factors, environmental impacts, and taxes, duties, and fees. Parameters or quantity measures used reflect preliminary models that do not precisely match actual technical or programmatic conditions. The conditions that may vary from the measurement basis include waste and spoilage allowance, accuracy of measurement (take-off) allowance, and specification, function, or content differences.

.4 Price the Cost Estimate

Pricing includes charging techniques that various stakeholders in the plan (bidders, contractors, etc.) apply to costs in the estimate to allow for overhead and profit, to improve cash flow, or to otherwise address market conditions and serve their business interests. It is important to distinguish between costs and prices. For example, contractors often *unbalance* a bid estimate by allocating costs to those items for which payment will be obtained early in a project; therefore, contract bid prices may not be a very useful reference source for developing a cost database. Activity-based costing (ABC) calls for minimizing arbitrary or unbalanced allocations so that optimum cost decisions or control may be obtained.

.5 Simulate and Optimize the Costs

The factors and parameters in an estimating algorithm may have a range of possible values that could occur, or that could be selected from within the scope. There may also be alternate algorithms that could be used for estimating. For estimating, simulation refers to methods that apply alternate factor and parameter combinations, or apply alternate algorithms so as to produce a distribution of possible outcomes. Optimization refers to methods that evaluate trade-offs between inputs, such as scope elements, so as to minimize or maximize the degree to which some set of objectives is met. Optimization commonly uses simulation or mathematical modeling techniques. Simulations and optimization is done concurrently with the costing and pricing steps as appropriate. These methods are useful for value analysis and engineering (see Section 7.5) to optimize scope decisions in terms of cost. They are also useful for evaluating cost risk (see Section 7.6).

.6 Budget Costs

Budgeting includes allocating the estimated cost of asset or project items into cost accounts against which cost performance will be measured and assessed. Budgeting results in a baseline for cost control performance assessment (see Sections 6.1 and 10.1). The cost accounts used from the chart of accounts must also support the cost accounting process (see Sections 5.1 and 9.1). Budgets are often time-phased in accordance with the schedule or to address budget and cash flow constraints.

.7 Analyze Cash Flow

To serve as a basis for *earned value* and other methods of cost control (see Section 7.1), the budget is time-phased to determine expected rates of cost incurrence and cash disbursement for each account or group of accounts including capital interest charges. As rates of investment are often constrained by the enterprise for financial reasons, the estimate and schedule are generally developed interactively to ensure that financial goals are achieved. The rate of investment may alternatively examine the rates of incurring cost (i.e., obligation made to expend) or actual cash disbursement.

.8 Bidding the Cost Estimate

For contractors, the end product of the estimating process may be submission of the bid or tender to another contractor or owner. A bid is a priced estimate (see Section 7.3.2.4). While the bid or tender is the final estimating task for the contractor, the bid is generally a cost input to the overall asset or project estimate (the dashed line in Figure 7.3-1).

.9 Review and Document the Estimate

Estimates are typically complex compilations of input from many stakeholders. To ensure the quality of an estimate (or budget or bid), a review process is called for. The review seeks to ensure that the estimate reflects the asset or project goals and scope, is suitable for cost accounting and control purposes, serves the stakeholders' financial requirements, and that all parties agree on and understand its content and probabilistic nature. Prior to the review, the *estimate basis* is documented to support the review and, after the review, it is updated as needed to support subsequent change management processes. The estimate should be benchmarked or *validated* against or compared to historical experience and/or past estimates of the enterprise and of competitive enterprises to check its appropriateness, competitiveness, and to identify improvement opportunities. Validation should always be done even if the reviewer also prepared the estimate (although preference should be given to an independent third party). Validation examines the estimate from a different perspective and using different metrics than are used in estimate preparation. A review may require that all or part of the estimate be recycled through any of the preceding steps of the process.

.10 Develop and Maintain Methods and Tools

The cost estimating process usually uses a wide variety of algorithms, data, software, forms, and so on. As was mentioned, historical reference cost data, including lessons learned, improve the reliability of cost estimating because it is a predictive process. Therefore, a key determinate of estimate output quality is the quality of the databases used.

Cost Estimating Database Development
All estimating algorithms are dependent upon having data such as labor and material unit rates, indices and factors, equipment costs, and other resource rate and cost factor information. The type of data that is used in the algorithm to convert scope quantification input to cost output is specific to the algorithm and estimating methodology used. Data are also used to support the review and validation process. The data may be obtained from published sources or they may be developed in-house. Published sources must be analyzed to determine adjustments needed to make the data applicable to the enterprise's situation (e.g., for location, culture, escalation, etc.).

Cost Estimating Algorithm Development
Estimating methods often require that custom algorithms be developed and maintained to support the estimating process. These algorithms are commonly based upon statistical analyses or modeling of historical or other cost information. The algorithms are needed to convert scope quantification input to appropriate cost output. For example, if early in design development, the only scope quantification available for a building is gross floor area, then an algorithm is needed to convert floor area into total cost;

i.e., Total Building Cost = (Gross Floor Area) x (Cost Per Unit of Floor Area). Cost models are a form of algorithm.

7.3.3 Inputs to Cost Estimating and Budgeting

.1 *Scope Definition.* The investment option (see Section 3.2) or project scope (see Section 7.1) is defined, and information needed to support development of the estimate is provided. The information needed depends on the desired classification of the estimate at that phase (see Section 7.3.1.1).

.2 *Technical Deliverables.* The scope definition is supplemented with documents, databases, and other detailed technical information (including contract documents) to support quantification of the scope. These deliverables are the output of work processes (e.g., engineering, design, and so on) that interface closely with, but are outside of, the TCM process.

.3 *Schedule Information.* While schedules are usually developed concurrently with cost estimates, expected schedule durations, constraints, and other schedule data are inputs to various steps of the estimating process.

.4 *Work Breakdown Structure (WBS).* The WBS (see Section 7.1) provides the overall organization of project work to be estimated. The chart or code of accounts (7.3.3.5) provides the mechanism for coding the WBS.

.5 *Chart or Code of Accounts.* Coding structures that support the work breakdown development (Section 7.1) and cost accounting process (see Sections 5.1 and 9.1) are provided. Each stakeholder with cost accounting and cost control responsibilities may have his own chart of accounts; coordination may require that stakeholders *map* their accounts with each other so that cost information can be exchanged. Budgeting allocates estimated costs to the proper cost accounts. There may also be a separate chart or code of accounts for cataloging information in a cost estimating database; this chart may differ from that used for cost budgeting and accounting.

.6 *Historical Cost Information.* The development and maintenance of cost estimating tools and data are often, but not always, based on feedback of actual asset and project (see Sections 6.3 and 10.4) cost performance information.

.7 *Estimate Information.* Information from previous estimates for this asset or project (or from other assets or projects as applicable) supports the development and maintenance of cost estimating tools and databases. Examples include parameters (e.g., ratio of building exterior skin area to gross floor area), factors (e.g., freight cost as a percentage of material cost), and rates (e.g., labor cost per hour).

7.3.4 Outputs from Cost Estimating and Budgeting

.1 *Cost Control Baseline.* A tabulation of costs in accounts that are formatted for cost accounting and cost control purposes. For some control methods, the costs are time-phased by account or group of accounts. As cost performance measures are made, they are assessed against the cost baseline (see Sections 6.1 and 10.1).

.2 *Resource Requirements.* Quantities of resources such as labor, material, and equipment are outputs of the estimating quantification process and costing algorithms. The resource requirements are used as a basis for resource planning (see Section 7.4) and procurement (see Section 7.7).

.3 *Cost Information for Analyses.* Investment decision making (see Section 3.3), value analysis and engineering (see Section 7.5), risk analysis (see Section 7.6), and procurement planning (see Section 7.7) all require cost information from the estimating process as their input. Risk analysis is typically performed concurrently with estimating. Among other planning and decision-making uses, risk analysis yields *contingency* costs used in estimating.

.4 *Estimate Basis.* Because cost estimates are approximations based in varying degree upon assumptions and interpretations of scope, plans, and objectives, stakeholders often misunderstand what a cost estimate represents. Communicating the basis of an estimate reduces misunderstanding, error, and misuse. The estimate basis generally includes a description of the scope, methodologies, references, and defining deliverables used, assumptions and exclusions made, and some indication of the level of risk and uncertainty. In general, the estimate basis (and all estimate backup) becomes the one deliverable that defines the scope of the project. As such, the estimate basis is also the basis for change management (see Section 10.3). After review of the estimate basis (and all estimate backup) by the project stakeholders, project scope definition and other inputs may need to be revised to ensure that all objectives have been achieved (i.e., estimate definition leads to refined scope definition).

.5 *Refined Scope Development.* Results and lessons learned from the estimating process often lead to modifications and refinements in the requirements, scope description, implementation plans, and WBS (see Sections 3.2 and 7.1.)

.6 *Refined Plan and Schedule.* Results and lessons learned from the estimating process often lead to modifications in asset or project work plans and schedules (see Sections 3.2 and 7.2.). The estimate and schedule are generally developed concurrently or iteratively.

.7 *Estimate Information.* Information from the estimate supports the development and maintenance of cost estimating tools and databases. The information may include all estimate detail data and documentation, factors, rates, and other metrics derived from the estimate, or any other estimating lessons learned.

7.3.5 Key Concepts for Cost Estimating and Budgeting

The following concepts and terminology described in this and other chapters and sections are particularly important to understanding the cost estimating and budgeting process of total cost management:

.1 *Activity Based Costing (ABC).* (See Sections 3.2 and 5.1). Cost management and control is improved when all costs are attributed or budgeted to the item or activity causing or driving the expenditure rather than through arbitrary or non-causal allocations.

.2 *Algorithm and Cost Estimating Relationship (CER).* (See Section 7.3.2.3).

.3 *Budgeting.* (See Section 7.3.2.6).

.4 *Chart or Code of Accounts.* (See Section 7.3.3.5).

.5 *Contingency.* (See Section 7.6.) Contingency is an amount added to an estimate to allow for unknown items, conditions, or events that experience shows will likely occur. Every project cost estimate should evaluate risk and uncertainty and include identifiable contingency costs in the estimate if needed.

.6 *Cost Accounting.* (See Sections 5.1 and 9.1). Accounting provides the measure of commitments and actual expenditures. The process, tools, and systems an enterprise uses to handle cost performance measurement information will often drive the *chart or code of accounts* and constrain how cost may be estimated and budgeted. Accounting also serves financial reporting purposes in addition to cost control purposes.

.7 *Cost Control Baseline.* (See Section 7.3.4.1).

.8 *Costing and Life Cycle Costing.* (See Section 7.3.2.3).

.9 *Estimate Basis.* (See Section 7.3.2.9).

.10 *Pricing.* (See Section 7.3.2.4).

.11 *Scope.* (See Sections 3.2 and 7.1). The scope is the sum of all the technical, programmatic, and other information that defines that which is to be estimated.

.12 *Quantification and Take-off.* (See Section 7.3.2.2).

.13 *Uncertainty.* (See Section 7.6 and 7.3.5.5). A cost estimate or budget is always an approximation. Therefore, understanding the probabilistic characteristics of the estimate is essential. Measures of uncertainty (range, confidence intervals, and so on) are often key determinants of estimate quality.

Further Readings and Sources

There are many texts and articles that describe cost estimating, budgeting, and related practices for various asset and project types in various industries. The following provide basic information and will lead to more detailed treatments.

- AACE International. *Cost Engineer's Notebook.* Morgantown, WV: AACE International (most recent revision.)

- Adithan, M., and B.S. Pabla. *Production Engineering, Estimating and Costing*. Delhi: Konark Publishers, 1989.
- Amos, Scott, J., Editor. *Skills and Knowledge of Cost Engineering*, 5th ed. Morgantown, WV: AACE International, 2004.
- Gransburg, Douglas D., Editor. *Professional Practice Guide (PPG) #6: Construction Cost Estimating*. CD ROM. Morgantown, WV: AACE International, 2000.
- Jones, Capers. *Estimating Software Costs*. New York: McGraw-Hill, 1998.
- Leo, Douglas W., Larry R. Dysert, and Bruce Elliott, Editors. *Professional Practice Guide (PPG) #13: Parametric and Conceptual Estimating*. CD ROM. Morgantown, WV: AACE International, 2002.
- Neil, James M. *Construction Cost Estimating for Project Control*. Englewood Cliffs, NJ: Prentice-Hall, Inc., 1981.
- Ostwald, Phillip F. *Cost Estimating for Engineering and Management*. Englewood Cliffs, NJ: Prentice-Hall, Inc., 2000.
- Stewart, Rodney D. *Cost Estimating*, 2nd ed. New York: John Wiley and Sons, 1991.
- Westney, Richard E., Editor. *The Engineer's Cost Handbook*. New York: Marcel Dekker, Inc., 1997.
- Winchell, William. *Realistic Cost Estimating for Manufacturing*, 2nd ed. Dearborn, MI: Society of Manufacturing Engineers, 1989.

7.4 Resource Planning

7.4.1 Description

Resource planning is the process of ascertaining future resource requirements for an organization or a scope of work. This involves the evaluation and planning of the use of the physical, human, financial, and informational resources required to complete work activities and their tasks. Most activities involve using people (i.e., labor) to perform work. Some activities involve creating an asset using component physical elements or parts (i.e., materials) as well as other items consumed during creation (i.e., consumables). Other tasks involve creating an asset using mainly information inputs (e.g., engineering or software design). Usually, people use tools such as equipment to help them. In some cases automated tools may perform the work with little or no human effort. Therefore, the goal of resource planning in TCM is to ensure that labor, materials, tools, and consumables, which are often limited in availability or limited by density, are invested in a project over time in a way that successfully, if not optimally, achieves project objectives and requirements.

Resource planning begins in the scope and execution plan development process (Section 7.1) during which the work breakdown structure, organizational breakdown structure (OBS), work packages, and execution strategy are developed. The OBS establishes categories of labor resources or responsibilities; this categorization facilitates resource planning because all resources are someone's responsibility as reflected in the OBS. These scope development deliverables are inputs to the schedule planning and development and cost estimating and budgeting processes (Sections 7.2 and 7.3, respectively). Resource estimating (usually a part of cost estimating) determines the activity's resource quantities needed (e.g., hours, tools, materials, etc.) while schedule planning and development determines the work activities to be performed. Resource planning then takes the estimated resource quantities, evaluates resource availability and limitations considering project and business circumstances (e.g., skills, location, resource markets, etc.), and then optimizes how the available resources (which are often limited) will be used in the activities over time. The optimization is performed in an iterative manner using the duration estimating and resource allocation steps of the schedule planning and development process (see Sections 7.2.2.4 and 7.2.2.6).

At the conclusion of the resource planning process, the resource "plan" becomes an inherent part of the project control budget and the resource-loaded schedule. Where appropriate, control budgets include both resource quantities and cost. The estimate and schedule deliverables include documents that describe the resource assumptions, limitations, and other resource considerations incorporated in the baseline project control plan. The resource plan is a key input to the procurement planning process (Section 7.7) that plans for acquisition of the planned resources in alignment with the execution strategy.

From the project control budget and the resource-loaded schedule, planned resource expenditure charts and tables can be developed that are then used as a control baseline against which actual resource use can be measured (Section 9.2) and assessed (Section 10.1). As changes are made to the project scope and/or plans, or performance trends are observed, changes to resource plans can be made through the change management process (Section 10.3).

Resource planning is a critical element of project control planning when the performance of the accounting process for project costs (Section 9.1) is poor as it is for many enterprises. This is because accounting for resource consumption (e.g., time cards, purchase order tracking, etc.) tends to be more detailed and more timely than accounting for costs. Many cost accounting systems report cost data too infrequently (e.g., monthly) and/or too indefinitely (e.g., not at an activity level) to effectively control most projects. This is reflected in the project control saying "control the hours to control the job."

Resource planning is often done at a strategic asset management level (Section 2.3) because the enterprise may have multiple projects competing for key resources (i.e., *portfolio management*). In that case, business management of the enterprise will have to decide on the best allocation of those key (i.e., strategic) resources between projects. Any such allocation or constraints will be addressed in the asset planning process (Chapter 3).

7.4.2 Process Map for Resource Planning

At its core, resource planning is an interactive optimization process that works in parallel with the schedule planning and development and cost estimating processes. This process is supported by the study and understanding of the criticality and availability of the various resources, which in turn is supported by historical productivity data and experience with resource issues. Figure 7.2-1 illustrates the process map for resource planning.

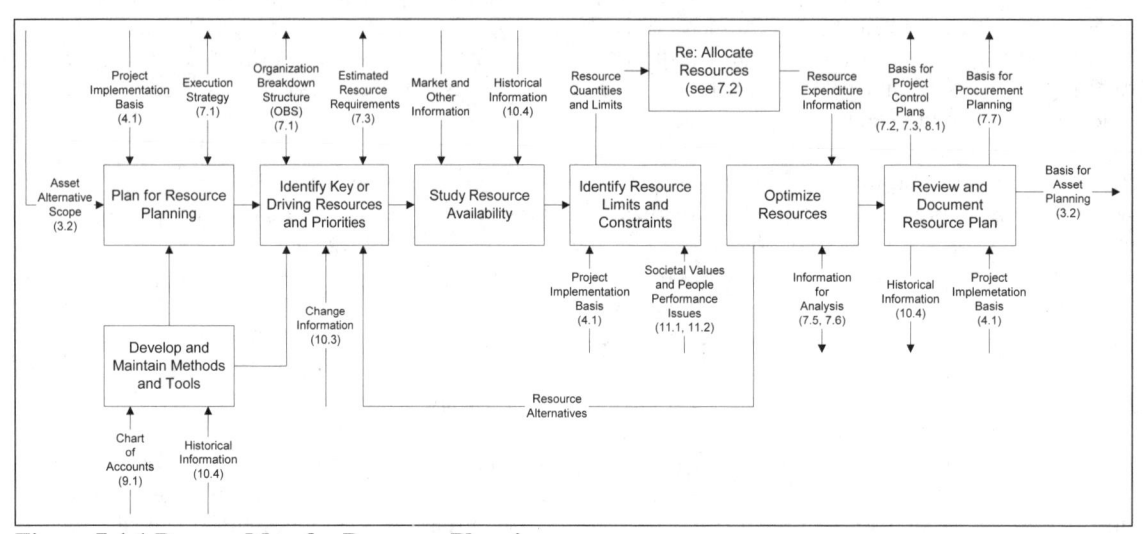

Figure 7.4-1 Process Map for Resource Planning

The following sections briefly describe the steps in the resource planning process.

.1 Plan for Resource Planning

Resource planning is a team effort. The team typically includes the project manager, planners, and other members such as schedulers, estimators, technical personnel (e.g., engineers, programmers), and managers (e.g., construction, programming, etc.). Often a scheduler leads the resource planning effort because the key step of resource allocation is a part of the schedule planning and development process. However, everyone on the project team with resource responsibilities (i.e., per the OBS) should have input to and buy-in for the resource planning aspects of the project control plans. The team and its activities for resource planning must be planned in conjunction with all the other project control planning processes as appropriate for the current phase of scope development. Resource planning tools are also identified that will facilitate the process, and past lessons learned are assessed for relevant guidance.

.2 Identify Key or Driving Resources and Priorities

Based on resource quantity availability and the requirements identified in the cost estimating process and from past project experience, resources are assessed and ranked in terms of how critical they are likely to be to project success. This information helps prioritize subsequent resource planning steps. Feedback from resource optimization may result in reassessment of resource criticality.

.3 Study Resource Availability

Methods for determining resource availability typically include site or field labor surveys, market analyses, and maintaining historical databases. Typically, a few resources will be both critical to success of a project or activity and highly limited in availability such as a highly specialized worker. For these activities, resource planning may result in additional estimated costs items (e.g., higher wages or labor incentives) and schedule activities (e.g., recruitment, training, etc.).

.4 Identify Resource Limits and Constraints

Resources are rarely in unlimited supply. Therefore, the supply limits must be identified so that thresholds can be set for the resource allocation step (see Section 7.2). Some of the limits may be dependent on market availability while others may be imposed as constraints by enterprise or project system management. There may also be physical constraints on the ability to apply resources (density of workers in a given area).

This step and the procurement planning process as a whole must also consider societal value and people performance issues (see Sections 11.1 and 11.2) that may somehow limit resource usage or performance (e.g., cultural attitudes, motivational issues, etc.).

.5 Optimize Resources

The allocation of resources during schedule development (see Section 7.2) may result in project scheduling challenges, opportunities, or risks that require an iterative evaluation of activity and schedule preferential logic alternatives. To optimize resource usage, the team may reassess which resources are critical and seek ways to obtain those resources (e.g., incentives, training, etc.). Optimization may also consider issues such as when and where material resources will be received as this will affect inventory and material handling costs. Cash flow and interest costs can be improved, and materials damages and losses reduced if orders are not placed too early and hoarding or stockpiling are avoided. Likewise, labor resources should not be mobilized earlier than necessary.

.6 Review and Document Resource Plan

Resource planning outputs (e.g., resource expenditure charts based on resource loaded schedules, recruitment and training plans, etc.) are reviewed by the project team to determine whether they are complete and suitable as a basis for planning, whether they meet project objectives and requirements, and whether they are competitive with industry's best practices and historical approaches.

.7 Develop and Maintain Methods and Tools

Resource planning is facilitated by having a database of historical resource data. These data should include past experiences with resource usage, availability, limitations, and similar information. The collection of historical resource planning data is generally a part of the project performance assessment process (Section 10.1) because resource plans and actual usage are in large part inherent to cost and schedule control records. Development and maintenance of resource planning tools (e.g., checklists, standard procedures, chart of accounts, etc.) is also a step in this process. A standard chart of accounts, along with the WBS/OBS, facilitates resource planning by establishing ways to consistently categorize resource information.

7.4.3 Inputs to Resource Planning

.1 *Project Planning Basis (Objectives, Constraints, and Assumptions).* The enterprise may establish requirements for resource planning such as constraints or limitations on the use of resources (see Section 4.1).
.2 *Changes.* During project execution, changes to the baseline project plans are identified in the change management process (see Section 10.3). Each change goes through the resource planning process so that it can be appropriately integrated into the project control plans.

.3 *Resource Quantities.* The cost estimating process (see Section 7.3) determines the quantities of labor hours, materials (counts, volumes, weights, etc.), equipment, tools, and consumable usage.

.4 *Resource Expenditure Information.* The rates or timing of resource expenditures are outputs from the scheduling resource allocation step (see Section 7.2).

.5 *Organizational Breakdown Structure (OBS).* The OBS, developed during the scope development process (see Section 7.1), documents the project organization and responsibilities for elements of the work in a logical, hierarchical manner. Much of the organization structure (i.e., functional discipline breakdown) may already be reflected in a standard chart of accounts.

.6 *Execution Strategy.* Plans are developed during scope development (see Section 7.1) that define how the project work will be implemented (i.e., the general approaches through which the work packages and activities will be performed). Elements of the strategy may affect resource planning.

.7 *Asset Alternative Scope.* If the process is being used in support of strategic asset planning, (see Section 3.2), the scope (usually conceptual) of the investment alternative is the primary process input.

.8 *Chart of Accounts.* The chart of accounts is a coding structure that allows all cost and resource information on a project to be uniquely identified. The chart of accounts often incorporates standard elements of the OBS (e.g., functional disciplines such as piping) as well as categorization of resource types (e.g., labor, material, etc.). The resource type categorization is sometimes called the *resource breakdown structure* (RBS). Each stakeholder with accounting, control, and reporting responsibilities may have its own chart of accounts; coordination requires that stakeholders *map* their accounts with each other so that cost and schedule information can be exchanged.

.9 *Societal Values and Performance Considerations.* (see Sections 11.1 and 11.2).

.10 *Historical Project Information.* Past project resource usage, availability, limitations, and similar information is used to support future project resource planning.

.11 *Information for Analysis.* Resource planning is iterative with the other project planning steps including value analysis and engineering and risk management (see Sections 7.5 and 7.6, respectively). These analytical processes may identify changes in resource plans that will increase value and/or reduce risks.

7.4.4 Outputs from Resource Planning

.1 *Resource Quantity Availability and Limitations.* The resource allocation step (see Section 7.2.) requires data on thresholds or limits for evaluating resource consumption over time. Examples of limitations include the availability of a particular skill, the total number of available workers with a particular skill set that belong to a local union, and the availability of a major crane or a specialized computer.

.2 *Basis for Project Control Plans and Plan Implementation.* The resource "plan" is an inherent part of the project control budget and the resource-loaded schedule. Control budgets should include both resource quantities and cost. The estimate and schedule deliverables include documents that describe the resource assumptions, limitations, and other resource considerations incorporated in the baseline project control plans.

.3 *Basis for Asset Planning.* If the process is being used in support of strategic asset planning (see Section 3.2), the resource plan (usually conceptual) is used to support feasibility analysis.

7.4.5 Key Concepts for Resource Planning

The following concepts and terminology described in this and other sections are particularly important to understanding the resource planning process of TCM:

.1 *Organization Breakdown Structure (OBS).* (See Section 7.1.2.3).

.2 *Resources.* In respect to the resource planning process covered in this section, resources include physical and human resources, in particular, labor (e.g., disciplines, trades, etc.), materials (e.g., steel, concrete, etc.), tools (e.g., construction equipment, computers, etc.), and consumables (e.g., welding rods, formwork, office supplies, etc.) used or employed in project activities. From a broader perspective, resources may also include physical space, monetary, and information resources.

.3 Resource Allocation. (See Section 7.2.2.6).
.4 Resource Availability, Limitations, and Constraints. (See Sections 7.4.2.3 and 7.4.2.4).
.5 Resource Management. (See Sections 1.1.2 and 1.4.2).
.6 Societal Values. (See Section 11.1).

Further Readings and Sources

There are many references describing resource planning and related practices for various project types in various industries. Resource planning, as addressed by the process in this section, is generally covered in project planning and scheduling texts, and less often as a subject in itself. Resource management, human resource management, and manufacturing or enterprise resource planning (MRP/ERP) are related but less relevant topics for which text references are not listed here. The following references provide basic information and will lead to more detailed treatments.

- Amos, Scott J. *Skills and Knowledge of Cost Engineering*, 5th ed. Morgantown, WV: AACE International, 2004.
- Callahan, Michael T., Daniel G. Quackenbush, and James E. Rowings. *Construction Project Scheduling*. New York: McGraw Hill, 1992.
- Canter, M. R. *Resource Management for Construction: An Integrated Approach*. Hampshire, London: MacMillan Press Ltd., 1993.
- Fleming, Quentin W. *Project Procurement Management: Contracting, Subcontracting, Teaming*. Tustin, CA: FMC Press, 2003.

7.5 Value Analysis and Engineering

7.5.1 Description

Value analysis (VA) and value engineering (VE), when applied as processes, are "the systematic application of recognized techniques which identify the functions of the product or service, establish the worth of those functions, and provide the necessary functions to meet the required performance at the lowest overall cost."[53] Typically, lowest overall cost refers to the lowest life-cycle cost. While VE is focused on the development of new assets, and VA on existing assets or projects, their representation in a basic process map is the same. This section refers to this process as VA/VE.

The concepts of "value" and "functions" are central to VA/VE. In general, value is a measure of the worth of a thing in terms of usefulness, desirability, importance, money, etc. While not the same as value, quality (i.e., as a measure of customer satisfaction) tends to be improved by VA/VE. In general, functions are attributes of an asset or project that give it a purpose (i.e., allow user/operator to accomplish work) and make it useful or desirable (i.e., to have value). In the VA/VE process, measures of a function's value are usually considered in relation to the cost of the function (i.e., a relative value; the function's monetary worth to the function's cost). While these general definitions will suffice for understanding the general concept, there are many types of value measures and functions considered in specific VA/VE methods and tools.[54]

The objective of VA/VE is to improve the value for the intended asset or project objectives as defined by the respective strategic asset requirements (see Section 3.1) or project implementation basis (see Section 4.1) inputs. However, unlike other practices used to improve "value" (e.g., suggestion lists, cost reduction exercises, etc.), VA/VE is based on rigorous function definition and alternative analysis. The outputs of VA/VE are asset and project scope alternatives with improved value, which must be decided upon by the strategic or project leadership.

7.5.2 Process Map for Value Analysis and Engineering

In TCM, the VA/VE process includes six basic steps: (1) planning and initiation, (2) function analysis, (3) creativity, (4) idea evaluation, (5) idea development and documentation, and (6) methods and tools development.[55] The value engineering process centers on steps that analyze functions and then assess their relative value. The outputs of value engineering are used primarily as inputs for the project implementation process. Figure 7.5-1 illustrates the process map for VA/VE, but keep in mind that the process is typically applied in a phased manner (i.e., more than once during a project) consistent with the project scope development phases described in Section 7.1

---

[53] SAVE International, *Value Methodology Standard (Glossary)*, 2003.
[54] SAVE International defines the many types of value (e.g., esteem, market, perceived, use, etc.) and functions (e.g., basic or essential, work, sell, etc.). Refer to the SAVE International *Value Terminology Dictionary*, 2005.
[55] SAVE International has established a standard it calls "Value Methodology"(VM). (See SAVE International, *Value Methodology Standard*, 2003, www.value-eng.org). VM delineates a process in the form of a "job plan." AACE International's VA/VE sub-process is conceptually consistent with the VM job plan phases, but the process is abstracted here in recognition of the different purposes and contexts of the two products. (Again, see SAVE International, *Value Methodology Standard*, 2003, www.value-eng.org).

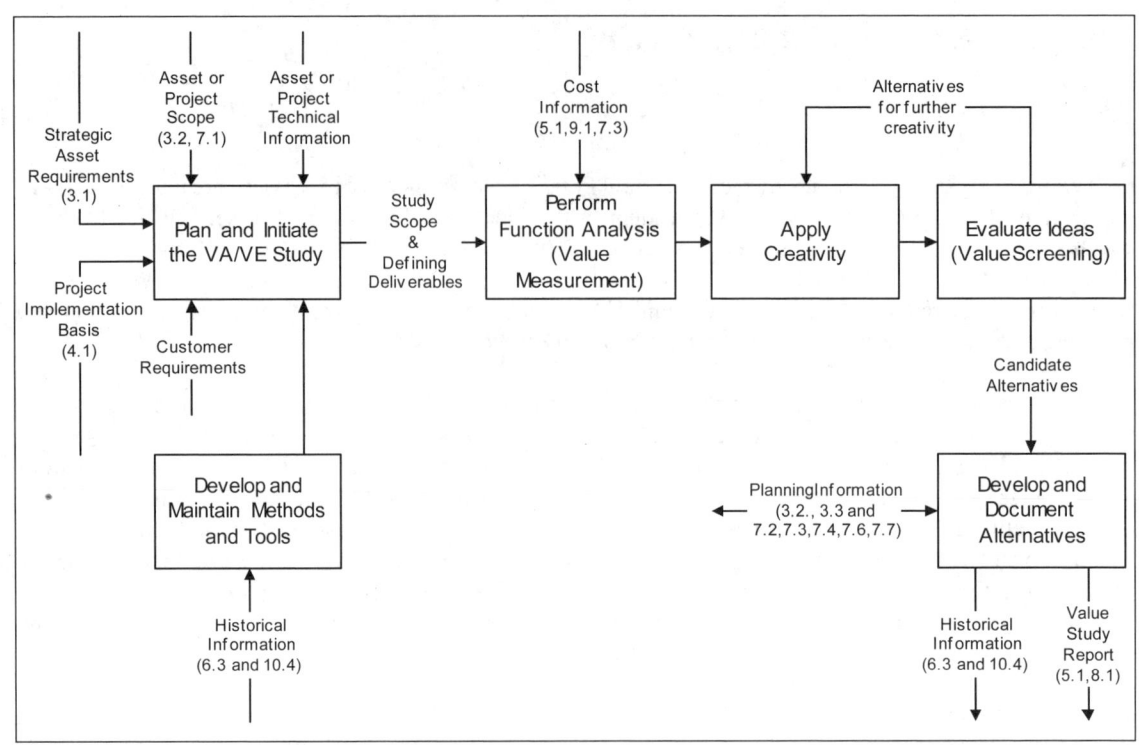

Figure 7.5-1 Process Map for Value Analysis and Engineering

The following sections briefly describe the steps in the value analysis and engineering process.

.1 Plan and Initiate the VA/VE Study

At the start of the process, VA/VE study leadership is established with the responsibility to plan and prepare for the main effort of the VA/VE study that will begin with function analysis. Preparation typically entails the following activities: (a) defining the subject asset or project including customer requirements for it and attitudes about it, (b) gathering information about and building models of the asset or project that will support the study, (c) establishing criteria for the study, (d) documenting the study scope, and (e) establishing a value study team.

Basic inputs to value study planning and initiation include the documented strategic asset requirements and project implementation basis (see Sections 3.1 and 4.1, respectively), and the current asset or project scope definition (see Sections 3.2 and 7.1). Additional technical and programmatic information and deliverables that define asset or project attributes are also inputs.

This basis scope information should be further evaluated to define the specific asset or project component to be studied, as well as the basic asset or project function that allows the customer to accomplish his task (i.e., why the asset exists or is needed). Furthermore, customer requirements for (i.e., wants and needs) and attitudes about the asset or project must be defined. Study leadership may use focus groups and/or surveys to determine the following:

   a. The prime buying or investing influence (i.e., who the customer really is);
   b. The importance of features and characteristics of the asset or project;
   c. The seriousness of user-perceived faults and complaints of the asset or project;
   d. How the asset or project compares to competing or similar assets or projects.

Much of this information gathering effort is focused on discovering the motivation for the customer to invest (despite faults) in this asset or project above all other alternatives. This information becomes the basis of the study team's value proposition to the user and the value delivery system to get it to them.[56]

The VA/VE study will also require technical and programmatic information that defines the physical attributes and performance characteristics of the asset or project (and any comparables that might be considered) such as drawings, specifications, test reports, and so on. The study leadership should gather the information needed for the study or at least make sure the information can be readily obtained or accessed when needed. Site visits, inspections, or walk-throughs can provide understanding that hard documents cannot convey. The study leadership may also obtain or build models of cost, energy use, and other attributes as might be appropriate for the study.

The study leadership also must establish the general criteria and measures that will be used to rate, rank, or decide upon value improvement ideas during the performance of the study. Finally, the VA/VE leadership must determine the appropriate study team members who will participate in or support the planned study activities, as well as lining up other resources required (e.g., meeting space, etc.).

The output of the planning and initiation step is documentation of the scope of the VA/VE study, as reviewed and agreed to by the study team and strategic or project leadership as appropriate. The scope describes the basis of the study (e.g., objective, methods, measures, assumptions, etc.) and defines what is or is not included in the study and what the team is or is not able to control or change.

Planning for VA/VE studies is facilitated when the enterprise has a project system that establishes guidelines for when and how VA/VE is to be applied and provides study support capabilities (i.e., methods, tools, and resources). VA/VE studies are typically applied in a phased manner consistent with the project scope development phases described in Section 8.1. The VA/VE process may be applied at any phase, but is most often applied at the initial phases of asset or project planning when scope definition is evolving and changes are least disruptive.

Many individuals in the strategic asset or project team may be involved in performing the VA/VE process. The value study team should be multidisciplinary. Management support of the process is vital to ensure that all the necessary resources are made available and are committed to the success of the process. Success is also facilitated by having an experienced cost or value specialist coordinate the effort.

.2 Perform Function Analysis

In this study stage, the study team uses function analysis to document the functions of the asset and/or its project components. The analysis is based on the study scope and defining deliverables described in the previous section. The primary method to analyze function is to model it using function hierarchy or function analysis systems technique (FAST). FAST is a diagramming technique to graphically show the logical relationships of the functions of a product in a hierarchical order (it is not a function flow diagram based on time sequence). The technique's value lies in the intensive questioning, challenging, and analysis of functionality that takes place during the diagram development. One aspect to challenge is the validity of constraints that dictated the original design, material, components, or procedures (i.e., constraints analysis).

Next, the study team quantifies function importance and cost metrics using value measurement techniques. These techniques provide quantitative measurements that indicate the relative strength of a respondent's perception of the item(s) or attributes of items. Value measurement techniques include rating, scaling, constant sum, pair comparison, criteria analysis, scoring model, ranking, and others. A "values index" is a common metric that is the ratio of the function's monetary worth to the function's cost.

The output of the function analysis stage is an ordered list of functions or items arrayed from the highest to lowest relative measured value as they currently exist.

---

[56] See Section 11.1 for a discussion of societal values.

.3 Apply Creativity

In this stage, the study team applies creative techniques to generate a list of alternative ways to replace, improve, or eliminate the low value functions or items identified in function analysis. This is a creative step that should be as unconstrained by habit and past thinking patterns as possible (i.e., "think outside the box"). Judgment of the quality of ideas is set aside at this stage. The objective of creativity is not to find ideas for asset design, but to find ideas for how to perform the functions, including unique combinations of functions.

.4 Evaluate Ideas

In this stage, the study team synthesizes ideas and selects the most feasible for final development and documentation. Value screening techniques are used to reduce the list of ideas to a manageable size. Screening techniques are usually qualitatively oriented, but they may quantify the attributes of items where numbers and scales indicate some measure of importance.

If none of the final ideas and combinations satisfactorily meet the study criteria, or if an apparently low value idea is considered a possible candidate for further improvement, the study team returns to the creativity stage. At the end of the evaluation stage, a ranked list of satisfactory alternatives is developed.

.5 Develop and Document Alternatives

Beginning with the highest rank value alternatives, the study team employs asset and project planning process methods (as covered in the sections of Chapters 3 and 7) to develop the scope of the alternative ideas and assess their impact on asset or project performance (e.g., cost, schedule, quality, risk, etc.). Based on the study team's understanding of the asset requirements and project objectives, the team identifies the best alternative(s) (if any) and document its basis. Typically, the study team prepares a study report that describes the performance of the study, its basis, and the team's recommendations. Project leadership then reviews the report and decides whether to implement the recommendations (see Section 4.1). If the project is in the later planning or execution phases, the recommendation may be handled through the change management process (see Section 10.3).

The value study report, and lessons learned about the study process, are captured in the project system historical database (see Sections 6.3 and 10.4). The value study team leadership may further track and assess the performance of the actions resulting from the value study. While it is difficult to parse the effects from any particular study, industry benchmarking has shown that there is a statistical correlation between the use of value improving practices and improved project cost outcomes.

7.5.3 Inputs to Value Analysis and Engineering

.1 *Strategic Asset Requirements and Project Implementation Basis.* (see Sections 3.1 and 4.1). These define the basis asset scope, objectives, constraints, and assumptions.
.2 *Asset or Project Scope.* (see Sections 3.2 and 7.1). Deliverables (asset options, work breakdown structure, work packages, and execution strategy) that define the current asset or project scope. Scope changes (see Section 10.3) for which VA/VE will be applied also channel through the scope development process.
.3 *Asset or Project Technical Information.* Deliverables that define the physical and performance attributes of the asset or projects to be studied.
.4 *Customer Requirements.* These requirements are the wants and needs of the user or other stakeholders. VA/VE must discover the motivation for the customer to invest (despite faults) in this asset above all other alternatives.
.5 *Planning Information.* (see Sections 3.2, 3.3, 7.2, 7.3, 7.4, 7.6, and 7.7). While VA/VE value measurements are focused on cost, outputs from other planning processes—such as schedule planning and development, risk management, and quality function deployment—are considered in evaluating

candidate alternatives. Specialists for applicable processes (e.g., estimating, scheduling, etc.) may be part of the value study team.

.6 *Cost Information.* (see Sections 5.1, 9.1, and 7.3). Value measurement is focused on relative cost and value measures. The cost information comes from cost estimating or accounting measurements.
.7 *Historical Information.* (see Sections 6.3 and 10.4). Past study approaches and results may help the plan the VA/VE study.

7.5.4 Outputs from Value Analysis and Engineering

.1 *Cost Information.* The VA/VE function analysis and evaluation steps apply the cost estimating methods covered in Section 7.3.
.2 *Planning Information.* (see Sections 7.2, 7.3, 7.4, 7.6, and 7.7). The VA/VE evaluation step applies the methods of the project planning processes.
.3 *Value Study Report.* (see Sections 4.1 and 7.1). Describes the performance of the study, its basis, and recommendations for implementation. The recommendations may be implemented at the asset management or project level as appropriate.
.4 *Historical Information.* (see Sections 6.3 and 10.4). The study approach and results are captured for use in future methods and tools development and VA/VE study planning.

7.5.5 Key Concepts and Terminology for Value Analysis and Engineering

The following concepts and terminology described in this and other chapters are particularly important to understanding the VA/VE process of TCM:

.1 *Value.* (See Section 7.5.1).
.2 *Functions.* (See Section 7.5.1).
.3 *Customer Requirements.* (See Sections 7.5.1 and 3.1).
.4 *Function Analysis.* A type of function model (See Section 7.5.2.2).
.5 *Value Measurement.* (See Section 7.5.2.2).
.6 *Value Screening.* (See Section 7.5.2.4).

Further Readings and Sources

Portions of this section are excerpted from Chapter 24 ("Value Analysis" by Del L. Younker) of the *Skills and Knowledge of Cost Engineering* referenced below. Also, as previously mentioned, this process is conceptually consistent with SAVE International's "Value Methodology Standard" (www.value-eng.org, 2003). SAVE International is the primary technical association for this technology. However, there are many references describing value analysis, engineering, management, and methodology for various asset and project types in various industries. The following provide basic information and will lead to more detailed treatments:

- Akiyama, K. *Function Analysis.* Cambridge, MA: Productivity Press, Inc., 1991.
- Amos, Scott J. *Skills and Knowledge of Cost Engineering*, 5th ed. Morgantown, WV: AACE International, 2004.
- Dell'Isola, Alphonse. *Value Engineering: Practical Applications.* Kingston, MA: R.S. Means, 1998.
- Fowler, T. C. *Value Analysis in Design.* New York: Van Nostrand Reinhold, 1990.
- Lawrence D. Miles Value Foundation (www.valuefoundation.org)
- Miles, L. D. *Techniques of Value Analysis and Engineering.* New York: McGraw Hill, 1961.
- Mudge, A. E. *Value Engineering: A Systematic Approach.* New York: McGraw Hill, 1971.
- Parker, Donald E. *Value Engineering Theory.* Washington, DC: The Lawrence D. Miles Value Foundation, 1995.
- Shillito, M. L., and D. J. DeMarle. *Value: Its Measurement Design and Management.* New York: John Wiley & Sons, Inc., 1992.

- Younker, Del L. *Value Engineering: Analysis and Methodology*. New York: Marcel Dekker, Inc., 2003.

7.6 Risk Management

7.6.1 Description

Risk management is the process of identifying risk factors (risk assessment), analyzing and quantifying the properties of those factors (risk analysis), mitigating the impact of the factors on planned asset or project performance and developing a risk management plan (risk mitigation), and implementing the risk management plan (risk control).[57] The goal of risk management is to increase the probability that a planned asset or project outcome will occur without decreasing the value of the asset or project. Risk management presumes that deviations from plans may result in unintended results (positive or negative) that should be identified and managed.

The risk management process is applied in conjunction with the other asset and project control planning processes (i.e., scope development, cost estimating, schedule planning and development, and resource and procurement planning). For example, when risk management identifies a risk factor and impact that can be mitigated using an alternative project plan, the alternative plan is developed using the applicable planning process (e.g., cost estimating, scheduling, etc.). This iterative planning approach of assessing and analyzing risk factors and developing alternative plan concepts that mitigate the risk impacts is applied until a baseline project control plan (including the risk management plan) is implemented.

.1 Uncertainty and Risk

Risk management is a process for addressing uncertainty in project outcomes. While uncertainty is generally understood to include both better and worse outcomes than planned (i.e., opportunities and threats), the term "risk" is not always interpreted to be the same as uncertainty. There are three conventions for defining the term "risk":

a. risk is the same as uncertainty (i.e., threats + opportunities),
b. risk is only the negative impacts of uncertainty (i.e., threats)
c. risk is the net impact of uncertainty (i.e., threats – opportunities).

In TCM, potential deviations from plans are all considered potentially adverse to overall performance (i.e., a perceived opportunity may also be a threat). However, properly managed, the asset management or project team may be able to capitalize on "opportune" uncertainties. Therefore, the term "risk" is defined in TCM as being the same as uncertainty; both threats and opportunities need to be assessed, analyzed, and controlled.

.2 Decision and Risk Analysis

The full risk management process, as mapped in this section, is designed for addressing uncertainty in project outcomes (i.e., from a project control context). However, the process generally applies and is critical to addressing uncertainty in the outcomes of any decision. As discussed in Section 3.3, a key challenge in strategic asset planning and investment decision making is bringing an awareness of risk and probability concepts to those processes whether they result in an implemented project or not. Traditional economic analysis used in investment decision making may be somewhat meaningless when there are significant risks.

7.6.2 Process Map for Risk Management

The risk management process centers on steps that assess risk factors and then analyze and mitigate their impacts. The primary outputs of risk management are baseline project scope definition and project

---

[57] These four phases were identified by AACE International's Risk Management Committee and published in the AACE International *Risk Management Dictionary* (Cost Engineering, vol. 37, no. 10, 1995).

control plans (including contingency) that address project risks, including a risk management plan for how to address risk factors that occur during project execution. Figure 7.6-1 is a process map for risk management.

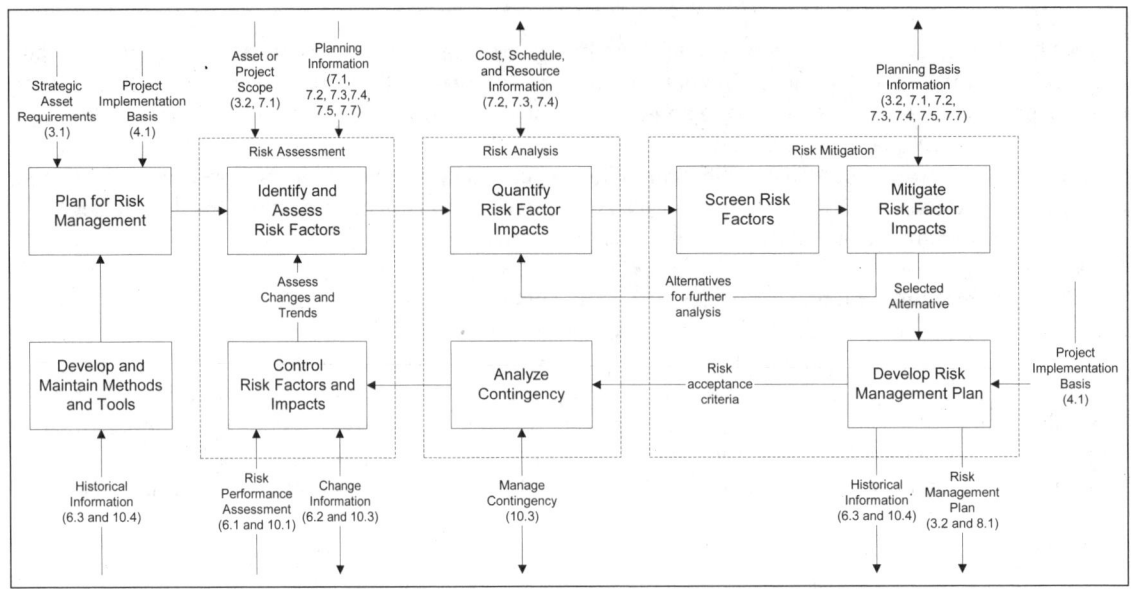

Figure 7.6-1 Process Map for Risk Management

The following sections briefly describe the steps in the risk management process.

.1 Plan for Risk Management

At the start of the process, risk management leadership is established with the responsibility to plan and prepare for the risk assessment, analysis, and mitigation efforts that will culminate in the risk management plan and risk control during execution. The leadership should establish the scope of risk management for the project (e.g., objective, methods, measures, assumptions, etc.). Roles and responsibilities should also be identified; this may include identifying a risk study team. The scope must be aligned with the strategic asset requirements and project implementation basis (see Sections 3.1 and 4.1, respectively) and with the current asset or project scope definition (see Sections 3.2 and 7.1).

Planning for risk management is facilitated when the enterprise has a project system that establishes guidelines for when and how risk management is to be applied and provides capabilities for the process (i.e., methods, tools, and resources).

Risk management is applicable to all enterprises and all asset or project life cycle stages. Risk assessment, analysis, and mitigation efforts studies are typically applied in a phased manner consistent with the project scope development phases described in Section 7.1.

During planning, it is especially important to understand the interrelated nature of value engineering (Section 7.5) and risk management. Changes to plans to address value issues affect risk and vice-versa. Therefore, as indicated in the process map in Section 2.4, the value engineering and risk management processes generally need to be revisited together.

Many individuals on the strategic asset or project team may be involved in the risk management process. Diversity of the risk management team is strongly encouraged, with participation by stakeholders and end users. However, risk management success is facilitated by having experienced cost management personnel coordinate the process because it is so closely linked to the other strategic asset and project control planning processes.

Management support of the risk management process is vital to ensure that all the necessary resources are made available and are committed to the success of the process. Also, the project team must clearly understand management's risk tolerance (i.e., willingness to accept or desire to avoid risks).

While the risk management process presented here appears somewhat mechanistic, experience and judgment, supported by good historical data about risk factors, are essential to effective risk management.

.2 Identify and Assess Risk Factors

Once the process has been planned, the risk study team identifies asset or project risk factors for analysis. Risk factors (or drivers) are events and conditions that may influence or drive uncertainty (i.e., either opportunities or threats) in asset or project performance. They may be inherent characteristics or conditions of the asset or project or external influences, events, or conditions such as weather or economic conditions.

Checklists or databases of common risk factors may be developed and used to facilitate this risk factor identification step. Checklists and similar tools are generally based on project historical data. For example, research of industry historical data has shown that one of the most significant project risk factors is having a poor level of project scope definition and planning. However, other risk factors may be unique to the asset or project; therefore, input from the entire project team about its risk perceptions should be obtained using creative processes such as brainstorming or other facilitated risk assessment meetings.

The output of this step is a list of potential risk factors or drivers. The list will generally include brief descriptions of each factor. Risk factors are also often classified by type. A common assessment classification is whether the project team can or cannot control the occurrence of the risk factor. For example, the project team cannot control the weather, but it can control the level of scope definition. For the weather, the project team can only mitigate impacts. However, for scope definition, the team can mitigate the risk factor itself (i.e., improve project definition before implementing the project control plan).

.3 Quantify Risk Factor Impacts

Once the risk factors have been identified, their quantitative impact on the asset or project plans is analyzed by the study team. Methods of quantification include (but are not limited to) subjective risk study team assessments (e.g., rating each factor's impact as high, medium, or low), manual estimates of the impact of each factor or group of factors, or complex simulation or parametric models.

There are two key challenges for risk analysis. First, the impacts of some risk factors are difficult to imagine or estimate, even for the most experienced project teams. Second, even if individual risk factors are understood, it is difficult to understand the interaction of risk factors (Is the occurrence of one risk factor dependent on the occurrence of others? Are risk factor impacts added or compounded?). Parametric modeling is one method that helps address these challenges. Parametric models are typically multi-variable regressions of historical risk factors versus actual project outcomes. Regression empirically quantifies the impact while allowing the dependency of risk factors to be examined. Regression models also provide useful probabilistic outputs, and results are replicable. There are also proprietary commercial project risk analysis systems available that help address the risk analysis challenges.

Simulation models can be created from project cost estimates, schedules, and any other plan component that can be expressed quantitatively. Monte Carlo simulations are often used because they provide probabilistic output that helps users understand the range of potential impacts of uncertainty on planned outcomes. However, if the simulation models are not empirically based, they tend not to adequately address the risk analysis challenges of properly addressing impacts and understanding risk factor interactions and dependencies.

The most robust risk analysis methods tend to combine subjective expert and team judgment and objective, empirical based modeling.

.4 Screen Risk Factors and Mitigate Impacts

Based on the understanding gained from initial risk analyses, the team should mitigate risk factors and/or their impacts and reduce uncertainty by identifying and analyzing project scope and planning alternatives that reduce risk without reducing the value of project outcomes. The risk factors of each mitigation alternative are then analyzed until the project team selects the project plan alternative to be implemented. In other words, risk analysis is done iteratively with risk mitigation.

As was mentioned, one of the most significant project risk factors is having a poor level of project scope definition and planning. Therefore, a common risk mitigation alternative is for the project team to continue with project planning until the project scope and plans are better defined. Most project systems establish guidelines for expected levels of scope definition.

Mitigating risks through alternative scope and plan development can be costly and time consuming. Therefore it may be useful to screen the risk factors to identify those for which mitigation efforts are most justified. Risk factors may be screened based on their properties, which include (but are not limited to) the following:

a. *Impact.* The cost, schedule, or other quantitative outcome of the risk factor.
b. *Probability.* The likelihood that a risk factor will occur. This may be based on an explicit or intuitive assessment and is often expressed as a measure from 0 to 100 percent.
c. *Immediacy.* The probability that the occurrence of a risk factor will vary over the life cycle of the asset or project, and the relative influence of the factor at any given time. Risk factors that gradually reveal themselves may be more amenable to mitigation than sudden events.

Figure 7.6-2 illustrates a common type of risk factor screening matrix. Risk mitigation is generally focused on those risk factors with both high impact and probability.

IMPACT	RISK FACTOR PROBABILITY OF OCCURRENCE	
	LOW	HIGH
LOW	Ignore these risk factors.	Analyze and manage where justified. Monitor where appropriate.
HIGH	Analyze and manage where justified. Monitor where appropriate.	**Focus effort to identify alternatives that eliminate this factor, reduce its probability of occurring, and/or reduce its impact. Monitor these factors.**

Figure 7.6-2. A Risk Factor Screening Matrix

.5 Develop a Risk Management Plan

As was mentioned, risk factors of each project scope and plan alternative are analyzed until the project team selects an alternative with acceptable risks for implementation. A risk management plan is then developed for this alternative in alignment with the project implementation basis (see Section 4.1). The risk management plan is part of the project control baseline plans (see Section 8.1).

The risk management plan will include plans for monitoring a project for the occurrence of key risk factors. The plan may also include optional contingency action plans for how the project team might respond to specific risk factors that might occur. For example, if a risk factor is the availability of people with a particular skill, the risk management plan may stipulate that, if fewer than a certain number of skilled people reply to a job posting (i.e., a threshold limit), a predetermined incentive pay program will be instituted.

Other project plans may incorporate aspects of risk management as well. For example, the project budget and schedule may include contingency allowances as discussed in the following section.

.6 Analyze Contingency

Contingency is an amount added to an estimate (of cost, time, or other planned resource) to allow for items, conditions, or events for which the state, occurrence, and/or effect is uncertain and that experience shows will likely result, in aggregate, in additional cost.[58]

The change management process (see Section 10.3) is used to incorporate changes in the project scope definition and baseline plans; contingency management is part of that process. In change management, if a project team takes an approved corrective action (within the project scope) that will cost more or less than the amount budgeted for the affected cost accounts, or will take more or less time than planned for affected activities, then budgeted funds or float, as approved, may be shifted from or to the contingency budget or float as appropriate.

Contingency analysis (a sub-step of risk analysis) quantifies the risk factor impacts after all mitigation efforts are complete. The team should guard against assumptions that the mitigation efforts will be entirely successful—or successful at all. Many mitigation efforts, themselves, can introduce additional variation in results that should be accounted for. The amount of contingency included in control plans depends in part on management's willingness to accept risk. The less risk that management is willing to accept that the project will overrun its budget or schedule, the more contingency that will be included in the control plans.

The risk management plan should document management's willingness to accept risk or desire to avoid it. If modeling techniques that produce probabilistic outcomes are used to quantify risk factor impacts, then the documentation of management's willingness to accept risk can be expressed simply as management's desired percentage confidence that the project will not overrun its budget or schedule (e.g., 50 percent confidence).

Contingency is normally controlled by the project team because experience shows that contingency will likely be required by the project. However, management may request that additional risk allowances be considered in the plans for objectives that it establishes. These allowances, typically controlled by management, are called reserves.

.7 Control Risk Factors and Impacts

After the project control plan is implemented (see Section 8.1), risk factors and impacts are monitored and measured in accordance with the risk management plan (see Section 10.1). If a monitored risk factor occurs or a risk impact threshold limit is crossed, then contingency action plans may be implemented or other corrective actions taken as appropriate. These changes are managed using the change management process (see Section 10.3). In some cases, further risk assessment, analysis, and mitigation may be required for changes, if performance trends occur, or new risk factors otherwise arise.

At the close of the project, historical data regarding risk factors and their impacts are captured in the project historical database (see Section 10.4).

.8 Develop and Maintain Methods and Tools.

Risk management uses a variety of methods (e.g., parametric or simulation models) and tools (e.g., risk factor checklists, report templates, etc.) that are developed and maintained. Historical risk factor

---

[58] AACE International Recommended Practices and Standards, *Standard Cost Engineering Terminology (10S-90)*, AACE International, Morgantown, WV.

occurrence and impacts, risk management approaches, and results are key resources for creating risk management methods and tools.

7.6.3 Inputs to Risk Management

.1 Strategic Asset Requirements and Project Implementation Basis. (see Sections 3.1 and 4.1). These define the basis asset scope, objectives, constraints, and assumptions, including basic assumptions about risks.

.2 Asset or Project Scope. (see Sections 3.2 and 7.1). Deliverables (asset options, work breakdown structure, work packages, and execution strategy) that define the current asset or project scope. Risk factors may be inherent characteristics or conditions of the asset or project scope. Scope changes (see Section 10.3) for which risk assessment and analysis will be applied also channel through the scope development process.

.3 Planning Information. (see Sections 3.2, 3.3, 7.1–7.5, 7.7). All planning components may be subject to risk factors that must be assessed. Also, alternate plans may be considered to mitigate risk factor impacts. Results from Value Engineering (7.5) are particularly important to assess.

.4 Cost, Schedule, and Resource Information. (see Sections 7.2, 7.3, 7.4). The quantification of risk factor impacts employs the methods and tools of the respective planning processes. Risk analysis is iterative with the other planning processes.

.5 Risk Performance Assessment. (see Sections 6.1 and 10.1). In the performance assessment processes, the asset or project status is monitored for the occurrence of risk factors. New risk factors identified during asset operation or project execution may require updated risk management planning.

.6 Change Information and Contingency Management. (see Section 10.3). During project execution, changes to the baseline scope definition and plans are identified in the change management process. In some cases, further risk assessment and analysis may be required for changes and trends. Additional contingency may be required to address changes and performance trends.

.7 Historical Information. (see Sections 6.3 and 10.4). Past risk factor occurrence and impacts, risk management approaches, and results are key resources for understanding asset and project uncertainty and for creating risk management methods and tools.

7.6.4 Outputs from Risk Management

.1 Cost, Schedule, and Resource Information (including Contingency). (see Sections 7.2, 7.3, 7.4). The quantification of risk factor impacts employs the methods and tools of the respective planning processes. Contingency is incorporated in project plans as appropriate.

.2 Planning Basis Information. (see Sections 3.2, 3.3, 7.1, 7.2, 7.3, 7.4, 7.5, 7.7). Alternate concepts and plans may be considered to mitigate risk factor impacts. Ultimately, one alternative is selected as the asset or project planning basis. It is particularly important to determine the extent that alternate concepts may affect value (Section 7.5).

.3 Risk Management Plan. (see Section 8.1). This plan becomes part of the overall project control plan that is implemented. A risk management plan may also be developed for non-project asset investment decision actions (see Section 3.3).

.4 Change Information and Contingency Management. (see Sections 6.2 and 10.3). Findings from risk assessment and analysis may influence the management of changes and contingency.

.5 Historical Information. (see Sections 6.3 and 10.4). Risk management approaches are key resources for future planning and methods development. Historical risk outcomes are reported from the asset and project performance assessment processes.

7.6.5 Key Concepts and Terminology for Risk Management

.1 Risk. (See Section 7.6.1.1).
.2 Uncertainty–Opportunities & Threats. (See Section 7.6.1.1).
.3 Risk Factors (or drivers). (See Section 7.6.2.2).

.4 Risk Assessment. (See Section 7.6.2.3).
.5 Risk Analysis. (See Section 7.6.2.3).
.6 Simulation and Modeling. (See Section 7.6.2.3).
.7 Risk Factor Properties. (See Section 7.6.2.4).
.8 Risk Factor Screening. (See Section 7.6.2.4).
.9 Risk Mitigation. (See Section 7.6.2.4).
.10 Risk Management Plan (See Section 7.6.2.5).
.11 Contingency Action Plans. (See Section 7.6.2.5).
.12 Contingency. (See Section 7.6.2.6).
.13 Risk Control. (See Section 7.6.2.7).

Further Readings and Sources

This process is based on and is conceptually consistent with risk management steps identified in AACE "International's Risk Management Dictionary" (see reference detail below). There are many other references describing risk analysis, management, and related practices for various asset and project types in various industries. Risk and decision analysis are often covered in the same texts. The following references provide basic information and will lead to more detailed treatments:

- AACE International. "Risk Management Dictionary," *Cost Engineering*, vol. 37, no. 10 (October 1995).
- Amos, Scott J., Editor. *Skills and Knowledge of Cost Engineering*, 5th ed. Morgantown, WV: AACE International, 2004.
- Ayyub, Bilal M. *Risk Analysis in Engineering and Economics*. Boca Raton, FL: Chapman & Hall/CRC, 2003.
- Curran, Michael W., Editor. *Professional Practice Guide No. 2: Risk*. CD ROM. Morgantown, WV: AACE International, 1998.
- Molak, Vlasta. *Fundamentals of Risk Analysis and Risk Management*, Boca Raton, FL: CRC Press/St Lucie, 1996.
- Schuyler, John R. *Risk and Decision Analysis in Projects*, 2nd ed. Upper Darby, PA: Project Management Institute, 2001.
- Uppal, Kul B., Editor. *Professional Practice Guide No. 8: Contingency*. CD ROM. Morgantown, WV: AACE International, 2001.

7.7 Procurement Planning

7.7.1 Description

Procurement planning is that part of the project control planning process that ensures that information about resources (e.g., labor, material, etc.) as required for project control is identified for, incorporated in, and obtained through the procurement process. The TCM process map does not explicitly include the procurement process. As with engineering, construction, programming, and similar functions involved with project execution, TCM only addresses the project control interface with procurement. The term *procurement* is used here in the broad sense of the collective functions that obtain labor, services, materials, tools, and other resources.

Asset owners usually obtain most of the labor, materials, and other resources used in projects from outside enterprises. These outside enterprises typically include vendors and fabricators for materials and contractors for labor. Even when the asset owner obtains resources from within their own enterprise, the project team's control of the internal resource supplying organization may be limited. In all these cases, procuring needed resources from these suppliers and contractors (and their suppliers in the *supply chain*) requires extra effort to plan and establish agreements. There are also additional concerns with assuring that other parties have acceptable values regarding society, ethics, environment, health and safety, and so on because problems with one party in this regard are likely to affect others with whom they have relationships (see Sections 11.1 and 11.2).

The relationship of suppliers and contractors with the project team, or between suppliers and contractors involved in the project, is defined by contracts, purchase orders, or other legal or procedural documents or agreements. Therefore, in order to institute a project control process, all interfaces of the suppliers and contractors with the project control process must be defined and established in the agreements that we refer to here as *contracts*. Contract clauses that define project control interfaces must be included in the overall project plan.

For project control, suppliers and contractors must be obligated to provide cost, resource, and schedule information as needed to plan the project (i.e., they may develop all or part of the project estimate and schedule), measure progress of the work, support change management, and support historical database needs. Payment methods to the suppliers and contractors and methods for resolving disputes with and between them must also be defined. The goal of procurement planning then is to ensure that labor, materials, tools, and consumables that are obtained from or through suppliers are obtained in a way that optimally achieves project objectives and requirements.

Interface between procurement and project control begins in the scope development process (Section 7.1) where the work breakdown structure, organizational breakdown structure (OBS), work packages and execution strategy are developed. The execution strategy identifies general approaches through which the work packages and activities will be performed, including the role of suppliers and contractors. As regards procurement, the primary execution strategy decisions involve determining the type of contracts to be used for various elements of the work. The decisions are based on a variety of factors such as the status of scope development, the owner's project control capability, perceived risks and *risk allocation* strategies, prevailing purchasing and contracting practices, and so on. Each contract type (e.g., lump sum, unit price, time and materials, cost-plus, etc.) has specific risk and project control interface implications.

For example, lump sum contracts are generally used when scope development is well advanced and design changes are unlikely, and/or when the owner has limited project control capability. Reimbursable or unit price contract types are used more often when the scope is less well developed, new technology is involved, and/or the owner has better project control capability (i.e., better able to measure and assess progress and direct corrective actions).

As was mentioned, suppliers and contractors must be obligated to provide cost, resource, and schedule information as needed for project control. Each supplier and contractor should be required to use a common chart of accounts at the information flow interfaces (i.e., they may use their own accounts internally, but they should use the common accounts for progress reports, billings, etc.). This facilitates project control and cooperation between all parties.

For planning and scheduling, suppliers and contractors generally prepare their own detailed plans and schedules, but any applicable milestones that are required by the overall schedule must be a contracted requirement. For costs, bid, and change order pricing, cost reports, billings, and other submittals should be in accordance with the project WBS/OBS and common chart of accounts (which is made part of the contract) to the level of detail needed to measure and assess the participant's progress and to capture in historical databases. Likewise, estimated and installed labor hour and material quantity information should be reported per the chart of accounts. Also as was mentioned, the owner must establish in the contract requirements for payment methods and timing, change management, and dispute resolution.

At the conclusion of the procurement planning process, all requirements for project control deliverables (e.g., schedule data, cost and progress reports, closeout data, etc.) from the suppliers and contractors and project control procedures they must follow will be incorporated in contracts as appropriate. Likewise, all the project control information (e.g., milestones, chart of accounts, etc.) that is needed by the suppliers and contractors will be incorporated in the contracts as well.

Project procurement planning may be affected by decisions made at a strategic asset management level (Section 2.3) when the enterprise has established relationships with key suppliers and contractors to support project work. In that case, business management of the enterprise will communicate strategic procurement planning requirements to the project team as appropriate (Section 4.1).

Procurement planning is facilitated by having a database of historical procurement data. These data should include past experiences with suppliers and contractors and the contract approaches used. Development and maintenance of procurement planning tools (e.g., checklists, standard procedures, contract terms, etc.) is also a step in the process. A standard chart of accounts, along with the WBS/OBS, facilitates procurement planning by establishing ways for all suppliers to consistently categorize and exchange project control information.

Procurement planning is a team effort. The team includes the project manager or project leader, the project control leads (e.g., estimating, scheduling, etc.), purchasing, contracting and legal personnel, and the managers or coordinators of the work that will be done by vendors, suppliers, and contractor officers. Because much of procurement planning involves issues of information flow between project participants, having an information technology person on the team is often desirable. Generally, the project control leader, in close cooperation with the purchasing and contracting functional leaders, leads the procurement planning effort as covered here. However, everyone on the project team with interface roles with suppliers or contractors should have input to and buy-in for the procurement planning aspects of the project control plans.

7.7.2 Process Map for Procurement Planning

At its core, procurement planning involves studying the capabilities of various resource providers and alternate procurement approaches, and establishing project control requirements for the relationships established. Historical information including lessons learned is a valuable asset in determining the best approaches. Figure 7.7-1 illustrates the process map for procurement planning.

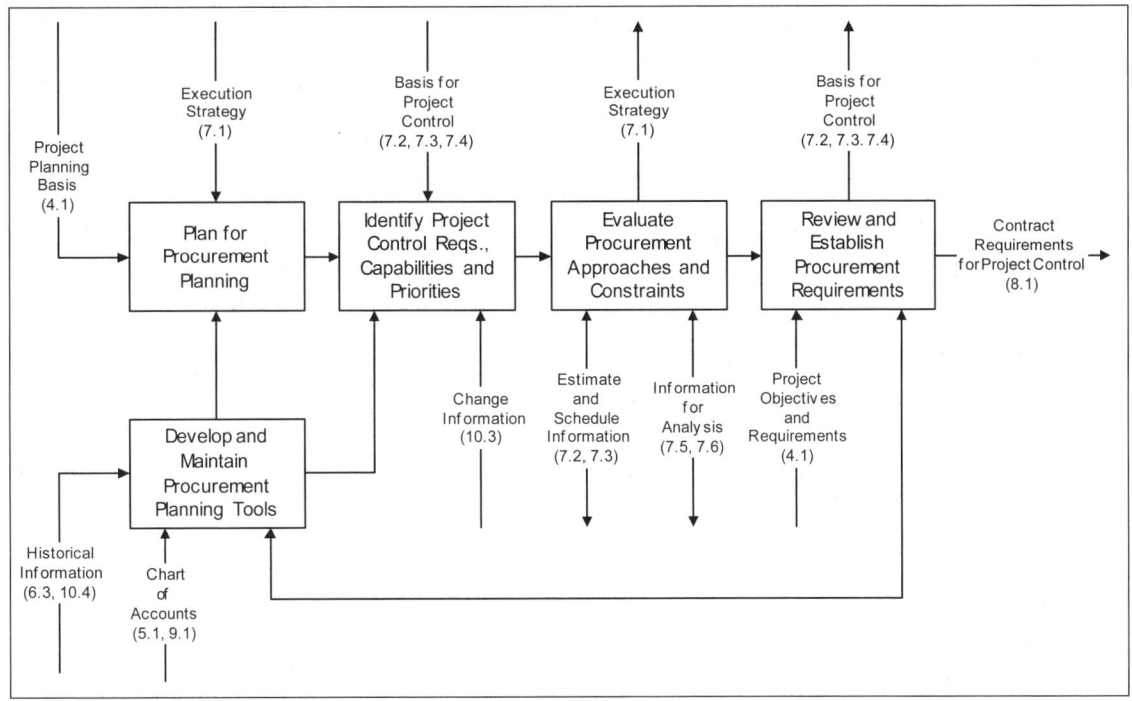

Figure 7.7.1 Process Map for Procurement Planning

The following sections briefly describe the steps in the procurement planning process.

.1 Plan for Procurement Planning

The procurement planning process requires activities and resources, so the work to be performed during the process needs to be planned. The project team identifies procurement planning tools that will facilitate the process, and the team assesses past project experience for lessons learned. Project requirements and initial execution strategies must also be considered.

.2 Identify Project Control Requirements, Capabilities, and Priorities

Based on initial overall project control plans (estimates and schedules), the initial execution strategy, and the scope of proposed changes, basic supplier, and contractor project control requirements are identified and prioritized. In addition, the project control capabilities of the project team need to be prioritized and evaluated.

.3 Evaluate Procurement Approaches and Constraints

Various approaches for establishing contract project control requirements for the various project suppliers and contractors need to be evaluated for their affect on project control plans and execution strategy. The affect of various procurement approaches on estimated cost and schedule (e.g., when to procure) also are evaluated. Opportunities to increase project value, reduce risks, and effectively allocate risks should also be assessed. The project control capabilities of the project team, suppliers, and contractors need to be considered.

.4 Review and Establish Procurement Requirements

The project team must review selected requirements for project control deliverables from the suppliers and contractors, and the project control procedures that they must follow. Likewise, all the project control information needed by the suppliers and contractors must be reviewed. The review ensures that project objectives and requirements are met. Resource planning outputs (e.g., resource expenditure charts based on resource loaded schedules, recruitment and training plans, etc.) are reviewed by the project team to determine whether they are complete and suitable as a basis for planning, whether they meet project objectives and requirements, and whether they are competitive with industry best practices and historical approaches.

.5 Develop and Maintain Procurement Planning Methods and Tools

Standard contract terms, procedures, and other tools for procurement planning must be created and maintained. Past project data (including project procurement approaches, suppliers and contractors used, and experiences with the same) must also be collected and maintained. Historical information and lessons learned are a key resource for evaluating the approach to use on future projects.

7.7.3 Inputs to Procurement Planning

.1 *Project Planning Basis (Objectives, Constraints, and Assumptions).* The enterprise may establish requirements for procurement planning such as the use of pre-selected vendors, alliance partners, and so on (see Section 4.1).
.2 *Changes.* During project execution, changes to the baseline project plans are identified in the change management process (see Section 10.3). Each change goes through the procurement planning process so that project control aspects can be appropriately integrated into contracts and project control plans. The change management process also concerns dealing with disputes and claims.
.3 *Basis for Project Control.* The integrated schedule, cost, and resource plans (Sections 7.2, 7.2, and 7.4) define the project control basis and requirements for the project.
.4 *Estimate and Schedule Information.* As alternate procurement approaches and requirements are assessed, the estimate and schedule effects are evaluated. The results of the evaluation support the procurement assessment. In addition, cost and schedule information provided by suppliers and contractors during the project control and procurement process is input for evaluation.
.5 *Execution Strategy.* Scope and execution strategy development (see Section 7.1) define how the project work will be implemented (i.e., the general approaches through which the work packages and activities will be performed). The strategy will generally specify the general contractual approaches to be used; however, it does not include the specific tactics, which are developed in procurement planning.
.6 *Chart of Accounts.* Coding structures that support the accounting and cost/schedule integration processes (see Sections 5.1 and 9.1) are provided. Each supplier will generally have its own chart of accounts; therefore, coordination requires that suppliers and contractors *map* their accounts to the one that is contractually required so that cost and schedule information can be exchanged.
.7 *Historical Project Information.* Past project procurement approaches, suppliers used, lessons learned, claims experience, and similar information is used to support future project procurement planning.
.8 *Information for Analysis.* Procurement planning is iterative with the other project planning steps including value analysis and engineering and risk management (see Sections 7.5 and 7.6, respectively). These analytical processes may identify changes in procurement plans that will increase value and/or reduce risks.

7.7.4 Outputs from Procurement Planning

.1 *Basis for Project Control.* Procurement requirements, as they affect the integrated schedule, cost, and resource plans (Sections 7.2, 7.3, and 7.4), are integrated into the project control basis.
.2 *Estimate and Schedule Information.* The results of procurement approach and requirements assessment are inputs to the planning and scheduling and estimating and budgeting processes (Sections 7.2 and 7.3).
.3 *Execution Strategy.* The results of procurement approach assessment are inputs to execution strategy development (Section 7.1).
.4 *Contract Requirements for Project Control.* All requirements for project control deliverables (e.g., schedule files, cost and progress reports, closeout data, etc.) from the suppliers and contractors and

project control procedures they must follow will be incorporated in contracts and purchase orders as appropriate. Likewise, all the project control information (e.g., milestones, chart of accounts, etc.) needed by the suppliers and contractors will be incorporated in the contracts as well.

7.7.5 Key Concepts for Procurement Planning

The following concepts and terminology described in this and other sections are particularly important to understanding the procurement planning process of TCM:

.1 *Procurement.* The acquisition (and directly related matters) of equipment, material, and services by such means as purchasing, renting, leasing (including real property), contracting, or bartering, but not by seizure, condemnation, or donation. Includes preparation of inquiry packages, requisitions, and bid evaluations; purchase order and contract award and documentation; and expediting, inspection, reporting, and evaluation of vendor or contractor performance.

.2 *Supplier.* A manufacturer, fabricator, distributor, or vendor that supplies materials, products, or goods for a project or for production. There may be some limited services associated with the supply of material or goods (e.g., technical support). Suppliers also generically applies to any internal resource suppliers that are not in the project team's direct control (i.e., with whom agreements must be established).

.3 *Contract.* A formal agreement between the project owner and resource suppliers or between project resource suppliers. Contracts also include purchase orders, work orders, and similar documents that establish working agreements. Procurement planning established the project control requirements to be incorporated in the contracts.

.4 *Contractor.* A business entity that enters into a contract(s) to provide services to another party. There may be some materials, products, or goods associated with the contracted service (e.g., construction services often include the provision of materials of construction).

Further Readings and Sources

There are many references describing procurement and contracting practices for various project types in various industries. However, procurement planning, as addressed by the process in this section, is generally covered in project management and control texts. The following references provide basic information and will lead to more detailed treatments.

- Amos, Scott, J. *Skills and Knowledge of Cost Engineering*, 5th ed. Morgantown, WV: AACE International, 2004.
- Fleming, Quentin W. *Project Procurement Management: Contracting, Subcontracting, Teaming.* Tustin, CA: FMC Press, 2003.
- Gransberg, Douglas D. and Keith Molenaar, Editors. *Professional Practice Guide (PPG) #10: Project Delivery Methods*. Morgantown, WV: AACE International, 2001.
- Heinze, Kurt. *Cost Management of Capital Projects*. New York: Marcel Dekker, 1996.
- Stukhart, George. *Construction Materials Management*. New York: Marcel Dekker, 1995.
- Zack Jr., James G., Editor. *Professional Practice Guide (PPG) #1: Contracts and Claims*. Morgantown, WV: AACE International, 2000.

CHAPTER 8

PROJECT CONTROL PLAN IMPLEMENTATION

8.1 Project Control Plan Implementation

8.1.1 Description

Project control plan implementation is the process of integrating all aspects of the project control plan; validating that the plans are comprehensive and consistent with requirements and ready for control; initiating mechanisms or systems for project control; and communicating the integrated project control plan to those responsible for the project's work packages. This process initiates project control for the current project phase for which work has been authorized by the project implementation process (Section 4.1). For example, control plans may be implemented at the start of each successive planning phase and then again prior to the final execution phase.

.1 Control Accounts

A key concept for project control plan implementation is the *control account* that functionally integrates the project control plan components (i.e., cost, schedule, resources, risk, and procurement). The control account relates directly to a work package component from the work breakdown structure (WBS) for which responsibility has been assigned (in accordance with the organizational breakdown structure [OBS] and the procurement plan), and for which cost budgets and resources have been assigned, and activities scheduled. However, a control account may include one or more work packages that are in the same branch of the WBS hierarchy and for which the same person in the OBS is responsible. Figure 8.1-1 illustrates the control account concept at the project execution phase.

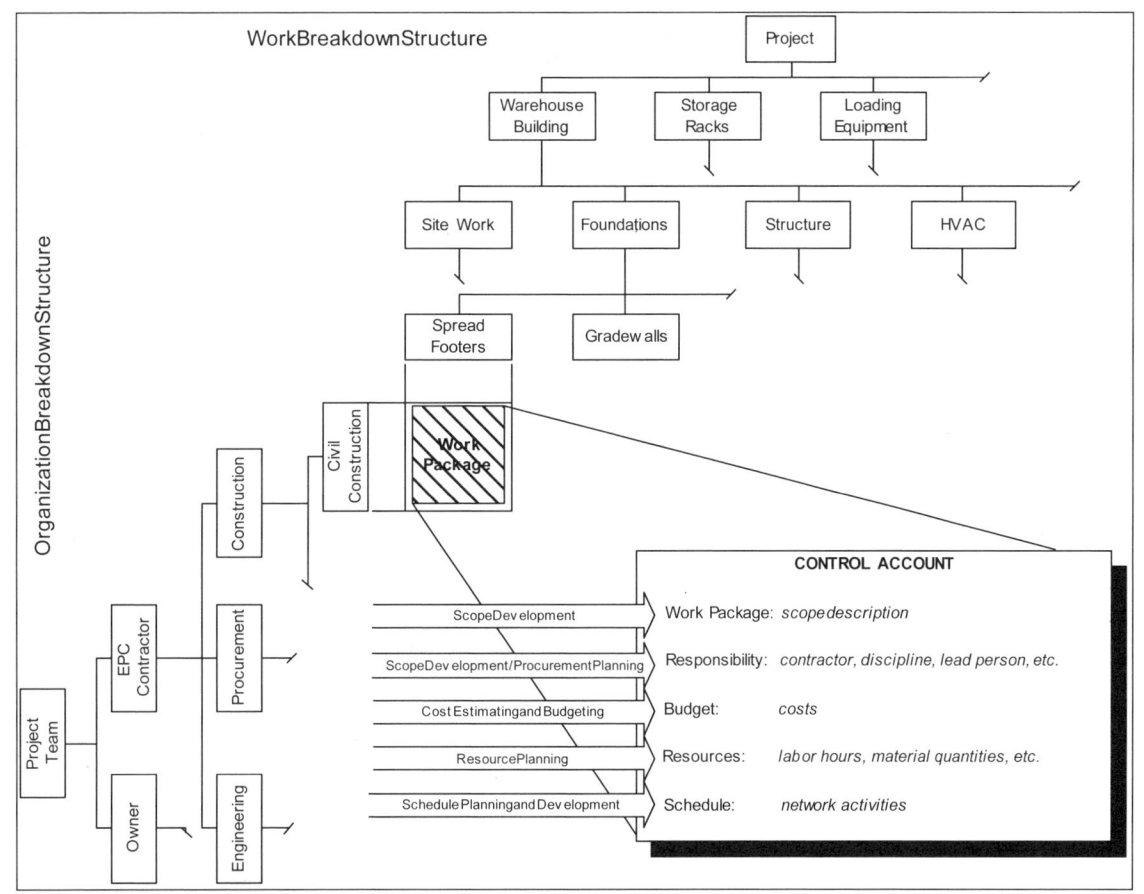

Figure 8.1-1 Example of the Control Account Concept

.2 Phased Control

As discussed in Section 4.1, the *project implementation* process uses *phases* and *gates* wherein a gate review is conducted at the end of each phase that results in updated direction (i.e., a decision to proceed to the next phase, request for additional work or information, or a halt to the project) and resource authorizations (i.e., phased project funding). After funds for a phase are authorized, the work for that phase usually begins in earnest. Therefore, a key concept for project control plan implementation is *phased control,* which recognizes that project control must start when work begins for a project phase. Implementation of project control cannot wait until the start of execution phase.[59]

For example, project control planning for the project execution phase (e.g., detailed engineering and construction) is performed during the preliminary design phase, and planning for the control of the preliminary design phase during the conceptual phase. Because the scope of work during the early phases is usually limited in extent (e.g., first or second level of the WBS, few people on the project team, few material purchases or contracts, etc.), project control planning is a simpler process than for the later execution phase when most of the work will be done.

8.1.2 Process Map for Project Control Plan Implementation

Figure 8.1-2 illustrates the process map for project control plan implementation. The primary inputs are control plan components and the primary outputs are control accounts, which are part of an integrated basis for project control for the next phase of work.

As was discussed, this process and the other project control planning processes are applied in a phased manner as project work is implemented (Section 4.1). Also, the input from the change management process (Section 10.3) is intended to illustrate that changes to the project control plan basis may be made that require implementation of a "revised" control plan. Implementations driven by changes follow the basic process but, depending on the scope of the changes, mid-phase implementation is usually quick with less effort. For mid-phase changes, the words "Maintain" or "Revise" apply to the steps rather than "Develop." However, the importance of communicating plan revisions to the project team is no less than for the initial plan implementation.

---

[59] For a well planned project, it is not uncommon for 5 to 10 percent of the project funds to be expended prior to the start of execution (e.g., prior to detailed engineering and construction). Unfortunately, in a misguided effort to reduce early "expenses," management may expect control planning for execution to wait until the start of the execution phase (e.g., wait until the contractor submits its plans). The result is increased risk of project failure because extensive early execution work is done without the benefit of control based on full understanding of the execution work.

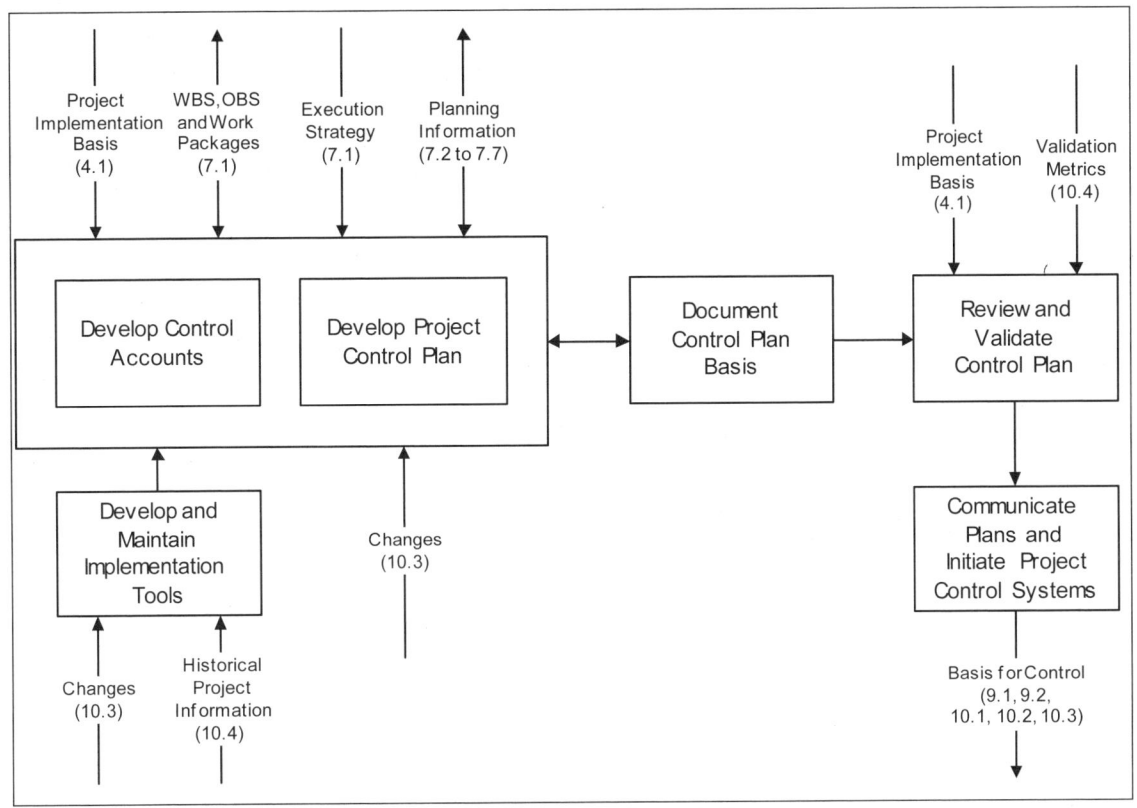

Figure 8.1-2 Process Map for Project Control Plan Implementation

The following sections briefly describe the steps in the project control plan implementation process.

.1 Develop Control Accounts

At the start of the process, the control accounts (see Section 8.1.1.1) are developed by the project control person or team. The process is generally more iterative with the various project control planning processes (Section 7.1 to 7.6) than indicated by Figure 8.1-2. As indicated by the "feedback" arrows, as the control accounts are developed, improvements to various aspects of the control plan may be made. Also, as discussed, if the process is initiated by a change, then control accounts are "maintained," rather than developed.

.2 Develop Project Control Plan

While control accounts functionally integrate the working aspects of the plan's components, a control plan procedure is also developed to communicate the plan. This deliverable is part of an overall project execution plan (PEP) that describes specific approaches that each functional entity (engineering, procurement, construction, safety, quality, etc.) will use. The project control plan is part of the PEP. The PEP is an extension of the execution strategy defined during scope development (Section 7.1).

The control plan describes specific systems and approaches to be used in project control. The plan is more of a narrative or qualitative representation (i.e., a communication tool) of the project control plan, while the control accounts, estimate, schedule, and so on represent the quantitative aspects.

The control plan will also outline both the control systems and the reports to be used. The control systems will have policies, procedures, and other aspects that guide and support effective project control.

.3 Document Control Plan Basis

The basis of the control plan components (i.e., cost, schedule, resources, risk, and procurement) and control accounts must be documented. This document describes how the control plan component was developed and defines the information used in support of that development. This document commonly includes, but is not limited to, a description of the scope included, methodologies used, references and defining deliverables used, assumptions and exclusions made, clarifications, adjustments, and some indication of the level of uncertainty. The basis of the plans and accounts must be well defined so that proposed changes can be evaluated to determine if there really is a change, and if so, to what extent (Section 10.3).

.4 Review and Validate Control Plan

The project control plan, control accounts, and documentation are reviewed by the project team to determine whether they are complete and suitable as a manageable basis for control, whether they meet project objectives and requirements, and whether they are competitive with industry best practices and historical approaches (i.e., validation). A useful tool for reviews is a readiness checklist for the project control function that helps assess that all aspects of the plan are complete and ready for implementation in all regards.

It is a challenge to develop "manageable" control accounts and systems. If measuring, reporting, and/or assessing control data is too burdensome (e.g., too detailed, frequent, difficult to understand, etc.), the process can stop working effectively (i.e., "analysis paralysis") and/or those responsible for the work will find ways to work around the project control system. Conversely, if the information is not detailed or frequent enough, or tools are inadequate, the control exercise can also become meaningless. Either way, the project is at risk for getting out of control. A good way to help determine if project control plans and accounts will be "manageable" is to develop and maintain standards and/or templates for successful approaches based on historical practices as captured in a historical database (Section 10.4).

Validation is applied specifically to plans to assess whether the plan results are appropriate and achieve the performance objectives. Validation usually involves benchmarking, which is a process that compares practices, processes, and relevant measures to those of a selected basis of comparison (i.e., the benchmark) with the goal of improving performance. The comparison basis includes internal or external best practices, processes, or measures. In validation, the "relevant measures" used are referred to as metrics; these metrics are developed in the project historical database management process (Section 10.4). While each plan element is usually reviewed and validated separately as it is developed; the project team should review and validate the integrated plan as a whole before implementation.

.5 Communicate and Initiate Project Control Systems

Those responsible for work packages must understand the project control plans and their control accounts. Those responsible for interfaces with the project control process (e.g., business accounting and financing) also need to understand those aspects of the project control plan that affect them. The PEP, including the project control plan, facilitates understanding; however, training may be required in the roles and the tasks that various responsible parties need to perform in support of project control.

If the responsibility for a work package lies with a supplier or contractor, the procurement planning process (Section 7.7) will have defined all the interfaces of the suppliers and contractors with the project control process. Suppliers, sub-contractors, and contractors generally prepare their own control plans and control accounting. However, these must be consistent with the overall control plans and control accounting to the extent required by the contract.

Once all parties are ready for control, the project control leader integrates the plans into mechanisms or systems for control. Information technology tools are at the core of the systems including software for scheduling, cost/schedule reporting, and project cost accounting as well as working databases used for or interfacing with this software. Initially the databases will contain the budgeted value, schedule, and resource data (these working databases are generally separate from the historical databases described in Section 10.4). As the project progresses, actual measured data are captured for assessment against the plans. At implementation, information security mechanisms must be established to control who may enter, change, delete, view, or otherwise use data and information in or from the database. In addition, the interaction/interface of owner, supplier, and contractor systems must be considered and resolved.

At the conclusion of project control plan implementation, the project control plan will have been documented and communicated to the project team, those responsible for work packages will understand their control responsibilities and their control accounts, and project control systems and tools will be set up and ready to support the project control measurement (Sections 9.1 and 9.2), performance assessment (Section 10.1), forecasting (Section 10.2), and change management (Section 10.3) processes.

It is important to note that no resources or funds should be committed without appropriate plans, budgets, and authorizations, as communicated by an initiation process such as described in this section.

8.1.3 Inputs to Project Control Plan Implementation

.1 *Project Implementation Basis.* The project implementation process (see Section 4.1) provides the asset scope, objectives, constraints, and assumptions basis for the project, as well as authorizing funds and resources. The project control plan must be consistent with the requirements established for the project.
.2 *Execution Strategy.* This defines the general approaches through which the work packages will be performed (Section 7.1); the project control plan must be consistent with the agreed upon approaches.
.3 *WBS, OBS, and Work Packages.* These deliverables from the scope development process (Section 7.1) define the scope of and responsibility for the control accounts.
.4 *Planning Information.* Project planning provides information that is incorporated in the control accounts. Schedule activities are inputs from schedule planning and development (Section 7.2), budgeted costs are input from cost estimating and budgeting (Section 7.3), and resource quantities are inputs from resource planning (Section 7.4). While each planning process considers risk, the risk management plan (Section 7.6) is also a component of the project control plan. Procurement planning (Section 7.7) defines supplier and contractor requirements for project control planning and control accounting.
.5 *Changes.* During project execution, changes to the baseline scope definition and plans are identified in the change management process (see Section 10.3). Each change goes through the project control planning processes so that it can be appropriately integrated into the project control plans and accounts.
.6 *Validation Metrics.* Historically based benchmarks and metrics (Section 10.4) are used in the validation step.
.7 *Historical Project Information.* Successful past project control plans and control account approaches are commonly used as project control plan implementation references.

8.1.4 Outputs from Project Control Plan Implementation

.1 *Basis for Project Control.* The project control plan and control accounts are integrated into systems for control. Information technology tools are at the core of the systems including software for scheduling cost/schedule reporting and project accounting, as well as databases used for or interfacing with software. The basis for project control also includes policies, procedures, and other documents that guide and support effective project control.
.2 *WBS, OBS, and Work Packages.* As control accounts are developed, improvements may be identified.

.3 *Planning Information.* As control accounts are developed, improvements to any of the project control planning components may be identified.

8.1.5 Key Concepts for Project Control Plan Implementation

The following concepts and terminology described in this and other chapters are particularly important to understanding the project control implementation process of TCM:

.1 *Control Accounts.* (See Section 8.1.2.1 and Figure 8.1-1).
.2 *Project Control Plan.* (See Section 8.1.2.2).
.3 *Project Execution Plan (PEP).* (See Section 8.1.2.2).
.4 *Basis.* (See Section 8.1.2.3).
.5 *Validation.* (See Section 8.1.2.4).

Further Readings and Sources

Project control plan implementation is generally covered in project management, project control, and project planning and scheduling texts, and not as a subject in itself. It is included as a separate process in TCM to highlight the importance of assuring that all aspects of the project control plan are integrated and validated as a whole, a step that is sometimes overlooked in treatments that focus on separate project control functions.

CHAPTER 9

PROJECT CONTROL MEASUREMENT

9.1 Project Cost Accounting

9.1.1 Description

Project cost accounting refers to the process of measuring and reporting the commitment and expenditure of money on a project. The measurement of money is a function of traditional accounting and payroll processes and systems. Project costs are measured so that commitments and expenditures of funds can be compared to the budget, and the funds can be evaluated as to whether they are too much or too little in consideration of the extent that work packages have been completed. The TCM process map does not explicitly include the cost accounting process; it only addresses the project control interface with cost accounting.

The "accounting" process excludes the "performance" measurement process (Section 9.2), which covers the measurement of the degree of completion or status of work packages (e.g., the status of materials shipments and inventory, the extent that materials have been installed, achievement of schedule milestones, etc.). In terms of information technology (IT), the distinction between cost accounting and other measurements is increasingly less distinct as materials or enterprise resource planning (MRP and ERP) systems increasingly encompass the measurement of all resource and performance data. However, disregarding the IT integration, cost accounting practice remains a unique function in itself.

9.1.2 Process Map for Project Cost Accounting

The project cost accounting process illustrated in Figure 9.1-1 includes not only the measurement of costs, but the review, classification, and accounting of them for project control purposes. The process is integrated with performance measurement (see Section 9.2). The measured costs are inputs to the project performance assessment process (Section 10.1)

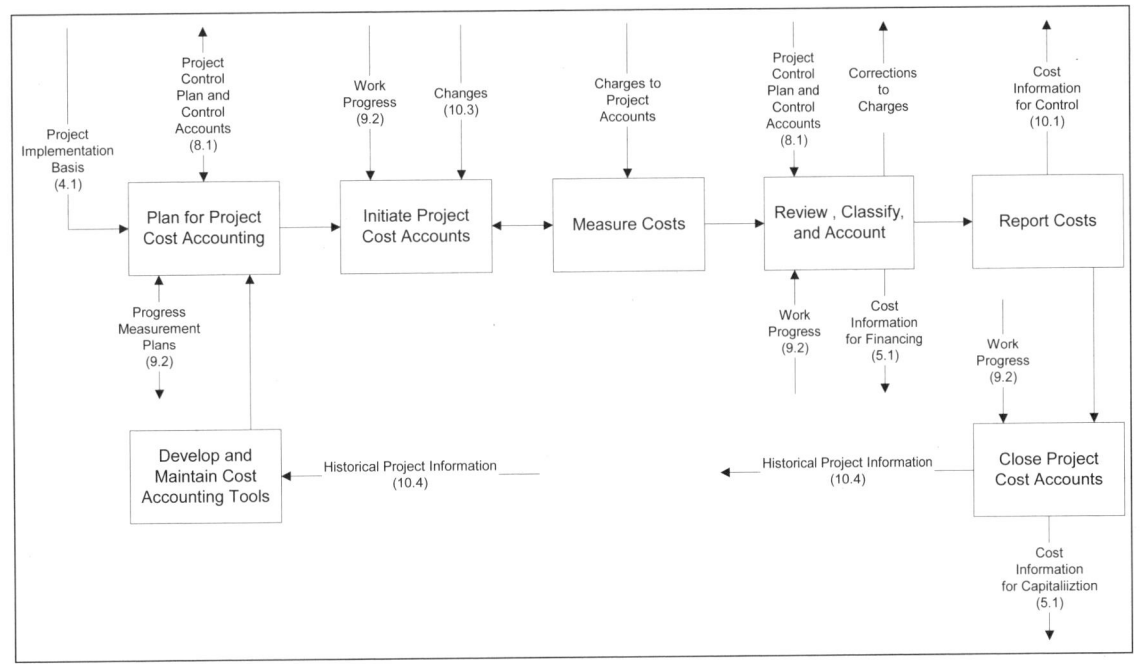

Figure 9.1-1 Process Map for Project Cost Accounting

The following sections briefly describe the steps in the project cost accounting process.

.1 Plan for Project Cost Accounting

The process for project cost accounting starts with planning for cost accounting. Initial planning starts with planning for the project scope and execution strategy development process (Section 7.1) and continues through development of control accounts during project control plan implementation (Section 8.1). Project control is facilitated when the cost accounting process measures and reports costs using the same coding structure as the control accounts. However, many accounting systems are not designed to support work package cost accounting (e.g., they may not have enough account coding data fields, their coding structures may be designed to address capitalization needs, etc.). Therefore, the interface (i.e., data transfer) between cost accounting and project cost control systems must be planned.

Planning ensures that the accounting system cost accounts are either consistent with the control accounts, or that processes and procedures are in place to classify, map, and transfer the accounting system cost data to the control accounts in the cost control system. The mapping may be automated by rule-based software or it may involve manual translation and reentry of data. For example, if the enterprise's accounting system only allows one actual cost entry or account per purchase order, but your project control accounts require cost data from individual line items within the purchase order, then the line item costs may have to be manually entered into the project cost control system. In addition, the interaction/interface of owner, supplier, and contractor accounting systems, if any, must be considered and addressed in cost accounting plans.

.2 Initiate Project Cost Accounts

After cost accounting has been planned, cost accounts are opened or initiated in the cost accounting system. The accounting plan will establish who may enter, change, delete, view, or otherwise use data and information in or from the system. To avoid mischarges, project cost accounts are generally opened only as needed, not all at once. Project control is responsible for interfacing with the accounting process to ensure that accounts are initiated in an appropriate and timely manner.

.3 Measure, Review, Classify, and Account Costs

Once accounts are opened, payments made to suppliers and contractors are recorded by the accounting process against the appropriate project cost account. Payments may also be made from one internal cost account to another within an enterprise. In any case, the project cost account ledger is debited to reflect the dispersal of funds. Similarly, accounting payroll systems capture labor expenditures (payments to the individuals) and these are also debited as costs to the project.

The project control function regularly checks that the costs recorded by the accounting process are appropriate. Cost data are commonly miscoded, misfiled, improperly invoiced, or otherwise mischarged. In addition, work may have been completed or materials received, but not yet invoiced; project control must review progress measurements (Section 9.2) to determine if costs have been incurred. Direct payments to suppliers, contractors, and individuals are generally captured by accounting (i.e., accounts payable) and can be reviewed in real-time with modern IT.

Some costs are not charged directly to the project cost accounts, but are initially charged to an indirect, overhead, or some other suspense cost center. For example, rent and utilities for an office building may be paid and charged to corporate overhead accounts; however, the project team housed in the building may be responsible for some of this cost. Periodically, these indirect or overhead costs are apportioned by the accounting process to other cost centers such as a project cost account. Indirect or overhead costs may be apportioned as a percentage markup on direct costs. The accounting process also periodically evaluates the markups and allocations used to ensure that the costs incurred are in balance with allocations. Project control may be responsible for establishing or reviewing the basis of indirect cost allocations to project cost accounts.

A methodology called *activity-based cost accounting (ABC)* seeks in part to ensure that indirect cost allocations are minimized and are proportional to the costs imposed by the activity (e.g., the allocation of building rent and utility cost to the project cost is based on the proportion of building floor area occupied and extent of building services used by the project team). ABC has a similar objective to the traditional practice of *job costing*—that is, to ascribe indirect costs appropriately to an order, job, or project.

The accounting process may charge to a cost account (i.e., book a debit to the project ledger) on a cash or accrual basis. Most project cost accounting is on a cash basis; that is, when the check is cut, the cost is recorded as expended. In accrual accounting, costs may be booked before the check is cut in recognition that while an actual payment has not been made, a commitment or liability to make that payment has been incurred (i.e., incurred costs). It may also be booked after the check is cut in recognition that while an actual payment has been made, the work or resource for which payment has been made has not yet occurred or been received. Project control may be responsible for establishing or reviewing the basis of accruals on projects.

Project control reports both accrued (i.e., incurred and committed) and cash (i.e., actual) expenditures. As will be discussed in the project forecasting Section 10.2, projects need to record both when project costs have been committed (i.e., work completed or materials received, but not yet paid) as well as actually expended so as to understand the project's liabilities and to support forecasts of remaining costs.

The costs described above are outflows or debits of funds from the project cost accounts. The project receives its funds from the enterprise and/or external project financiers. It is a project control responsibility to prepare committed and actual cash flow forecasts (Section 7.3) so the finance function can obtain funds (or approvals of funds) in a timely manner from whoever is financing the project.

.4 Report Project Costs

The project accounting system reports costs as they are debited and credited to the various cost accounts in the ledgers. As was discussed, if the accounting system cost accounts are inconsistent with the control accounts, the project control process must transfer the reported cost to the project cost control system. Unfortunately, such transfers are commonly required, consuming significant, if not all, project control resources on the project (this effort and resources must be planned). As a result, what is called cost control on many projects, really only consists of recording the amounts expended; by themselves, expenditure data are largely useless for control because they say nothing about whether the expenditures are too much or too little in consideration of the extent that work packages have been completed. Best practices for project performance assessment and reporting (e.g., *earned value*) are covered in Section 10.1.

.5 Close Project Cost Accounts

Project cost accounting ends when the cost accounts are closed in the cost account system. Before closing the accounts, it is generally a project control responsibility to ensure that all charges to cost accounts are complete (i.e., there are no outstanding invoices or charges) and that costs are recorded in the right accounts. To avoid mischarges, project cost accounts are generally closed as quickly as possible after the work is complete on that work package. Project control is responsible for interfacing with the accounting process to ensure that accounts are closed in an appropriate and timely manner.

After accounts are closed, capital costs must be booked to the asset ledger so depreciation can begin. It is generally a project control responsibility to ensure that costs are allocated to the appropriate asset account in a timely manner (the capitalization process is covered in Section 5.1). It is common for the enterprise financial functions to be more concerned with capitalization (i.e., the final cost data from project closeout) than project control (i.e., the working cost data during project execution). The result is that enterprise accounting systems are often set up to support asset accounts, rather than control accounts.

Therefore, project control practitioners often find themselves heavily involved in helping to change and improve accounting systems as more companies add ERP and project management capabilities.

9.1.3 Inputs to Project Cost Accounting

.1 *Project Implementation Basis.* The implementation basis includes project cost accounting requirements that are usually consistent with business finance and accounting management (Section 4.1).
.2 *Project Control Plan and Control Accounts.* The project control plan (Section 9.1) describes specific systems and approaches to be used in project control including interface with accounting systems. The control accounts (Section 8.1) are work packages from the WBS for which responsibility has been assigned in accordance with the OBS and the procurement plan, and for which cost budgets and resources have been assigned, and activities scheduled. Accounting cost account structures may or may not align directly with the control account structure; plans must address this and cost allocations may need to be made for project control purposes.
.3 *Progress Measurement Plans.* Plans for measuring work completion (Section 9.2) and resource usage should be aligned with cost measurement plans as appropriate. Alignment may consider the frequency of measurements, alignment with control accounts, etc.
.4 *Work Progress.* The time of initiation and closing of cost accounts is partly dependent on planned work package activity start and actual completion dates (Section 9.2). Also, work progress is compared to payments made to identify committed costs.
.5 *Changes.* During project execution, changes to the baseline scope definition and plans are identified in the change management process (see Section 10.3). Change may result in changes to project cost accounting.
.6 *Charges to Project Accounts.* In the accounting process (steps of which are not part of the TCM process map), payments made to suppliers and contractors are recorded by the accounting process against the appropriate project cost account. Payments may also be made from one internal cost account to another within an enterprise.
.7 *Historical Project Information.* Successful past project cost accounting approaches are commonly used as future planning references.

9.1.4 Outputs from Project Cost Accounting

.1 *Project Control Plan and Control Accounts.* Project cost accounting planning may identify improvements to aspects of project control plan implementation (Section 8.1).
.2 *Project Measurement Plans.* Project cost accounting planning may identify improvements in plans for measuring work completion (Section 9.2).
.3 *Corrections to Charges.* Project control review of project costs may identify corrections that need to be made in the accounting process (e.g., mischarges, mistaken invoices, etc.).
.4 *Cost Information for Financing.* Project control prepares forecasts of committed and actual cash flow so the finance function can obtain funds (or approvals of funds) in a timely manner from whoever is financing the project. Information may also be needed for taxation and other enterprise financial purposes (Section 5.1).
.5 *Cost Information for Capitalization.* After accounts are closed, project control provides information about the allocation of project costs to assets so capital costs can be booked to the asset ledger and depreciation can begin (Section 5.1).
.6 *Cost Information for Control.* Cost commitment and expenditure information is used in earned value performance assessments, project cost forecasting, and cash flow assessment (Sections 10.1 and 10.2).
.7 *Historical Project Information.* The project's cost accounting approaches are captured for use as a future planning reference. Project cost data are also captured in the project historical database (Section 10.4).

9.1.5 Key Concepts for Project Cost Accounting

The following concepts and terminology described in this and other chapters are particularly important to understanding the project cost accounting process of TCM:

- .1 *Control and Cost Accounts.* (See Section 8.1).
- .2 *Expenditures.* A cost that is charged to an account when a payment or disbursement is made.
- .3 *Commitments.* The sum of all financial obligations made, including expenditures as well as obligations, which will not be performed or received until later. May also be referred to as an accrued expenditure.
- .4 *Cost Allocation (overhead, markups, etc.).* The process of evaluating, classifying, and shifting or transferring costs from one account to another so that reported costs for a work package are consistent with the basis for the cost included in the work package budget.
- .5 *Cash Flow Analysis.* (See Section 7.3) The process of time phasing the budgeted or forecasted costs to determine the expected rates of cost commitment or expenditure. The analysis provides the financing function with the input it needs to ensure that sufficient funds are available or approved for the expenditure or commitment.
- .6 *Cash and Accrual Accounting.* In cash accounting, costs are accounted for when expended (i.e., payments are made or cash disbursed). In accrual accounting, costs are accounted for when an obligation to make an expenditure is incurred, even if cash will not be expended or disbursed until a later time.
- .7 *Capitalization and Depreciation.* Some project costs are charged (i.e., expensed) as immediate or current expenses. However, capital project costs are held in suspense as work-in-progress (i.e., a suspense account), until the capital asset is put in service. Prior to being put in service, the capital project costs are allocated to items in the capital asset ledger and balance sheet (i.e., capitalized), and these costs are then charged or recognized over time in the profit statement as a depreciation expense. Capital and expense designations and depreciation rules are usually defined by government tax authorities. Project control personnel generally assist the finance function in making the cost allocations.
- .8 *Activity-Based Costing (ABC).* A method to allocate costs in a way that the costs budgeted and charged to an account truly represent all the resources consumed by the activity or item represented in the account (i.e., the allocation is not arbitrary, but reflects what drives the cost).

Further Readings and Sources

The interface of project control with cost accounting is generally covered in project management, project control, and cost management texts. The following references provide basic information and will lead to more detailed treatments.

- Amos, Scott J., Editor. *Skills and Knowledge of Cost Engineering*, 5th ed. Morgantown, WV: AACE International, 2004.
- Humphreys, Kenneth K., Editor. *Project and Cost Engineer's Handbook*, 4th ed. New York: Marcel Dekker, Inc., 2005.

9.2 Progress and Performance Measurement

9.2.1 Description

Progress and performance measurement is the process of measuring the expenditure or status of non-monetary resources on a project (e.g., tracking the receipt of materials or consumption of labor hours) and the degree of completion or status of project work packages or deliverables (e.g., the extent that materials have been installed, deliverables completed, or milestones achieved), as well as observations of how work is being performed (e.g., work sampling). Together with project cost accounting measures of the commitment and expenditure of money (Section 9.1), progress and performance measures are the basis for project performance assessment. Performance assessment methods such as earned value analysis, forecasting, work sampling productivity analysis, and so on are covered in Sections 10.1 and 10.2.

9.2.2 Process Map for Progress and Performance Measurement

The progress and performance measurement process illustrated in Figure 9.2-1 includes a variety of work, resource, and process performance measurement steps. The process is integrated with project cost accounting measurement (see Section 9.1). The measurements are inputs to the project performance assessment process (Section 10.1)

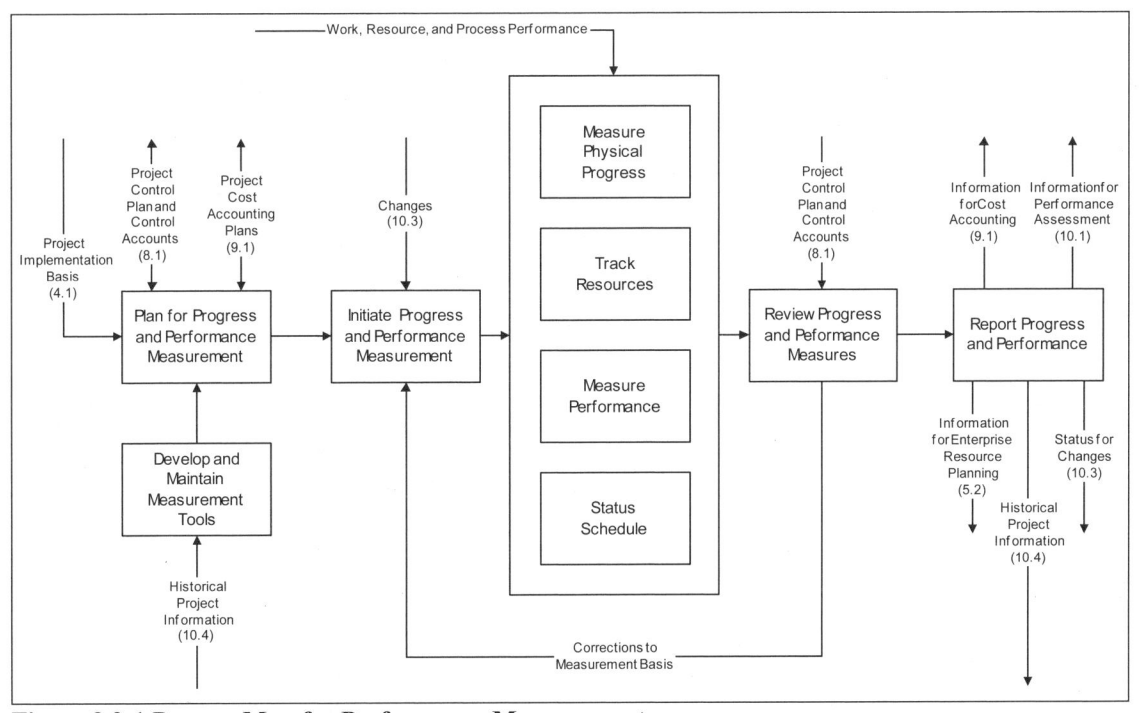

Figure 9.2-1 Process Map for Performance Measurement

The following sections briefly describe the steps in the progress and performance measurement process.

.1 Plan for Progress and Performance Measurement

The process for progress and performance measurement starts with planning for the measurements. Initial planning starts with planning for the project scope and execution strategy development process (Section 7.1) and continues through development of control accounts during project control plan implementation (Section 8.1). A requirement of work package and control account development is that the resources, activities, and deliverables for each work package and control account be measurable. Because the measurements are done to support the assessment methods that will be used, planning for measurement and assessment (Section 10.1) must be done together.

One aspect of planning includes assigning specific roles and responsibilities for measuring the progress and performance of each work package. That planning is done in consultation with those responsible for each work package (as determined during scope development). Another aspect to plan is the interface (i.e., data transfer) between measurement systems (e.g., payroll systems, material management systems, etc.) and systems used for project control (e.g., scheduling software). Finally, the use of enhanced performance measurement and assessment methods such as work sampling must also be planned.

Planning ensures that the measures captured in and reported by various systems are either consistent with the control and cost accounts, or that processes and procedures are in place to obtain measures and/or translate them to the account basis. This may involve manual measurement, translation, and entry of data. For example, if the enterprise's material management system does not report procurement milestones for each line item in a purchase order (i.e., item shipment date, item receipt date, etc.), but your control account activity measures require milestone dates for individual line items within the purchase order, then the line item milestone dates may have to be obtained by some other means (e.g., calling the procurement department) and manually entering the data into the project control system. In addition, the interaction/interface of owner, supplier, and contractor reporting systems, if any, must be considered and addressed in progress and performance measurement plans.

After progress and performance measurement has been planned, measurement processes or systems are initiated for each resource type for which consumption or status is to be measured and each work package activity or deliverable type for which the degree of completion will be measured. The progress measurement plan will establish who may enter, change, delete, view, or otherwise use data and information in or from each system. Project control is responsible for interfacing with the design management, material management, and other processes to ensure that measurement is initiated in an appropriate and timely manner. Methods such as work sampling may require consultation and/or negotiation with those whose work will be observed to ensure that the method is understood.

.2 Measure Physical Progress (to Support Earned Value Performance Assessment)

Each control account manifests at a work package level the overall project plan for activities to produce project deliverables (i.e., the schedule), the use of resources (i.e., the resource and procurement plans), and the commitment and expenditure of funds (i.e., the cost budget). Progress against each of these plan elements is measured to support earned value analysis and forecasting.

The earned value assessment method (as covered in more detail in Section 10.1) starts with the premise that control accounts have resource values (typically cost or labor hours) that can be summed to the total value for the project. The percent progress of any sub-component of the WBS, at any point in time, is then the sum of the value of each control account in that WBS component that has been "earned" at that point, divided by the total value of that component of the WBS. The earned value for each control account is the value of the control account multiplied by the percent "physical progress" of the scope included in that control account. For example, if the work package was construction of a building concrete foundation, with a budgeted cost of $10,000, and the construction physical progress at a certain time was measured as 40 percent complete, the earned value for that foundation control account at that point of time would be $4,000 (i.e., 0.4 x $10,000).

The earned value method is typically applied at the cost account level. For example, a work package may include installation of a piece of equipment for which there are cost accounts for the equipment purchase (i.e., material cost account) and installation of the piece of equipment (i.e., labor cost account). The labor and material progress will be measured separately, and then, using earned value methods, the weighted progress for any work package, component of the WBS, or cost type can be determined.

If the work package is the responsibility of suppliers or contractors, they will not only use measurements to control their own work, but may also use them as a basis for billing for their work depending on the billing method specified in their contract type.

The following describes the traditional physical progress methods for measuring the extent of completion of the scope of a work package.

Units Completed

This measurement method can be used when work package scope can be further decomposed into fairly homogenous units of work (e.g., units of material, drawings, lines of code, function points, etc.) that each require approximately the same level of effort to produce, and for which work is usually completed, and can be measured, for some units while work continues on others.

For example, if a work package's labor cost account scope was to pull 10,000 meters of wire through conduit, and the wire was made up of many short lengths of wire pulled at different times, then a meter of wire pulled could be considered a valid "unit" of measurement. Therefore, if 4,000 meters had been pulled as of a given point in time, then the labor cost account would be considered 40 percent complete (i.e., 4,000/10,000). For the work package's material cost account, if 8,000 meters of the wire had been received at the site at the same point in time, then the material cost account would be considered 80 percent complete (i.e., 8,000/10,000).

Incremental Milestone

This measurement method can be used when work package scope is one deliverable (i.e., not many units as described above) or a set of deliverables done together, for which multiple activities must be performed in sequence and for which the completion of incremental tasks can be observed. In this case, based on estimates or past experience, a percent completion value can be credited for completion of key incremental tasks or "milestones." For example, if a work package's labor cost account scope was to install a piece of equipment that had a sequence of 5 activities to perform (i.e., receive, set, align, test, and accept), then the percent cost account completion at completion of each activity can be estimated (i.e., 15, 60, 75, 90, and 100 percent, respectively). The estimated percents would be called the rules of credit. Therefore, when the equipment piece was set, the work package would be considered 60 percent complete. The work package's material cost account would be considered 100 percent complete when the equipment arrived at the site.

In some cases (usually hard to measure minor work packages), the incremental milestones may simply be the start and finish (e.g., earn 30 percent when you start, and 100 percent at completion), or just the finish (i.e., earn 100 percent at completion and nothing until then).

Weighted or Equivalent Units Completed

This measurement method is a hybrid of units completed and incremental milestones. It is used when the work package scope includes non-homogenous units of work and/or work tasks that overlap such that the other methods don't work well. In this case, based on estimates or past experience, a percent completion value can be credited for completion (and possibly intermediate milestones) of specific scope components or units. For example, if a work package's scope was to landscape a site, the scope may include many different components (i.e., trees, turf, shrubs, etc.) for which the installation sequence is non-sequential and flexible depending on vagaries of the weather. Units completed or incremental milestones alone do not readily apply. In this case, the estimated weighting or rules of credit are 60 percent when all trees are planted, 20 percent when the turf is laid, and 20 percent when the shrubs are planted. If at a point in time the turf is laid and trees planted, the percent complete would be 60 percent (i.e., 40 plus 20).

Resource Expenditure (Level of Effort)

This measurement method is generally used when the work package scope does not include discrete deliverables or milestones and for which the activities are of long duration and of a relatively constant level of effort. These most often include management and support labor cost accounts (e.g., project management, project control, quality assurance, etc.). For these, the percent complete may be estimated based on the percent of the total planned or forecast duration, hours, or cost spent for the control account. For example, if a work package's scope is project control during construction, the project control staff is relatively fixed throughout construction, and the forecasted execution duration is 16 months, the percent complete at the end of the 4th month can be estimated as 25 percent (i.e., 4/16).

Judgment

This measurement method is the most subjective and is used when more objective methods are not reasonable. In this method, the person responsible for the work package estimates the percent complete based on his or her informed judgment. For example, if a work package's scope was to landscape a site, the scope may include many different components of many sizes (i.e., trees, turf, shrubs, etc.) for which the installation sequence is flexible depending on vagaries of the weather. Units completed or incremental milestones do not readily apply. If landscaping is a minor component of the project scope, then the landscaping supervisor may simply be asked to provide an estimate of percent completion.

.3 Track Resources

In addition to the physical progress measures that support earned value performance assessment, the status of resource procurements and resource usage need to be tracked to support productivity analysis (Section 10.2), to support forecasting and change management (Sections 10.3), and to track resource risk factors identified in the risk management process (Section 7.6).

Labor Hours

For labor cost accounts, hours are often used as a basis for earned value performance assessments rather than costs. By controlling the hours, you can effectively control the cost. Part of the reason is that hours data are typically captured at more frequent intervals (i.e., daily or weekly) than accounting and payroll systems book costs or make payments (often monthly). Cost accounting requires adjustments and allocations (e.g., for overhead) and this creates a lag in reporting. A monthly assessment cycle is too long for many projects. If hours are used for earned value methods, then the hours spent on a control account will need to be captured for comparison to the budgeted hours. Hours data will also be used in the assessment of labor productivity, either through earned value or work sampling. Project payroll systems are often closely linked or part of project cost accounting systems.

Material Management and Fabrication

For material cost accounts, earned value measurements are most often done on the basis of units completed or interim milestones (i.e., material cost account completion is credited in proportion to the percent of units received by the project, or in accordance with rules of crediting). However, the current status of each material procurement or fabrication is of greater interest to project controls than just for progress measurement.

For example, project control is at risk if material is not received in time and/or in the sequence planned; therefore, interim material status data are needed to assess the likelihood of this risk. Also, the change management process requires that the status of material procurements be known so that the effect of a change or trend on material costs or schedule can be estimated. Furthermore, shipments that come too early may look good on a progress report, but may lead to increased inventory and material handling costs, and so on.

Therefore, the status of order placement, fabrication, shipments, inventories, and so on is measured. Increasingly, material or enterprise resource planning (MRP/ERP) systems capture material management information that can be used effectively for project control.

.4 Status the Schedule

As with tracking labor and material resources, the resource of time must be tracked. As activities in the project schedule are started and completed, or when milestones are achieved, the actual start, finish, or milestone date will be captured in the project schedule database (often called the project management information system [PMIC]). During the assessment process (Section 10.1), the effect of project progress on the scheduled work remaining will be evaluated.

.5 Measure Work Process Performance (i.e., "how" work is being done)

Physical progress measurement and earned value assessment do not provide much information about why performance is better or worse than planned. Project control also requires information about the specific causes of performance problems. For material cost accounts, the material management expediting and quality management inspection functions provide such information about supply chain performance. Work sampling is a method that can be used to assess project labor performance (and in some respects material). The safety inspection process may also provide useful performance information for project control. Finally, quality management processes (i.e., work process improvements by functions working on or supporting the project) may contribute to project performance improvement.

Expediting is a process in which a representative of the buyer assists the material supplier in achieving its contractual obligations. The representative expedites the flow of information, obtaining approvals, and so on. Inspection is a process in which a representative of the buyer helps ensure that the supplier conforms with contract specifications and that any required processes and procedures are followed. The work and products of both suppliers and contractors are subject to inspection. Both the expediting and inspection functions provide project control with information about potential and actual control problems and their causes.

Work sampling measurement involves observing and recording what people are doing during the hours they are charging to the project. In projects, it is most typically applied to the construction and maintenance processes. In manufacturing processes, the equivalent method may be referred to as time and motion studies. In work sampling, a statistically planned sample of project activities is chosen for observation. During the assessment process, the measurements are compared to standard expectations or metrics for how long particular tasks should take and how they should be done. Observations also help identify productivity improvement ideas. For example, work sampling may identify that materials are stored too far from the work site and that workers are taking too much time to acquire supplies or materials. Because individuals will often try to make their own work more efficient, it may also be observed that some crews are creating local hoards of materials to avoid the long walk, resulting in damage to or loss of materials. These are examples of the type of information work sampling provides to help assess and improve project performance.

The safety management and inspection process will provide information on how to perform work tasks more safely. Any safety changes to or observations concerning work tasks (e.g., re-sequence work to avoid overcrowding in an area) are in effect measures that must be assessed in the project control process. Likewise, any quality (i.e., process improvement) changes to or observations concerning work tasks must be addressed.

.6 Review Progress and Performance Measures

The project control function regularly checks that the basis of project progress and performance measurements is appropriate and in alignment with the project control plan and control and with cost accounts. Measures are also reviewed to ensure timeliness and accuracy.

A risk to be aware of with progress measurements and schedules of payment based on progress is that contractors responsible for work packages can benefit financially by over-reporting progress and/or assigning too much money for payment for work that is performed early in the project. This is called front-end loading of the payment schedule. Front-end loading improves a contractor's cash flow at the expense of the owner. Its also contributes to poor project control. Therefore, it is important to use objective measures of progress whenever possible, and carefully review progress measurements (especially if the judgment method is used) and payment schedules.

Most measurements are not made directly by those responsible for the project control process. Physical progress (e.g., quantities installed, drawings completed, lines coded, etc.) is generally measured and reported by whoever is responsible for the work package. Labor hour status is reported from accounting payroll systems, and material status is reported from material management systems. Work sampling may be performed by a specialist in industrial engineering. However, those with project control responsibility should spot check the work progress and performance measurements to some extent (i.e., informal work sampling, questioning responsible leaders, etc.) to ensure that the data being received and reviewed are reliable, appropriate, and understood.

.7 Report Progress and Performance Measures

After review, measurement information is reported to the performance assessment process (Section 10.1). Information includes physical progress measures for earned value performance assessment, work sampling measures for work productivity and process improvement evaluations, current status data for the forecasting of work yet to be completed, and so on.

Schedule status data (e.g., completion dates for activities and milestones, etc.) are entered into the scheduling system (i.e., PMIS). If an integrated cost/schedule control system is used, the physical progress measures are entered there as well. If not, the progress data are entered into the cost control system.

Measures of work package progress and milestone achievements are reported to the project cost accounting process (Section 9.1) to support the initiation and closing of cost accounts. Also, the measures or progress and tracking of resources identifies costs that the project has become obligated to pay (i.e., incurred costs).

In addition, measurement data are used in the evaluation of changes and trends in the change management process (Section 10.3). These data may also be used in the enterprise resource planning system (Section 5.2).

Finally, historical project information is captured. The information is used to help improve measurement tools such as software, forms, checklist, procedures, and so on. Measurement data, including experiences and lessons learned about past measurement practices, are used for planning project progress and performance measurement practices on future projects.

9.2.3 Inputs to Progress and Performance Measurement

.1 *Project Implementation Basis.* The implementation basis includes progress and performance measurement requirements (Section 4.1).
.2 *Project Control Plan and Control Accounts.* The project control plan (Section 8.1) describes specific systems and approaches to be used in project control, including interface with measurement and assessment (cost/schedule control) systems. The control accounts (Section 8.1) are work packages from the WBS for which responsibility has been assigned in accordance with the OBS and the procurement plan, and for which cost budgets and resources have been assigned, and activities scheduled. Measurement plans must address how planned measures align with the planned control accounts (i.e., the measurement basis). During reviews, this alignment is assessed and corrected as needed.
.3 *Project Cost Accounting Plans.* Plans for measuring cost commitments and expenditures (Section 9.1) should be aligned with progress and performance measurement plans as appropriate. Alignment may consider the frequency of measurements, alignment with control accounts, etc.

.4 *Work, Resource, and Process Performance.* As project work packages are executed, information about the progress and performance of their activities and resources is captured by those responsible as determined in the project control plan and control accounts. Also, measures, observations, and other information about "how" work activities and work processes are being done or improvement ideas are captured (e.g., work sampling, safety observations, quality improvement ideas, etc.).

.5 *Changes.* During project execution, changes to the baseline scope definition and plans are identified in the change management process (see Sections 10.3). Change may result in changes to project cost accounting.

.6 *Historical Project Information.* Successful past project progress and performance measurement approaches are commonly used as future planning references. Historical cost and schedule data are also captured at project closeout.

9.2.4 Outputs from Progress and Performance Measurement

.1 *Project Control Plan and Control Accounts.* Measurement planning may identify improvements to aspects of project control plan implementation (Section 8.1).

.2 *Project Cost Accounting Plans.* Project progress and performance measurement planning may identify improvements in plans for cost accounting (Section 9.1)

.3 *Corrections to Measurement Basis.* Project control review of project measurement may identify corrections that need to be made in the measurement process (e.g., timeliness, quality of measures, etc.).

.4 *Information for Enterprise Resource Planning.* Resource tracking measurement data may be used directly by the enterprise resource planning system (Section 5.2).

.5 *Measurement Information for Project Cost Accounting.* Measures of work package progress and milestone achievements are reported to the project cost accounting process (Section 9.1) to support the initiation and closing of cost accounts. Also, the measures of progress and tracking of resources identifies costs that the project has become obligated to pay (i.e., committed costs).

.6 *Measurement Information for Performance Assessment.* Measurement information includes physical progress measures for earned value performance assessment, work sampling measures for work productivity and process improvement evaluations, current status data for the forecasting of work yet to be completed, and other assessments included in Section 10.1.

.7 *Status Information for Change Management.* Measurement data are used in the evaluation of changes and trends (Section 10.3). In order to evaluate the effect of a change, it is necessary to know if the work has already been performed, if the material has already been shipped, etc.

.8 *Historical Project Information.* The project's performance measurement approaches are captured in a database (Section 10.4) for use as future planning references. Final measures are captured as part of the project's cost and schedule performance data.

9.2.5 Key Concepts for Progress and Performance Measurement

The following concepts and terminology described in this and other chapters are particularly important to understanding the project cost accounting process of TCM:

.1 *Earned Value.* (See Section 10.1).

.2 *Productivity.* (See Section 10.1 and 11.2).

.3 *Progress.* Development to a more advanced stage. In network scheduling, progress indicates activities have started or completed, or are in progress.

.4 *Physical Progress.* (See Section 9.2.2.2).

.5 *Expediting.* A procurement process in which a representative of the buyer assists the supplier in achieving its contractual obligations, particularly as regards schedule. The representative, or expeditor, facilitates or expedites the flow of information, the obtaining of approvals, and so on.

.6 *Inspection.* A process for examining or measuring to verify whether an activity, component, product, or service conforms to specified requirements. The inspection may be focused on quality or safety; both provide useful information for project control.

.7 *Work Sampling.* A productivity improvement method that involves observing a sample of the work tasks that people are doing on a project, and the time they spend doing them, and comparing the observations and measurements to standard expectations or metrics.

Further Readings and Sources

The project performance measurement and assessment process is covered in a variety of sources. Most project management and control texts address basic earned value and earned value management systems and resource tracking to some degree. Direct measurement and assessment of supplier performance, work processes, and productivity are more thoroughly covered by procurement and material management, quality management, and industrial engineering texts. The following references provide basic information and will lead to more detailed treatments.

- Amos, Scott J., Editor. *Skills and Knowledge of Cost Engineering*, 5th ed. Morgantown, WV: AACE International, 2004.
- Fleming, Quentin W., and Joel M. Koppleman. *Earned Value Project Management*, 2nd ed. Upper Darby, PA: Project Management Institute, 2000.
- Humphreys, Kenneth K., and English, Lloyd, Editors. *Project and Cost Engineer's Handbook*, 3rd ed. New York: Marcel Dekker, Inc., 2005.
- Maynard, Harold B., and Kjell B. Zandin. *Maynard's Industrial Engineering Handbook*, 5th ed. New York: McGraw-Hill, 2001.
- Stumpf, George R., Editor. *Professional Practice Guide No. 5*: *Earned Value*. CD ROM. Morgantown, WV: AACE International, 1999.

CHAPTER 10

PROJECT CONTROL PERFORMANCE ASSESSMENT

10.1 Project Performance Assessment

10.1.1 Description

Project performance assessment is the process of comparing actual project performance against planned performance and identifying variances from planned performance. It also includes general methods of identifying opportunities for performance improvement and risk factors to be addressed. After the variances, opportunities, and risks are identified, actions to address them, and the potential effects of the actions on project outcomes, are further assessed and managed through the forecasting and change management processes (Sections 10.2 and 10.3, respectively). Corrective or change actions are then implemented as appropriate through updated project control planning (Chapter 7), which closes the project control cycle. At project closeout, the final assessments of project performance are captured in the project historical database (Section 10.4) for use in future project scope development and planning.

Performance against each aspect of the project plan must be assessed. Project cost accounting measures of the commitment and expenditure of money (Section 9.1) are compared to the cost plan or budget. Resource tracking measures (e.g., the receipt of materials or consumption of labor hours) are compared to the resource plans. Schedule status (as reflected in the statused network schedule) is compared to the baseline or target schedule. Also, the project status is assessed to determine if any risk factors, identified in the risk management plan or otherwise, are imminent or occurring.

During the early planning phases of a project life cycle, work performance is assessed against the project control plan established specifically for that phase (per Section 8.1) and for which partial funds and resources have been authorized (per Section 5.1). At the same time, the effects of scope development on the overall capital budget and schedule targets for the project are assessed In other words, day-to-day performance of planning activities is assessed against the project control budget for that phase, while the scope being planned is assessed against the capital budget.

The level of understanding of project performance is increased when the assessment integrates the evaluation of each aspect of the project plan. One method of integrating schedule and budget assessment is called *earned value management*. Some branches of the United States government require that this project control technique be used on their capital projects (sometimes referred to as Cost/Schedule Control systems Criteria or C/SCSC). The method is objective, quantitative, and effectively identifies variances from planned schedule and budget performance.

For complete performance assessment, earned value techniques must be augmented with practices that identify opportunities and risks, not just variances. For materials, resource tracking based on material management system data and expediting and inspection observations provides a wealth of information for assessing performance that may be affected by materials issues. Likewise for labor, work sampling measures, work inspection observations, and other surveillance inputs provide information for assessing labor productivity issues (and to some extent material issues as well).

10.1.2 Process Map for Project Performance Assessment

The project performance assessment process illustrated in Figure 10.1-1 is the initial problem and opportunity "identification" stage of the project control assessment processes. The primary inputs are performance measurements (see Sections 9.1 and 9.2). The initial performance assessments of these measurements are the outputs for further analysis in the forecasting and change management processes (Sections 10.2 and 10.3, respectively).

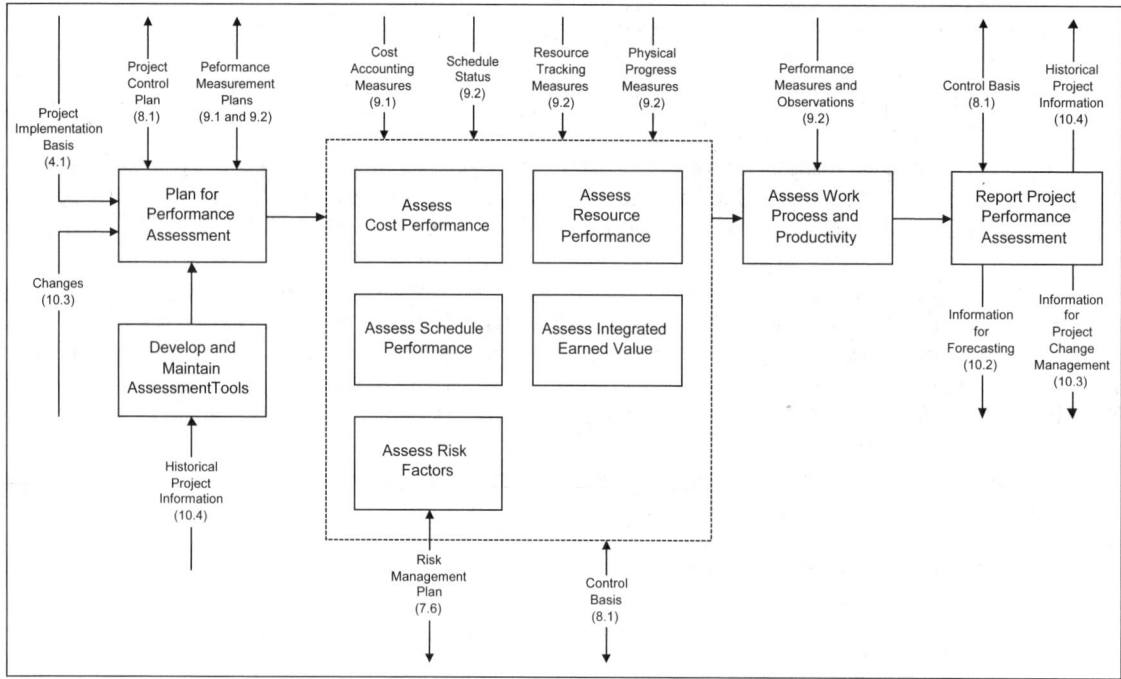

Figure 10.1-1 Process Map for Project Performance Assessment

The following sections briefly describe the steps in the project performance assessment process.

.1 Plan for Performance Assessment

The process for performance assessment starts with planning for the assessments. Initial planning starts with development of the execution strategy and work packages during scope development (Section 7.1) and continues through development of control accounts during project control plan implementation (Section 8.1). A requirement of work package and control account development is that the resources, activities, and deliverables for each work package and control account be measurable and therefore suitable for quantitative assessment. Planning for measurement (Sections 9.1 and 9.2) and assessment must be done together. Planning ensures that the quantitative measurement and assessment practices used (e.g., earned value) are consistent with the control and cost accounts.

The use of each assessment method (e.g., earned value, work sampling, etc.) should be planned in a way that optimizes the identification of variances, opportunities, and risks for all aspects of the project plan. Also, planning assigns specific roles and responsibilities for assessing project performance. Unlike the measurement process for which much of the day-to-day responsibility of measuring performance (e.g., units completed) lies with those responsible for the work packages, assessment is generally a function performed by cost engineers in a project control role supporting the project manager. However, those responsible for the work packages should make their own subjective assessments of their performance, and provide other observations that help project management understand their performance.

Another aspect to plan is the interface (i.e., data transfer) between measurement systems (e.g., payroll systems, material management systems, etc.) and systems used for assessment (e.g., scheduling software). In addition, the interaction/interface of owner, supplier, and contractor reporting systems, if any, must be considered and addressed in performance measurement and assessment plans.

After project performance measurement and assessment has been planned, and measurement processes or systems have been initiated, the use of assessment methods begins.

.2 Assess Cost Performance

Cost performance is generally assessed using the *earned value* method. That method starts with the premise that control accounts have a resource value (typically cost or labor hours) that can be summed to the total value for the project (or some branch of the cost account structure such as labor costs). The percent progress of any sub-component of the work breakdown structure (WBS) or cost account structure branch, at any point in time, is then the sum of the value of each control account in that branch that has been "earned" at that point, divided by the total value of that account structure branch. The earned value for each control account is the value of the control account multiplied by the percent "physical progress" measurement (see Section 9.2) of the scope included in that control account. For example, if the work package was construction of a building's concrete foundation, with a budgeted cost of $10,000, and the construction physical progress at a certain time was measured as 40 percent complete, the earned value for that foundation control account at that point of time would be $4,000 (i.e., 0.4 x $10,000).

The earned value is then compared to the expended costs to determine if there is a cost or budget variance for that item (or for that branch of the cost account structure). Using the previous example, assume that $5,000 had been expended on the concrete foundation, and the earned value was $4,000. In this case, the foundation's work package is $1,000 or 25 percent over budget. This variance would be further evaluated by reviewing status reports by and/or speaking to the foreman responsible for this work package (or their supervisor), as well as by reviewing material management reports, work sampling reports, and so on. All of this information would be used in forecasting the foundation work and cost remaining (see Section 10.2). The cost performance variance (i.e., earned minus expended) of all work packages can then be summed to determine overall project cost variance.

The earned value method is typically applied at the cost account level. For example, a work package may include installation of a piece of equipment for which there are cost accounts for the equipment purchase (i.e., material cost account) and labor to install the piece of equipment (i.e., labor cost account). The labor and material progress will be measured separately. For example, assume the material cost budget for the equipment item purchase was $8,000, and the labor cost budget for its installation was $2,000. Further, the equipment, which actually cost $10,000, had been shipped to the site but installation, which had cost $1,000 to date, was only 50 percent complete. The weighted work package percent progress would be the total earned value/total budget or [(100 percent x $8,000)+(50 percent x $2,000)]/($8,000 + $2,000) = $9,000/$10,000 = 90 percent. The work package is also $2,000 over budget (i.e., $11,000 expended minus $9,000 earned). In this way, you can view the cost from a work package perspective (i.e., it is $2,000 over budget), or a cost account perspective (i.e., the material is $2,000 over budget, but the labor is on budget).

The cost assessment is usually reported using both tables and charts. A typical cost report table or chart might include the budgeted, expended, and earned costs tabulated against the project date. The charts are typically cumulative distribution function diagrams (often called "S" curves because the typical plot is shaped like a flattened letter S). To support such a table or chart, the budget must be time phased. The time phasing is determined by the resource allocation methods as described in Section 7.2.

These observations—along with schedule, resource, productivity, and work process and performance assessments—will be used in the forecasting process (Section 10.2) to evaluate the budget for remaining work, and to address trends and changes (Section 10.3).

.3 Assess Schedule Performance

Schedule performance assessment starts by entering the actual start, finish, and milestone achievement dates for activities in the project schedule (usually using scheduling software). If earned value techniques are used, the percent complete information is also documented for each activity. However, schedule performance is based on the remaining duration needed to complete the work of the activity, which is then used to evaluate the percent of schedule completion. Performance is assessed by calculating the revised durations and completion dates of remaining activities and of the project as a whole using scheduling algorithms (again, usually using scheduling software). This does not change the planned schedule but is only used to evaluate progress and determine if some corrective action is needed to maintain the planned schedule. Corrective action is usually applied to the activities in progress or the immediately following activities.

Schedule performance variance may be expressed as either the amount of time or the percent of the planned duration that the schedule is ahead or behind. For example, a project may be 2 months behind schedule (i.e., schedule slippage) or 10 percent behind the planned project duration of 20 months. The variance can be reported for any activity, a group of activities, or the project as a whole.

If earned value techniques are used, schedule performance variance can also be expressed in terms of cost, hours, or other resource value used. Using earned value, schedule variance is the earned value less the value of the work that was planned or scheduled to be complete. If the earned is greater than the planned value, then the project is ahead of schedule (see Section 10.1.2.5). Earned value and scheduling (i.e., critical path analysis) must both be used because earned value will only indicate if sufficient resources are being applied. Critical path scheduling will tell if the correct activities are being worked on.

The schedule will also be assessed to determine if the logic for the remaining work is still valid (e.g., is the actual performance now out of sequence). This observation, along with cost, resource, productivity, and work process and performance assessments (i.e., trends) will be used in the forecasting process (Section 10.2) to evaluate the plan and schedule for remaining work, and to address trends and changes (Section 10.3).

The schedule assessment is usually reported using a schedule plot (e.g., a bar chart) showing the planned (i.e., target) and actual schedule activity status. The assessment can also be displayed in a table showing a percentage or factor that expresses the extent that the schedule is ahead or behind at given points in time. To help assess management priorities, additional schedule status reports may include lists of activities sorted by pending planned start dates (activities requiring immediate attention), pending planned finish dates, or by total float (activities with most immediate potential impact to project completion).

.4 Assess Resource Performance

In addition to cost and schedule assessment, the status of resource procurements (i.e., materials) and resource expenditures (i.e., labor hours) against resource plans needs to be assessed.

Labor Hours

Industry data indicate that for most well-defined projects the labor cost account experiences the most variance. For that reason, there is a common saying: "control the hours and control the project." Hour assessments can be used because labor costs are usually proportional to labor hours, at least on the average for a particular discipline, trade, or craft.

Another reason that labor hour assessment is considered particularly valuable is that labor hour measurements are usually performed more frequently than cost measurements. The cost accounting system (Section 9.1) for many project systems reports costs on a monthly basis. If the project's major activities or phases are measured in days (e.g., a process plant shutdown) or weeks, cost performance assessment may be inadequate to support effective, timely project control.

Labor hour performance is usually evaluated the same way as cost performance using basic earned value methods. The methods previously described for cost assessment all apply, with the exception that labor hours are used as the resource "value" measure, rather than cost. Another exception is that total project cost performance cannot be based on using labor hours because not all cost accounts are labor accounts (and, if they were, the cost of labor hours for different people will vary).

As with cost, the labor hour assessment is usually reported using both tables and charts. A typical labor hour report table or chart might include the budgeted, expended, and earned hours tabulated or plotted against the project date (after forecasting, the report may also include forecasted hours to complete or totals at completion). To support such a table or chart, the hours must be time phased. The time phasing is determined by the resource allocation step described in Section 7.2.

Variances in labor hour performance often result from labor productivity differing from the estimate used in the plan. The assessment of labor productivity is discussed later in this section.

The labor hour observations, along with cost, material resource, productivity, and work process and performance assessments, will be used in the forecasting process (Section 10.3) to evaluate resource plans for work remaining, and to address trends and changes (Section 10.4).

Material Management and Fabrication

Often, material supply and fabrication activities in project schedules start with preparation of the bid packages, and finish with the receipt or acceptance of the material item(s) at the project location. These basic milestones are usually adequate to support project activity logic (e.g., an item cannot be installed until it is received) and earned value assessments (e.g., an item's cost value is earned when it is received). Because the material supply chain is usually complex, all the supply chain incremental activities (e.g., order placement, intermediate materials shipment, fabrication, product shipments, shipping status, inventories, and so on) are usually not included in a master project schedule unless the schedule logic requires them or it is desirable to earn value for the material progress in increments. However, it is a project control responsibility to assess the supply chain status to some degree in order to identify project performance opportunities and risk. This can be facilitated by using a materials tracking database, which may also include the pre-order approval submittals.

The status of materials is usually reported by an enterprise's material management system. This system may be integrated with or part of a material or enterprise resource planning (MRP/ERP) system. The reports will include the current status of each material item in its supply chain (e.g., planned start/finish dates of intermediate activities and supporting notations). In essence, the material management system is an extension of the project scheduling and progress reporting system and in some cases may be linked to it. In any case, project control assesses these reports for performance opportunities and risks.

For example, the project schedule status shows that a vessel was ordered on schedule. However, material management reports show that the vessel fabricator has not achieved an intermediate inspection milestone date. Having observed this, the project control person may forecast and evaluate the effect of a late delivery, and/or may communicate to the procurement department how critical the vessel is.

The change management process also requires that the status of material procurements be known so that the effect of a change or trend on material costs or schedule can be estimated. Furthermore, shipments that arrive at the project site unreasonably early may look good on a progress report, but may lead to increased inventory and material handling costs, exposure to damage or loss, and so on.

Material status assessments are usually reported as qualitative findings to be considered in cost and schedule forecasting and change management. The time-phased cumulative planned and actual use or receipts of key materials can be plotted for the plan during the project's duration versus the periodic status dates. The planned use is obtained from the resource planning process (Section 7.4).

.5 Assess Integrated Earned Value (i.e., Integrated Cost and Schedule Performance Assessment Using an Earned Value Management System [EVMS])

An earned value management system (EVMS) integrates the assessment of the project budget and schedule. A full description of such systems is not provided here, but the basis assessment methods are described.

EVMS cost/schedule integration starts with establishment of a WBS and control accounts (Section 8.1). Each control account has a budget and is represented by at least one activity in the project schedule.

EVMS integrates cost and schedule by time phasing the cost and resource budget plans. The budgeted cost or resource for any time period (typically by month) is the budget for all work packages planned to be performed in full within that time period, plus, for any work package planned to be in-progress during that time period, the percent of the work package budget planned to be performed during that time period. The budget for that time period is called the *planned* value of work scheduled.

Next, the planned value of work performed or *earned* value is determined for the time period. This is the budgeted cost or resource for all work packages actually performed in full within that time period, plus, for any work package actually in-progress during that time period, the percent of the work package budget (based on actual percent progress) performed during that time period.

Next, the actual cost or resource usage for work performed is determined for the time period. This is the actual amount incurred on the work packages completed or in-progress during the time period and is called the *actual* value.

Using the above time-phased values, cost, resource, and schedule "variances" for the project (or some portion of the WBS) can be assessed as follows:

- Schedule Variance (SV) = Earned – Planned
- Cost or Resource Variance (CV) = Earned – Actual

A negative variance (i.e., the earned value is less than that expended) may reflect an unfavorable trend (i.e., an overrun or schedule slip). The variances can also be reported as performance indices or factors as follows:

- Schedule Performance Index (SPI) = Earned/Planned
- Cost or Resource Performance Index (CPI or RPI) = Earned/Actual

An index less than 1.00 reflects unfavorable performance (i.e., earned value is less than that expended). These performance factors can be used in forecasting (Section 10.2). However, the SPI will approach 1.00 as the project nears completion and then loses its utility for forecasting.

Finally, the percent complete for the project (or some portion of the WBS) can be assessed as follows:

- Percent Complete = Cumulative Earned Value/Total Budget (for the project or WBS component as appropriate).

The strengths of an EVMS are that it integrates cost and schedule performance assessment of variances from plans while being objective and quantitative. However, the method in itself does not explain why the performance is what it is, nor how performance can be improved. It simply waves a red flag when there are problem areas that need further assessment, or when positive performance needs to be assessed for potential reduction in project costs and/or early completion.

Another challenge is that EVMS relies on cost as its "value" measure. As was mentioned in the labor hour assessment discussion, cost accounting systems often report expended costs monthly. If the project's major activities or phases are measured in days or weeks, the red flags may be too late for effective project control.

.6 Assess Work Process and Productivity

In general terms, labor productivity is defined as the ratio of the value that labor produces to the value invested in labor. In an absolute sense, it is a measure of the extent to which labor resources are minimized and wasted effort is eliminated from a work process (i.e., work process efficiency).

In earned value assessment, productivity is a ratio (i.e., a factor) that compares the labor effort expended to that which was planned (sometimes called the "spent-earned ratio"). In earned value terms, productivity is calculated as follows:

- Labor Productivity Factor = Expended Hours / Earned Hours,
  where the earned hours = percent physical progress x control budget hours

To be useful, the control budget must reflect the current scope and quantities. This is the same method defined previously in the labor performance assessment description. However, in this case, a factor less than 1.00 is favorable. For example, if work was 60 percent complete on the labor cost account of a work package that had a budget of 200 hours, and 100 hours had been spent, then the productivity factor is 0.83 (i.e., = 100/(0.6 x 200). Care must be taken to understand the nature of any productivity factor that is quoted because alternate sources may use the inverse (i.e., a factor less than one is not favorable).

Another related way to measure the value of labor input to the work output is to calculate the ratio of labor cost or hours spent to the quantity of work performed. Example ratios are hours per line of code developed, hours per design deliverable, or hours per tonne of steel erected. These types of ratios are often the basis of the control budget labor estimates. A difference between the actual ratio and the ratio used as a basis of estimate indicates whether actual productivity is better or worse than planned.

These factors and ratios are useful for forecasting (Section 10.2), but they provide no information as to whether wasted effort exists in the work process. In other words, a project's use of labor may be unproductive in an absolute sense, while still achieving a favorable productivity factor if the plan also reflects unproductive use of labor. If a project objective is to optimize cost competitiveness, then a relative productivity assessment alone may be inadequate.

To optimize the use of labor, as well as control it, a direct method of measuring and assessing labor productivity is needed; one such method is *work sampling*. This method provides the specific information needed to eliminate wasted effort. Work sampling provides systematic observations of work activity at the work site to:

1) determine the proportion of labor hours being spent in non-productive work activity and delays versus productive work activity,
2) analyze factors that cause non-productive activity or delays, and
3) identify opportunities to reduce non-productive activity and delays.

Assessment of work sampling data allows for prompt removal or reduction of roadblocks, optimizing the work process by making the work convenient for the workers (i.e., they have all necessary tools, materials, supplies, information, and supervisory support readily available at all times). Optimizing the convenience of the work is a strong motivating factor and motivation is a key driver of work productivity.

A full description of the work sampling process is not provided here, but the basic method involves recording a sample of worker activities according to established, pre-defined activity category classifications. The percentages of observations in each productive and non-productive activity category are computed and applied to the total labor-hours available to determine the time spent on each category. The resulting data show the overall crew utilization for the period of work sampled. The goal is to optimize the direct time by analyzing the utilization roadblocks and constraints that have been observed and recorded.

Short of a full work sampling effort, a project can use limited or informal sampling, manpower surveys, time card notations, and other approaches to capture information about the roadblocks and constraints that workers are experiencing. Time lapse photography of critical work areas is also used. In all cases, the methods must focus on assessing the process, not the worker (i.e., planning and management is the problem).

Another direct method of assessing and improving absolute productivity is quality work process improvement. In this case, the workers, in a planned quality improvement program, identify, assess, and implement work process improvements as a part of their job responsibility. In this case, project control has a role in helping the workers assess the effect of their improvement ideas on project performance.

Finally, expediting and inspection reports may indicate that the supplier or contractor is experiencing some sort of process problem (e.g., difficulty in obtaining a critical raw material, difficulty in hiring a critical labor skill, etc.). Project control has a role in helping identify and assess improvements in their work process as they affect project performance.

If changes in the work process that might improve performance are identified in the performance assessment process, then change requests should be initiated in the change management process (Section 10.3).

.7 Assess Risk Factors

Each of the assessment methods described above may identify imminent or occurring risk factors, as anticipated in risk management planning (Section 7.6) or otherwise. The risk management plan includes plans for monitoring anticipated risk factors. Risk assessments are considered in the forecasting and change management process.

.8 Report Project Performance Assessment

The results of assessments (i.e., variances, opportunities, and risks) are reported to the forecasting and change management processes (Sections 10.2 and 10.3, respectively). At project closeout, the final project performance assessment is captured in the project historical database (Section 10.4) for use in future project scope development and planning.

It is also a project control responsibility to give those responsible for work packages immediate feedback on performance assessments. This feedback may be accomplished by having frequent project team performance review meetings in addition to the progress status meetings. While objective measurements and assessments are required for effective project control, subjective assessments by of those responsible for and with expertise in project control are invaluable.

Quantitative assessment reports tend to consist of tables and charts (e.g., "S" curves) as were described with each of the assessment methods above. Schedule reports tend to be activity plots (e.g., bar charts, etc.). In each case, the report must clearly show the variance from the plan that must be addressed and controlled.

Graphical representations are particularly useful when there is no bottom line variance (e.g., cost is on budget), but the measure is unpredictable over time or between accounts indicating a potential risk to address (i.e., your good performance is the result of luck, not good control). Also, cost and schedule performance assessments are most useful when reported in an integrated manner.

Quantitative assessments must be supported by observations of the probable cause of any significant variances identified. In addition to probable causes, opportunities and risks should be noted as identified by methods such as work sampling, expediting, inspection, work process improvement, and so on.

At the close of the process, historical project information, including experiences and lessons learned about assessment practices, is used to improve assessment tools such as software, forms, checklists, procedures, and so on.

10.1.3 Inputs to Project Performance Assessment

.1 *Project Implementation Basis (Objectives, Constraints, and Assumptions).* The enterprise may establish requirements for performance assessment, such as the use of an EVMS system and so on (see Section 4.1).
.2 *Project Control Plan.* The project control plan (Section 8.1) describes specific systems and approaches to be used in project control including interface with measurement and assessment (cost/schedule control) systems.
.3 *Performance Measurement Plans.* Plans for cost and resource commitment, incurrence, and expenditure measurement (Section 9.1) and progress and performance measurement (9.2) must be planned with the assessment process.
.4 *Risk Management Plan.* Project status is monitored for the occurrence of risk factors. Risk management plans (Section 7.6) provide the basis for risk monitoring and assessment.
.5 *Project Control Basis.* The control accounts (Section 8.1) are work packages from the WBS for which responsibility has been assigned in accordance with the OBS and the procurement plan, and for which cost budgets and resources have been assigned, and activities scheduled. These plans are the baselines against which performance measures are assessed.
.6 *Performance Measures and Observations.* Cost accounting (Section 9.1), and schedule status, resource tracking, and physical progress measures (Section 9.2) are captured and reported for assessment against baseline plans. Also, direct observations of work are used to identify work process and productivity improvements.
.7 *Changes.* During project execution, changes to the baseline scope definition and plans are identified in the change management process (Sections 10.3). Change may result in changes to project performance assessment.
.8 *Historical Project Information.* Successful past project progress and performance measurement and assessment approaches are used as future planning references and to help improve assessment tools.

10.1.4 Outputs from Project Performance Assessment

.1 *Project Control Plans.* Performance assessment plan considerations are considered in overall project control planning.
.2 *Performance Measurement Plans.* Plans for cost commitment and expenditure measurement (Section 9.1) and progress and performance measurement (Section 9.2) must be planned with the assessment process.
.3 *Risk Management Plan.* Project status is monitored for the occurrence of risk factors. New risk factors identified during project execution may require updated risk management planning (Section 7.6).
.4 *Project Control Basis.* Performance measures are assessed against the control plan baselines. The assessment may raise issues about the appropriateness of the baseline.
.5 *Information for Forecasting.* Assessments of project progress, performance variances, and past productivity are used in forecasting (Section 10.2) the performance of the remaining work scope.
.6 *Information for Project Change Management.* Performance variances are evaluated as to the need for and scope of corrective actions as determined in the change management process (Section 10.3). Also, a change request may be originated for any work process change that might improve performance.
.7 *Historical Project Information.* The project's performance measurement and assessment approaches are used as future planning references and to help improve assessment tools.

10.1.5 Key Concepts for Project Performance Assessment

The following concepts and terminology described in this and other chapters are particularly important to understanding the project performance assessment process of TCM:

.1 *Earned Value.* (See Section 10.1.2.2 and 10.1.2.5).
.2 *EVMS.* (See Section 10.1.2.5).
.3 *Productivity.* (See Section 10.1.2.6 and 11.2).

.4 *Variance*: An empirical difference between actual and planned performance for any aspect of the project control plan.
.5 *Trend*: Non-random variance of actual asset or project performance from that which was planned. Analysis of performance measurements is required to determine if an observed performance variance is a trend (i.e., predictable) or a random outcome (i.e., unpredictable), and that determination will influence subsequent control actions and forecasts.
.6 *Work Process Improvement*. (See Section 11.4).

Further Readings and Sources

The project performance measurement and assessment process is covered in a variety of sources. Most project management and control texts address basic earned value and earned value management systems and resource tracking to some degree. Direct measurement and assessment of supplier performance, work processes, and productivity are more thoroughly covered by procurement and material management, quality management, and industrial engineering texts. The following references provide basic information and will lead to more detailed treatments.

- AACE International. *Recommended Practice No. 22R-01. Direct Labor Productivity Measurement as Applied on Construction and Major Maintenance Projects*. AACE International, 2004.
- AACE International. *Recommended Practice No. 25R-03. Estimating Lost Labor Productivity in Construction Claims*. Morgantown, WV: AACE International, 2004.
- Amos, Scott J., Editor. *Skills and Knowledge of Cost Engineering*, 5th ed. Morgantown, WV: AACE International, 2004.
- Fleming, Quentin W., and Joel M. Koppleman. *Earned Value Project Management*, 2nd ed. Upper Darby, PA: Project Management Institute, 2000.
- Humphreys, Kenneth K., and Lloyd English, Editors. *Project and Cost Engineer's Handbook*, 3rd ed. New York: Marcel Dekker, Inc., 2005.
- Maynard, Harold B., and Kjell B. Zandin. *Maynard's Industrial Engineering Handbook*, 5th ed. New York: McGraw-Hill, 2001.

10.2 Forecasting

10.2.1 Description

Forecasting is the process of evaluating project control plans and control baselines in consideration of assessments of ongoing project performance. The forecasting process should be performed in a proactive, systematic way on an established evaluation schedule, rather than being performed in reaction to performance problems because problems often become apparent only through forecast evaluations.

The forecasting process is used to assess each applicable element of the project control plan (i.e., scope, schedule, budget, resources, and risks) that is affected by a deviation, trend, change request, or opportunity. The inputs to the process include plans, performance and progress assessments, and change management information. The primary forecasting process outputs are "forecasts" (i.e., best predictions) for the performance and outcome of each control plan element. These forecasts should be reported in a way that highlights performance variances and issues that need project management attention.

The forecasting methods and tools used are the same as those used in the project control planning processes (Chapter 7). However, during forecasting, the methods are applied in the context of a project that is progressing while demanding quick (or at least expeditious) and effective project control decisions.

The first objective of forecasting is to support the identification of efficient means (i.e., corrective actions), with acceptable risks, for the project to achieve its objectives when past and/or current performance is at variance with baseline plans. Secondarily, opportunities to improve future performance are evaluated, even when performance conforms with baseline plans. Finally, forecasting incorporates the results of the evaluations of performance data and opportunities into control plans by communicating the forecasted (i.e., predicted) cost, schedule, and resources to complete the project or achieve specific milestones. At the start of the project, the approved control baseline plans and forecasts are the same; they will differ as the project progresses because the baseline was made from estimates of future performance.

Forecasting also supports the change management process (Section 10.3) in that it is used to evaluate not only deviations and trends, but requests for changes to the project scope definition or plan. The forecasting process provides the mechanism to bring all deviation, trend, and change information together, allowing for a comprehensive analysis and perspective when considering individual changes.

10.2.2 Process Map for Forecasting

Figure 10.2-1 illustrates the process map for forecasting. The forecasting process applies the project control planning processes in the context of a project in progress (i.e., integrated with the performance assessment and change management processes).

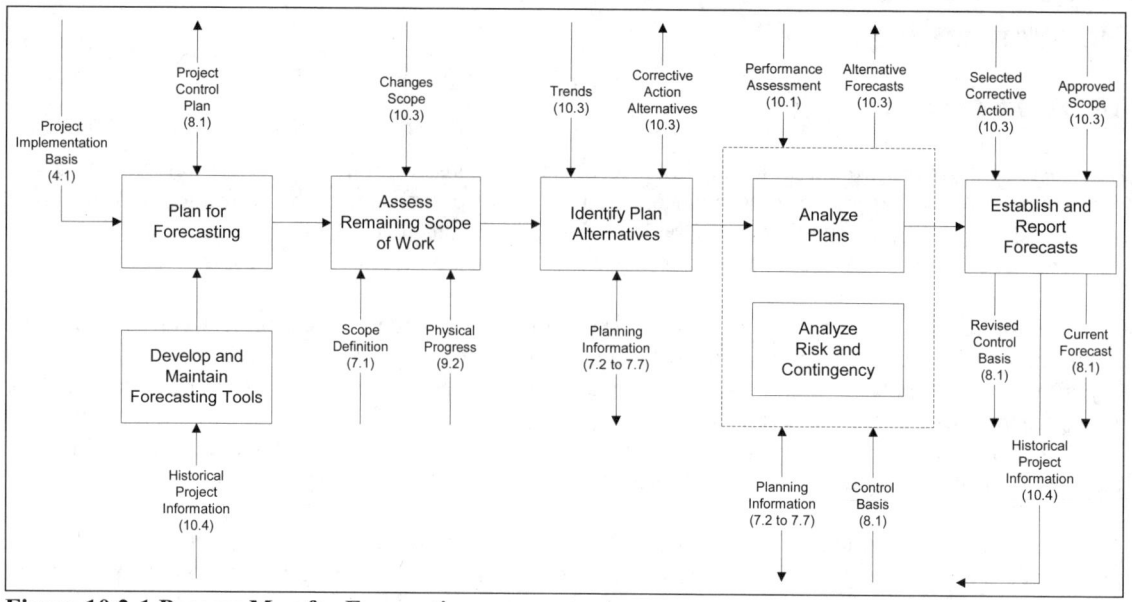

Figure 10.2-1 Process Map for Forecasting

The following sections briefly describe the steps in the forecasting process.

.1 Planning for Forecasting

The forecasting process starts with planning. Initial planning starts with development of the execution strategy and work packages during scope development (Section 7.1) and continues through development of control accounts during project control plan implementation (Section 8.1). Because forecasting applies many of the methods of integrated project planning, the basis or description of how those planning methods were initially applied must be documented at the time of control plan implementation.

Planning for forecasting establishes the timing of forecasts, how forecasts are communicated or reported, methodologies and systems/tools to be used, and specific roles and responsibilities for forecasting. Forecasts should be prepared and issued on an established schedule that is appropriate for the pace of work on the project (e.g., a round-the-clock plant turnaround will require more frequent evaluations). The forecasting schedule is often linked to when accounting systems can provide current and accurate historical data, but accounting should not drive forecasting if there is a need for more frequent evaluations. Communication or reporting of forecasts needs to consider the audience and how actionable information is best provided to decision-makers and project stakeholders.

Another aspect to plan is the use of tools and systems for forecasting (e.g., scheduling software). For example, forecasting is facilitated if the software used for, and the files and databases from, the initial planning process are available for use. In addition, the interaction/interface of the owner, suppliers, and contractors in forecasting, if any, must be addressed in forecasting plans.

Forecasting, like other aspects of performance assessment, is generally a function performed by cost engineers in a project control role supporting the project manager. However, those responsible for the work packages affected by forecasts, and the project team as a whole, should be included in the forecast assessment effort as appropriate.

After the forecasting effort is planned and measurement processes or systems have been initiated, the use of forecasting methods begins.

.2 Assess Remaining Scope of Work

Forecasting of any aspect of the control plan (i.e., cost, resources, schedule, etc.) starts with an assessment of the current status of the work scope. The scope development process (Section 7.1) established the original scope as reflected in the project WBS. Physical progress measurements methods (Section 9.2) establish the scope that has been completed. If no changes to the scope have been identified by the change management process (Section 10.3), then the remaining scope is simply defined as the WBS components not completed or in-progress.

The change management process (Section 10.3) defines the scope of any changes that have been identified. The forecasting process then assesses the scope definition of the proposed change in consideration of the scope of the planned remaining scope.

.3 Identify Plan Alternatives

The change management process may initially identify alternative actions to implement changes and to modify performance deviations and trends (including process improvements). These are generally simple action statements (e.g., "revise preferential schedule logic"). The forecasting process develops the proposed action statements into actionable control plan alternatives for further assessment (e.g., "complete activity B before activity A"). Additional alternative actions may be identified in this process.

If no deviations, trends, or changes or have been identified, this process step is skipped because the plan for the remaining work is still valid and remains unchanged.

.4 Analyze Plans

Forecasting applies the methods of integrated project planning (Chapter 7) in the context of a project that is progressing. As such, the descriptions here make extensive reference to the Chapter 7 sections.

Forecasted Cost

Cost forecasting begins with the current status of commitments and expenditures for the work packages or cost accounts being updated (to reflect actual amounts as of the date of the forecast). Performance assessments (Section 10.1) provide current productivity and other useful information for forecasting. In the change management process (Section 10.3), any cost performance deviations and variances are assessed as to whether they are trends (i.e., non-random). Also, performance improvement opportunities may have been identified as potential changes.

If changes or trends have been identified, the cost of the work scope remaining is then estimated using the methods of the cost estimating and budgeting process (Section 7.3). The total project cost forecasted then is the expended amount for completed work plus the estimated cost for the remaining work scope. The forecasted estimate must consider the performance to date, any improvement or correction actions proposed, and risk factors (as would any project estimate).

An alternate, quick, but simplistic method for estimating the cost of the work scope remaining is to use the cost performance index (CPI) as computed in an earned value management system (i.e., budgeted cost of work performed/actual cost of work performed or BCWP/ACWP). In this method, the cost of work remaining is estimated by simply dividing the budgeted cost of work remaining (i.e., total budget minus the BCWP) by the CPI. However, it should be kept in mind that more often than not, the remaining work scope will occur at a different rate than that experienced to date due to learning curve, closeout, miscellaneous punch list work, and so on.

Cost forecasts are developed for each plan alternative that has been identified. Cost forecasts, as with baseline planning, should be prepared in an integrated manner with schedule and resource forecasts. The alternate forecasts (along with associated schedule, resource, and other forecasts) are inputs to the change management process during which a decision will be made on a selected course of action. If no changes or trends have been identified, the cost forecast is simply the actual cost of work performed plus the budgeted cost of work remaining.

Forecasted Schedule

Schedule forecasting starts with the statused network schedule (Section 10.1). The schedule statusing will also have identified if the logic for the remaining work is still valid (e.g., is the actual performance now out of sequence). In the change management process (Section 10.3), any schedule performance variances are assessed as to whether they are trends (i.e., non-random). Also, performance improvement opportunities may have been identified as potential changes.

If changes or trends have been identified, the plan and schedule for the work scope remaining is then developed using the methods of the schedule planning and development process (Section 7.2). The project schedule forecast is then revised reflecting the current status integrated with the schedule for the remaining work scope. The revised schedule must consider the performance and productivity to date, resource allocation, any improvement or correction actions proposed, and risk factors. Creating a revised schedule entails of the schedule development steps, and therefore is done only infrequently when conditions invalidate the planned schedule because it can no longer be attained.

Schedule forecasts are developed for each plan alternative that has been identified. Schedule forecasts, as with baseline planning, are prepared in an integrated manner with cost and resource forecasts. The alternate forecasts (along with associated cost, resource, and other forecasts) are inputs to the change management process during which a decision will be made on a selected course of action. If no changes or trends have been identified, and the project status is as planned, the schedule forecast is simply the existing schedule.

Forecasted Resources

Resource forecasting begins with the current status of material procurement and labor expenditures. In the change management process (Section 10.3), any resource performance variances are assessed as to whether they are trends (i.e., non-random). Also, performance improvement opportunities may have been identified as potential changes. Variances in labor hour performance often result from labor productivity differing from the plan. Assessments of labor productivity should be carefully analyzed to determine crafts and/or trades impacted by the productivity variances and to apply trends associated with specific trades to those trades alone and not uniformly across all future labor.

If changes or trends have been identified, the resources for the work scope remaining are then estimated using the methods of the resource planning process (Section 7.4). The total resource forecast then is the expended resources for completed work plus the estimated resources for the remaining work scope. The forecasted estimate must consider the performance to date, any improvement or correction actions proposed, and risk factors (as would any project estimate).

Resource forecasts are developed for each plan alternative that has been identified. Resource forecasts, as with baseline planning, are prepared in an integrated manner with schedule and cost forecasts. The alternate forecasts (along with associated cost and schedule forecasts) are inputs to the change management process during which a decision will be made on a selected course of action. If no changes or trends have been identified, the resource forecast is simply the actual resource expenditures or use on work performed plus the resource planned for work remaining.

.5 Analyze Risks and Contingency

Each forecast alternative is evaluated using the risk management process (Section 7.6). That process evaluates and quantifies the impact of any risk factors inherent to the alternative plan(s). The quantification includes estimating the contingency required for the remaining work. Contingency must be forecast like any other cost account.

After an alternative course of action is decided upon, the risk management plan is updated as appropriate and the contingency cost account is managed through the change management process.

.6 Establish and Report Forecast

The forecasting process results in projections of the performance and outcome for each control plan element. The forecasts for the scope of work, including approved changes, result in a revised project control baseline against which performance will be measured and assessed (Section 10.1) for the remaining project until such time that the forecasting process results in a further revised project control baseline.

However, performance trends cannot always be corrected or mitigated. Therefore, the forecasts for the scope of work, including both approved changes and trends, that could not be corrected are reported so that management is always aware of the most accurate projected project outcome. Additional funding approvals may have to be obtained if the forecasted cost exceeds delegated authority limits. Approvals to obtain additional labor or material resources may also have to be obtained.

It is also a project control responsibility to keep those responsible for work packages appraised of the approved control baselines and current forecasts. As previously mentioned, communicating the forecast information is critical to its successful use and will facilitate input from project team members during the forecast preparation.

At the close of the process, actual project information, including experiences and lessons learned about forecasting practices, is used to improve forecasting tools such as software, procedures, roles and responsibilities, and so on.

10.2.3 Inputs to Forecasting

.1 *Project Implementation Basis.* (See Section 4.1). This defines the basis asset scope, objectives, constraints, and assumptions, including basic assumptions about forecasting approaches.
.2 *Project Control Plans.* The project control plan (Section 8.1) describes specific systems, policies, procedures, and approaches to be used in project control, including forecasting (and all other aspects of measurement and assessment).
.3 *Scope of Changes.* (See Section 10.2.2.2).
.4 *Scope Definition.* (See Section 10.2.2.2).
.5 *Physical Progress.* (See Section 10.2.2.2).
.6 *Trends.* Trends, as identified in the change management process (Section 10.3), must be considered in any plan alternatives and forecast analyses.
.7 *Corrective Actions (Alternatives and Selected).* The change management process (Section 10.3) initially identifies possible corrective actions. Later, based in part on forecasting outcomes, corrective actions are selected.
.8 *Planning Information.* Forecasting applies the methods of integrated project planning (Chapter 7) in the context of a project that is progressing.
.9 *Project Control Basis.* Forecasts must be developed in consideration of the current control baseline plans as well as changes and trends.
.10 *Approved Scope.* The forecasts for the scope of work, including approved changes, become the revised project control baseline. The approved scope of changes is determined in the change management process (Section 10.3).
.11 *Historical Project Information.* Successful past forecasting approaches are used as future planning references and to help improve forecasting methods and tools.

10.2.4 Outputs from Forecasting

.1 *Project Control Plans.* Forecasting plans are considered in overall project control planning (and all other aspects of measurement and assessment planning).

.2 *Planning Information.* Forecasting applies the methods of integrated project planning (Chapter 7) in the context of a project that is progressing (i.e., planning during forecasting must consider the project status).

.3 *Corrective Action Alternatives.* The change management process (Section 10.3) initially identifies possible corrective actions. Forecasting may identify other alternative actions as well.

.4 *Alternative Forecasts.* The change management process (Section 10.3) considers and decides upon alternative actions based in part on forecasting outcomes.

.5 *Project Control Basis.* The cost, schedule, and resource forecasts for the scope of work, including approved changes, become the revised project control baseline (Section 8.1).

.6 *Historical Project Information.* The project's forecasting approaches are used as future planning references and to help improve forecasting methods and tools.

10.2.5 Key Concepts for Forecasting

The following concepts and terminology described in this and other chapters are particularly important to understanding the forecasting process of TCM:

.1 *Forecast.* The project team's estimate of the most likely outcome for a given element of the project plan (e.g., cost forecast, schedule forecast, etc.).

.2 *Forecasting.* (See Section 10.2.1). The process of evaluating project control plans and control baselines in consideration of assessments of ongoing project performance. The result of the process is a forecast.

.3 *Trend.* Non-random variance of actual asset or project performance from that which was planned. Analysis of performance measurements is required to determine if an observed performance variance is a trend (i.e., predictable), or a random outcome (i.e., unpredictable), and that determination will influence subsequent control actions and forecasts.

.4 *Variance.* An empirical difference between actual and planned performance for any aspect of the project control plan.

.5 *Change Management.* (See Section 10.3). A process to control any change to a scope of work and/or any performance trend from or change to an approved or baseline project control plan. The process includes the identification, definition, categorization, recording, tracking, analyzing, and disposition of trends and changes.

.6 *Change.* Alteration or variation to a scope of work and/or any other approved or baseline project control plan (e.g., schedule, budget, resource plans, etc.).

.7 *Corrective Action.* A task or activity performed or direction given with the intent to mitigate or otherwise address a variance from planned project performance (i.e., to recover performance or improve or restore control).

Further Readings and Sources

The forecasting process is covered in most project management and control texts. The following references provide basic information and will lead to more detailed treatments.

- Amos, Scott J., Editor. *Skills and Knowledge of Cost Engineering*, 5th ed. Morgantown, WV: AACE International, 2004.
- Gransberg, Douglas D., and James Koch, Editors. *Professional Practice Guide No. 12: Construction Project Controls*. CD ROM. Morgantown, WV: AACE International, 2002.
- Humphreys, Kenneth K., Editor. *Project and Cost Engineer's Handbook*, 4th ed. New York: Marcel Dekker, Inc., 2005.
- Stumpf, George R., Editor. *Professional Practice Guide No. 5: Earned Value*. CD ROM. Morgantown, WV: AACE International, 1999.

10.3 Change Management

10.3.1 Description

Change management refers to the process of managing any change to the scope of work and/or any deviation, performance trend, or change to an approved or baseline project control plan. The change management process is used to approve or disapprove changes in the scope and baseline plans, thereby closing the project control cycle loop. The process includes the identification, definition, categorization, recording, tracking, analyzing, disposition (i.e., approval or disapproval for incorporation into approved or baseline project control plans), and reporting of deviations, trends, and changes.

Change management imposes the required structure and discipline in the project control process by protecting the integrity of the control basis as a valid baseline (i.e., it represents a project plan in alignment with project objectives and requirements) for performance measurement. The process objective is not to limit or promote change, but to manage and report it. Change can be good or bad, but it must always be carefully evaluated, approved or rejected, and, upon approval, methodically incorporated into the revised baseline plan. Changes most often require the project manager's approval; however, in any case, a formal process for how change progresses from identification through incorporation into the project must be understood by all project team members.

Most project systems seek to limit changes during project execution because the difficulty of managing change increases with their number and extent (i.e., "analysis paralysis"), and change is a known project performance risk factor. Changes during project execution—particularly if they result in cost increases, drawdown on contingencies, delays, disputes, and/or rework—can be highly demoralizing. The best approach to limit change is to establish and use a strong scope development and integrated planning process (Chapter 7). Projects that begin execution with clear objectives and requirements, integrated project teams, and thoroughly defined scope and project execution plans will experience fewer deviations and less need for changes.

With change management playing such a central role in the project control process, it is important that the procedure be well planned, disciplined, and documented, as well as formally communicated to all project team members. It is critical to change management that each project team member understand the process and roles and responsibilities for identifying, tracking, communicating, approving, and incorporating change as it will occur throughout the project lifecycle.

.1 Deviations, Variances, Trends, Changes, and Corrective Actions

As used in this section, the terms *deviations*, *trends*, and *changes* have unique definitions. Changes are alterations or variations to the scope of work and/or any other approved or baseline project control plan (e.g., schedule, budget, resource plans, etc.). A deviation is a departure, intentional or otherwise, in a work product or deliverable from established requirements (e.g., nonconformance with contract documents, the design basis or specifications, an imperfection or defect in a material, etc.). A trend is a non-random variance of actual project performance from that which was planned. Variance analysis is a method used to determine if a variance is a trend by identifying the root cause of the difference from plan and categorizing the difference for tracking and final disposition. Trends are commonly the result of changing market prices of labor or material, or varying labor productivity rates. While deviations, variances, and trends could be considered "changes" in the general sense of a change in status or conditions or changing performance over time, discussion of changes in this section are in reference to changes in scope or plans. In fact, one objective of the process is to help ensure that deviations, variances, and trends do not result in "changes."

In that respect, change management outputs include not only actions to incorporate changes in the scope and baseline plans, but corrective or improvement actions as well. Corrective actions are tasks or activities performed or directions given with the intent to mitigate or otherwise address a deviation in a work product, or a variance from planned project performance (i.e., to recover performance or improve or restore control). Improvement actions are tasks or activities performed or directions given with the intent to further improve upon an establish trend identified or to take advantage of new information, technology, market conditions, etc.

.2 Change Management and Associated Processes and Practices

The forecasting process (Section 10.2) is closely allied with change management because forecasting is used to assess each applicable element of the project control plan that is affected by a deviation, trend, change request, or opportunity (the effects often resulting from corrective or improvement actions). The forecasting process is linked to change management at its beginning with identification of change and at its finish when change is approved or rejected and the impact of change is incorporated into the revised forecast.

The risk management process (Section 7.6) is also closely allied with change management because not only is change a risk factor in itself, but the contingency cost control account (established in the risk management process to address risk impacts), which is typically the responsibility of the project manager, is managed through the change management process. Each non-scope change evaluated must be assessed within the context of the contingency allocated to the project. Furthermore, it is important to understand how the proposed change will impact the future risk profile of the project by introducing greater or less risk than considered in the baseline risk planning and contingency funds allocated.

Managing contract change is a part of the change management process. As was discussed in the procurement planning section (7.7), contracts are legal agreements between project suppliers, contractors, and the owner. Change often requires that new or revised agreements be established through the procurement process. However, change increases the risk that there will be disputes and legal claims; these are generally detrimental to project performance. Therefore, developing plans and applying methods for resolving disputes and claims are part of the change management process.

10.3.2 Process Map for Change Management

Figure 10.3-1 illustrates the process map for change management. As was mentioned, the change management process closes the project control cycle loop. It is largely a governing process that is characterized by extensive interaction between the forecasting (Section 10.2) and project control plan implementation (Chapter 8.1) processes.

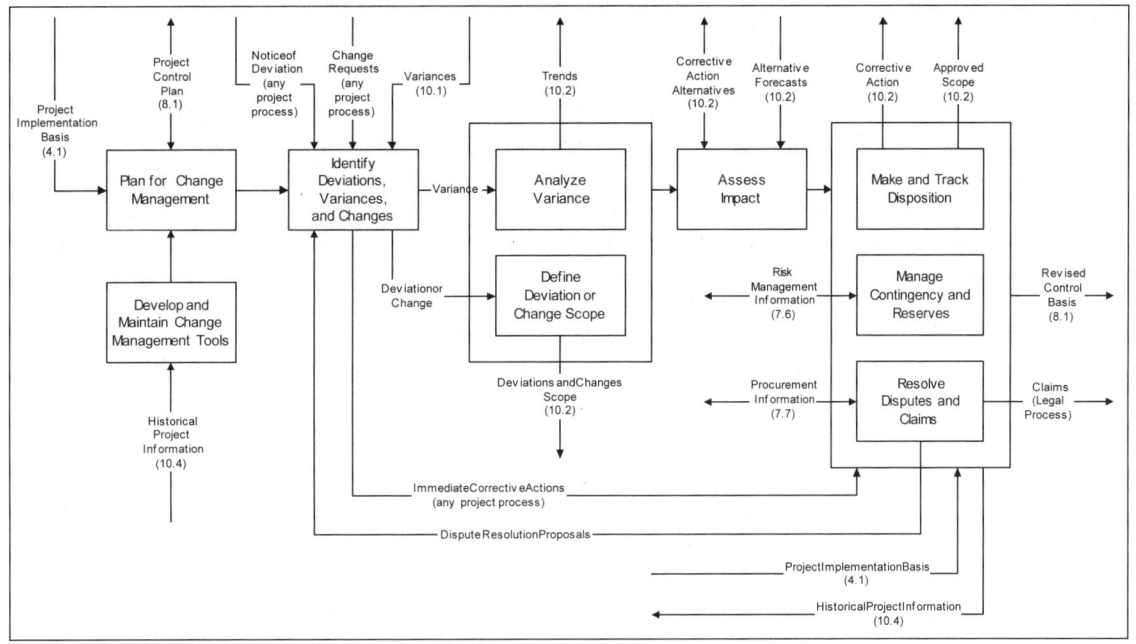

Figure 10.3-1 Process Map for Change Management

The following sections briefly describe the steps in the change management process.

.1 Plan for Change Management

Change management starts with planning. Initial planning starts with development of the execution strategy and work packages during scope development (Section 7.1) and continues through development of control accounts during project control plan implementation (Section 8.1). It is critical that the basis of each aspect of the project control plan be thoroughly documented because all deviations, change requests, and trends are assessed relative to that basis. The change management plan itself should describe specific systems and approaches to be used in change management in alignment with the other project control planning, measurement, and assessment processes.

Successful change management starts with good integrated project planning. Even the best planned and executed change management processes and systems (and project control as a whole) have been known to collapse under the burden of the avalanche of deviations, change requests, and trends that will result if initial project planning was poor.

Planning also assigns specific roles and responsibilities for change management. It is often said that change management is the responsibility of everyone involved with the project because the success of the process depends on everyone actively watching for and notifying project management of any potential or actual deviation or change. However, once that notice is made, change management, like other aspects of performance assessment, is generally a function performed by cost engineers in a project control role supporting the project manager. However, those responsible for the work packages affected by change, and the project team as a whole, will be included in assessments as appropriate; this creates a significant communication challenge. Change management for a large project may be a full time job for one or more people during project execution.

Another aspect to plan is the use of tools and systems for change management (e.g., deviation notice and change request forms, etc.). In addition, the interaction/interface of the owner, suppliers, and contractors in change management, including dispute and claims resolution processes, must be addressed in contracts and change management plans.

.2 Identify Deviations, Variances, and Change

The change management process depends on everyone with project work package responsibilities actively watching for and notifying project management of any potential or actual deviation or change. In addition, the performance assessment process (10.1) identifies and notifies project management of performance variances.

The initial notification should be immediate (e.g., verbal, e-mail, etc.), allowing the project manager to make immediate disposition (e.g., reject, direct an action, etc.) as appropriate. Immediate disposition may be appropriate if the correction action clearly has no significant impact on the project scope, plans, or performance of other activities. However, if the issue cannot be disposed of without further analysis of its nature and consequences, the notification is done in writing, usually using a previously established change notification form.

Notification forms have many names (e.g., deviation notices, change requests, etc.) but all have the same purpose of providing project management with a basic description of the nature of the deviation or change, a quick assessment of its cause and general impact, and basic descriptive data (e.g., name, date, location, etc.).

Once notified, project management records and begins tracking the deviations and change requests (i.e., using a change log or logs) to ensure that the change management process addresses each one appropriately. Notices should be categorized in the logs by source (e.g., business, engineering, etc.), engineering discipline/account category, cause (e.g., safety, environmental, constructability, etc.), and so on so that management can better understand the project change drivers. Applying greater levels of definition and categorization to notices during the logging process allows for improved analyses later in the process when root causes for change drivers are being sought and lessons learned are being determined. For contracted work, the contract will establish mechanisms for handling change requests.

Notification of performance variances is typically part of regular project status reporting. However, project management must be notified of variances observed outside of the normal assessment and report cycle as well. As with deviations and change requests, immediate disposition may be appropriate if the performance correction action clearly has no significant impact on the project scope, plans, or performance of other activities.

For those deviations, change requests, and variances for which disposition is not immediate, further definition and analysis is required before corrective actions can be taken.

.3 Analyze Variance

Variance analysis is a process to determine if a variation is a trend or a random occurrence and whether the variation is acceptable. If the variation is not acceptable, variance analysis also determines the most likely cause of the variation (whether it is a trend or random) and identifies potential corrective actions that address the cause. Corrective action alternative development is integrated with the forecasting process (Section 10.2).

Most project teams recognize that an unfavorable performance trend, being non-random, indicates that future performance is also likely to be similarly unfavorable unless corrective action is taken. However, the risk is less apparent, but no less in need of corrective action, when there is no bottom-line variance (e.g., cost is on budget), but the measure is unpredictable over time or between accounts. In other words, if the apparent good bottom-line performance is the result of luck, corrective action is needed to establish control.

.4 Define Deviation or Change Scope

The scope of deviations and change requests for which disposition is not immediate must be defined. The cause must also be assessed. The individual notification should include a basic description of the nature of the deviation or change, a quick assessment of its cause and general impact, and basic descriptive data (e.g., name, date, location, etc.).

After notification, it is usually a project control responsibility to further define the scope as needed to assess the change impact on overall project scope and plans. This scope definition step is integrated with the forecasting process (Section 10.2) that uses the methods of scope development (Section 7.1) as appropriate. At the same time, the most likely cause must be determined so that corrective actions can be developed that will both address the cause and mitigate impacts.

.5 Assess Impact

Having defined the nature and cause of trends and the scope and cause of deviations and change requests, corrective action alternatives are developed and assessed using the forecasting process (Section 10.2). Forecasting applies the methods of integrated project planning (Chapter 7) in the context of a project that is progressing while demanding quick and effective change management decisions.

The change management process may initially identify alternative actions to implement changes and to correct performance trends (including process improvements). These are generally simple action statements (e.g., "revise schedule logic"). The forecasting process develops the proposed action statements into actionable control plan alternatives for further assessment (e.g., "complete activity B before activity A"). Additional alternative actions may be identified in this process.

.6 Make and Track Disposition

Based on the impact assessment, a correction action is decided upon and implemented as appropriate. Project management records and tracks the trends, deviations, and change requests (i.e., using a trend log, change log, etc.) to ensure that the change management process addresses each one appropriately. If the disposition affects a supplier or contractor, and/or requires additional costs, then several other change management steps apply as described in the following paragraphs.

.7 Manage Contingency and Reserves

If an approved corrective action will cost more or less than the amount budgeted for the affected cost accounts, then budgeted funds, as approved, may be shifted from or to the contingency budget as appropriate. However, if the change represents a change of the project objectives and requirements, then additional or excess funding needs to be obtained or returned to the enterprise as appropriate. In some cases, the enterprise may have established a reserve account for such changes, and in that case, the funds may be obtained from that account with enterprise management approval.

The contingency account should be regularly assessed as to the contingency required for the remaining work. This is done using the methods of the risk management process (Section 7.6). That process evaluates and quantifies the impact of any risk factors inherent to the revised scope and plans. After a corrective action is decided upon, the risk management plan is updated.

The practices for assessing and managing the contingency cost account are sometimes called *contingency drawdown methods*. In some project systems, if the contingency required for the remaining work is less than the amount remaining in the contingency account, the excess contingency is returned to the enterprise so the strategic asset management process can use the funds for other investments. In other project systems, the excess funds, if any, are not returned until the project is closed out.

The advantage of periodic drawdowns is that they efficiently manage the enterprise's limited resources, and project teams are less likely to spend contingency funds on work outside of the current approved baseline project scope. The risk of periodic drawdowns is that if not prudently managed more contingency could be needed than available after drawdown. In this case, the project team may resort to risky control actions or inappropriately cutting scope rather than going through the process of replenishing contingency, which can by painful or problematic in organizations new to managing contingency in this manner .

.8 Resolve Disputes and Claims

Managing contract change is a part of the change management process. The interactions/interfaces of the owner, suppliers, and contractors in change management are addressed in contract documents and change management plans. However, change sometimes results in disputes and claims if the parties cannot agree on some aspect of the change in relation to contract agreements (i.e., scope, compensation, relief, damages, delay, etc.). Disputes are generally best resolved by the project team using the established contract mechanisms (i.e., dispute clauses), which may include arbitration.

However, if the dispute cannot be resolved by the project team, a claim may result. A claim is a written statement by one of the contracting parties seeking adjustment (e.g., additional time and/or money) or interpretation of an existing contract because of acts or omissions during the preparation of or performance of the contract. Unresolved claims are filed with the courts and from there the legal claims resolution process (which varies widely depending on the nature of the claim, jurisdictions, etc.) takes over. Claims resolution can become a project in itself, led by the legal function, often continuing well after the project from which it originated has been completed and otherwise closed out. Enterprises may establish objectives for the legal process that bear no relationship to the project from which the claim originated (e.g., establish legal precedence for the validity of a novel claim basis to be applied on current or future projects).

Claims resolution uses many of the planning, measurement, and assessment methods in the project control process, but in a forensic context to achieve the objectives of the parties to the claim. Any aspect of the planned and actual performance may be subject to dispute, analysis, negotiation, and resolution.

.9 Revised Control Basis

The change management process, in integration with the forecasting process (Section 10.2), results in a revised project control baseline against which performance will be measured and assessed (Section 8.1) for the remaining project. It is a project control responsibility to keep those responsible for work packages appraised of the approved control baselines.

The approved changes should be incorporated into the control basis using work package and control account methods. For project control, each control account must represent a discrete package of work and set of activities that are measurable and for which responsibility is assigned. For example, consider an approved change titled "Install a spare (bypass) pumping system." Change management assessment determined that this change affects work packages for the pump system, as well as the electrical system (i.e., the motor control center), and affects labor and material costs and includes activities for several disciplines and trades (e.g., mechanical, electrical, etc.). In other words, it affects many control and cost accounts for which the budget, resources, and activities will be revised accordingly.

Some projects incorporate changes in the control basis by establishing new control accounts for the entire change (e.g., "Install a spare (bypass) pumping system."). However, except for changes of the most limited nature, this approach violates project control principles (discrete packages of work and set of activities that are measurable and for which responsibility is assigned). If enough changes are implemented this way, the control basis will cease to be reliable (e.g., the electrical responsibility will no longer have a handle on the work they need to do).

At the close of the change management process, historical project information, including experiences and lessons learned about change management practices, is used to improve change management tools such as notification forms, logs, procedures, etc.

10.3.3 Inputs to Change Management

.1 *Project Implementation Basis.* (See Section 4.1.) This defines the basis asset scope, objectives, constraints, and assumptions, including basic assumptions about forecasting approaches. All changes must be evaluated with respect to their alignment with the project implementation basis.
.2 *Project Control Plans.* The project control plan (Section 8.1) describes specific systems, policies, procedures, and approaches to be used in project control, including change management.
.3 *Deviation Notices and Change Requests.* Anyone associated with the project may notify project management of a potential or actual deviation or change.
.4 *Variances.* Performance assessment (Section 10.1) identifies differences between actual and planned performance for any aspect of the project control plan for variance analysis in the change management process.
.5 *Corrective Action Alternatives.* Alternative designs, specifications, activities, activity logic, and so on are identified in concert with the forecasting process (Section 10.2).
.6 *Alternative Forecasts.* Forecasting (Section 10.2) provides expected plan and performance results for alternate corrective actions. Change management considers and decides upon the alternatives based in part on forecasting outcomes.
.7 *Risk Management Information.* Change management applies the methods of risk management (Section 7.6) to analyze risks of correction actions and to manage contingency.
.8 *Procurement Information.* Change management applies the methods of procurement planning (Section 7.7) to help avoid and resolve disputes and claims.
.9 *Historical Project Information.* Successful change management approaches are captured and applied as future planning references and to help improve change management methods and tools.

10.3.4 Outputs from Change Management

.1 *Project Control Plans.* Change management plans are considered in overall project control planning (and all other aspects of measurement and assessment planning).
.2 *Trends.* Trends, as identified through variance analysis, are considered in forecast analyses (Section 10.2).
.3 *Scope Definition.* (See Section 10.3.2.4) After identification of a deviation or change, it is usually a project control responsibility to further define the scope as needed to assess the change impact on overall project scope and plans. This scope definition step is integrated with the forecasting process (Section 10.2), which uses the methods of scope development (Section 7.1) as appropriate.
.4 *Selected Corrective Actions and Approved Scope.* The approved scope of changes and corrective actions is determined in the change management process and used in forecasting (10.2).
.5 *Corrective Action Alternatives.* The change management process initially identifies possible corrective actions. Forecasting (Section 10.2) may identify other alternative actions as well.
.6 *Alternative Forecasts.* The change management process considers and decides upon alternative actions based in part on forecasting results (Section 10.2).
.7 *Project Control Basis.* The revised scope of work and plans, including approved changes, becomes the revised project control baseline (Section 8.1).
.8 *Historical Project Information.* The project's change management approaches are captured and applied as future planning references and to help improve change management methods and tools.

10.3.5 Key Concepts for Change Management

The following concepts and terminology described in this and other chapters are particularly important to understanding the change management process of TCM:

.1 *Change Management*. (See Section 10.3.1).
.2 *Change*. (See Section 10.3.1.1).
.3 *Claim*. (See Section 10.3.2.8).
.4 *Contingency*. (See Section 7.6). Risk and uncertainty are quantified and incorporated in baseline cost, schedule, and other plans. The quantification is called contingency.
.5 *Corrective Action*. (See Section 10.3.1.1). Also improvement action.
.6 *Deviation*. (See Section 10.3.1.1).
.7 *Dispute*. (See Section 10.3.2.8).
.8 *Forecast*. (See Section 10.2). The project team's estimate of the most likely outcome for a given element of the project plan (e.g., cost forecast, schedule forecast, etc.) Forecasts are a basis for selecting corrective actions.
.9 *Reserves*. (See Section 7.6). Funds included in an approved budget, but are not expected to be needed to address originally defined project baseline requirements. In general, reserves may only be released for expenditure by enterprise management.
.10 *Trend*. (See Section 10.3.1.1).
.11 *Variance*. (See Section 10.3.1.1).
.12 *Variance Analysis*. (See Section 10.3.1.1).

Further Readings and Sources

The project control change management process is covered in most project management and control texts (i.e., see readings for Section 2.4). The following references provide basic information and will lead to more detailed treatments.

- Amos, Scott J., Editor. *Skills and Knowledge of Cost Engineering*, 5th ed. Morgantown, WV: AACE International, 2004.
- Gransberg, Douglas D., and James Koch, Editors. *Professional Practice Guide No. 12: Construction Project Controls*. CD ROM. Morgantown, WV: AACE International, 2002.
- Humphreys, Kenneth K., Editor. *Project and Cost Engineer's Handbook*, 4th ed. New York: Marcel Dekker, Inc., 2005.
- Uppal, Kul B., Editor. *Professional Practice Guide No. 8: Contingency*. CD ROM. Morgantown, WV: AACE International, 2001.
- Zack, James G., Editor. *Professional Practice Guide No. 1: Contracts and Claims*. CD ROM. Morgantown, WV: AACE International, 2000.

10.4 Project Historical Database Management

10.4.1 Description

Project historical database management is a process for collecting, maintaining, and analyzing project historical information so that it is ready for use by the other project control processes and for strategic asset management. Empirical information is the most fundamental project planning resource available and it is manifested in the form of quantified and documented historical data and information. The historical database management process captures empirical information and retains this experience within the institutional memory to support the development of continually improving project plans as well as improved methods and tools. The purpose of the process is not to repeat history, but to learn from it (i.e., to enable continuous improvement in the project system).

To illustrate historical data's importance, Figure 10.4-1 provides a simplified block flow diagram of the information flow in the project control process. Each block represents a project control process that incorporates data manipulation methods or tools (e.g., cost estimating system). The interconnecting lines show the general flow of data and information products among the processes. Clearly, if you remove the historical block from the diagram, there is no closure in the information flow. Without the historical data process, project planning methods and tools have no other basis other than the personal knowledge of the project team members; no institutional memory is developed and no opportunity of a learning organization exists.

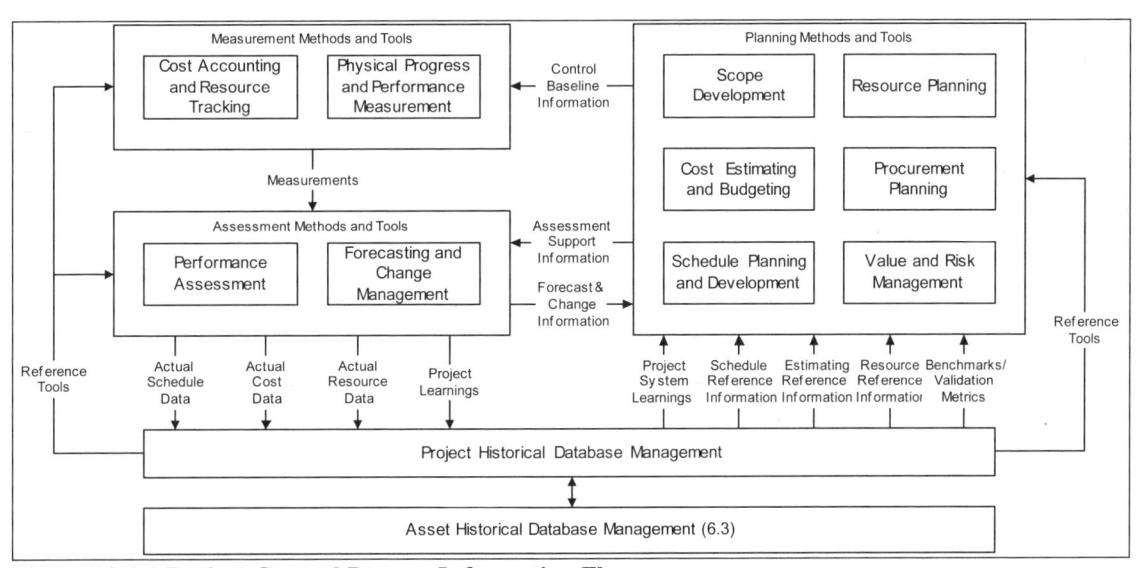

Figure 10.4-1 Project Control Process Information Flow

Figure 10.4-1 is essentially the same as Figure 6.3-1 (Section 6.3) for the asset historical database management process. While the figures show separate blocks for the asset and project processes, the distinction between them is somewhat artificial. Both processes have similar needs for performance benchmarks, cost references, and other information. If an enterprise's project system is viewed as a strategic asset of the enterprise, the asset database can be viewed as the master. In any case, through a relational database structure or some other means, the databases should be integrated, allowing users to access life cycle information about the asset and project portfolios.

10.4.2 Process Map for Project Historical Data Management

Figure 10.4-2 illustrates the process map for asset historical database management. The two main steps of the process include collecting data of various types and processing it into useful information products.

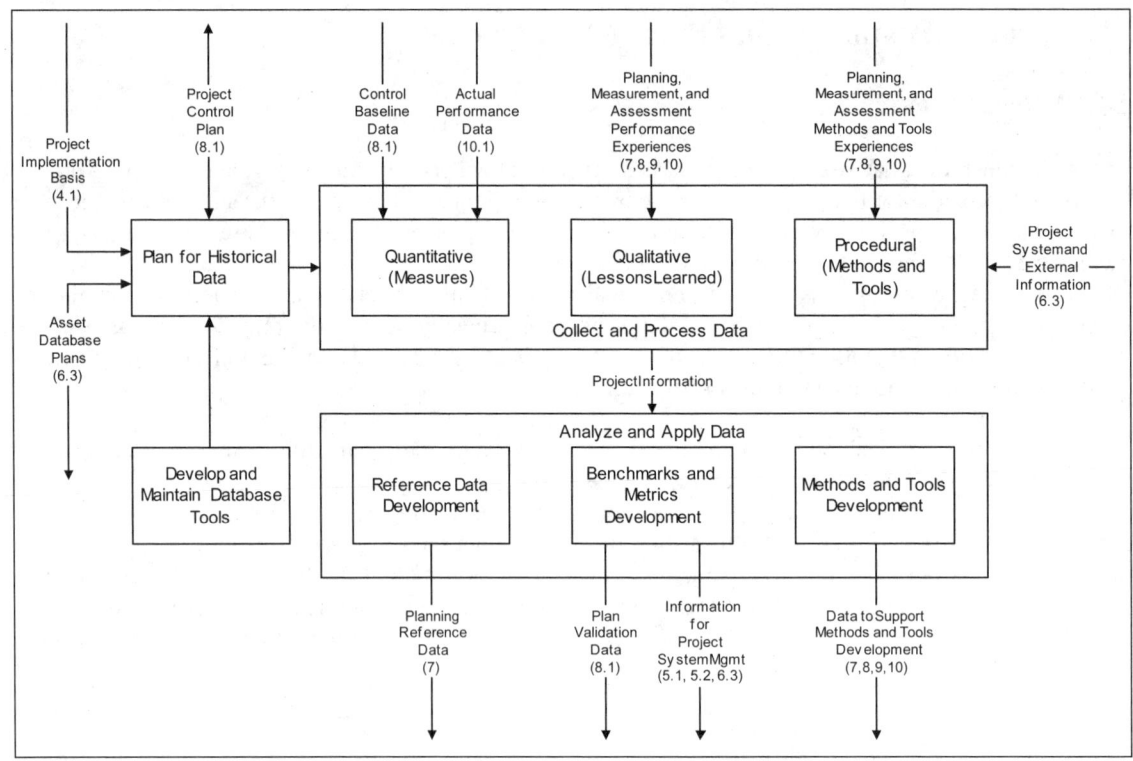

Figure 10.4-2 Process Map for Project Historical Database Management

The following sections briefly describe the steps in the project historical database management process.

.1 Plan for Historical Database Management

Project historical database management starts with planning. The database is a strategic asset of the enterprise. As such, planning the database management process for a given project must first consider the status and requirements of the master database(s). The database plan must then address the interface/interaction of the project data inputs and outputs with the master database as well as issues such as data format and level of granularity.

The project inputs include planned and actual quantitative data and qualitative information about the performance of project work and control methods and tools. The quantitative data (e.g., cost estimates, actual costs, schedules, etc.) must be processed. Processing includes cleaning, organizing, and normalizing the data as required for inclusion in the master database(s) for continued use. The qualitative information (e.g., learnings, etc.) must be cleaned, organized, and standardized as required for inclusion as well. These collection and processing activities, many of which are done at the time of project completion (i.e., project closeout), must be planned and resources allocated for their performance.

The processed quantitative data are then used for the development and maintenance of reference databases for planning (e.g., estimating line-item database), metrics for plan validation (e.g., check estimate competitiveness), and tools development (e.g., estimating algorithm development, templates, etc.). The processed information, including lessons learned, helps guide the effective application of the data in the development and maintenance tasks, but also serves as a direct reference to aid project planning. Much of this analysis and development is done on a project system or programmatic level (Section 6.3); however, a given project may require special data products that need to be developed for use on that project (e.g., estimating algorithms for equipment using new technology).

The plan for project historical database management must address the collection and processing work that will be somewhat project specific, but also the project's interface with the existing or future master database (i.e., guidelines, procedures, and systems used by all the enterprise's assets and projects). Planning topics may include, but are not limited to, the following:

- roles and responsibilities
- allocated resources
- collection methods (during the project and at closeout)
- data structure and format (i.e., work breakdown or cost code structure)
- level of detail and comprehensiveness of records
- data and record quality
- storage and maintenance (tools and systems)
- access and retrieval (methods and access rights)
- analysis methods (where applicable)
- information product quality (data validation)
- legal issues (retention, claims issues, etc.)

Databases may capture both electronic and hard-copy information; each type of datum has specific considerations. In whatever form it is captured, the goal is to store the data in a way that is easy to find, retrieve, update, and use. Additionally, there may be multiple databases that support specific purposes and each must be considered while planning to ensure that the data collection process captures required information/data at the proper levels of granularity (e.g., databases specific to an estimating system for a particular technology). Finally, some enterprises have limits or restrictions on retaining original data and records that must be adhered to as a matter of policy and must be addressed (e.g., use the raw data to create metrics, then discard the original data).

Data collection and processing activities may be a responsibility of cost engineers in a project control role supporting the project manager. The project data collected and processed are typically channeled to a single project control professional responsible for overall master database maintenance, analysis, and development supporting the enterprise's overall project system. These parties must coordinate their efforts in order to develop, implement, and maintain an effective database. Another aspect to incorporate into the data collection and processing plan is the interaction/interface of suppliers and contractors with the owner's data collection methods and format. Others on the project team are also likely to have roles in providing and processing raw data. Giving prior consideration to the available data format and granularity may significantly ease data integration into the database or facilitate the data's later use.

.2 Collect and Process Data

Quantitative (Measures)

The database inputs include estimated, planned, and actual quantitative data about the performance of project work. The quantitative data (cost, hours, schedule durations, etc.) must be collected and processed.

Data collection is usually performed as a part of the project closeout process. Data are often collected by completing a form or forms that are set up with a standard coding structure and level of detail consistent with master database requirements. The forms should also capture information that identifies and characterizes the project in terms of name, location, project type, execution strategies used, and so on. Schedule durations can be captured in form tables, but it is also useful to keep a copy of the electronic schedule or a printout so that the schedule logic is retained.

Data processing includes cleaning, organizing, and normalizing as appropriate to incorporate the data into the master database(s) for continued use. Data cleaning refers to ensuring that data are complete and acceptably accurate for database purposes, which may differ from accounting and finance purposes. Organizing data refers to ensuring that data are coded in accordance with the code of accounts and/or other structures used by the database and are otherwise identifiable (e.g., meaningful account titles, category descriptions, etc.).

It should be noted that cost data as reported directly from cost accounting systems are useful, but are usually neither clean nor organized in a manner that best supports project control planning, methods and tools development, and so on.

Normalizing data is a more complex step that involves translating the data so that they are on a standard or "normal" basis in terms of time, location, and currency. For example, if the project was located in Canada in 2005, and costs are in Canadian dollars, but all the other projects in the database were U.S. projects, entered in 1998 U.S. dollars, then the project's cost would need to be adjusted (for currency exchange rate and time value of money differences) before entry into the database. After processing, the data may then be entered in an electronic database and/or kept in hard-copy form.

Qualitative Data (Process Lessons Learned)

Database inputs also include qualitative information about the performance of the project process or system. This information may include assessments of how successful the project was in achieving its objectives, and what factors contributed to the project's success or failure. Subjective information may be captured through the use of surveys, narrative descriptions, interviews, or formal lessons learned workshops. More objective information can be obtained by benchmarking the project. Benchmarking involves comparing the project's practices and performance to selected projects or project systems that used the best practices and achieved the best performance.

The qualitative information must also be cleaned, organized, and standardized as required for incorporation into master database(s). After processing, the data may then be entered in an electronic database and/or kept in hard-copy form. The goal is to capture qualitative information that will allow the next project team to build on successful approaches, avoid repeating unsuccessful ones, and provide context for assessing quantitative data.

Procedural (Methods and Tools Lessons Learned)

In an extension of the above methods, additional qualitative information is captured about the performance of project control methods and tools. In this case, the goal is to capture information that will support efforts by the enterprise to develop or improve methods and tools (e.g., new or updated templates, forms, information systems, etc.) for the project system.

For example, the process lessons learned may identify that project control results were poor because the cost accounting processes did not provide timely cost measurement to support performance assessment. In that case, lessons learned about accounting system methods and tools would be examined to find ways to improve project cost accounting timeliness.

.3 Analyze and Process Data

Reference Data Development

Many planning and assessment methods and tools rely on reference databases of some sort. For example, the reference database for a cost estimating system may contain standard unit hours, unit costs, adjustment factors, and similar measures of work or material item cost and resource requirements. The reference data provide an empirical basis for planning.

The reference data should be consistent, reliable, and competitive with a well defined basis (e.g., assumptions, conditions, etc.) such that any project team can determine how its requirements and basis conditions differ from the reference and adjust accordingly. The quality of a reference database is not judged by how correct or accurate its entries are in terms of representing the absolute cost or duration of any given item or activity on any given project. Rather, it is judged by how reliable it is a planning "base" in terms of competitiveness and consistency with consistency meaning that the basis is known and is consistent between similar items and does not change over time unless its change has been justified by analysis.

Reference data are typically normalized to a standard basis (i.e., in terms of time, location, currency, conditions, etc.). Project data may be normalized at the time of collection and processing, or at the time that the reference database is created or updated. Established reference databases generally do not require constant updating; annual updates are common. At the time of review and update, the data from projects collected over the period are analyzed to determine if the existing data are still good references. If new reference data are developed, the basis must be consistent and well documented.

Benchmarks and Metrics Development
Benchmarks and metrics are a form of reference data, but the purpose is primarily to support the validation of project plans (Section 8.1). Benchmarking is a process that compares practices, processes, and relevant measures to those of a selected basis of comparison (i.e., the benchmark) with the goal of improving performance. The comparison basis includes internal or external competitive or best practices, processes, or measures. Validation is a form of benchmarking applied specifically to plans to assess whether the plan results are competitive and achieve the performance objectives.

A planning tool reference database typically contains data that support deterministic (i.e., bottoms-up or detailed) planning of low level components of the work breakdown. A metrics database will typically contain data (e.g., factors, ratios, etc) that support assessment of top levels of the work breakdown structure. For example, an estimating systems reference database may contain standard unit hours for discrete items of work (e.g., 2 hours per cubic meter to install rebar for a concrete spread footer) while a metrics database may contain standard unit hours for aggregated items of work (e.g., 8 hours per cubic meter to install all process plant cast-in-place concrete). Metrics are also useful references for stochastic (i.e., top-down or conceptual) planning methods and tools.

Methods and Tools Development
Each of the project control processes includes a step for methods and tools development (e.g., new or updated templates, forms, systems, etc.). Each of these processes has historical information as an input for development of methods and tools. This information typically includes examples of methods and tools used on other projects and lessons learned from their use. In addition to qualitative analyses to promote continuous improvement, quantitative data can be used to support the development of planning algorithms (e.g., regression analysis of inputs and outputs to develop parametric estimating or scheduling models). Models are particularly critical to the asset planning process (see Section 3.2).

10.4.3 Inputs to Project Historical Data Management

.1 *Project Implementation Basis.* (See Section 4.1.) This defines the basis asset scope, objectives, constraints, and assumptions. The historical database management plans must be evaluated with respect to their alignment with project objectives and requirements including the status and requirements for the master database(s).
.2 *Project Control Plans.* The project control plan (Section 8.1) describes specific systems and approaches to be used in project control including historical database management.
.3 *Control Baseline Data.* The historical database captures plan data (Section 8.1) as well as actual performance data.
.4 *Actual Performance Data.* Performance assessment (Section 10.1) feeds actual performance data to the historical database management process, most often at the time of project closeout.
.5 *Performance and Methods and Tools Experiences.* Qualitative lessons learned are collected from all project control processes (Chapters, 7, 8, 9, and 10).
.6 *Project System and External Information.* The strategic asset management process (Section 6.3) provides both internal project system and external industry benchmarking data.

10.4.4 Outputs from Project Historical Data Management

.1 *Project Control Plans.* Historical database management plans are considered in overall project control planning (and all other aspects of measurement and assessment planning).
.2 *Planning Reference Data.* Many planning methods and tools (Chapter 7 sections) rely on historically based reference data.
.3 *Plan Validation Data.* Benchmarking and validation methods (Section 8.1) rely on historically based benchmarks and metrics.
.4 *Data to Support Methods and Tools Development.* Each of the project control processes (Chapters 7, 8, 9, and 10) includes a step for methods and tools development and each of these steps has historical project information (e.g., go-bys, lessons learned, modeling inputs, etc.) as an input.
.5 *Information for Project System Management.* Project data are inputs to the strategic asset management measurement processes (Sections 5.1 and 5.2) and asset management database (Section 6.3). The database itself is a strategic asset of the enterprise.

10.4.5 Key Concepts for Project Historical Data Management

The following concepts and terminology described in this and other chapters are particularly important to understanding the project historical database management process of TCM:

.1 *Database.* Any collection of data or information that is retained for future use. The database is the documented manifestation of experience.
.2 *Reference Data.* Any database data or information that is used by a system to support its function (primarily empirical, quantitative data). Reference data quality is judged by how reliable it is as a planning "base" in terms of competitiveness and consistency, with consistency meaning that the basis is known, is consistent between similar items, and does not change over time unless its change has been justified by analysis.
.3 *Lessons Learned.* Qualitative information that describes what was learned during the performance of a process, method, or tool. Lessons learned are captured in a database to support development or improvement of processes, methods, and tools.
.4 *Metric.* Database data (primarily empirical, quantitative factors, ratios, etc.) that are used to assess the results of a process, method, or tool (see *Validation*).
.5 *Benchmark.* A metric that supports the benchmarking process.
.6 *Benchmarking.* A measurement and analysis process that compares practices, processes, and relevant measures to those of a selected basis of comparison (i.e., the benchmark) with the goal of improving performance.
.7 *Validation.* In project control, a form of benchmarking applied specifically to project plans to assess whether the plan results are competitive and achieve the project's performance objectives (see *Benchmarking*).
.8 *Continuous Improvement.* Quality or process management methods that continuously identify, assess, and implement ideas to improve process performance. The methods use quantitative performance measurements of the process to identify improvement opportunities and ideas and to assess the results of implemented ideas. Databases are often used to retain measurement data.
.9 *Normalization.* To adjust data to a standard (i.e., normal) basis in terms of time, location, currency, technology, or other characteristics that define the normal basis.
.10 *Project Closeout.* A process performed at the end of a project to ensure that all project work, obligations, measurements, and transactions (e.g., charges, payments, etc.) are complete and systems are closed; to perform and report final project performance assessments; and to ensure that all required data, information, lessons learned, and deliverables are collected and processed for the appropriate historical database.
.11 *Basis.* Documentation that describes how an estimate, schedule, or other plan or database component was developed and defines the information used in support of development. A basis document commonly includes, but is not limited to, a description of the scope included, methodologies used,

references and defining deliverables used, assumptions and exclusions made, clarifications, adjustments, and some indication of the level of uncertainty.

.12 *Code of Accounts.* Systematic coding structures for organizing and managing asset, cost, resource, and schedule activity information. An index to facilitate finding, sorting, compiling, summarizing, and otherwise managing information that the code is tied to.

Further Readings and Sources

Despite the importance of empirical data to cost engineering processes and methods, the project historical data management process is not well covered by industry texts. The following references provide some basic information and will lead to more detailed treatments.

- Amos, Scott J., Editor. *Skills and Knowledge of Cost Engineering*, 5th ed. Morgantown, WV: AACE International, 2004.
- Hollmann, John K. "Project History—Closing the Loop," *AACE International Transactions*. Morgantown, WV: AACE International, 1995.
- Humphreys, Kenneth K., Editor. *Project and Cost Engineer's Handbook*, 4th ed. New York: Marcel Dekker, Inc., 2005.

IV. TOTAL COST MANAGEMENT ENABLING PROCESSES

CHAPTER 11

ENABLING PROCESSES

11.1 The Enterprise in Society

11.1.1 Description

This section concerns the *value* of the *enterprise* and its *strategic assets* to *society*. A premise of the TCM process is that the enterprise and its strategic assets (including the resources and processes it uses, products it makes, and so on) should have a positive sustainable value to society and should continually strive to improve that value. Before proceeding with the discussion, the terms in the opening sentence must be clearly understood:

- *Value* (re: Section 7.5 and 11.5): A measure of the worth of a thing in terms of usefulness, desirability, importance, money, etc.
- *Enterprise* (re: Section 1.4): Any endeavor, business, government entity, group, or individual that owns or controls strategic assets.
- *Strategic Asset* (re: Section 1.4): Any unique physical or intellectual property of some scope that is of long term or ongoing *value* to the enterprise.
- *Society*: The human environment in which the enterprise exists as defined by its economic, political, legal, and other attributes. Society's stakeholders are its citizens, including enterprises.

.1 Societal Values

This section is included because the TCM processes have been primarily described from a quantitative, monetary perspective with the primary end of the process being the wealth or monetary welfare of the enterprise's owners. We need to remind ourselves that TCM, at least in the investment decision making process (see Section 3.3), should be concerned with *economic costs*. Economic costs consider that the value of money is relative to time, currency, and context, including the societal context; that is, an amount of money saved to benefit both the enterprise and society has a greater value than the same amount of money saved to benefit only the enterprise. All *societal values* must be considered in planning, measurement, and assessment.

A challenge with considering societal values is in how to measure them. They tend to be highly subjective and differ between individuals, groups, cultures, locales, and so on. It is also difficult to determine who the stakeholders in society are for a given situation. There is lively debate and much active research in the social, economic, and decision science fields (e.g., welfare economics, industrial ecology, etc.) around the issues of measuring and assessing social and environmental values and considering them in economic decisions. Much of the work involves very complex valuation modeling. Some social scientists consider it nearly impossible to make an economic-based decision with any certainty that it will maximize social welfare; however, enterprises are increasingly expected by society (politically, legally, or otherwise) to make the attempt.

In TCM, these issues arise mainly in the strategic asset planning processes (Chapter 3). For example, starting in Section 3.1, customer and stakeholder needs and desires are elicited and requirements result from analyzing this input. Among those needs and desires are subjective societal values. To simplify and ensure consistency in the requirements elicitation and analysis process (and asset planning and investment decision making later), many enterprises establish *policy* (i.e. *decision policy*) in regards to social values. For example, enterprise policy may establish a requirement that all its facilities around the globe must meet the most stringent environmental, health, and safety (EHS: Section 11.5) standards regardless of the value the local citizens place on these social issues. An enterprise must also consider the policies of other enterprises that it works with or establishes relationships with (partners, contractors, etc.). Such policies are important considering that the cost to an enterprise for making a wrong social value judgment may be extreme.

.2 Ethics

At all times, each person in the enterprise must judge the means and the ends of a process against personal and societal values and rules of conduct. These values and rules of conduct are referred to as *ethics*. In judging, people and organizations must ask questions about the means and ends such as: Are they fair, respectful, responsible, honest, and honorable? Society sets the framework for this questioning, but individuals and organizations make the judgments and set the rules. Discussions of society values therefore often involve a discussion of ethics or ethical values. Most enterprises will have an ethics policy if none other concerning social values.

This brief discussion is a lead in to Section 11.2, which continues this discussion in regards to individuals, teams, and organizations, which are subsets of the enterprise and society. Section 11.6 discusses the environment, health, safety, and security, which are key concerns for society.

11.1.2 Key Concepts for the Enterprise in Society

The preceding discussions briefly touch on a few considerations regarding society. The starting premise for the TCM process is that the enterprise and its strategic assets should have a positive sustainable value to society and should continually strive to improve that value. The following concepts and terminology described in this section are particularly important to understanding the enterprise in society for TCM.

.1 *Societal Values.* (Section 11.1.1.1).
.2 *Economic Costs.* (Section 11.1.1.1).
.3 *Decision Policy.* (Section 11.1.1.1).
.4 *Ethics* (Section 11.1.1.2).

Further Readings and Sources

The references from the social sciences, economics, decision science, and related fields are too numerous to mention. Professionals should familiarize themselves with their enterprise's ethics code and related social decision policy, if any. The AACE International Canon of Ethics (part of its Constitution and Bylaws) includes the following statements: "The AACE member…will apply knowledge and skill to advance *human welfare*," and further, "Members will hold paramount the safety, health, and *welfare of the public*, including that of future generations."

11.2 People and Performance Management

11.2.1 Description

TCM is the sum of the practices and processes that an enterprise uses to manage the total life cycle cost investment in its portfolio of strategic assets. Costs include any investment of resources, with human resources being a major category along with materials, time, money, and information. Therefore, the effective utilization of human resources is an integral part of TCM. However, in the process sections of the *TCM Framework*, resources, including human resources, are generally described from a quantitative perspective as something to plan, measure, and assess. The goal of this section is to highlight some unique qualitative considerations for managing human resources.

11.2.2 Leadership and Management of People[60]

.1 Leadership

Leadership is not about imposing control, but about obtaining commitment from people to support enterprise goals and objectives. It is about positively influencing people's behavior toward self control and enhanced individual and group performance. To obtain commitment from people around objectives, a leader must first understand those enterprise objectives, develop a personal vision of their purpose, and communicate the vision and get other stakeholders to see that they have a shared purpose. For this, a leader must develop an environment of mutual trust.

Behavioral scientists have advanced a number of theories about leadership. Without detailing each theory, they collectively indicate that successful leaders have an attitude of trust and respect for people and their opinions; a balanced concern for individuals, people, and relationships versus organization, process, and production; and an understanding of motivating factors (e.g., a challenging job, good working conditions, etc.). The theories also indicate that to be a good leader, or team member, one must understand and challenge one's own attitudes and assumptions about people and their behavior.

.2 Teams

Few endeavors of an enterprise are undertaken by individuals acting alone. Significant and challenging activities can only be accomplished through integrated efforts of several individuals. However, high-performing, successful teams do not just happen; they are built by leaders who can obtain the team member commitment, despite sometimes differing personal objectives, to support enterprise goals and objectives. There are many challenges to effective team building including team members' differing motivations and expectations, and differing attitudes and assumptions about people, work, and accountability. It is a leader's responsibility to communicate to the team clear goals that are tied to overall business objectives and customer requirements and then work with the team to address the challenges and obtain commitment to work together toward the common goals.

Team members' differences are both challenges and opportunities. Differences in the way team members think and act (e.g., some are intuitive, others logical) can be leveraged so that a team takes a balanced approach to problems. Differences in team members' cultural backgrounds can be taken advantage of in the same way. However, the attributes that add richness to a team may also add more complications for the leader to work through. Significant differences and conflicts should always be addressed, not ignored. One more important aspect of team building is that team members' goals and

---

[60] This subsection is largely abstracted from Levin, Ginger, "Leadership and Management of Project People" (Chapter 22) in *Skills and Knowledge of Cost Engineering*, 5th edition, AACE International, Morgantown, WV, 2004. That text and, by extension, this one include excerpts from Flannes, Steven W., and Ginger Levin, *People Skills for Project Managers*, Vienna, VA: Management Concepts Inc., 2001; Reprinted with permission.

objectives may not coincide with the enterprise's goals and objectives. The team leader must be aware of that fact and work toward team integration or minimizing the gaps between diverse goals.

.3 Leadership Roles: Leading, Managing, Facilitating, and Mentoring

The most effective leaders have the ability to assume different roles through the life cycle of managing assets or projects. The appropriate role—leader, manager, facilitator, or mentor—is assumed depending on the team member's respective needs for shared vision, structure and discipline, path clearing, or personal guidance.

The role of leader takes priority when the team loses sight of its shared purpose. The manager role of providing structure and discipline is called for when self-control is not keeping things on track. Facilitation is needed when roadblocks such as conflicts between teams, resource shortages, or other obstacles call for the leader's influence to clear the way or help the team members find paths to do their jobs. The role of mentor or coach is important when an individual's skills, knowledge, or behavior need development or improvement and some guidance, assistance, feedback, or role modeling might help that individual and, by extension, also help the team.

.4 Motivation

When people are involved in a process or system such as TCM, successful performance toward a goal often depends on the motivation of the people involved. However, in the TCM process, the questions asked regarding performance measurement, assessment, and actions toward a goal are focused on impersonal attributes such as: What are the asset or project value drivers? The cost drivers? The risk drivers? The question TCM has not asked is: What is driving the team member's performance or behavior toward the goal? What are the personal value, cost, and risk equations that individuals consciously or unconsciously measure, assess, and act upon? As was mentioned, a good leader must understand what motivates team member behavior that supports effective individual and team performance.

The drivers (i.e., motivators or demotivators) may come from either intrinsic or extrinsic sources. Sources of intrinsic motivation rise from within people, such as a personal desire to learn or to help others. Extrinsic sources originate from outside the person, such as rewards or improved working conditions. To have an impact, extrinsic sources must either counter or complement intrinsic sources. For example, if a person has no desire to learn, an offer of reimbursement for education costs is unlikely to have an effect on that person's actions. If, however, that person has a desire for money or esteem, an opportunity for higher pay or a better title with an increased level of education may have an effect. A leader must understand a person's intrinsic motivations in order to find extrinsic motivators or *incentives* that will improve behavior and performance without violating anyone's ethics.

As with leadership, behavioral scientists have advanced many theories about motivation. These have characterized the subject from the perspectives of evolution, biology, drives, needs, and social influence. The many theories will not be described here, but each of these perspectives is in agreement that individuals display a wide range of motives. Each theory also begins with the premise that motivation involves goal-directed behavior.

.5 Ethics

The preceding discussions concern how leaders influence people's behavior and the performance of actions (i.e., the means) toward enterprise goals, objectives, and purpose (i.e., the ends). As discussed in Section 11.1, at all times, each person in the enterprise must judge the means and the ends against personal and societal values and rules of conduct. In judging, people and organizations must ask questions about the means and ends, such as: Are they fair, respectful, responsible, honest, and honorable? Society sets the framework for this questioning, but individuals and organizations make the judgments and set the rules. Most organizations have ethics programs or rules of conduct. For example, AACE International has a

Canon of Ethics, which if violated by a member, may subject that individual to expulsion from the Association.[61]

11.2.3 Organizations[62]

The preceding discussion of leadership focused on people working in teams. However, teams are part of an enterprise's organizational structure. Therefore, TCM process activities as well as the concepts of leadership, motivation, and ethics must be considered in the context of the established or changing organizational structure.

.1 Organization Structure Design and Development

An organizational structure can be considered a strategic asset of the enterprise, and it can be managed using the TCM process. Organizational requirements and plans should be based on the needs and objectives of the enterprise; performance should be measured and assessed, changes controlled (i.e., *organizational development*), and so on. As with any asset or project, the structure and scope must be well defined and communicated to the stakeholders so they understand how they are tied to the enterprises' objectives.

Traditionally, the design of an organization structure must consider the following principles:

- *Division of labor.* Consider departmentalization or specialization.
- *Unity of command.* Consider lines or chains of command.
- *Unity of directions.* Consider authority and responsibility.
- *Span of control.* Consider levels of control and degree of centralization.

Traditionally, there are three structural design frameworks used, for which the preceding principles are considered:

- *Functional.* Focused on division of labor or specialization (e.g., cost engineering)
- *Divisional.* Focused on unity of command and direction concerning product lines and/or regions. Typically, each division is organized functionally.
- *Matrix*: Focused on tasks. Typically, task managers draw resources from functional and divisional organizations as needed.

Typically, each design will have lateral or "dotted line" relationships, liaisons, and temporary attributes to meet special needs. Many enterprises also have hybrid organizational designs because each design has advantages and disadvantages in terms of the efficient and effective use of resources, decision making, and encouragement of expertise development.

Functional designs encourage expertise development and avoid duplication of resources, but tend to be "siloed" or more focused on the needs of the specialty than the integration of specialties needed to serve processes, products, or customers. Divisional designs improve the focus on product and customers and decision making concerning them, but tend to use resources inefficiently because each division uses functional organization, which may foster detrimental rivalries. Matrix designs use resources efficiently and have a focus on the task (i.e., process, product, project, or customer), but they complicate decision making and allocation of resources because lines of authority are less clear (e.g., a person may have two supervisors: functional and project). In today's complex world, organization structures tend to be complex

---

[61] The introduction to the Canon of Ethics reads: "The AACE member, to uphold and advance the honor and dignity of Cost Engineering and the Cost Management profession and in keeping with the high standards of ethical conduct will (1) be honest and impartial and will serve employer, clients, and the public with devotion; (2) strive to increase the competence and prestige of their profession; and (3) will apply knowledge and skill to advance human welfare."

[62] Some of this subsection is abstracted from Bent, James A., "Project Organization Structure" (Chapter 19), in *Skills and Knowledge of Cost Engineering*, 5th edition, AACE International, Morgantown, WV, 2004.

models that integrate the three traditional designs into one structure that can dynamically serve an enterprise's overall strategies.

.2 Organization Structure Design and Development for TCM

In TCM, a key organization concern is the *authority* to make decisions as to a commitment or investment of enterprise resources (i.e., time, people, or money). Authority is a concern because the *matrix* type of organization design is commonly used in TCM, particularly for *project management*. A matrix works well because asset and project management are task and product-focused efforts using teams with resource needs that vary over the life cycle of the effort. A matrix is a flexible and efficient design for drawing resources from functional and divisional organizations as needed. Organization charts for a matrix organization are dynamic and must constantly be revised.

However, the matrix design complicates decision making because team, functional, and divisional managers may have conflicting authority over resources. Team members that report to multiple supervisors may become confused as to whom they should listen. This situation places a premium on leadership and planning. Specifically, leadership ensures that everyone shares a clear vision of common purpose to avoid rivalries and conflict. Planning ensures that there is unity of direction; that is, it clearly establishes guidelines of who has authority for different types of decisions. Enterprises that have project systems (see Section 4.1) will have such established guidelines. The authority of the team manager must be adequate to allow efficient day-to-day operations. Planning also makes sure that resources are allocated wisely.

Each TCM process map includes a planning step in which roles, authority, and responsibility are established. Also, the resource planning (Section 7.4) and procurement planning (Section 7.7) processes must consider the owner and contractor organization structures and how they will interact. These processes must also consider whether the owner or contractor has sufficient qualified resources for specific roles and activities.

Because of their intimate knowledge of asset and project cost investments, cost engineers are expected to be good stewards of the enterprise's resources. Some organizations institutionalize this idea by having them report to a functional or division manager rather than the team manager; that is, they become in part an internal auditor of the team's function. However, this can lead to mistrust; the cost engineer should be a close and trusted advisor to the team manager. A better way to ensure cost engineers' independence to fairly assess and report cost issues is to have team managers direct them, but ensure that no one team manager has an undue influence on their future career (e.g., make sure performance appraisals are balanced).

While the TCM project control process almost always employs teams organized in a matrix structure, it is more common to find a divisional structure used for the strategic asset management process because the division usually "owns" and operates the asset (i.e., *operational management*) and has a less temporary focus than a project team. A division may have its own established *capital management* or *strategic planning* department, function, or team that handles much of the asset management process. However, when separate divisions within the enterprise are given authority to decide on major investments for their part of the asset portfolio, there is a risk that the decisions will be biased, often unintentionally, by their parochial needs and desires and by competitive instincts (i.e., "pet projects"). Yielding to biases, or lacking a unified vision, a division's assets may evolve through many small upgrade and maintenance projects into something that no longer meets the enterprise's strategic requirements in some regard.[63] While TCM does not address business strategy development (strategy is an input), the effective application of TCM in deploying that strategy requires strategic alignment between organizations and calls for planning, measuring, and assessing the enterprise's asset portfolio as a whole.

---

[63] Mintzberg, Henry, *The Rise and Fall of Strategic Planning*. New York: The Free Press, 1994.

.3 Competencies

Competencies are the skills and knowledge required of an individual or organization to perform a job or function. Knowledge is an understanding gained through experience or study, and skills are abilities that transform knowledge into use.[64] Enterprises must assess where and with whom competencies should reside in the organization structure. Often, organizational effectiveness is improved if some jobs or functions are performed by individuals or organizations outside the enterprise (i.e., outsourced). In general, most enterprises retain in-house those jobs and functions that are essential to its operations and effectiveness. These are generally called the "core competencies" of the organization.

An individual's core competencies are those that are essential to the successful performance of their specific job. Organizational effectiveness is enhanced when individual and enterprise competencies are tied together in a model. Lepsinger and Lucia define competency models as ". . . a descriptive tool that identifies the skills, knowledge, personal characteristics, and behaviors needed to effectively perform a role in the organization and help the business meet its strategic objectives."[65] In other words, for best performance a model should define the skills and knowledge needed for a job as well as the expected levels of performance. Furthermore, the model should tie skills and knowledge to organizational roles, and tie everything back to business objectives and strategies.

A basic competency model for a particular job or function can be displayed as a table. In the first column each competency is listed. The expected level of performance for each step of competency development or maturity is then shown in adjacent columns. These models are effective tools for training and career planning and performance management. Many professional societies, including AACE International, have developed consensus competency models for standardization and professional certification purposes.

11.2.4 Productivity and Performance Management[66]

The preceding discussions concerned positively influencing people's behavior toward self control and better individual and group *performance* within the context of the organization. In TCM, labor performance is measured and assessed as objectively as possible; the measurement is usually referred to as *productivity*. In Section 10.1, labor productivity was defined in general terms as the ratio of the value that labor produces to the value invested in labor.

It is expected that an enterprise will to do everything possible to promote performance and productivity. Performance begins with having capable or competent people. Figure 11.2-1 illustrates a typical performance expectancy model in which the individuals have basic capabilities that result from many factors. The performance outcome of the individual's activities partly depends on effectively developing and using that capability. Competency models help assure that appropriate skills and knowledge are developed and experience is obtained over the course of an individual's career. For example, an individual's performance of competencies in the model can be rated, with overall performance being weighted for the importance of each competency to the organization's objectives. Identified performance gaps can be addressed through training, new assignments, coaching, mentoring, and so on.

Enterprises can either facilitate or constrain capability development and deployment. One goal of performance management is to manage the constraints. Figure 11.2-1 illustrates the types of potential constraints. The previous sections covered the role of leadership and organizational design and

---

[64] AACE International. Recommended Practice 11R-88, *Required Skills and Knowledge of Cost Engineering*, AACE International, Morgantown, WV, 2005.

[65] Lepsinger, Richard and Anntoinette D. Lucia, *The Art and Science of Competency Models: Pinpointing Critical Success Factors in Organizations*, Jossey-Bass/Pfieffer, San Francisco, 1999.

[66] Some of this subsection is abstracted from Neil, Dr. James M., "Performance and Productivity Management (Chapter 17)," *Skills and Knowledge of Cost Engineering*, 5th edition, AACE International, Morgantown, WV, 2004.

development in making sure that the individual's capability and performance is promoted and not restricted.

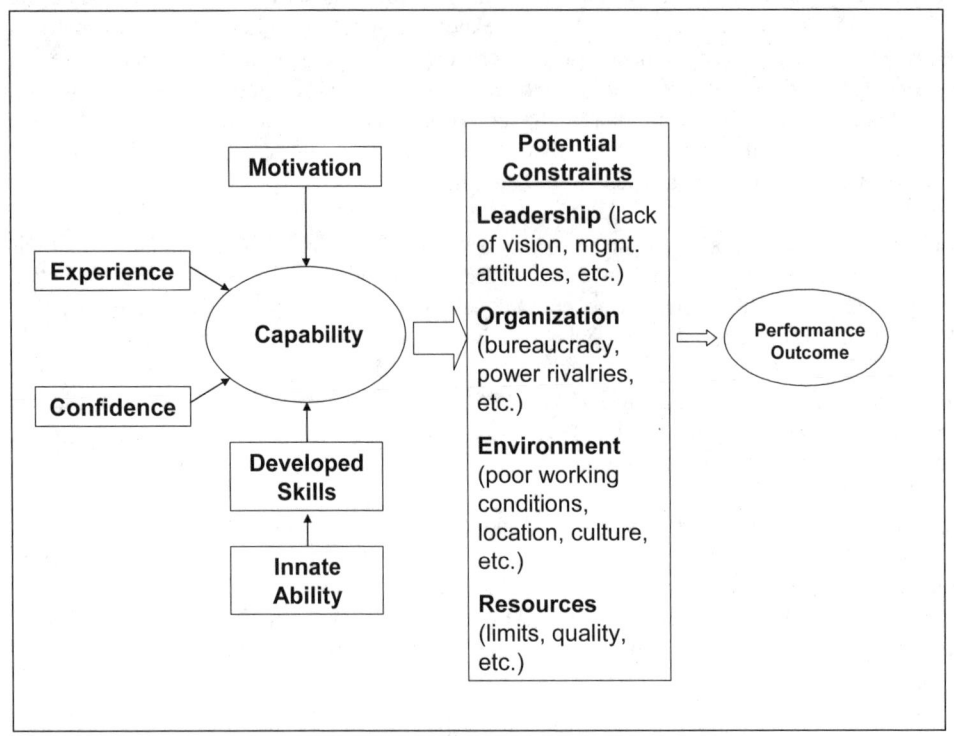

Figure 11.2-1 Performance Expectancy Model

In Section 10.1, labor productivity was defined in an absolute sense as a measure of the extent to which labor resources are minimized and wasted effort is eliminated from a work process (i.e., work process efficiency). Figure 11.2-2 illustrates how performance potential is lost through inefficiency and waste.

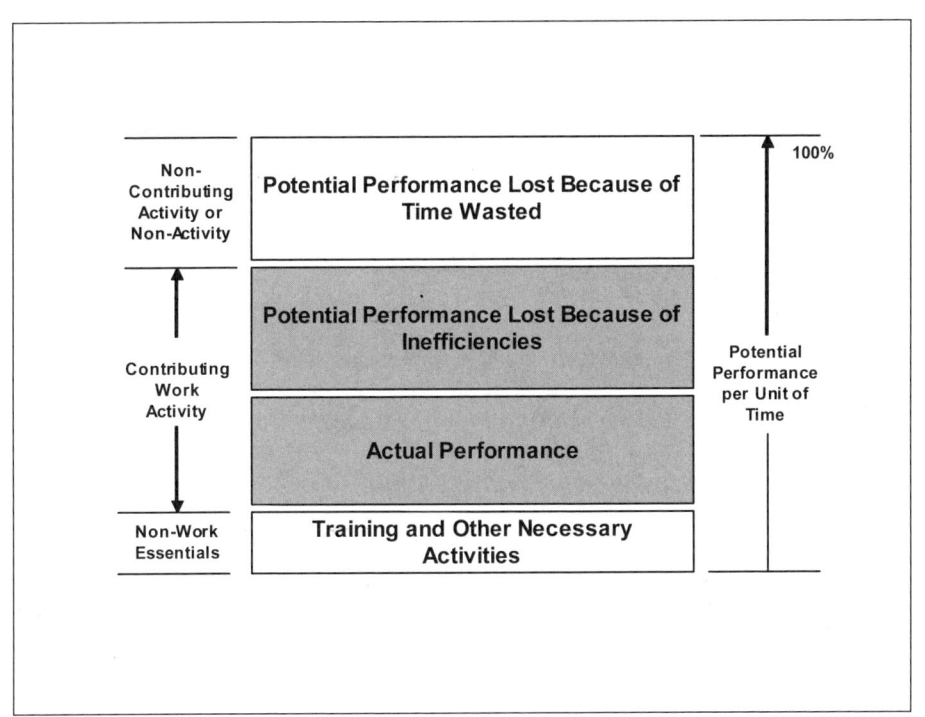

Figure 11.2-2 The Performance Problem

The goal must be to eliminate or minimize the factors contributing to that degradation. The solution to the performance problem is the TCM process; that is, planning, measuring, and assessing the work through an integrated process while making sure that leadership and organization promote its success.

11.2.5 Key Concepts for People and Performance Management

The preceding discussions touched on a few principles and considerations regarding people and performance management for the TCM process. A key point to emphasize is the important role of leadership in promoting performance, particularly for the matrix organizations typically used for asset and project management. Some people and performance management application issues are covered in other sections, particularly resource planning (Section 7.4), procurement planning (Section 7.7), and project performance (including productivity) assessment (Section 10.1).

The following concepts and terminology described in this section are particularly important to understanding people and performance management in relation to TCM:

.1   *Leadership.* (Section 11.2.2.1).
.2   *Teams.* (Section 11.2.2.2).
.3   *Leadership Roles.* (Section 11.2.2.3).
.4   *Motivation/Incentives.* (Section 11.2.2.4).
.5   *Ethics.* (Section 11.2.2.5).
.6   *Organization Design.* (Section 11.2.3.1). Including traditional principles and frameworks for organization design.
.7   *Matrix Organization.* (Section 11.2.3.2). A common design used for asset and project management.
.8   *Competencies and Competency Modeling.* (Section 11.2.3.3).
.9   *Productivity.* (Sections 10.1 and 11.2.4). Including the problems of *waste* and *inefficiency*.

Further Readings and Sources

The references on people and performance management are too numerous to mention. However, this section was in large part abstracted from AACE International's *Skills and Knowledge of Cost Engineering*, which in turn reflects material from the texts of the contributing authors listed below.

- AACE International. Recommended Practice 11R-88, *Required Skills and Knowledge of Cost Engineering*, AACE International, Morgantown, WV, 2005.
- Amos, Scott J. *Skills and Knowledge of Cost Engineering*, 5th ed. Morgantown, WV: AACE International, 2004.
- Bent, James A. *Effective Project Management Through Applied Cost and Schedule Control*. New York: Marcel Dekker, Inc., 1996.
- Flannes, Steven W., and Ginger Levin. *People Skills for Project Managers*. Vienna, VA: Management Concepts Inc., 2001.
- Kezsbom, Deborah S., and Katherine A. Edward. *The New Dynamic Project Management: Winning Through Competitive Advantage*. New York: John Wiley & Sons, 2001.

11.3 Information Management

11.3.1 Description

TCM is an integrative process in which the practices and methods all rely on the creation, collection, communication, understanding, analysis, and/or use of data, information, and knowledge. This is evident in each TCM process map in which the arrows represent rudimentary flows of information between process steps (see Chapter 2). In applying TCM, cost engineers not only use information (e.g., process steps of estimating, scheduling, etc.), but facilitate its flow (i.e., communication) in respect to cost management. This section of the *Framework* provides a few basic information management principles that will help cost engineers understand the nature of information and how it is managed.

Specifics of information technology (IT) are not described in this section given its rapid evolution. IT evolution continues to alter the concepts of time, location, and resource management for TCM and other business processes. Not only is more information available faster, but also IT increasingly allows work to be done at any time, in any location where someone with the skills, knowledge, and resources is available. It is also fostering the integration of work processes as common information can be more readily shared and accessed. A penalty is that the amount of information is growing so rapidly that it has become more challenging to find the information needed and to ascertain its quality.

The information management process includes the gathering and processing of cost related *data*, the conversion of this to *information*, and finally, the presentation and delivery of this information within the enterprise and those it interacts with so that they can obtain useful *knowledge* about the cost behavior of the enterprise and its business environment. Information management is concerned with ensuring that this process takes place economically, efficiently, and effectively with the objective of obtaining the maximum cost knowledge yield for asset and project data inputs.

.1 Data, Information, and Knowledge

Data are the raw material of information management. Data include text, numbers, images, and so on that are generally not organized in a way to make them useful. For example, data about project cost expenditures are not very useful for project control until they have been assessed to identify variances from plan and whether the variances represent trends for which knowledge about causes and potential corrective actions can be obtained.

Information is data that has been processed and presented in a way that makes it useful; that is, it enables knowledge to be obtained. In the previous example, the recognition of performance variances and trends is useful information to a cost engineer.

Knowledge is learning from information about the past, present, and possible future. It confirms that past activities have or have not resulted in desired outcomes. It enables people to start altering their behavior to optimize future results (i.e., continuous improvement), or to speculate in the possible ways inputs may be related to outputs for the processes they are interested in. In the previous example, the cost engineer can use the trend and related information to identify corrective actions and possible future risks of those actions; these are obtained from personal knowledge and experience and/or the knowledge base of the enterprise.

.2 Data and Database Management

Knowledge management is composed of two separate but related areas: data management and information control or database management. *Data management* is concerned with the safe and effective storage of the enterprise's information assets, including raw data, processed information, and knowledge (e.g., lessons learned). These assets may be generically referred to as a *database*. Data management can be considered the first tier or back room operation of knowledge management concerned with data back-up, making sure data are not captured twice, configuration management (see Section 6.2), data quality, and so on. Data management also includes maintaining and controlling an inventory of the various data elements (i.e., a single type of data such as a project start date or a monetary expenditure) used by the enterprise; this inventory is sometimes referred to as a *data dictionary*. Cost engineers may be involved in data management in areas such as creating codes or charts of accounts (see Section 7.3) that form a data dictionary.

Information control or *database management* is concerned with the way data are formed into information (i.e., collated and organized into databases) and made available to the enterprise. Database management personnel work closely with information system designers and users to determine the best ways to store, access, and maintain the databases that support information systems. Information security is a growing concern. The TCM strategic asset management and project control processes each include database management sub-processes. Cost engineers may be directly responsible for some database management (e.g., a specialized database that supports a cost estimating system). In other cases, cost engineers must understand the database supporting their work, such as an enterprise resource planning (ERP) system database supporting project control or a business intelligence (BI) system supporting asset management.

.3 Information Systems

Information systems are the mechanisms or tools by which knowledge is delivered to the enterprise and those it interacts with. They include hardware and software *information technology* (IT), which may include not only computers, but also telecommunication hardware, the Internet, or even a cork bulletin board. Information systems also include specific methodologies to build, select, and deliver IT solutions.

Information systems increasingly consist of two components. One is the traditional system to process daily transactions, and the other is called *data warehousing*. Data warehousing stores data that were gathered from multiple databases, analyzes it, and produces reports for multiple knowledge purposes. For example, the project control systems of various projects may collect the actual cost for a particular item for control purposes; a data warehouse would allow the cross-project price trends for this item to be analyzed and reported for purposes other than project control.

There are information systems applicable for all the steps in the TCM process whether accounting, estimating, scheduling, decision making, and so on. Some systems support day-to-day business operations and others are more specialized systems such a specialized cost analysis model. Each TCM process map has a step for development and maintenance of methods and tools and often these are IT tools of some sort. However, IT is just a tool; for the most part it does not, by itself, perform the TCM processes. In general, relying on IT tools in TCM without the support of cost engineering expertise is detrimental to successful TCM implementation. The misuse of scheduling software by inexperienced personnel is a particular source of problems.

Cost engineers may be directly responsible for building, selecting, or delivering information systems in respect to cost management. For example, the asset planning, investment decision making, and performance analysis processes rely heavily on cost and economic models, which must often be created or customized by cost engineers for a particular application. In other cases, cost engineers must understand the system supporting their work (e.g., an ERP or BI system).

When evaluating requirements, planning, and making decisions for information system investments, it is important for cost engineers to recognize that knowledge gained from the system is the benefit—not the quantity of data acquired, processed, and handled. Many large IT investments are considered failures by the users because the system provides them with lots of data, but no more knowledge than they had originally using a simple spreadsheet based on some basic inputs.

Another common error in implementing information systems is to assume that these tools are a canned product (usable and effective right out of the box); this is rarely true. Information systems should be implemented and managed like any other project of the enterprise. Because information systems often affect many stakeholders and their needs, and are integrated to one degree or another, projects to implement them are often among the most challenging and the most likely to fail. Another common error is to fail to consider the service and maintenance of the information system. Again, the system should be managed like any other asset of the enterprise and all of its life cycle costs must be considered.

Information systems are tools used by individuals to perform tasks. That means potential social and personal impacts must be considered during the planning and implementation of any information system. Many information system projects fail because they were developed for purely technical reasons with no consideration of the social impacts on the system users.

.4 Communication

Communication systems are a subset of information systems, but an area of concern for cost engineers because of their role as translators and communicators in TCM. They may translate customer needs to requirements, requirements to technical scope, technical scope to cost plans, cost plans to measures, and measures to knowledge about the scope that can be acted upon. The translation is generally hindered by noise in the form of uncertainty and statistics. At each translation, cost engineers must communicate their knowledge to the asset and project team to answer their questions: What does this mean? What should be done? What will the likely result be? Cost engineers are also observers and inquirers and must ask their own questions: What are your needs? What progress have you made? What corrective actions do you suggest? For TCM to be successful, information systems must facilitate this communication, and cost engineers must make sure that knowledge is communicated effectively. Each communication raises questions about the best approach, for example: Do we use text, tables, or charts? Do we issue hard copy or online reports? Do we call or e-mail? Do we display ranges or point values? Good communication can make the difference between asset and project performance success or failure no matter how good the planning, measuring, and assessment are.

11.3.2 Key Concepts for Information Management

The preceding discussions touched on a few principles and considerations regarding information management for the TCM process. A key point to remember is that information and information systems are assets of the enterprise to be managed like any other. Cost engineers are not only involved in helping manage IT projects and using IT tools, but may also be responsible for developing and managing specialized databases and information systems related to cost management.

The following concepts and terminology described in this section are particularly important to understanding information management in relation to TCM:

.1 *Data, Information, and Knowledge.* (Section 11.3.1.1).
.2 *Databases and Database Management.* (Sections 6.3, 10.4, and 11.3.1.2).
.3 *Information Technology (IT) and Systems.* (Section 11.3.1.3).

Further Readings and Sources

The references on information management are too numerous to mention and are particularly prone to becoming outdated. The most relevant sources are the most current; e.g., *AACE International Transactions*, AACE's *Cost Engineering Magazine*, and so on.

11.4 Quality and Quality Management

11.4.1 Description

There are many definitions and perceptions of what quality and quality management are. In simple terms, quality in TCM is conformance of an asset (product, service, process, etc.) with requirements and expectations. Quality management is what an enterprise does to ensure that its assets meet these requirements and expectations. In TCM, quality management is not a separate process; TCM, including strategic asset management and project control, are quality processes. The TCM processes, as discussed in Section 2.1.2, are based on the plan, do, check, assess (PDCA) model; this model is a time honored quality management approach sometimes called the Deming or Shewhart cycle. TCM is what an enterprise does to ensure that its assets meet the requirements in respect to cost.

The International Organization of Standardization (ISO) has identified 8 principles that should guide quality management practice.[67] These principles, with how TCM addresses them, are as follows:

- *Customer focus.* The entry process to TCM is requirements elicitation and analysis (i.e., focusing on the customer needs and expectations).
- *Leadership.* TCM establishes a unity of purpose and direction for cost management throughout the asset and project life cycles in alignment with the enterprise's strategies.
- *Involvement of people.* TCM recognizes the roles and responsibilities of everyone involved in asset and project management. By linking all efforts to enterprise strategy, people involved have a greater sense of ownership and motivation.
- *Process approach.* TCM is by definition a process for applying the skills and knowledge of cost engineering. Each component process is based on the PDCA model.
- *System approach to management.* TCM is focused on identifying, understanding, and managing its component processes as a system in alignment with the enterprise's strategies.
- *Continuous improvement.* TCM is not about repeating history, but improving on it by performance-focused planning. The PDCA model is specifically a continuous improvement model.
- *Factual approach to decision making.* The TCM investment decision making process focuses on objective, economic analysis as the basis for decision making. It also stresses using empirical data as a basis for planning, and objective analysis as a basis for change management.
- *Mutually beneficial supplier relationships.* TCM focuses on proactive team approaches, including the involvement of suppliers, contractors, and stakeholders other than owner. Quality management principles guide the resource and procurement planning processes of TCM.

These principles guide the actions an enterprise takes to achieve quality or conformance to requirements. Key actions to achieve conformance are measurement and control. TCM, based on the PDCA cycle, inherently stresses measurement and control in both its strategic asset management and project control processes. When people think of quality measurement and control, they often think of *quality assurance (QA)* and *quality control (QC)*; these are key functions found in most enterprises that create and operate assets and manage projects. What is not often recognized is that the cost engineering function, applying the TCM process, is as much associated with quality as the QA/QC functions.[68]

---

[67] www.iso.org/iso9000-14000/iso9000/qmp.html
[68] Brian R. McConachy discusses how project control could cover quality management for project execution in his article "Concurrent Management of Total Cost and Total Quality," AACE International Transactions, 1996.

.1 The Relationship of Cost and Quality

Chapter 3 of the *TCM Framework* outlines a series of integrated asset management processes that start with business strategy and an identified business problem, elicit customer needs and establish requirements for any solution to the problem, translate those requirements into alternate asset scope, and then decide upon the alternatives based on economic cost measures. Cost measures are then critical to assessing asset performance. Subsequently, Chapter 7 outlines a series of project control planning processes that, again, winnow project scope down to a set of measures, of which cost is a key measure used to assess project performance. What is notable here is the translation of business strategy and customer needs to costs.

Philip Crosby, one of the most recognized authorities on quality management, established four "absolutes" of quality management[69]:

1. Quality is defined as conformance to requirements, not "goodness."
2. The system for causing quality is prevention, not appraisal.
3. The performance standard must be zero defects, not "close enough."
4. The measurement of quality is the Price of Nonconformance™, not indices.

In other words, Crosby is saying that quality comes from planning and design, and the best measure of quality is cost. From that perspective, cost engineering, applied in the TCM process, is arguably a more central function to quality management than quality assurance and control. Crosby goes on further to say that quality is too important to be left to the quality control department, meaning that management must create a system that results in quality; a system in which TCM and cost engineers should play a key role.

.2 Quality Policy and Standards

As discussed in Section 3.1, some requirements for a process or product may be voluntarily or involuntarily imposed on the asset or project management system by enterprise management, government, or some other authority. In TCM, quality policy is an imposed requirement, meaning the enterprise's quality management strategy and approach is already established; TCM is a process to deploy that policy. In TCM, it is assumed that quality policy will reflect the ISO principles outlined in Section 11.4.1.

Another type of imposed requirement is accepted and agreed upon standards. Most industries have some established standards for the products they produced. There are also standards for how processes are performed. Possibly the most widely recognized authorities for establishing and maintaining standards are the International Organization for Standardization (ISO) and the American National Standards Institute (ANSI).[70] In regard to TCM, the standards of most relevance are ISO 9000 (quality management systems-fundamentals and vocabulary) and ISO 10006 (quality management guidelines to quality in project management).

ISO 9000 (and its "family" of related standards) is focused on an enterprise having, maintaining, and following a documented quality process and procedures (i.e., QA). Enterprises apply and seek certification in the standard to assure their customers that they have a quality management system in place. ISO 10006 is similar, but is focused specifically on project management. As mentioned, TCM can be the basis for creating a cost management process in an enterprise's quality management system in accordance with these standards.

---

[69] Crosby, Philip B., *Quality is Free*, McGraw-Hill, New York NY, 1979.
[70] As an example application, AACE International works with ANSI to establish standard terminology for cost engineering (e.g., ANSI Z94.2 or most recent release).

.3 Quality Planning and Improvement

J.M. Juran also emphasizes the importance of prevention or design to quality management. In his Juran Trilogy™, he emphasizes three aspects of quality management:[71]

- *Quality Planning:* Identifies the quality features to be provided and plans for delivering them without deficiencies.
- *Quality Improvement*: Reduces or eliminates deficiencies in current goods, services, or processes.
- *Quality Control*: Maintains the results achieved through the previous two practices.

Juran's *quality planning* is essentially the steps in Chapter 4 of the *TCM Framework*; that is, identify the problem and discover customer needs (i.e., requirements); develop the product and features that respond to the needs and processes able to produce the features (i.e., asset planning); and develop and transfer a control basis (i.e., decision making and project implementation). Again, *quality planning* is not a separate process or function, but an integrated way of planning directed toward satisfying customer needs. To plan for quality is not a separate plan, rather it is the way you plan. Using TCM, that way is based on the PDCA model for each component process. Every TCM component process starts with the planning step to determine how the rest of the PDCA process will be executed.

In Juran's view, planning and quality management must be guided by a "breakthrough" way of thinking. *Quality improvement* should emphasize not just traditional *continuous improvement*, but also breakthrough changes, which are "a dynamic, decisive movement to new, higher levels of performance." He further describes breakthrough as "the creation of good (or at least necessary) changes, whereas control is the prevention of bad changes." The mindsets of breakthrough (make change) and traditional control (prevent change) are so different that management must establish expectations for breakthrough to happen. Asset performance assessment and planning are where most breakthrough ideas will originate and be developed. The TCM sections on change management emphasize that the purpose of change management is not to limit change, but to manage it.

.4 Quality Assurance and Control (QA/QC)

While a goal of quality management may be zero defects or deficiencies, the reality is that humans and systems are imperfect and that goal is rarely achieved. There must be strong quality control to achieve the planned results. Furthermore, the quality and cost engineering control functions must interface because quality measures have cost attributes (i.e., cost of quality).

QA includes practices focused on providing confidence that requirements will be fulfilled while QC includes practices focused on fulfilling the requirements. QA is generally focused on measuring and assessing conformance of the quality management system and processes with its requirements. As such QA does not ensure quality assets or products, but provides confidence that nothing stands in the way of quality being achieved (e.g., Do you have a quality management process? Is it being followed?). QC focuses on measuring and assessing the conformance of products with their requirements (e.g., Is the product in accordance with specification?).

The measurement methods employed in QA/QC may be continuous (e.g., measurement devices on a production line) or may involve sampling, testing, inspection, or auditing. The methods generally employ statistics to analyze variances to determine if non-conformance is random or a trend. Non-conformance generally affects costs, schedule, productivity, and other measures of concern to cost engineers. Therefore, cost engineers often interface with QA personnel to impose proper process controls and with QC personnel in analyzing the causes of variance and identifying potential corrective actions. Generally, QA/QC requirements are also a critical part of contracts, and a source of performance issues that cost engineers are

---

[71] Juran, J.M., *Managerial Breakthrough*, Revised Edition, New York: McGraw-Hill, 1995.

likely to have a part in addressing. TCM and QA/QC both rely on change management processes to maintain effective performance measurement control baselines.

.5 Quality Management Methods in TCM

While the component processes of TCM each represent a link in a quality management system, a number of the processes and methods are commonly associated with or are key to quality management. Some of these are briefly recapitulated in the following paragraphs with the reference sections shown.

Quality Function Deployment (re: Sections 3.1 and 3.2)
QFD is a methodology for translating requirements into design. In QFD, requirements are often called the "voice of the customer," and the QFD approach allows the designer to merge the "voice of the customer" with the "voice of the product or process." It is possible to consider cost as well as quality requirements in QFD; this variation has been called *cost deployment*.

Value Analysis and Engineering (VA/VE) (re: Section 7.5)
Crosby points out that the system for providing quality is prevention. Juran points out the need for breakthrough quality improvements. VA/VE supports both prevention and breakthrough improvement. Specifically, the intensive questioning, challenging, and analysis of functionality and validity of constraints that takes place during VA/VE *function analysis* is a method for building quality into an asset (i.e., preventing failure). In respect to breakthroughs, the VA/VE *creativity* step looks for ideas for how to perform functions. The step is supposed to be performed as unconstrained by habit and past thinking patterns as possible (i.e., "think outside the box") so that breakthrough opportunities can be discovered.

Benchmarking (re: Section 6.1)
Benchmarking is a measurement and analysis process that compares practices, processes, and relevant measures to those of a selected basis of comparison (i.e., the benchmark) with the goal of improving performance. The comparison basis includes internal or external competitive or best practices, processes, or measures. The method can support both continuous and breakthrough improvements depending on whether "best" practice benchmarks are viewed as goals to be achieved or exceeded (i.e., breakthrough).

Cost of Quality (re: Section 6.1)
Cost of quality analysis is the key method for assessing performance against functional requirements and constraints. Cost of quality refers to the cost of both conforming and not conforming (i.e., at variance) with requirements. Costs of quality are generally analyzed in the following four categories: prevention, appraisal, internal failure, and external failure. Prevention costs are the QA costs (e.g., training) and appraisal costs are the QC costs (e.g., testing). These costs are essentially designed into the asset or process during asset planning (i.e., costs of conformance that are fixed or controllable by design), so performance assessment tends to focus on the "resultant" cost of failure or variance during the asset's use (i.e., costs of nonconformance are more variable by nature).

For strategic asset management and project control, the cost of quality is manifested in estimates, schedules, and resource plans as appraisal costs, activities, and personnel (e.g., inspection). In actual performance, failure costs are manifested in poor productivity, scrap materials, rework, and often claims and disputes because contracts usually establish QA/QC requirements.

Change Management (re: Sections 6.2 and 10.3)
For project control, change management refers to the process of managing any change to the scope of work and/or any deviation, performance trend, or change to an approved or baseline project control plan. For asset management, change management refers to the process of managing any change to documented information defining the scope of an asset or the basis of measuring and assessing its performance over its life cycle. Change management helps ensure that requirements always address customer needs. By ensuring that the basis of performance measurement is always consistent with established requirements, change management is also a key element of *quality control*.

Configuration Management (CM) (re: Section 6.2)

CM is a change management process that has traditionally been focused on controlling engineering documentation, but has evolved in recent years to encompass the entire business process infrastructure, including any information that could impact safety, quality, schedule, cost, profit, or the environment. CM, as with QFD, has been used most frequently in the software, product development, and military program arenas.

11.4.2 Key Concepts for Quality and Quality Management

This chapter touches on a few key quality and quality management principles that guided development of the TCM process. A key point of this section is to highlight that quality management is not a separate process, but a way that processes should work. TCM is a quality management process. Another key point is the relationship between cost and quality; that is, cost may be the best single measure of quality.

The following concepts and terminology described in this section are particularly important to understanding the quality and quality management in relation to TCM:

.1 *Quality.* (Section 11.4.1). See conformance to requirements.
.2 *Conformance to Requirements.* (Section 11.4.1 and 11.4.1.1). The definition of quality.
.3 *Quality Management.* (Section 11.4.1). TCM is a quality management process.
.4 *Plan-Do-Check-Assess (PDCA).* (Section 11.4.1). The basis model for TCM.
.5 *Quality Measurement.* (Section 11.4.1.1). In some views, cost is the best single quality measurement.
.6 *Quality Policy.* (Section 11.4.1.2). In TCM, quality policy is an imposed requirement that is assumed to be guided by accepted quality management principles (e.g., ISO principles in Section 11.4.1).
.7 *Quality Standards.* (Section 11.4.1.2). Imposed requirements (e.g., ISO 9000 standards).
.8 *Quality Planning.* (Section 11.4.1.3). An integrated way of planning directed toward satisfying customer needs.
.9 *Quality Improvement.* (Section 11.4.1.3). Includes both continuous and breakthrough improvements.
.10 *Continuous Improvement.* (Section 11.4.1 and 11.4.1.3). The traditional result of the PDCA process.
.11 *Quality Assurance.* (Section 11.4.1.4). Actions that provide confidence that the requirements will be fulfilled.
.12 *Quality Control.* (Section 11.4.1.4). Actions focused on fulfilling requirements.

Further Readings and Sources

The references on quality are too numerous to mention. However, the following references and sources provide basic information and will lead to more detailed treatments.

Associations:
- American Society for Quality (ASQ) (www.asq.org)
- International Organization of Standardization (ISO) (www.iso.org)
- American National Standards Institute (ANSI) (www.ansi.org)

Texts:
- Cokins, Gary. "Quality Management." Chapter 7 in *Skills and Knowledge for Cost Engineering*. Morgantown, WV: AACE International, 2004.
- Crosby, Philip B. *Quality Is Free.* New York: McGraw Hill, 1979.
- Crosby, Philip B. *Quality Is Still Free.* New York: McGraw Hill, 1996.
- Juran, Joseph M. *Managerial Breakthrough*, rev. ed. New York: McGraw-Hill, 1995.
- Juran, Joseph M., and A. Blanton Godfrey. *Juran's Quality Handbook*, 5th ed. New York: McGraw-Hill, 1999.
- McConachy, Brian R. "Concurrent Management of Total Cost and Total Quality." In *AACE International Transactions*. Morgantown, WV: AACE International, 1996.

- Project Management Institute. *A Guide to the Project Management Body of Knowledge*, 3rd ed. Upper Darby, PA: Project Management Institute, 2004.

11.5 Value Management and Value Improving Practices (VIPs)

11.5.1 Description

As with quality, there are many definitions and perceptions of what value and value management are. In simple terms, *value,* as defined in TCM is a *measure* of the worth of a thing in terms of usefulness, desirability, importance, money, etc. *Value management* in TCM is what an enterprise does to ensure that its assets provide or maintain the usefulness and/or value that the various stakeholders require.[72] The concept of value management is intimately tied to *quality*, which in TCM is defined as conformance with requirements. *Quality management* ensures that customer requirements are established and conformed to while value management ensures that the requirements and processes comprehensively address customer values.

As with quality, there is no value management process in TCM. That is because, as with quality management (see Section 11.4), TCM, including strategic asset management and project control, is a value management process that focuses on value while recognizing that costs, broadly defined, are often the best *measure* of value or worth. However, while there is no separate value management process, there are many practices included in or related to TCM that are *value improving practices* (VIPs) in that they have a specific focus and/or significant effect on getting the most value from the process.

Some would call a practice a *VIP* only if it meets criteria that set the practice apart from "business as usual." For example, some criteria to be considered a VIP may include:

- a formal, planned process with assigned responsibilities
- a facilitated effort led by an independent practice expert
- involves all the key stakeholders
- documents, communicates, and follows up on the results

Generally, VIPs should consider cost over the *life cycle* of the asset and project (see Section 2.1) because the ultimate goal of most enterprises is long term profitability. VIPs must also be used in the early design and planning phases because the ability to influence value diminishes rapidly as scope definition and design progress. Figure 11.5-1 illustrates this concept, which is called the *influence curve*.

---

[72] The general concept of value as discussed here should not be construed as "appraised" value, which is narrowly defined as a monetary measure of an asset's worth (see Section 3.2).

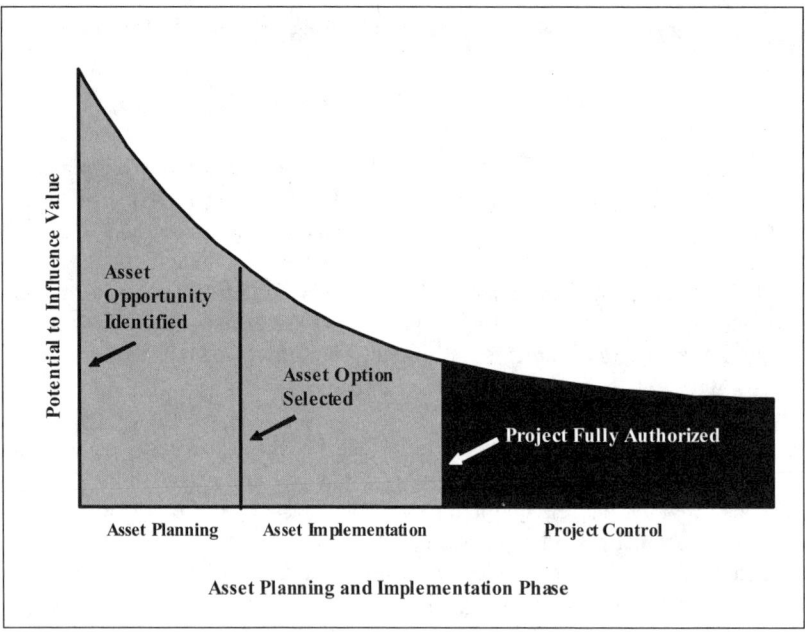

Figure 11.5-1. The Influence Curve

.1 The Relationship of Cost and Value

Lawrence D. Miles, the founding authority on value analysis and engineering, stated that the "best value is determined by two considerations: performance and cost."[73] This statement recognizes that customers rarely are willing to pay *any* cost for performance and if customers can get the performance at *no* cost, they will almost certainly be most satisfied. However, very little is free, and in a competitive environment, the goal is usually to obtain equal or better performance at a lower cost than before and at a lower cost than the competition in consideration of risk.

Performance measures are central to the TCM process, starting with the requirements elicitation and analysis process (Section 3.1), which translates customer and stakeholder needs and wants into *performance requirements*. Any practice after that which can obtain the same performance at lower costs is a *value improving practice*.

.2 Value Analysis and Value Engineering (VA/VE)

Of all the processes in TCM, VA/VE is the most cogent to value and value management. As defined in Section 7.5, VA/VE is "the systematic application of recognized techniques which identify the *functions* of the product or service, establish the worth of those functions, and provide the necessary functions to meet the required performance at the lowest overall cost."[74] Given that *functions* are attributes of an asset or project that give it a purpose and make it useful or desirable (i.e., anything that provides what a customer wants or needs), VA/VE is arguably the most important VIP as it is directed straight at the issue of value.

.3 Other Value Improving Practices (VIPs) in TCM

While all TCM processes are important to managing value, the TCM process includes several processes and methods besides VA/VE that are generally recognized as being most central to value management. As mentioned before, some may have criteria for performing a practice before it is label it as a VIP.

---

[73] Miles, Lawrence D., *Techniques of Value Analysis and Engineering*, 3rd edition, Washington, D.C.: Lawrence D. Miles Foundation, 1989.
[74] SAVE International, *Value Methodology Standard* (Glossary), www.value-eng.org, 2003.

Requirements Elicitation and Analysis

Understanding performance requirements of the customer and stakeholders, as described in Section 3.1, is a prerequisite to improving both quality and value. In practice, some enterprises may apply and label requirements elicitation practices as a specific VIP to put special emphasis on a particular aspect (e.g., *classes of facility quality* evaluations in the process industries).

Target Costing and Cost Deployment

As described in Section 3.2, these methods have improved traditional design and planning by making cost a consideration in design (i.e., a requirement or constraint) from the very beginning rather than leaving it until the last step when it is often too late to give it proper attention.

Decision Analysis

As described in Section 3.3, decisions are generally based on analyses that translate values to monetary measures. To the extent that values are consistently and properly analyzed, this process leads to better decisions based on those values.

Life Cycle Costing (LCC)

As described in Section 3.3, decision analysis should examine the life cycle costs, which include the investment (e.g., acquisition, production, construction, etc.), operation, maintenance, use, and disposal of an asset or project. Most VIPs end with making decisions on alternative courses of actions, and therefore should apply LCC methods.

Risk Management

As described in Section 7.6, risk is the same as uncertainty and includes both opportunities and threats. The risk management process is very similar to VA/VE with the exception that risk management is focused on "risk factors" rather than functions. It tends to be more focused on uncertain extrinsic influences on an asset or project rather than their more deterministic intrinsic properties and function.

Optimization

The schedule planning and development process (Section 7.2), cost estimating and budgeting process (Section 7.3), and investment decision making (Section 3.3) process include steps or methods for optimization. These steps often involve simulation using modeling techniques. The value equation of achieving performance at the least cost is inherently suited to these methods, which seek optimal solutions. Optimization may also be applied to costs for specific elements of a design (e.g., *energy optimization* for a chemical process).

Benchmarking

The asset assessment process (Section 6.1) includes *benchmarking,* which is a measurement and analysis process that compares practices, processes, and relevant measures to those of a selected basis of comparison (i.e., the benchmark) with the goal of *improving performance.* Value is improved if performance is improved at less or no extra cost.

Review and Validation

Each TCM process includes a review and validation step that in part assures that the process and its outcome meet the established *performance* requirements, which often include cost and schedule requirements (e.g., target costs, milestones, etc.). In that sense, the review can be considered part of a *value assurance* process.

.4 Other Value Improving Practices (VIPs)

There are many VIPs not explicitly included in the TCM process because they are more closely related to design, construction, operations, or other work processes. However, as VIPs, they are inherently important to TCM and its focus on value.

Arguably, cost engineers, or someone with equivalent skills and knowledge, should play a key role in <u>all</u> VIPs because they all result in *decisions* based on best *value,* which by definition is a function of *cost.* To include those knowledgeable about performance, but exclude those most knowledgeable about value and cost, is folly.

One group of VIP methodologies involves analyzing "abilities," specifically how "executable" a project or work process is and how "operable" or usable the resultant asset, product, or service is. Some of the more widely used methods are *manufacturability* and *constructability* analyses, which are focused on execution, and *reliability, availability, and maintainability (RAM)* analysis, which is focused on operations. Their common goal is to find the best value alternative approach. They are similar to VA/VE except the focus is on the relation between design and how a process is performed (an ability). Some common principles apply for each of these methods including:

- always consider safety
- use a formal, focused analytic process
- apply the method early in the design process
- involve all the key stakeholders
- evaluate the applicable life cycle cost (LCC)
- document, communicate, and follow up on the results

Manufacturability Analysis

Manufacturability is used during asset planning to optimize product and production system design in consideration of the effective performance of manufacturing and related activities. Alternate materials, manufacturing technologies, and standardization are key considerations (e.g., use common parts for different products).

Constructability Analysis

Constructability is used during construction project planning and it involves methods to optimize the design in consideration of the effective performance of construction activities. Alternate materials, unique construction sequencing (i.e., activity logic), and construction technologies are key considerations.

Reliability, Availability and Maintainability (RAM) Analysis

RAM is used primarily during asset planning. It involves using quantitative methods to optimize the performance or operation (i.e., operability) of process systems and their components. RAM methods generally employ predictive modeling and simulation that consider future asset performance.

The above are some of the more common VIPs. However, the same concepts can be applied to analyzing the value of any process. For example, designability analysis would examine the value of using alternate design technologies (e.g., 3D CAD) in consideration of the scope of what was being designed, biddability analysis could examine the value of alternate procurement or contracting bidding approaches in consideration of the scope of the bid package, and so on.

The list of practices that could be labeled VIPs is nearly endless. It is important to keep in mind that no project can or should apply all of them; analysis tends to yield diminishing returns and uses limited resources ineffectively. The use of VIPs should be prioritized and carefully planned.

11.5.2 Key Concepts for Value and Value Management

This chapter touches on a few key value and value management principles that guided development of the TCM process. A key point of this section is to highlight that value management is not a separate process, but a way that processes should work. TCM is a value management process. Another key point is the relationship between value, performance, and cost; you improve value when you get the required performance at a lower cost.

The following concepts and terminology described in this section are particularly important to understanding the value and value management in relation to TCM:

.1 *Value Improving Practices (VIPs).* (See Section 11.5.1)
.2 *Influence Curve.* (See Section 11.5.1)
.3 *Performance Requirements.* (See Section 11.5.1.1)
.4 *VA/VE.* (See Sections 7.5 and 11.5.1.2)
.5 *Life Cycle Costs.* (See Section 11.5.1.3)
.6 *Manufacturability.* (See Section 11.5.1.4)
.7 *Constructability.* (See Section 11.5.1.4)
.8 *Reliability, Availability, Maintainability (RAM).* (See Section 11.5.1.4)
.9 *Operability.* (See Section 11.5.1.4)

Further Readings and Sources

Most references on value management are focused on VA/VE (see references in Section 7.5). There are currently no books devoted to the topic of VIPs as discussed in this section.

11.6 Environment, Health, and Safety Management

11.6.1 Description

Environment, health, and safety (EHS) concerns the physical well being and stewardship of people, other life forms, and the space, air, land, and water they occupy and interact with. Security is also increasingly recognized among EHS concerns. Security is a somewhat unique concern because it has to do with securing well being from malicious intent.[75] Other EHS risk factors and drivers may be intentional but are generally not malicious nor hold much threat of violence. Concern for such matters is spawning what McDonough and others have termed the "next industrial revolution."[76]

EHS issues are concerns for all stakeholders in TCM and must be addressed in one way or another in all TCM processes. EHS is not a separate process, but rather a recognition that there are critical stakeholder and customer EHS needs and expectations that must always be considered in the application of the TCM process. In other words, EHS is viewed from a quality management perspective. Section 11.4 defines quality management as what an enterprise does to ensure that its assets meet the requirements, which are focused on customer needs.

In TCM, the health, safety, and security of the stakeholders, including the environment, is assumed to be a main priority of the enterprise's business strategy that will be translated into requirements.[77] The well-worn phrase "safety first" is increasingly being recognized by enterprises to mean "EHS first."

After decades of often ineffective efforts to manage EHS issues, changes in how enterprises manage EHS issues are underway and gaining traction worldwide. Specifically, there is a growing recognition and acceptance that attention to EHS issues can no longer be treated as an after the fact concern, but rather must be integrated into all aspects of everyday living. At the consumer level, interest in recycling and in "green" products and processes is an example of this new paradigm. In industry, this translates into the recognition that EHS (like quality management) is not just the job of an EHS department, but it is "everybody's" job; it must be built into the management system. Enterprises have learned that a reputation for poor EHS performance can damage the bottom line as much as a reputation for poor quality. Continuous improvement must become a cornerstone of EHS performance, just as it has become a cornerstone of quality management.

Building EHS into management strategy makes sense because enterprises that position themselves to perform effectively in an EHS sense will enjoy a competitive advantage over those who don't. This is true because the enterprise's stakeholders all have EHS performance high on their needs and expectations list; these stakeholders include the public, investors, lenders, the media—and perhaps most importantly—customers. The competitive advantage can be negated by getting locked into business relationships with other enterprises prone to accidents, pollution incidents, or lack of concern for employee or public health; that is, enterprises have learned they can't outsource the problem. They are also learning that EHS is not a challenge to hide from; building EHS requirements into a quality management system can spawn innovations that yield both cost savings and better business performance than can be achieved through just "compliance" with regulations. So, in reality, EHS expenditures are not so much "cost" as "investment" issues for which a return on investment can and should be expected.[78]

In addition to the inherent benefits of a quality management EHS approach, governments sometimes offer economic incentives that provide an additional competitive advantage. These include advantageous

---

[75] Information security is covered in Section 11.3.
[76] McDonough, William and Michael Braungart, "The Next Industrial Revolution," *Atlantic Monthly*, October 1998.
[77] The environment (land, air, water, other life forms, etc.) can alternately be viewed as a stakeholder in any business problem or opportunity, or as a societal asset; that is, it is an encompassing, multi-dimensioned entity upon which society, including the enterprise, ultimately and collectively depends for its health, safety, and well being.
[78] Hoffman, Andrew J., *Competitive Environmental Strategy—A Guide to the Changing Business Landscape*, Washington, DC: Island Press, 2000.

tax structures, tradable permits, rewards for best practices, or exemption from some regulatory requirements if best practices are used.[79]

Building EHS requirements into a quality management system like TCM has a profound impact on how corporations view EHS costs and account for them. In the past (and too often at present), management focus was on minimizing the costs of *compliance* and control (i.e., cost of non-conformance)—inspection, fines, penalties, treatment facilities, site remediation, and so on. However, more proactive enterprises are taking TCM's quality management approach and focusing on cost *prevention* through better design while considering the life cycle costs of their assets. TCM plans, measures, and assesses the full economic costs (including hidden opportunity costs) of the enterprise's asset and project portfolio including prevention, appraisal, and failure costs in regard to EHS requirements.

11.6.2 Key Environment, Health, and Safety Considerations for TCM

This section highlights some key considerations for addressing EHS issues using TCM's quality management approach for assets and projects. These can be categorized as process and stakeholder considerations.

.1 Process Considerations

EHS Functional and Supply Chain Integration

EHS issues come into play in all aspects of an enterprise. Consequently the management of these issues must be strategically integrated into management of the business, not just tacked on at the end. As noted previously, the traditional approach of viewing EHS matters as separate functions or processes is giving way to viewing them and managing them as integrated components of a common whole. As was also mentioned, management must concern itself with the entire supply chain for its assets and projects; EHS failure in any link can affect the others. Finally, regulations for environmental, health, and safety issues are beginning to cross reference each other, and costly management redundancy can be eliminated when the three areas are managed more holistically.[80]

Life Cycle Awareness

Assets, products, and services have potential EHS effects throughout all aspects of their creation and delivery. No longer can concern be limited to addressing failures (e.g., injuries, illness, emissions, etc.) that occur during asset operation or project execution. From the early phases of asset planning or product development, many decisions must be made on how to prevent EHS failures and improve performance. The consumption of resources (e.g., raw materials), use of processes (e.g., methods of manufacture), and product features (e.g., recycleability) must be planned and decided. How a product is distributed must also be considered. Consumption or use of the product, and the potential for misuse and the EHS effects of these also merit close attention. And final disposal of the product and by-products, in whatever waste stream it is likely to find its way to, is also a major source of EHS effects that needs to be considered from the early planning and design stages.[81]

Sustainable development is another life cycle issue to consider. As economic development proceeds throughout the world, development actions must be carried out in a fashion that does not use resources in a manner or degree that compromises the ability of future generations to sustain such development. In other words, as a matter of strategy for an enterprise, planning must not only consider the life cycle of the asset, but the life cycle of the environment and its asset value as *natural capital*.[82]

---

[79] Hirsch, Dennis D., "Second Generation Policy and the New Economy," *Capital University Law Review*, Vol. 29, Number 1, 2001.

[80] Global Environmental Management Initiative (GEMI). New Paths to Business Value: Strategic Sourcing—Environment, Health & Safety, 2001.

[81] Gibson, Will. Chapter 26 in *A Practical View of Life-Cycle Assessment: Implementing ISO 14000,* Tom Tibor and Ira Feldman, Editors. Chicago, IL: Irwin Professional Publishing, 1997.

[82] Barcott, Bruce, "What's Wilderness Worth?" *Outside Magazine*, March 2005.

Standards and Performance Beyond Compliance
Governments at all levels have established EHS standards of compliance. These establish legal responsibilities regarding EHS issues. For example, in the United States, the federal Comprehensive Environmental Response, Compensation and Liability Act (CERCLA), Superfund Amendments and Reauthorization Act (SARA), and Resource Conservation and Recovery Act (RCRA) identify hazardous contaminants, specify the levels of contamination that require cleanup actions to be initiated, and establish cleanup or disposal methods that are acceptable.

However, enterprises increasingly recognize a broader duty to society, if not moral responsibility, to do more than the minimum legally required. In that respect, organizations are increasingly developing voluntary codes of EHS conduct and charters. These are used as models for companies to benchmark their EHS performance and they often establish more stringent requirements than government standards for compliance. The number of organizations and standards is enormous, often addressing just a small segment of an industry. However, one example of an industry-wide EHS standard is the Responsible Care® program that is used by much of the international chemical industry in the United States.

For environmental management, arguably the most significant voluntary standard is the International Organization of Standardization (ISO) ISO 14000 standard. As with ISO 9000 (see Section 11.4), the ISO 14000 series of standards pertain to the management systems that an organization employs to manage environmental matters, not to the environmental performance of the organization. The standard provides a framework for setting environmental requirements and for implementing them and assessing performance against them. ISO also publishes numerous safety standards that are usually for very specific applications.

For safety and health management, a consortium of international standards organizations developed the Occupational Health and Safety Assessment Series (OHSAS) 18000 standards. The OHSAS 18000 series was developed to be compatible with the ISO 14000 environmental management series.

Also worthy of note in the environmental arena is the ICC (International Chamber of Commerce) Business Charter for Sustainable Development. This Charter contains 16 principles that hundreds of companies worldwide have adopted voluntarily as a public expression of their commitment to apply the concept in their business management.

Continuous improvement is one of the principle goals of any quality management system. For the regulated community, EHS performance will increasingly be judged by standards in addition to regulatory compliance. These standards may be explicit and readily imposed such as the industry examples provided, or they may represent unstated needs and expectations that must be elicited from stakeholders. In any case, compliance should be considered "table stakes"; that is, the minimum expected to have the privilege of being in business.

Risk Awareness
In TCM, risk is considered the same as uncertainty; that is, it includes both opportunities and threats. Stakeholders often perceive EHS issues as threats. Therefore, their EHS needs and expectations for a solution to a business problem can be driven by fear or other strong emotions, particularly if the EHS issue affects the stakeholder personally. Some of the emotion can be dealt with through communication or other means (see Section 11.1). However, the risks are often real as evidenced by the many EHS disasters that appear regularly in the media. The risks should be addressed directly and objectively by using the risk management process (Section 7.6). However, as systems become more complex and less understood by the stakeholders (e.g., nuclear power, genetics, etc.), it becomes more challenging to address the issues.

Adding to the challenge is the issue of security. As was mentioned, security has to do with securing EHS well being from malicious intent. The challenge comes from the fact that the threats are malicious, possibly violent, and purposeful in seeking to bypass prevention features.

.2 Stakeholder Considerations

Consumers

Consumers are becoming increasingly sensitive to the EHS performance of enterprises and their products. In response, some major companies such as Wal-Mart have set environmental standards for the products they carry. Increasingly, companies that respond to consumer interests in "greener," safer, and healthier products will enjoy a degree of competitive advantage over those that do not. The trends are unmistakable in areas such as automobile safety and emissions, concern with food additives and labeling, and so on. However, special care must be exercised not to send contradictory messages to EHS literate consumers; a heavy price in lost business (or even malicious action) can be levied for misrepresentation.[83]

Employees

Just as the EHS sensitivity of consumers is on the increase, so is the sensitivity of employees. People like to work for EHS responsible companies, and are taking more interest in the EHS performance of their employers. Companies that acknowledge and respond to this interest will gain an advantage in competing for highly skilled and trained employees.

Stock Investors

The investor community has also developed an interest in the EHS performance of companies. In 1993, the Sun Company, Inc. became the first large corporation to endorse the CERES Principles, a 10-point code of corporate conduct for environmental performance and accountability. CERES stands for Coalition for Environmentally Responsible Economies and represents groups of socially concerned investors that control several hundred billion dollars of investment capital.[84]

Investor interest is not limited to social goals; however, investors are also concerned with bottom line returns on their investment. Companies with below par EHS performance may acquire liabilities that can significantly detract from the value of their stock.[85]

Financial Institutions

Banks and other lenders are more willing to lend money to companies that manage EHS performance in a preventative way because they are better financial risks. Banks are also becoming more interested in the EHS overtones of proposed uses of borrowed money. Few financiers are willing to loan money for major development projects with particularly significant EHS effects (e.g., the Three Gorges Dam). For smaller projects, they are increasingly requiring verification that the asset being constructed will not be soon rendered uneconomic or regulated out of existence due to environmental or related health and safety factors.

Similarly, insurance companies are much more amenable to writing coverage for companies with a good EHS performance track record. Again the reasons are very pragmatic—such companies are a better business risk. And from the insured's point of view, a clean record is a definite asset in negotiating lower rates.

In summary, for an enterprise to compete and succeed, the EHS agendas of stakeholders, in addition to those of regulators, will have to be tended to. Expanding stakeholder interests in corporate EHS performance will go hand in hand with more public scrutiny. Mandated public reporting requirements will increase. More proactive companies have voluntarily begun to publish corporate EHS annual reports. For example, some consider the guidelines developed by the Global Reporting Initiative as a "gold standard" for such reports.

---

[83] Piasecki, Bruce, *Better Products Better World*, Saratoga Springs, NY: The AHC Group, Inc. (in press for 2006).
[84] *Guide to the CERES Principles*, The Coalition for Environmentally Responsible Economics, Boston, MA, 1994.
[85] Goodman, Susannah Blake, Jonas Kron, and Tim Little. *The Environmental Fiduciary—The Case for Incorporating Environmental Factors Into Investment Management Policies*, The Rose Foundation for Communities and the Environment, 2004.

As discussed, EHS is not a separate TCM process. EHS is factored into TCM by making sure that customer and other stakeholder EHS needs and expectations are always considered in the application of the process.

11.6.3 Environment, Health, and Safety Methods for TCM

While each TCM process must consider EHS issues, the processes themselves do not include any specific methods for EHS management. For example, the schedule planning and development process (Section 7.2) must consider EHS activities (e.g., permitting, inspection, safety meetings, reviews, etc.), but the activities themselves and the methods used in their performance are not TCM processes and methods. However, two TCM processes hold particular relevance for EHS issues from a prevention viewpoint: value analysis and engineering (VA/VE; Section 7.5) and risk management (Section 7.6).

VA/VE supports prevention through the intensive questioning, challenging, and analysis of the functionality and validity of constraints that takes place during VA/VE *function analysis*. In general, functions are attributes of an asset or project that give it a purpose (i.e., allow user/operator to accomplish a task) and make it useful or desirable (i.e., have value). When function and value are viewed from an EHS perspective, the VA/VE process supports the prevention through design philosophy.

The risk management process includes steps for identifying asset or project risk factors (or drivers), analyzing them, and mitigating them as appropriate. Risk factors are events and conditions that may influence or drive uncertainty (i.e., either opportunities or threats) in asset or project performance. EHS and security issues, particularly the effects of failures (e.g., injuries, illness, emissions, etc.), should be evaluated using risk analysis. Based on the risk analysis outcomes, the EHS risk factors and/or their effects should be mitigated by planning alternatives that reduce the risk without reducing the value of the outcomes.

11.6.4 Environmental Assets and Projects

As was mentioned, the environment (land, air, water, other life forms, etc.) can be viewed as an asset on which society, including the enterprise, ultimately and collectively depends for its health, safety, and well being. Increasingly, society's expectation is that enterprises will not only do no harm to the environment, but will also remediate harm done in the past by the enterprise or others that may have owned or controlled the asset before them. These expectations mean that most enterprises now monitor and assess the environment in relation to the life cycle of their asset ownership and operation and remediate the environment through projects for which measurement and assessment (or regulations) demonstrate a need.

The measurement process entails evaluating the environmental conditions and effects of the asset, including the history of asset (e.g., Who owned the site and how did they affect it?) and development of a baseline (e.g., water, soil, and air quality parameters) against which environmental performance can be effectively measured. As with any resource managed through TCM, if there are performance problems, corrective actions must be evaluated and taken as appropriate. Risk management (Section 7.6) may also indicate that mitigating actions should be taken before a risk factor becomes an environmental failure.

Because of societal and political concern for the environment, which is often charged with emotion, environmental mitigation and remediation projects require an open and comprehensive approach to establishing requirements and resolving such issues as cost growth, environmental regulation concerns that impact the schedule and cost of a project, static and dynamic baseline development, cost estimating, calculating contingency, risk and uncertainty analysis, innovative claims, and dispute avoidance.

Because environmental mitigation and remediation projects are often associated with other projects, one goal is to be cost effective without disrupting the other projects. The control systems for risks, safety, health, and quality as well as for cost, and schedules for associated projects should complement each other. The development of a baseline that integrates the scope of work, cost, and schedule becomes an important management tool that allows for early identification of potential schedule delays and/or cost overruns.

Environmental remediation is a particularly difficult operation that generally combines unique construction expertise (e.g., ability to work with hazardous materials) with unique scientific and engineering requirements. The planning of remediation projects is arduous because environmental and work conditions are often variable and uncertain, and environmental restrictions present problems that often require unique execution strategies, construction practices, and so on. Some examples of the types of special planning concerns and cost drivers for an environmental remediation construction project include:

- hazardous or contaminated waste material and waste water handling
- personal protection required (e.g., encapsulation)
- energy (kilo calories) expended by and productivity of encapsulated workers
- medical examinations
- first aid facilities
- worker decontamination
- vehicle, equipment, and tools decontamination
- testing and monitoring equipment
- field laboratory setup and operation
- site communication and emergency warning systems
- site security
- special permits
- dust and emissions control and mitigation
- environmental due diligence
- community and public relations

These and other uncertain or hidden costs associated with remediation work often have to be accounted for through assumptions, allowances, and contingency. The issue of cost drivers and cost growth has plagued environmental projects for several decades. Consequently, risk management and the ability to adequately estimate and manage contingency for environmental projects has become a critical project control process (see Section 7.6).

11.6.5 Key Concepts for Environment, Health, and Safety

The preceding discussions touched on a few principles and considerations regarding EHS in the TCM process. A key point to remember is that EHS is not a separate process—EHS issues are considered in TCM by making sure that customer EHS needs and expectations are addressed. By doing so, assets and projects are managed with a view toward prevention of EHS failures and continuously improving EHS performance through design. This is a quality management perspective; therefore, Section 11.4 on quality management is a lead-in to EHS management.

The following concepts and terminology described in this section are particularly important to understanding EHS management in relation to TCM:

.1 *Quality Management.* (Section 11.4 and 11.6.1). TCM is a quality management process and EHS issues are considered using this process approach.
.2 *EHS Standards/Compliance.* Compliance with minimum standards and regulations should be considered the minimum behavior expected to have the privilege of being in business.
.3 *Non-Conformance/Prevention.* (Section 11.6.1). As in quality management, management effort should be focused on preventing non-conformance with EHS requirements and improving performance rather than after the fact appraisal, failure, and correction.
.4 *Sustainable Development.* (Section 11.6.2.1). Enterprises should not use resources in a manner or degree that compromises the ability of future generations to sustain such development. It extends TCM's perspective from the life cycle of an asset alone to include the life cycle of the environment and its asset value as *natural capital*.

.5 *Natural Capital.* (Section 11.6.2.1). The monetized value of the earth's ecosystem services.

Further Readings and Sources

The references on EHS are too numerous to mention. However, the following references and sources provide basic information and will lead to more detailed treatments.

- Barcott, Bruce. "What's Wilderness Worth?" *Outside Magazine*, March 2005.
- BSI, OHSAS 18001, www.bsi-global.com.
- Brauer, Roger L. *Safety and Health for Engineers.* New York: John Wiley & Sons, 1994.
- Gibson, Will. "A Practical View of Life-Cycle Assessment." In *Implementing ISO 14000* by Tom Tibor and Ira Feldman, Editors. Chicago, IL: Irwin Professional Publishing, 1997.
- Global Environmental Management Initiative (GEMI). *New Paths to Business Value: Strategic Sourcing–Environment, Health and Safety.* Washington, DC: GEMI, 2001.
- Global Reporting Initiative. *Sustainability Reporting Guidelines.* Washington, DC: GEMI, 2002.
- Goodman, Susannah Blake, Jonas Kron, and Tim Little. *The Environmental Fiduciary–The Case for Incorporating Environmental Factors into Investment Management Policies.* Oakland, CA: The Rose Foundation for Communities and the Environment, 2004.
- Hawkins, Paul, Amory Lovins, and L. Hunter Lovins. *Natural Capitalism–Creating the Next Industrial Revolution.* New York: Little Brown and Company, 1999.
- Hirsch, Dennis D. "Second Generation Policy and the New Economy." *Capital University Law Review*, vol. 29, no. 1, 2001.
- Hoffman, Andrew J. *Competitive Environmental Strategy–A Guide to the Changing Business Landscape.* Washington, DC: Island Press, 2000.
- International Organization for Standardization (ISO), www.iso.org.
- Juran, Joseph M., and A. Blanton Godfrey. *Juran's Quality Handbook*, 5th ed. New York: McGraw-Hill, 1999.
- McDonough, William, and Michael Braungart. "The Next Industrial Revolution." *Atlantic Monthly*, October 1998.
- Morris, Alan S. *ISO 14000 Environmental Management Standards: Engineering and Financial Aspects.* New York: John Wiley & Sons, 2003.
- Reed, O. Lee, Peter J. Shedd, Jere W. Morehead, and Robert N. Corley. *The Legal and Regulatory Environment of Business*, 13th ed. New York: McGraw Hill College, 2005.
- Selg, Richard A. *Hazardous Waste Cost Control*, 1st ed. New York: Marcel Dekker, Inc., 1993.
- Selg, Richard A., Editor. *Professional Practice Guide (PPG) #11: Environmental Remediation.* Morgantown, WV: AACE International, 2002.
- Stavins, Robert N. *Economics of the Environment*, 4th ed. New York: W.W. Norton & Company, 2000.

APPENDICES

APPENDIX A—AACE INTERNATIONAL RECOMMENDED PRACTICE NO. 11R-88
REQUIRED SKILLS AND KNOWLEDGE OF COST ENGINEERING

aace International

AACE International Recommended Practice No. 11R-88

REQUIRED SKILLS AND KNOWLEDGE OF COST ENGINEERING

Recommended Practice No. 11R-88
Required Skills and Knowledge of Cost Engineering

January 17, 2006

This recommended practice has the following purposes:

- define what *core* skills and knowledge of cost engineering a person is required to have in order to be considered a professional practitioner, and in doing so,
- establish the emphasis of *core* subjects for AACE International education and certification programs.

It is also hoped that enterprises will find this useful as a reference or guide for developing their own competency models. *Knowledge* is an understanding gained through experience or study, and *skills* are abilities that transform knowledge into use. *Core* subjects are those whose usage is occasional to frequent and are considered by AACE International as being required for professional practitioners of cost engineering to know and be able to use.

This recommended practice lists these core subjects and provides general *performance statements* (i.e., "be able to" describe, perform, etc.) to represent the level of proficiency expected in each subject area. These statements are representative or guiding examples only.

This text is an outline that is intended to be the structural foundation for products and services developed by the Educational and Certification Boards. It will continue to be modified as current practice changes.

BACKGROUND AND SCOPE UPDATE

The original recommend practice *Required Skills and Knowledge of a Cost Engineer* was developed by the AACE International Education Board and published in 1988 based on their evaluations of a membership survey. Until that time, AACE International lacked a formal definition of professional cost engineering in terms of skills and knowledge. Based on the recommended practice findings, the Education Board then published the first *Skills and Knowledge of Cost Engineering* text to provide an educational product to elaborate on the core skills and knowledge subjects. The earlier text has been regularly updated by the Education Board.

Since the original publication, the AACE Technical Board was given the charter to define the technology of cost engineering and total cost management. In 2005, the Technical Board completed development of the *Total Cost Management Framework* which describes a systematic process (i.e., TCM process) through which the skills and knowledge of cost engineering are applied. It also provides an integrated structure upon which the Technical Board can organize its development of recommended practices, including this one.

This update of the *Required Skills and Knowledge of a Cost Engineer* retains most of the content of the earlier versions while incorporating those elements of the TCM process that the AACE associate boards (Technical, Education and Certification) determined are required for a professional practitioner of cost engineering to know. It also incorporates a more systematic organization of the subjects, based on TCM developments, to better differentiate between general *supporting knowledge* used in more than one practice or process (e.g., statistics, elements of cost, etc.), and specific *practice knowledge* used in particular functions or processes (e.g., cost estimating, planning and scheduling, etc.)

INTRODUCTION

A professional cost engineering practitioner must first be able to articulate the meaning of the terms *cost engineering* and *total cost management (TCM)*. Practitioners will frequently be asked these questions. Given the importance of this first knowledge requirement to the understanding this recommended practice, the questions are answered here. Elaboration of all other skills and knowledge requirements is left for subsequent Education Board products.

What are Cost Engineering and TCM?
The AACE International *Constitution and Bylaws* defines cost engineering and total cost management as follows:

> **Section 2.** The Association is dedicated to the tenets of furthering the concepts of *Total Cost Management* and *Cost Engineering*. Total Cost Management is the effective application of professional and technical expertise to plan and control resources, costs, profitability and risk. Simply stated, it is a systematic approach to managing cost throughout the life cycle of any enterprise, program, facility, project, product or service. This is accomplished through the application of cost engineering and cost management principles, proven methodologies and the latest technology in support of the management process.
>
> **Section 3.** Total Cost Management is that area of engineering practice where engineering judgment and experience are utilized in the application of scientific principles and techniques to problems of business and program planning; cost estimating; economic and financial analysis; cost engineering; program and project management; planning and scheduling; and cost and schedule performance measurement and change control.

In summary, the list of practice areas in Section 3 are collectively called *cost engineering*; while the "process" through which these practices are applied is called *total cost management* or TCM.

How is cost and schedule management an "engineering" function?
Most people would agree that "engineers" and engineering (or more generally, the "application of scientific principles and techniques") are most often responsible for creating functional things (or *strategic assets* as we call them in TCM). However, engineering has multiple dimensions. The most obvious is the dimension of physical design and the calculation and analysis tasks done to support that design (e.g., design a bridge or develop software). However, beyond the physical dimension of design (e.g., the bridge structure), there are other important dimensions of *money, time*, and other *resources* that are invested in the creation of the designed asset. We refer to these investments collectively as *costs*. Using the above example, someone must estimate what the bridge might cost, determine the activities needed to design and build it, estimate how long these activities will take, and so on. Furthermore, someone needs to monitor and assess the progress of the bridge design and construction (in relation to the expenditure of money and time) to ensure that the completed bridge meets the owner's and other stakeholder's requirements. Someone must also monitor and assess the cost of operating and maintaining the bridge during its life cycle.

Returning to the *Constitution and Bylaws* definition, understanding and managing the cost dimensions requires skills and knowledge in "business and program planning; cost estimating; economic and financial analysis; cost engineering; program and project management; planning and scheduling; and cost and schedule performance measurement and change control." No significant asset has ever been built without dealing with these cost dimensions in some way, and the more systematically and professionally these dimensions are addressed, the more successful the asset performance is likely to be. Therefore, cost *engineering* recognizes that cost is a necessary extension of traditional engineering (and other creative functions such as systems analysis, etc.), and that there is an intimate connection between the physical and cost dimensions of the asset.

Do cost engineering practitioners need to have a traditional "engineering" background?
The skills and knowledge required to deal with *costs* (i.e., cost estimating, planning and scheduling, etc.) are quite different from those required to deal with the physical design dimension. From that difference, the field of *cost engineering* was born. Cost engineering practitioners work alongside of and are peers with engineers, software analysts, play producers, architects, and other creative career fields to handle the cost dimension, but they do not necessarily have the same background. Whether they have technical, operations, finance and accounting, or other backgrounds, cost engineering practitioners need to share a

common understanding, based on "scientific principles and techniques", with the engineering or other creative career functions.

Do cost engineering practitioners all have the same function?
Cost engineering practitioners tend to be: a) specialized in function (e.g., cost estimating, planning and scheduling, etc.); b) focused on either the asset management or project control side of the TCM process; and c) focused on a particular industry (e.g., engineering and construction, manufacturing, information technology, etc) or asset type (e.g., chemical process, buildings, software, etc.). They may have titles such as cost estimator, quantity surveyor, parametric analyst, strategic planner, planner/scheduler, value engineer, cost/schedule engineer, claims consultant, project manager, or project control lead. They may work for the business that owns and operates the asset (emphasis on economics and analysis), or they may work for the contractor that executes the projects (emphasis on planning and control). But, no matter what their job title or business environment, a general knowledge of, and skills in, all areas of cost engineering are required to perform their job effectively. In summary, the purpose of this document is to define the *required skills and knowledge of professional cost engineering*.

THIS DOCUMENT'S OUTLINE STRUCTURE AND ITS RELATIONSHIP TO PARTICULAR FUNCTIONS AND AACE INTERNATIONAL CERTIFICATIONS

Figure 1 illustrates the hierarchical structure of the Required Skills and Knowledge of Cost Engineering. The first level of the structure differentiates between general *supporting knowledge* used in more than one practice or process, and specific *practice knowledge* used in particular functions or process steps. Succeeding levels further break down the content to whatever level is appropriate for each skills and knowledge area. The location of a skill or knowledge element in the level of the outline does not reflect on its relative importance.

On the process and functional side, the structure is organized in accordance with the plan, do, check, (or measure), and assess (PDCA) process model that serves as the basis for the TCM process through which all the skills and knowledge of cost engineering are applied. It is not structured by a practitioner's work function. For example, cost estimators will not find all of their required skills and knowledge under one heading. Their particular function's required skills and knowledge will include elements of supporting knowledge, as well as elements of planning, measuring, and assessing that are appropriate to their function.

This document includes the required skills and knowledge that certified cost engineers and consultants (CCE/CCCs) must have. Its scope is broad and represents the comprehensive skills and knowledge that business management may expect someone with overarching responsibilities in an organization to have (e.g., supporting overall capital program or project system management).

For specialty certifications [e.g., planning and scheduling professionals (PSP)], the Certification Board will document appropriate skills and knowledge requirements. These will include elements from this overall outline as they apply to the scope of the particular function. They may also include more detailed skills and knowledge than included here. The scope of those requirements will not be as broad, but will be deeper, representing the skills and knowledge that business management may expect from a manager of or expert in the particular function.

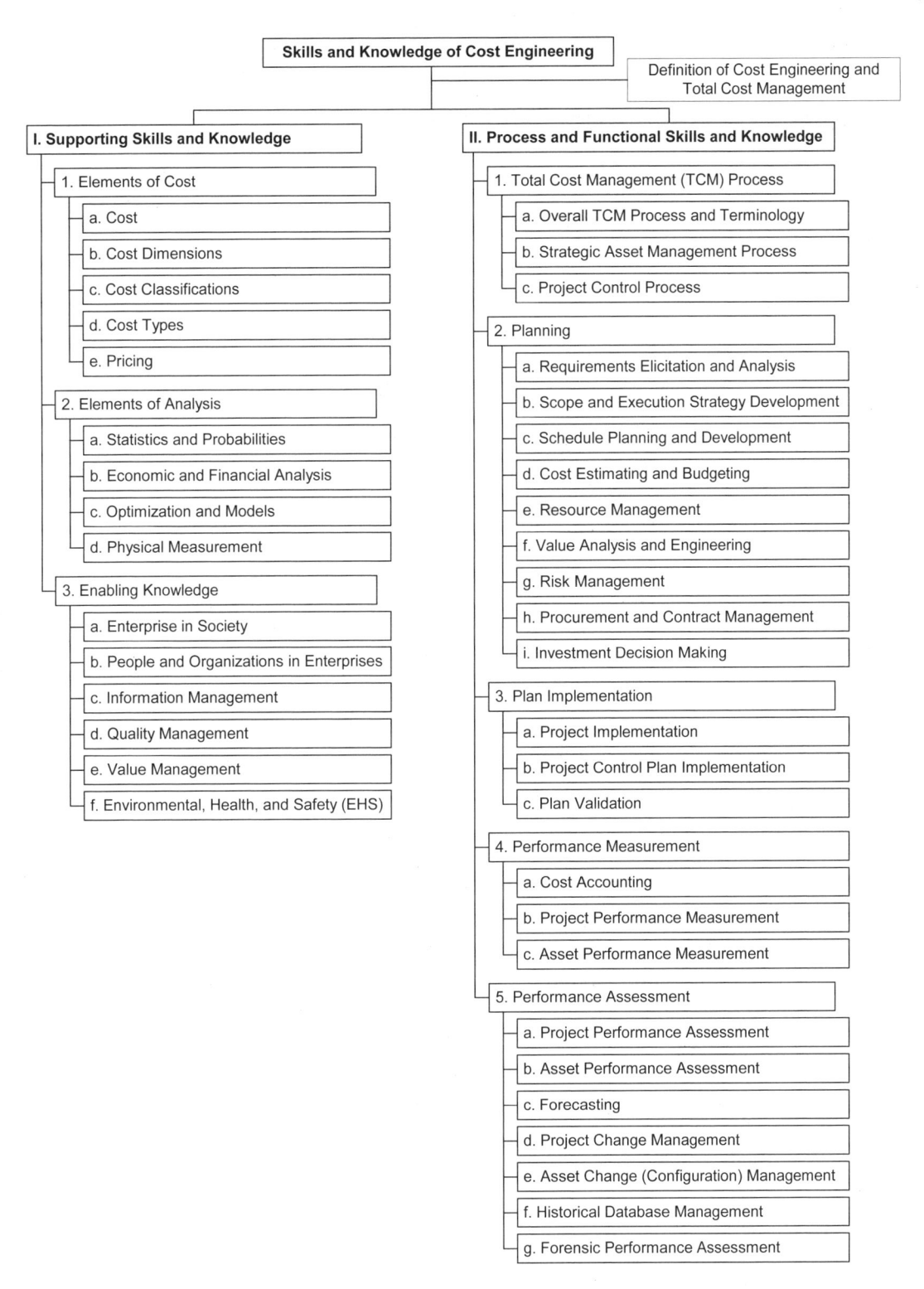

```
Skills and Knowledge of Cost Engineering
├── Definition of Cost Engineering and Total Cost Management
├── I. Supporting Skills and Knowledge
│   ├── 1. Elements of Cost
│   │   ├── a. Cost
│   │   ├── b. Cost Dimensions
│   │   ├── c. Cost Classifications
│   │   ├── d. Cost Types
│   │   └── e. Pricing
│   ├── 2. Elements of Analysis
│   │   ├── a. Statistics and Probabilities
│   │   ├── b. Economic and Financial Analysis
│   │   ├── c. Optimization and Models
│   │   └── d. Physical Measurement
│   └── 3. Enabling Knowledge
│       ├── a. Enterprise in Society
│       ├── b. People and Organizations in Enterprises
│       ├── c. Information Management
│       ├── d. Quality Management
│       ├── e. Value Management
│       └── f. Environmental, Health, and Safety (EHS)
└── II. Process and Functional Skills and Knowledge
    ├── 1. Total Cost Management (TCM) Process
    │   ├── a. Overall TCM Process and Terminology
    │   ├── b. Strategic Asset Management Process
    │   └── c. Project Control Process
    ├── 2. Planning
    │   ├── a. Requirements Elicitation and Analysis
    │   ├── b. Scope and Execution Strategy Development
    │   ├── c. Schedule Planning and Development
    │   ├── d. Cost Estimating and Budgeting
    │   ├── e. Resource Management
    │   ├── f. Value Analysis and Engineering
    │   ├── g. Risk Management
    │   ├── h. Procurement and Contract Management
    │   └── i. Investment Decision Making
    ├── 3. Plan Implementation
    │   ├── a. Project Implementation
    │   ├── b. Project Control Plan Implementation
    │   └── c. Plan Validation
    ├── 4. Performance Measurement
    │   ├── a. Cost Accounting
    │   ├── b. Project Performance Measurement
    │   └── c. Asset Performance Measurement
    └── 5. Performance Assessment
        ├── a. Project Performance Assessment
        ├── b. Asset Performance Assessment
        ├── c. Forecasting
        ├── d. Project Change Management
        ├── e. Asset Change (Configuration) Management
        ├── f. Historical Database Management
        └── g. Forensic Performance Assessment
```

Figure 1. High Level Outline of the *Skills and Knowledge of Cost Engineering*

Required Skills and Knowledge of Cost Engineering

Note: In the outline that follows, the **bold** or *italic list* words signify key concepts for which the practitioner should at least be able to provide a basic description. Regular text is for representative performance statements.

I. SUPPORTING SKILLS AND KNOWLEDGE

1. **Elements of Cost**

    a. **Costs**: be able to define/explain these general concepts in relation to each other and to assets and/or activities.
    - i. **Resources**
    - ii. **Time**
    - iii. **Cost**

    b. **Cost Dimensions**:
    - i. **Lifecycle**: be able to describe this term and differentiate the life cycle of an *asset* and a *project*
    - ii. **Process (product vs. project)**: be able to describe and differentiate the cost characteristics and types (see cost types below) that make up *product* and *project* costs.
        1. be able to distinguish among products, co-products, and byproducts.
    - iii. **Responsibility**: be able to describe and differentiate the cost perspectives of an owner and a contractor/supplier
    - iv. **Valuation**: be able to describe and differentiate cost from *cash/monetary* versus economic/**opportunity costs** (also see **economic analysis**) perspectives.
    - v. **Influence:** be able to explain the concept of the *cost influence curve*
    - vi. **Legal**:
        1. be able to explain how cost and schedule analysis practices might differ when applied for *forensic* versus traditional planning and control purposes.
        2. be able to describe some potential legal consequences that may result from using poor or unethical cost management practices (e.g., anti-trust, claims, Sarbanes-Oxley, etc)

    c. **Cost Classifications:** for the following classifications, be able to:
    - i. explain the general differences between the ways costs are classified for various cost management purposes
    - ii. given a problem with appropriate cost classification inputs (e.g., indirect cost using ABC classification method), be able to calculate how the cost would be accounted for in a *project* or *product* estimate.
        1. **Operating (Production, Manufacturing, Maintenance, etc.) vs. Capital**
        2. **Capital vs. Expense**
            a. *Depreciation*
            b. *Amortization*
            c. *Accrual*
        3. **Fixed vs. Variable**
        4. **Direct vs. Indirect**
            a. *Activity-Based Costing (ABC)*
            b. *Job Costing*

    d. **Cost Types**: for the following cost types, given cost type and classification inputs, be able to apply them in a project or manufacturing estimating application (i.e., for *project* or *product* cost)
    - i. **Materials**:
        1. **Materials types**: be able to describe the types and their cost drivers:
            a. *Raw*
            b. *Bulk*
            c. *Fabricated*
            d. *Engineered or designed*

e. Consumables
2. **Purchase costs**: be able to describe these terms/concepts and their influence on the cost of materials:
    a. market pricing (pre-negotiated vs. competitively bid, etc.)
    b. order quantity
    c. taxes and duties
    d. carrying charges
    e. cancellation charges
    f. demurrage
    g. hazardous material regulations
    h. warranties, maintenance and service
3. **Materials management costs**: be able to describe these terms/concepts and their influence on the cost of materials:
    a. delivery schedule
    b. packing
    c. shipping and freight
    d. freight forwarding
    e. handling
    f. storage and inventory
    g. agent cost
    h. surveillance or inspection
    i. expediting
    j. losses (shrinkage, waste, theft, damage)
    k. spare parts (inventory or start-up)
    l. surplus materials
4. **Capital Equipment**: (i.e., fabricated or engineered items)
    a. **Rent vs. lease vs. purchase**:
        i. be able to explain the mechanics and cost considerations.
        ii. given a problem with useful life, fixed and operating cost, credits, depreciation, taxes, etc., be able to determine the most economical option
    b. **Valuation**: be able to explain these concepts:
        i. reproduction costs
        ii. replacement costs
        iii. fair value
        iv. market value
        v. book value
        vi. residual or economic value
        vii. operating vs. economic life
5. **Temporary Equipment**: (expensed items for construction, maintenance, etc) be able to explain the cost implications of *rent, operators, maintenance, scheduling, etc.*

ii. **Labor**
1. **Labor Wage Rate or Salary**:
    a. be able to describe the differences in mechanics of compensation for wage and salaried employees including the meaning of *exempt* and *non-exempt*.
    b. Be able to calculate an effective wage rate allowing for:
        i. *overtime premium*
        ii. *other premium pays*
        iii. *shortened shift time*
        iv. *travel time*
        v. *show-up pay*
2. **Benefits and Burdens (mandated and fringe)**:
    a. be able to describe the basic mechanics of benefits and burdens such as:
        i. *retirement (social security),*
        ii. *unemployment insurance*
        iii. *workers compensation*
        iv. *insurance*

v. *paid time off (sick, vacation, holiday)*
b. be able to identify typical differences between industrialized and non-industrialized countries and between populated and remote areas.
3. **Overhead and profit**: be able to describe the basic mechanics of charging various overhead and profit cost elements to direct labor costs such as:
   a. *Indirect labor (home office, administrative and similar costs)*
   b. *small tools*
   c. *profit*
4. **Union**: be able to explain the cost differences between union and open shop labor

iii. **Subcontract**: be able to explain the cost implications of the following issues:
1. *reimbursable vs. non-reimbursable costs*
2. *overhead and profit (including contract administration and legal costs)*
3. *license, fees or royalties*
4. *bonds (bid, payment, or performance)*
5. *retainage*
6. *performance guarantees*
7. *liquidated damages*

iv. **Cost of money**: be able to describe these costs:
1. *escalation*
2. *inflation*
3. *currency exchange rates*

v. **Risk and Uncertainty**: be able to describe these costs:
1. *contingency*
2. *allowance*
3. *reserve*

e. **Pricing**
   i. **Cost vs. Pricing**: be able to explain the difference
   ii. **Price strategy**:
   1. be able to describe how business strategy and market forces may affect pricing.
   2. be able to describe from an owner or buyer perspective concerns about pricing (i.e., risks, competitiveness, cash flow, etc).
   3. be able to describe how profit affects pricing
   4. be able to describe how profit may be determined how the different types of contracts may influence the amount

2. **Elements of Analysis**

   a. **Statistics and Probability**
      i. **Samples and Populations**: be able to describe the relationship of the mean of a sample to the mean of a population, and the general affect of sample randomness, bias and size on the reliability of the sample statistics .
      ii. **Descriptive Statistics**
         1. **Basic Statistics**: given a set of data, be able to determine the arithmetic *mean, median, mode, standard deviation and variance.*
         2. **Normal Distribution**: be able to provide the percent of observations within one and two standard deviations of the mean for a *normally* distributed variable.
         3. **Non-Normal Distributions**: be able to describe the following concepts:
            a. *skewness (symmetry)*
            b. *kurtosis (central tendency relative to normal).*
         4. **Histograms, Cumulative Frequency**: given a tabular distribution for a variable that is other than normal, be able to draw a histogram and resultant cumulative frequency curve (frequency distribution), and determine the percent probability of the variable not being less than or more than a given number
      iii. **Inferential Statistics**

1. **Probability:** given a curve of normal distribution and an accompanying table of areas under the curve, be able to determine the probability of a) the variable being between two given numbers, b) not being higher than a given number, or lower than that number, and c) given a confidence interval or range in terms of percentage probability, give the corresponding low and high number of the interval or range.
2. **Regression Analysis:** be able to describe the concept of the methodology as well as diagnostic statistics (*R2, root mean square error (RMSE), and t*)
3. **Statistical Significance**:
   a. Be able to describe the purpose and use of chi-squared and t-tests
   b. Be able to interpret the t-statistic for comparing two sets of normally distributed data.
   c. Be able to interpret of the chi-squared statistic for comparing two sets of data that may not be normally distributed.

b. **Economic and Financial Analysis**
   i. **Economic Cost**: be able to define concepts of **opportunity cost** and assigning monetary value to non-cash values, costs and benefits.
   ii. **Cash Flow Analysis**:
      1. be able to calculate simple and compound interest rates and solve interest problems using the basic single payments, uniform series, and gradient formulas.
      2. given a set of cost and revenue forecasts calculate a cash flow for an asset investment option
   iii. **Internal Rate of Return**: be able to determine discounted rate of return of a cash flow series.
   iv. **Present/Future Value Analysis**: be able to calculate present value, future value, and equivalent uniform annual value of a cash flow series.

c. **Optimization**
   i. **Model**:
      1. be able to describe the concept of a quantitative representational *models* and *parameters*.
      2. given an optimization goal involving a result Y which is a function of X, use graphical or incremental methods to determine the optimum value of Y.
   ii. **Linear Programming**: be able to describe the types of problems amenable to this mathematical optimization technique (i.e., find extreme points of a function given a set of constraints).
   iii. **Simulation:** be able to describe the use of a model for analysis of a cost problem.
   iv. **Sensitivity Analysis**: be able to perform a sensitivity analysis of a modeled problem.

d. **Physical Measurements:** be able to convert basic metric and imperial weight and dimensional measurements.

3. **Enabling Knowledge**

   a. **Enterprise in Society**
      i. **Societal Values**: be able to generally describe societal concerns and needs that should be considered in asset and project planning.
      ii. **Decision Policy**: be able to describe how to translate societal values to policy so that an enterprise can consistently address societal values in everyday practice.
      iii. **Ethics**:
         1. be able to explain the need to judge the means and the ends of a practice or process against personal and societal values and rules of conduct.
         2. be familiar with AACE International's ethics policy (Canon of Ethics).

   b. **People and Organizations in Enterprises**
      i. **Leadership**: Be able to explain why it is important to obtain team *commitment* and clearly communicate the *purpose* of a task or project, and how this might be done.

Required Skills and Knowledge of Cost Engineering

1. **Leadership Roles**:
   a. be able to explain why the need for *leading, managing, facilitating, and mentoring* roles may vary by situation.
   b. discuss the meaning and provide examples of "*participative management.*"
2. **Motivation/Incentives (Behavioral Science):**
   a. be able to discuss *motivator/demotivator* affects on labor attitude and performance
   b. given a list, be able to describe the basic themes of two or more generally accepted behavioral science theories:
      i. *McGregor- Theory X and Y*
      ii. *Herzberg-Motivation-Hygiene*
      iii. *Argyris-Effects of organization like on individuals*
      iv. *Likert-Four model systems*
      v. *Mouton-Managerial grid*
      vi. *Other current theories*
3. **Performance/Productivity Management:**
   a. Be able to describe the concept of *productivity* (and its difference from the term *production*).
   b. be able to describe the affect on performance of these factors in terms of *motivation* and *waste/inefficiency*, and how performance could be improved and at what cost (e.g., leadership role, work process change, etc.):
      i. *individual worker skills*
      ii. *crew balance of skills*
      iii. *immediate supervision competence*
      iv. *overall supervision competence*
      v. *worker and supervision attitudes*
      vi. *work force sociological, cultural and demographic characteristics*
      vii. *absenteeism and turnover*
      viii. *overtime*
      ix. *level of technology used*
      x. *learning curve*
      xi. *work area environment*
      xii. *weather*
      xiii. *geographic location*
      xiv. *proximity to other work and contractors*
      xv. *job layout*
      xvi. *work rules*
      xvii. *safety practices*
      xviii. *quality control practices (including quality circles)*
      xix. *materials and tools availability*
      xx. *wages, salaries and benefits.*

ii. **Organization Structure**
   1. **Organizational Design**: be able to describe the issues that organizations must address (*division of labor, unity of command, unity of directions, and span of control*) and how each may affect performance.
   2. **Basic Structures**:
      a. be able to draw and example chart and explain the differences between, and advantages/disadvantages of traditional *functional, divisional, and matrix* structures
   3. **Teams:**
      a. be able to explain how and why teams are used in enterprises and why they are typically used to manage projects.
      b. be able to describe typical team organization (i.e., matrix) and operation and the roles, responsibilities, and methods for its successful performance.
   4. **Typical Organizations in TCM**: be able to generally describe the typical roles of *capital investment management* (business planning), *operations management*, and *project management* in TCM (i.e., where cost engineers usually work).

c. **Information Management**
   i. **Data, Information, and Knowledge**: be able to explain the difference between these three types of "information"
   ii. **Databases and Database Management**. Be able to define and explain the following concepts:
      1. **History**: the importance of historical and empirical information to most cost engineering practice
      2. **Reference Data**: the need that specific methods and tools for specific processed data
      3. **Lessons Learned**: the need for data that is qualitative in nature.
      4. **Metric**: the need that benchmarking or validation methods have for specific processed quantitative data
      5. **Validation**: the need to assure the reliability and sometimes competitiveness of data
      6. **Basis**: the need to understand the basis of all data and information in a database
      7. **Normalization**: be able to adjust data to a common basis in currency, time, location, etc.
   iii. **Information Technology (IT) and Systems**: be able to explain that information systems are the mechanisms or tools by which knowledge is delivered to the enterprise and those it interacts with (i.e., includes communication).
      1. **Enterprise Resource Planning/Management (ERP/ERM)**: be able to describe the goal of these types of systems (support efficient business processes, including project management, through shared or common databases)

d. **Quality Management**: be able to explain the following concepts:
   i. **Quality**: be able to define this as conformance to *requirements* (which are based on customer needs).
   ii. **Requirements**: (see **Requirements Elicitation and Analysis** practices)
   iii. **Quality Planning**: be able to describe this as an integrated way of planning directed towards satisfying customer needs.
   iv. **Quality Management**: be able to describe this as a process for managing quality and understand that TCM is a quality management process focused on continuous cost performance improvement.
   v. **Quality Assurance**: be able to describe this as actions that provide confidence that the requirements will be fulfilled.
   vi. **Quality Control**: be able to describe this as actions focused on fulfilling requirements
   vii. **Continuous Improvement**: be able to describe this as a common goal of quality management processes (the traditional result of the PDCA process).
   viii. **Plan-Do-Check-Assess (PDCA)**: be able to describe this as the basis model for TCM and many other management processes.
   ix. **Quality Measurement**: be able to explain that in some views, cost is the best single quality measurement because so many measures can be expressed in cost terms.
   x. **Quality Policy**: be able to explain that this as an imposed requirement that is assumed guided by accepted quality management principles
   xi. **Quality Standards**: be able to describe these *imposed requirements*.
      1. **ISO 9000** standard quality management series
      2. **ISO 10006** quality in project management
   xii. **Quality Focused Practices in TCM** be aware that these key practices (covered in later sections) have particular importance to quality management
      1. *Benchmarking*
      2. *Cost of Quality*
      3. *Value Analysis/Engineering*
      4. *Change Management*

e. **Value Management:**
   i. Be able to explain the following general concepts (i.e., not in the context of Value Analysis and Engineering practice):

1. **Value** (i.e., a measure of the worth of a thing in terms of usefulness, desirability, importance, money)
2. **Value Management** (i.e., what an enterprise does to ensure that its assets provide or maintain the usefulness and/or value that the various stakeholders require.)
3. **Value Improving Practices** (i.e., practices that have a specific focus and/or significant effect on getting the most value from a process and meet criteria that set the practice apart from "business as usual".)

ii. Be able to describe the purposes and general approach of these value improving practices (also see the section on Value Analysis and Engineering):
1. **Manufacturability Analysis**
2. **Constructability Analysis**
3. **Reliability, Availability and Maintainability (RAM) Analysis**

f. **Environment, Health, Safety, and Security (EHS)**: be able to explain the following concepts:
  i. **Quality Management**. be able to describe why TCM is a quality management process and EHS issues are considered using this process approach (i.e., through establishing EHS *requirements* and managing to them).
  ii. **Non-Conformance/Prevention**. be able to explain why it is important, as in quality management, to focus on preventing non-conformance with EHS requirements and improving performance rather than after the fact *appraisal, failure and correction*.
  iii. **EHS Standards/Compliance**. be able to explain why compliance with minimum standards and regulations should be the minimum expected.
    1. **ISO 14000**: management systems that an organization employs to manage environmental matters.
  iv. **Sustainable Development**. be able to explain why enterprises should not use resources in a manner or degree that compromise the ability of future generations to sustain such development.

II. PROCESS AND FUNCTIONAL SKILLS AND KNOWLEDGE

1. **Total Cost Management (TCM) Process**

   a. **Overall TCM Process and Terminology**
      i. Basic Terminology: be able to explain the following:
         1. *Plan-Do-Check-Assess (PDCA):*
         2. *Strategic asset*
         3. *Project*
         4. *Portfolios and Programs*

      ii. **TCM Processes:** be able to sketch the **TCM, strategic asset management,** and **project control** processes in basic **PDCA** format and explain the following:
         1. the cost management purpose of the overall processes
         2. how the two component subprocesses differ, but are related to each other
         3. the benefits of an integrated, systematic cost management approach over the life cycle of assets and projects

   b. **Strategic Asset Management Process**
      i. given a representation of the strategic asset management process map (or some portion of it), be able to describe the basic purpose of each step and how it relates to the other steps in the map.

   c. **Project Control Process**
      i. given a representation of the project control process map (or some portion of it), be able to describe the basic purpose of each step and how it relates to the other steps in the map.
      ii. be able to describe the *Earned Value* management process as a specific way of applying the project control process (i.e., in what ways is it specialized)

2. **Planning**

   a. **Requirements Elicitation and Analysis**: be able to describe the following concepts
      i. **Stakeholders/Customers**: be able to describe how to identify these in relation to various business problems
      ii. **Needs, wants, or expectations of stakeholders**: be able describe challenges of eliciting this information from various stakeholders
      iii. **Requirements**: be able to describe the characteristics of a good requirement for use in asset or project control planning
      iv. **Cost requirements**: be able to describe the following asset planning methodologies for which cost may be a requirement
         1. *Target costing (including design-to-cost, and cost as an independent variable)*
         2. *Quality-function deployment*
      v. Other Concepts:
         1. **Asset vs. Project:** be able to explain how requirements for an asset or product might differ from those for a project.

   b. **Scope and Execution Strategy Development**: be able to describe the following concepts
      i. **Asset scope**: be able to describe this as the physical, functional and quality characteristics or design basis of the selected asset investment
         1. **Functional decomposition**
      ii. **Project scope**: be able to describe this as the scope of work to deliver the asset
         1. **Project scope breakdown (work decomposition)**
      iii. **Work Breakdown Structure (WBS):** be able to diagram a WBS for a basic scope provided in narrative form

iv. **Organization Breakdown Structure (OBS)**: be able to diagram an OBS for a basic scope provided in narrative form
v. **Work package**
vi. **Deliverables**
vii. **Execution strategy**

c. **Schedule Planning and Development**: be able to describe the following concepts:
  i. **Schedule Planning**
    1. **Activities**
    2. **Activity Logic and Logic Diagramming**:
       a. given a series of logic statements, be able to draw a *logic diagram*.
       b. given a *soft-logic* work package with no strict activity interrelationships, be able to describe ways to do schedule planning for this work.
       c. be able to describe how schedule planning differs between a *batch and a continuous process*.
       d. Be able to describe the concept of *linear scheduling*
    3. **Activity Duration**
    4. **Critical Path**: be able to define and identify the critical path(s) in a project schedule
    5. **Float**: be able to describe the relationship and significance of *total and free float* in the scheduling of an activity.
    6. **Schedule Models**: Using the PDM method, and given a logic diagram and durations for activities, be able to calculate the early start and finish, late start and finish, and total and free float times for all activities. Identify minimum project completion time.
       a. **Precedence Diagram Method (PDM)**: in using this method include at least on each finish-start, finish-finish, start-finish, and start-start relationships with lags and identify critical path(s)
       b. **Bar chart/Gantt chart**:
          i. be able to explain the difference between this and a logic diagram
          ii. given network activity durations, early and late start and finish times, and total float, be able to draw a bar chart based on early start of all activities, and show total float of activities where applicable.
    7. Historical Data: be able to describe the importance of historical, empirical data and databases to schedule planning and schedule development
  ii. **Schedule Development**: describe difference from schedule planning
    1. **Milestones**
    2. **Resource Loading**
    3. **Resource Leveling or Balancing**: for a simple PDM network with resource inputs, be able to resource level the network within early and late start limits, and draw a histogram of worker-loading for early start, late start, and resource leveled configurations.
  iii. **Schedule Control Basis**
    1. **Schedule Control Baseline**
       a. Be able to describe the concept of short interval scheduling (SIS) in relation to an overall project schedule control baseline.
    2. **Planned Schedule**
    3. **Schedule Basis**
  iv. Other Concepts:
    1. **Programs and Portfolios**: be able to explain these concepts and how schedule planning and development might be handled for groups of projects
    2. **Operations/Production:** be able to explain how production scheduling differs from project scheduling
    3. **Schedule strategy**
       a. be able to describe the characteristics and risks of a *fast track* schedule

b. be able to describe alternate schedule strategies in regards to potential changes and claims that a contractor may apply in developing a network schedule (e.g., crashing).
c. be able describe the characteristics and risks of *just-in-time (JIT)* scheduling.
4. **Schedule Development:**
   a. be able to describe the concept of development by *schedule level*
   b. be able to describe the concept of *rolling wave* development.
5. **Schedule Change Management:** be able to describe how schedule changes might be managed.
6. **Critical Chain:** be able to describe the concept
7. **Linear Scheduling:** be able to describe the concept
8. **Schedule Contingency:**
   a. be able to define the term including what it is supposed to cover
   b. be able to describe several typical ways that it can be assessed

d. **Cost Estimating and Budgeting**: be able to describe the following concepts:
   i. General Concepts (must also understand *Elements of Cost and Analysis*):
      1. **Cost Estimate Classification**. Be able to describe AACE's recommended practice and its basis on scope definition (also see *project implementation* for discussion of scope development phases).
      2. **Uncertainty**.(also see *Risk Management*)
         a. **Probability**: Be able to describe the *probabilistic* nature of cost estimates and the concept of *ranges* and *accuracy*, and the importance of communicating these to the project team.
         b. **Accuracy**: Be able to describe asset and project characteristics likely to affect the accuracy of cost estimates, and the relationship of estimate classification to accuracy.
         c. **Contingency**:
            i. be able to define the term including what cost it is supposed to cover
            ii. be able to describe several typical ways that it can be estimated
      3. **Algorithms and Cost Estimating Relationships (CER).**
         a. **Algorithm types**: Be able to describe the basic characteristics of these algorithm types:
            i. **Stochastic or parametric**
               1. given the inputs, be able to perform a *"scale of operations"* estimate
               2. be able to explain why this algorithm type is most often applied in *asset planning*.
            ii. **Deterministic or definitive:** be able to explain why this algorithm type is most often applied in *project control planning*.
         b. **Factors**:
            i. be able to describe some typical uses of *factors, ratios, and indices* in algorithms of various types.
            ii. given a set of project characteristics and associated factors, be able to adjust a cost estimate from one time, location, situation, currency, etc. to another.
      4. **Chart or Code of Accounts**: be able to describe the characteristics of a good code account structure and its benefits for estimating and project control
      5. **Historical Data**: be able to describe the importance of historical, *empirical* data and databases to cost estimating
   ii. Practices: be able to describe the basic mechanics of these estimating steps
      1. **Quantification and Take-off**:
         a. be able to describe how the practices vary by level of scope definition and the algorithm type to be used for costing

b. be able to describe ways that this step is sometimes automated, and considerations for using the results of automated take-off
2. **Costing and Life Cycle Costing** (see algorithms); be able to explain the concept of project versus life cycle costing
3. **Cash Flow and Forecasting**:
   a. be able to discuss the importance of integrating estimating and scheduling practices (incorporating the element of timing in quantification and costing)
   b. be able to discuss the affects on planning and cost estimating when cash flow is restricted
   c. given a schedule and set of cost inputs, be able to develop a *cost flow curve*.
4. **Pricing**:
   a. be able to discuss some business considerations for establishing pricing (risk, competition, desired rate of return, current economic conditions, etc.).
   b. given a basic set of cost inputs and production plans be able to calculate a *break-even product price*
5. **Bidding**
   a. be able to discuss some considerations for using someone else's bid as an input to your cost estimate.
   b. be able to describe the purpose and mechanics of *unbalancing* or *front-end loading* a bid
6. **Budgeting**: be able to describe the mechanics of creating a control budget from a cost estimate
7. **Cost Control Baseline**: be able to describe how cost and schedule control baselines can be integrated
8. **Estimate Basis**: be able to describe the typical content of estimate basis documentation

iii. Other Concepts:
1. **Product vs. Project costs:** be able to explain how estimating *product* (i.e., output of manufacturing) cost differs from *project* cost

e. **Resource Management:** be able to describe how this process is tied closely to cost estimating (e.g., quantification) and schedule development (e.g., resource allocation). Also see *performance / productivity management* considerations

i. **Resource availability**: be able to discuss ways to assess availability and potential consequences of not doing so
1. be able to describe the types of resources and their appropriateness to analysis
2. be able to discuss potential sources for resources
3. be able to discuss methods for validation of initial estimates

ii. **Resource limits and constraints**: be able to discuss typical limits and constraints that may occur or be imposed
1. be able to discuss the role supervision and span of control has on resource limits
2. be able to describe how optimal and maximum crew sizing may play a part
3. be able to discuss the effects of physical workspace limits

iii. **Resource allocation**: be able to describe the mechanics of this step in *schedule development*
1. forward vs. backward allocation: be able to explain the differences in the methods
2. smoothing vs. maximum limits: be able to explain the difference in the terms
3. maximum vs. over-maximum allocation: be able to explain the differences in the terms

f. **Value Analysis and Engineering**: be able to describe the following concepts:
i. General Concepts:
1. **Purpose**:

a. be able define the concept (i.e., "the systematic application of recognized techniques which identify the functions of the product or service, establish the worth of those functions, and provide the necessary functions to meet the required performance at the lowest overall cost." Where overall cost is usually life-cycle cost).
b. distinguish among the terms "lowest life-cycle cost," "best quality," and "best value."
c. be able to describe how value analysis/engineering differs from other cost or scope reduction exercises.
d. be able to describe how value analysis and engineering differs from other value improving practices such as manufacturability and constructability.

2. **Value:** be able to explain the this general concept as well as the meanings, using examples if desired, of these four kinds of value that may be associated with an item:
   a. Use value
   b. Esteem value
   c. Exchange value
   d. Cost value

3. **Functions**

ii. Process/Practices; be able to describe the purpose and mechanics of these steps:
   1. **Function Analysis** (*Value Measurement*)
   2. **Creativity**
      i. Describe each of the following problem solving techniques:
         1. Brainstorming
         2. Checklists
         3. Morphological analysis
         4. Attribute listing
   3. **Value Screening**

g. **Risk Management**: be able to describe the following concepts:
   i. General Concepts
      1. **Risk and Uncertainty**: be able to define risk in terms of opportunities and threats
      2. **Risk Factors** (or drivers) and *Risk Factor Properties*
      3. **Risk Management Plan**
      4. **Contingency Action Plans**
      5. **Contingency** (see cost estimating and schedule development)
         a. be able to describe the appropriate level of authority for managing contingency
         b. be able to describe typical criteria for its use (i.e., as opposed to a slush fund).
   ii. Practices: be able to describe the purpose and mechanics of these risk management process steps:
      1. **Risk Assessment**
      2. **Risk Analysis**
      3. **Risk Factor Screening**
      4. **Risk Mitigation or Acceptance**
      5. **Risk Control**

h. **Procurement Planning and Contract Management**
   i. **Contract types**: be able to explain the advantage and disadvantages of these types of contracts from the owner and contractor viewpoints:
      1. *Fixed price (with fixed, incentive, or award fees)*
      2. *Unit price*
      3. *Cost-plus (with fixed, incentive, or award fees)*
      4. *Time and materials (T&M)*

ii. **Risk Allocation**: be able to explain how each contract type above allocates risks between the contracting parties.

iii. **Contract Documents:**
1. be able to describe the general contents and purposes of the following elements of bidding and contract documents:
    a. invitation to bid or request for proposal
    b. bid form
    c. agreement
    d. general conditions
    e. supplementary or special conditions
    f. technical specifications
    g. drawings
    h. addenda
    i. modifications
    j. bid bond and contract (performance) bond
    k. performance guarantee
    l. warranties
2. be able to explain the role of contract documents in avoiding and resolving disputes, changes and claims (also see Change Management).
3. be able to describe the various types of insurance that may be required as part of a contract
4. be able to explain the term "*retention*" and be able to calculate its effective cost given the terms of the contract and time-value of money.
5. be able to distinguish between "Job (project) overhead" and "general overhead' and provide examples of each.
6. be able to explain what is meant by a contract payment term such as "2/15 net 30", and given a payment timing and time value of money scenario, be able to determine the method of payment that is economically most advantageous under these terms.

iv. **Integrated Project Control**:
1. be able to explain the basic mechanics of how the project control process might be integrated between parties to each type of contract. (e.g., how to *measure and report progress, integrate schedules*, etc.).
2. be able to explain the role of contract documents in avoiding and resolving disputes, changes and claims (also see *Change Management*).

v. **Changes and Claims:** (see *Change Management* and *Forensic Performance Assessment*)

vi. Other Concepts:
1. **Supply chain:** be able to explain this concept and how it might affect procurement planning.
2. **Supplier relationships:** be able to explain this concept and how it might affect procurement planning (e.g., initial price versus life cycle cost)
3. **Schedule of values:** be able to explain this concept in regards to contracts, change management, and project control for contracted work.

i. **Investment Decision Making**
   i. General Concepts:
   1. be able explain the concepts and perform the analyses covered previously in the **Economic and Financial Analysis** section.
   2. **Decision Policy / Criteria**:
       a. be able to describe the role of decision policy in consistent asset *investment strategy deployment*
       b. be able to explain why decision policy for most corporations establishes *net present value and return on investments* (or equivalent) as primary decision criteria.
   ii. **Decision Analysis:**

1. **Decision Model**:
   a. be able to able to explain the benefits of using a cost-based, quantitative decision model that addresses probabilities
   b. be able to describe the mechanics of addressing non-cash value and risk considerations in a monetary decision model.
   c. be able to evaluate and select the best alternative from several alternatives using these methods.
      i. **Net Present Value**
      ii. **Decision Tree** (probability weighted present value):
      iii. **Discounted Rate of Return** (breakeven)
      iv. **Cost/Benefit Ratio**
2. **Sensitivity Analysis and Monte Carlo Simulation**: be able to discuss mechanics of using a decision model to assess probable outcomes.

iii. **Business Decision Basis or Business Case**: be able to describe the information (e.g., objectives, assumptions, constraints, etc) that should be communicated to the project team.

iv. **Capital Budgeting**. be able to describe the mechanics of investment decision making in a typical enterprise capital budgeting process.

v. **Portfolio Management**. be able to describe the affect of portfolio considerations (multiple and often competing assets and projects) on investment decision making and capital budgeting processes.

3. Implementation

    a. **Project Implementation**: be able to explain the following concepts:
       i. **Phases and Gates Process**: be able to describe the typical stages in respect to project planning and funding authorization and the benefits of an established process
          1. **Front-end loading (FEL):** be able to describe this concept and its benefits in terms of risk management and project control planning
       ii. **Project Implementation Basis** or **Scope Statement**: be able to describe the typical information in this deliverable at project initiation and the importance of business and project team agreement and communicating this information to all stakeholders.

    b. **Project control plan implementation**: be able to explain the following concepts:
       i. **Control Accounts**: describe this concept and its content in relation to WBS and earned value application
       ii. **Project Control Plan and Basis**: be able to describe the typical information in this deliverable at the start of project execution and the importance of integrating, agreeing on and communicating this information to the project team.

    c. **Validation**: be able to describe how the quality and competitiveness of plans might be assessed before implementation and why the process is important. Also explain the value of historical, empirical information.

4. **Performance Measurement**

    a. **Cost Accounting**: be able to describe the interface of the accounting process with cost engineering practice
       i. **Cash and Accrual Accounting**. Be able to describe these concepts
       ii. **Control and Cost Accounts**: be able to discuss the role of the **chart or code of accounts** with integrating project control
          1. **initiation/closure**: be able to discuss the importance of timely management of cost accounts
          2. **review/correct**: be able to discuss ways to deal with and the affects on project control of mischarges.

iii. **Classify and account**: be able to explain the role of the cost engineer in assuring that cost accounting information is accounted for so as to align with the control basis. Be able to describe these cost accounting concepts:
1. **Expenditures** (i.e., cash disbursements)
2. **Incurred Costs** (i.e., expended plus cost of work performed but not paid for yet)
3. **Commitments** (i.e., including expended costs and financial obligations)
4. **Cost Allocation**
5. **Activity-Based Costing (ABC)**

iv. **Capitalization and Depreciation**: be able to explain these concepts and the typical role of the cost engineer in working with the finance function to assure it is done effectively

v. **Asset vs. Project Accounting**:
1. be able to describe how traditional asset operation and finance focused accounting differs from that needed for project control
2. be able to describe how legacy or contractor cost accounting system accounts are often not consistent with project control needs, and how the inconsistency may be addressed.

b. **Project Performance Measurement**
  i. General Concepts
  1. **Earned Value:** be able to explain the general concept and the importance of and reliable control basis and objective, quantitative physical progress measures
  ii. Practices
  1. **Physical Progress**: be able to explain the general concept and the following methods, and, given input information, be able to calculate percent complete.
      a. *units completed*
      b. *incremental milestone*
      c. *weighted or equivalent units completed*
      d. *resource expenditure*
      e. *judgment*
  2. **Track Resources**
      a. **Labor hours**: be able to explain the advantages and disadvantages of tracking labor hours instead of cost as the basis for earned value
      b. **Material management and fabrication**: be able to discuss how material progress/status can be measured
  3. **Measure Performance** (how work is being done)
      a. be able to discuss why earned value measures alone have limited value in finding ways to improve performance.
      b. be able to discuss the mechanics of the following methods, how they can help find ways to improve performance, and their strengths and weaknesses:
          i. *Work sampling*
          ii. *Time and motion studies*
          iii. *Time lapse photography and video monitoring*
          iv. *Expediting*
          v. *Inspection*
  4. **Status Schedule**: be able to discuss the mechanics of statusing and updating a schedule

c. **Asset Performance Measurement**: be able to explain how earned value methods do not apply for operations and performance is measured against metrics established by the *requirements*.
  i. **Functional Performance**: be able to explain how measures capture what an asset does and how it does it including quality control attributes, cycle time, and so on.
  ii. **Utility measures:** be able to discuss ways to capture user or customer perceptions of how well the asset meets their wants and needs.

iii. **Measure Activity Factors**: be able to explain how if ABC/M methods are used, *cost assignment network tracing* ties expenses to activities whose performance must be measured.
iv. **Track Resources**: be able to explain how *ERP systems* increasingly handle these measures in operation facilities

5. **Performance Assessment**

   a. **Project Performance Assessment**: be able to explain the concepts
      i. General Concepts
         1. **Variance**: be able to describe this concept as an empirical difference between actual and planned performance for any aspect of the control plan.
         2. **Trends**: be able to describe the difference between random and non-random variance and how this might influence subsequent control actions and forecasts
      ii. Practices for **control assessment**: be able to describe methods for assessing and reporting performance (variances and trends) against the following baseline plans:
         1. **cost**:
            a. be able to describe basic earned value methods
            b. be able to describe and prepare tabular and cumulative distribution charts ("s-curves") for reporting
         2. **schedule**:
            a. be able to describe methods to identify variance (e.g., calculate slip, earned value methods, etc), assess critical path and remaining float.
            b. Be able to describe performance reporting methods (e.g., schedule plot showing the planned and actual schedule activity status), tables showing a percentage or factor that expresses the extent that the schedule is ahead or behind at given points in time, lists of activities sorted by early start date or total float, etc.).
         3. **resources**
            a. **labor**
               i. be able to describe basic earned value methods
               ii. be able to describe and prepare tabular and *cumulative distribution charts ("s-curves")* for reporting
            b. **material and fabrication**: be able to describe the use earned value, schedule assessment, material management reports, and so on.
         4. **risk**: be able to explain the monitoring and assessment of risk factors in accordance with a risk a management plan
      iii. Practices for **integrated earned value (Earned Value Management System or EVMS) assessment**
         1. be able to explain and calculate all the basic *earned value measures and indices (Planned and/or Budget [was BCWS], Earned [was BCWP], and Actual [was ACWP], SV, CV, SPI, CPI)*
         2. be able to describe the advantages and disadvantages of a fully integrated EVMS assessment using costs
      iv. Practices for **work process and productivity improvement**
         1. **Productivity assessment**
            a. **Labor productivity factor**: be able to calculate this using earned value and explain its significance
         2. **Work process improvement**.
            a. **Work sampling**: be able to describe the mechanics of the method and how it can be used to eliminate *wasted effort* and improve the work process
            b. be able to describe other methods such as *informal sampling, manpower surveys, time card notations, quality circles, inspection observations*, etc.

b. **Asset Performance Assessment**: be able to explain how for operations, earned value methods do not apply and performance is measured against metrics established by the requirements.
  i. **Measurement Basis**: be able to describe these concepts for measuring and assessing asset management performance (profitability being the most common metric):
   1. **Balanced Scorecard**
   2. **Key Performance Indicators (KPI)**
  ii. **Practices**
   1. **Profitability**: see *return on investment*
   2. **Cost of Quality**:
      a. be able to describe the mechanics of the method and *costs of prevention, appraisal and failure*.
      b. be able to explain how the method can lead to corrective actions
   3. **Benchmarking**: be able to describe the purpose and mechanics of a benchmarking study
   4. **Lessons Learned**. be able to explain the purpose and mechanics of capturing and evaluating lessons learned
   5. **Risk Assessment**: be able to explain the monitoring and assessment of risk factors in accordance with a risk a management plan

c. **Forecasting**
  i. **Forecast and Forecasting**.
   1. be able to describe the concepts of forecasts and forecasting
   2. be able to describe how the project control planning concepts (e.g., estimating, scheduling, etc.) are applied in the context of work in progress, performance assessment findings, change management, and corrective actions.
  ii. **Earned Value Methods**:
   1. be able to explain and calculate the basic earned value concepts related to forecasting (*BAC, EAC, labor productivity factor*)
   2. be able to explain why earned value measures alone may not be an appropriate basis for a forecast; explain what else must be considered.

d. **Project Change Management**
  i. Basic Terminology: be able to describe the concepts
   1. **Scope:** be able to describe how the meaning of the term "scope" differs in the contexts of owner project funds authorization versus contracting
   2. **Deviations**
   3. **Trends** (also see *performance assessment*):
   4. **Changes**: be able to explain the difference between scope and non-scope changes in an owner funding context
   5. **Changes and Contract Types:** be able to explain how the change order process may differ with different contract types.
   6. **Disputes and Claims**
   7. **Contingency, Allowances, and Reserves** (see *Risk Management*)
  ii. Practices: be able to describe the concepts
   1. **Variance or trend analysis**: be able to describe the difference between performance variance and a trend
   2. **Impact assessment**: be able to describe how the project control planning concepts (e.g., estimating, scheduling, etc.) are applied in change management
      a. Be able to describe the concept of *time impact analysis* related to schedule change
   3. **Make and track disposition**
      a. **Corrective action** (also improvement action): be able to describe what these are and why they might be needed.
      b. be able to describe ways that change management findings and dispositions (actions) are recorded, reported, and incorporated in the *project control plans*

4. **Manage contingency and reserves**:
    a. **Draw down**: be able to describe methods for managing contingency
    b. be able to describe ways to assess the need for contingency for work in progress
5. **Resolve contract disputes and claims:** be able to discuss the concept of changes and change management in respect to contract agreements (also see *Forensic Performance Assessment*)

e. **Asset Change (Configuration) Management**
   i. **Requirements**: Be able to explain how managing the scope of the "asset" in respect to its requirements in strategic asset management differs from managing the scope of "work" in project control.
   ii. **Configuration Management**: be able to describe the role of this practice area in managing change in information that defines the asset

f. **Historical Database Management** (see basic concepts in *Information Management*)
   i. **Empirical Data**: be able to explain why empirical information is the most fundamental planning resource available (why is it critical for asset and project planning?)
   ii. **Project Closeout**: be able to describe the mechanics and challenges of closing out a project in respect to project control systems, data and information.

g. **Forensic Performance Assessment**
   i. be able to describe how *forensic* assessment differs from typical project control performance assessments (i.e., the primary purpose is to relate *causation* and *responsibility (or entitlement)* to performance to resolve disputes in a legal context and/or to gain knowledge to support long term performance improvement.
   ii. be able to describe the difference between changes and claims (for *scope, compensation, relief, damages, delay*, or other disagreements)
   iii. be able to describe major reasons for contract changes including the role of *project scope definition*
   iv. be able to describe various types of schedule **delay** in respect to contract changes and claims:
      1. *excusable*
      2. *non-excusable*
      3. *compensatory*
      4. *concurrent*
   v. be able to describe the potential affects of disputes on project performance
   vi. be able to discuss role of these costs (see **Elements of Cost**) in context of disputes and claims (*bonds, retainage, performance guarantees, liquidated damages, demurrage, legal costs, etc.*)
   vii. be able to discuss means and methods of resolving disputes and claims through *negotiation, mediation, arbitration*, and/or *litigation* (or other forms of *alternative dispute resolution*) including being able to discuss potential good points and bad points of each forum.
   viii. Be able to describe the terms *discovery process, depositions* and *interrogatory*.
   ix. Be able to describe why it is import to distinguish between *supposition* and *fact*.

**APPENDIX B—AACE INTERNATIONAL
MEMBERSHIP INFORMATION**

It's About Time...

aace International

Join **AACE International** and gain access to a wealth of resources that will save you time and money! You'll stay informed about the complexities of the cost and management profession -- plus you'll have access to discounts on educational programs, publications, insurance and more!

It's About Information...

Visit AACE's website, www.aacei.org, and locate thousands of technical papers and publications at the Online Bookstore. AACE's database is keyword searchable for quickly locating appropriate reference articles. Check out AACE's E-ployment page where members can post resumes at no additional cost.

AACE offers numerous distance learning courses on estimating and project management. The AACE Approved Educational Provider program helps maintain high quality development courses and providers. AACE also holds many seminars throughout the year.

AACE is an advocate for education. AACE annually awards scholarships to college and graduate students.

Join cost and management practitioners from around the world to learn, network, and expand your career at AACE International's Annual Meeting. With over 100 technical presentations and seminars by global experts in the cost and management field as well as networking and social events, the Annual Meeting is a world-class event.

It's About Resources...

Cost Engineering Journal - AACE International's monthly publication features cost estimating, project control, economic and financial analysis, planning and scheduling, cost engineering, and project management technical articles for cost professionals around the world. Through the mail or via the AACE International website, the *Cost Engineering* Journal is a great resource for members.

AACE's Virtual Library - The Virtual Library (VL) is a fully searchable database that contains over 40 years of the Association's full-text technical articles available electronically in Adobe Acrobat (PDF) format. AACE offers two versions of this member's only benefit -- one for our Corporate Sponsors and one for our individual members. The VL will continue to expand as newly published articles are scanned and added to the library.

Technical Development - Increase your knowledge and expertise by joining one of AACE International's many technical committees, subcommittees, and Special Interest Groups (SIG's) at no additional cost to members. Discuss industry problems with your peers or help experts develop new and improved techniques and practices for the profession.

The Bookstore - Purchase all the leading estimating and cost management books and CD's, as well as Professional Practice Guides and Annual Meeting Transactions online 24 hours a day.

It's About Networking...

Expand your contacts through AACE International. Attend AACE local section or Annual Meetings for interesting speakers, informational tours, social dinners and much more. Join one of our many technical committees and their listservs -- a great resource! Plus, the price is right -- they are free to all AACE members!

It's About Excellence...

AACE's Certified Cost Consultant (CCC), Certified Cost Engineer (CCE), or Interim Cost Consultant (ICC), Earned Value Professional (EVP) certification, and Planning and Scheduling Professional (PSP) certification programs are third-party credentials that are recognized as signifying specialized cost and management capabilities. The CCC/CCE programs are accredited by the Council of Engineering and Scientific Specialty Boards. AACE certifications are internationally recognized in the cost management field.

It's About You!

AACE International -- **Promoting the Planning and Management of Cost and Schedules.** AACE is your professional partner bringing you information and support you can trust. Join and become part of a unique network of individuals who are dedicated to improving the cost and management profession.

AACE International is a 501(c)3 non-profit professional association **Promoting the Planning and Management of Cost and Schedules**.

Since 1956, AACE International has provided its members with the resources they need to enhance their performance and ensure continued growth and success. With about 5,500 members world-wide, AACE International serves cost management professionals: planners and schedulers, project controls managers, cost managers and engineers, project managers, estimators, and bidders AACE has members in 78 countries and currently includes 70 local sections.

Get a leg up on networking...join AACE today!

It's easy, just complete the application below and send it to AACE International:
- **Address:** 209 Prairie Avenue • Suite 100 • Morgantown, WV 26501 U.S.A.
- **Fax:** +1.304.291.5728

Or complete the application online:
- **Website:** www.aacei.org

AACE International Membership Application

Send completed application along with a check, money order, or credit card information to **AACE International, 209 Prairie Avenue, Suite 100, Morgantown, WV 26501, USA.** Canadian checks or money orders must include the currency differential between US and Canadian dollars.

Application is for:
- ☐ **Member** (US$130 annually)
- ☐ **Student Member** (US$25 annually)
  - Projected Graduation Date _____
  - Degree/Program _____

General Information

NAME _____
First   Middle   Last (Family)

BUSINESS (OR SCHOOL) ADDRESS:

Company Name   Title
Street Address
City   State/Province   Postal Code   Country
Phone   Fax
E-mail Address

HOME ADDRESS:

Street Address
City   State/Province   Postal Code   Country
Phone   Fax
E-mail Address

PREFERRED CONTACT INFORMATION: ☐ Business   ☐ Home
PUBLISH IN DIRECTORY: ☐ Yes   ☐ No
DEMOGRAPHIC INFORMATION: ☐ Male   ☐ Female
DATE OF BIRTH: _____

Background & Payment Information

EDUCATION INFORMATION:
- College/University _____
- City, State or Province, Country _____
- Degree and Major _____
- Date Received _____

There is an additional US$10 fee for all new membership applications.

☐ Check or money order made payable to **AACE International** enclosed
☐ Visa   ☐ Mastercard   ☐ American Express
☐ Eurocard   ☐ Access

Credit Card Number _____
Card Expiration Date _____
(Credit Card Charges in US$.)
Name on Card _____
Full Signature _____

WORK EXPERIENCE:
- From: _____ To: _____
- Title: _____
- Company Name: _____
- Supervisor: _____
- Job Duties: _____